Advanced Information and Knowledge Processing

Series Editors
Professor Lakhmi Jain
lakhmi.jain@unisa.edu.au

Professor Xindong Wu
xwu@cs.uvm.edu

T0142922

Dirk Husmeier, Richard Dybowski and Stephen Roberts (Eds)
Probabilistic Modeling in Bioinformatics and Medical Informatics
1-85233-778-8

Ajith Abraham, Lakhmi Jain and Robert Goldberg (Eds)
Evolutionary Multiobjective Optimization
1-85233-787-7

K.C. Tan, E.F. Khor and T.H. Lee
Multiobjective Evolutionary Algorithms and Applications
1-85233-836-9

Nikhil R. Pal and Lakhmi Jain (Eds)
Advanced Techniques in Knowledge Discovery and Data Mining
1-85233-867-9

Amit Konar and Lakhmi Jain
Cognitive Engineering
1-85233-975-6

Miroslav Kárný (Ed.)
Optimized Bayesian Dynamic Advising
1-85233-928-4

Marcus A. Maloof (Ed.)
Machine Learning and Data Mining for Computer Security
1-84628-029-X

Yannis Manolopoulos, Alexandros Nanopoulos, Apostolos N. Papadopoulos and
Yannis Theodoridis
R-trees: Theory and Applications
1-85233-977-2

Sanghamitra Bandyopadhyay, Ujjwal Maulik, Lawrence B. Holder and Diane J. Cook (Eds)
Advanced Methods for Knowledge Discovery from Complex Data
1-85233-989-6

Sifeng Liu and Yi Lin
Grey Information
1-85233-995-0

Mitra Basu and Tin Kam Ho (Eds)

Data Complexity in Pattern Recognition

 Springer

Mitra Basu, PhD
Electrical Engineering Department
City College
City University of New York
USA

Tim Kam Ho, BBA, MS, PhD
Bell Laboratories
Lucent Technologies
New Jersey
USA

British Library Cataloguing in Publication Data
A catalogue record for this book is available from the British Library

Advanced Information and Knowledge Processing ISSN 1610-394
e-ISBN 1-84628-172-5
ISBN-13: 978-1-84996-557-6   e-ISBN-13: 978-1-84628-172-3

Printed on acid-free paper

Printed in the United States of America   (MVY)

9 8 7 6 5 4 3 2 1

springer.com

Preface

Machines capable of automatic pattern recognition have been fascinating subjects that capture much popular imagination. Algorithms for supervised classification, where one infers a decision boundary from a set of training examples, are at the core of this capability. Over the last few decades, tremendous progress has been made on inventing and refining such algorithms. Yet, automatic learning in many simple tasks in daily life still appears to be far from reach. So we ask, what is missing from these efforts? When the automatic classifiers are not perfect, is it a deficiency of the algorithms by design, or is it a difficulty intrinsic to the classification task? How do we know whether we have exploited to the fullest extent the knowledge embedded in the training data?

A well-known description of the intrinsic difficulty of a classification problem is the Bayes error, which can be computed if complete knowledge is given on the probability distribution of each class in the feature space. But empirical observations suggest that, from the perspectives of automatic classifiers given limited training data, problems can be difficult for different reasons even if they have the same Bayes error. This results in strongly data-dependent performances of classifiers. Factors affecting accuracy can be, for example, the shapes of the classes and thus the shape the decision boundary, the amount of overlap among the classes, the proximity of two classes, and the number of informative samples available for training. Classifiers respond to these factors in their unique ways. A recent realization is that the complexity of the data must be weighed in when evaluating the performance of various classifiers.

Besides pattern recognition, classification is also a central topic in several related disciplines such as machine learning, neural networks, and data mining. Practical applications are also numerous, in image, video, and speech signal processing, biometrics, digital libraries, biomedical studies, financial engineering, military decisions, and many other areas of scientific, engineering, and business data analysis. A prerequisite for setting proper expectations on classification performance is to understand the complexity of a specific data set arising from an application. To understand the data complexity is to find out whether, or to what extent, patterns exist in the data. It is also to obtain guidance on selecting specific classification techniques. We believe that this is the key to further advances in classification.

We have seen relevant attempts to understand data characteristics in several major methodological areas. However, the huge and diverse literature of the field has made it extremely difficult for one to keep up with the progress. In addition, because of background and terminology differences, it has become a sad state of affairs that many researchers are often unaware of concurrent developments under slightly different names. Motivated by this, we collected in this book a set of reviews, commentaries, and case studies on data complexity and its role in shaping the theories and techniques in different areas.

The book consists of two parts: (I) Theory and Methodology, and (II) Applications. Part I begins with several chapters that propose measures of data complexity from different perspectives. Chapter 1 describes several measures of geometrical and topological characteristics of point sets in high-dimensional spaces, and their utility in analyzing data sets with known or controlled complexity. Chapter 2 focuses on a dissimilarity based representation of objects and addresses the intricate relationship between the intrinsic complexity of a data set, the chosen object representation, the apparent complexity determined by the sampling density with respect to this representation, along with the implications of these on classifier choices. Chapter 3 discusses the possibilities and difficulties in estimating data complexity when the data models are assumed to be in a known form, such as an isotropic Gaussian, for which certain simple classifiers are suitable. Examples are shown where the same problem may appear easy or difficult depending on the classifier being used, due to influences of the density parameters and the sample size on the relevant measures. The chapter concludes with an interesting remark that estimating such measures is not necessarily easier than training a classifier for the task.

Various aspects of data complexity can affect the behavior of different families of classifiers in different ways. Among the earliest concerns is the role of linear separability on the effectiveness of linear classifiers. This concern is carried into recent studies on support vector machines that are linear classifiers in a transformed feature space. Chapter 4 reviews descent procedures for linear classifier training, and discusses the effect of linear separability on the behavior of such procedures. Chapter 5 relates data complexity to the inductive learning principle and the control of model complexity. Two approaches to control classifier complexity are compared: a margin-based approach and an adaptive parameterization approach. Experiments are shown that highlights conditions under which the margin-based approach is more effective.

Chapter 6 describes the influence of data geometry on the performance of a popular genetic algorithm based classifier, XCS. The chapter continues to use several geometrical complexity measures to analyze the regions in the complexity space where XCS performs favorably. This study is extended to six classifiers in chapter 7, where the domains of dominant competence are found for three traditional classifiers and three types of ensemble classifiers.

Grammatical inference has received much attention recently. Concerted efforts from diverse disciplines to find tractable inference techniques have added new dimensions and opened up unexplored territories. Chapter 8 studies the data complexity issue in grammatical inference at three concentric levels: representational level (strings, trees, and graphs), class of languages, and the issue of membership. Choices made at one level may affect data complexity as seen at another level. For example, the choice in the representational level may make the later tasks easier or harder. The author reviews necessary basic concepts and presents discussions on how stochastic and other languages have evolved to address the needs.

The question of data complexity affects all applications of classification, in revealing or rejecting existence of dependences, suggesting and justifying a particular classification method, and determining the utility of predictions. For example, studies on data complexity can help explore the existence of patterns in occurrences of diseases, characteristics of dependencies in retail transactions, reliability of biometrical authentication techniques, feasibility of earthquake prediction by seismic waveforms, and the practicality of categorizing regular text, email message, and web pages. Similar problems also occur in many other areas of science and engineering.

In Part II, we collected studies of several key applications on their sources of difficulties and how data complexity influences the complexity and behavior of their solutions.

Chapter 9 features a large set of detailed analyses of properties of pattern distributions in a high-dimensional feature space associated with a symbol recognition problem, both from theory and from empirical observations. The tools and arguments developed there can be useful to many other application areas involving natural or artificial patterns.

Chapter 10 proposes a set of graph-representation–based methods suitable for document comparison, with special motivations for usage in a web mining context. The methods feature compact representation, practical speed, and comparable or even favorable accuracy over traditional vector-based methods. This exemplifies how methods are designed to adapt to the difficulty of a problem.

Chapter 11 reviews clustering algorithms that are applied to microarray data, showing that the classical algorithms are inadequate to extract the underlying characteristics. The authors call attention to issues facing the bioinformatics community and describes attempts in this community to redesign clustering algorithms that are sensitive to data complexity in biological data.

Chapter 12 presents the problem of classifying magnetic resonance spectra where high dimensionality of the raw feature space and extreme sample sparsity have caused many difficulties. Classification accuracies are strongly influenced by the problem representation using different extracted features. Geometrical complexity offers an explanation for this influence.

Chapter 13 gives a tutorial introduction to the problem of tropical cyclone tracking in weather forecasting, and discusses the various aspects of the problem where complexities in the data have strong impacts on the prediction accuracy.

Chapter 14 argues strongly for involving humans in the loop of developing a solution to a visual pattern recognition problem where automatic methods may not be able to fully adapt to data complexity. The chater describes the CAVIAR software that serves as a proof of the concept.

Finally, is classification complexity always something to be avoided? It turns out that there are occasions where one actually wishes to exploit the difficulty of a machine vision problem for some good use. Chapter 15 describes a new topic of study called "human interactive proof," where the security of an information system is guarded by "reverse Turing tests" that present patterns difficult for machines but easy for human to recognize.

Data complexity is a fundamental, important, and far-reaching topic. Our attempt in this book captures only a snapshot of the recent activities related to this theme. There have been many other related investigations in statistics and information theory. Although it is not possible to survey all the relevant past and current works in this single volume, we hope this collection will bring attention to this topic, and that the references included here will provide some background to researchers interested in following up this development in pattern recognition. It is our belief that making these discussions accessible to a wider audience will stimulate further exchanges among various communities dealing with data analysis.

We are grateful to all the contributors and reviewers who have made this endeavor an enjoyable and exciting learning experience. The editorial and production staff at Springer have provided valuable support during the preparation of the manuscript. We are also in debt to Anil Jain, Robert Duin, and George Nagy, who kindly provided much encouragement in the early phases of this study. Tin thanks the support of Bell Labs management on her pursuits, and in particular, Lawrence Cowsar, Wim Sweldens, Al Aho, Margaret Wright, and Bill Coughran, for hosting visits from Mitra, George, Ester, and Martin over the last few years while this work developed.

Mitra Basu, Arlington, VA
Tin Kam Ho, Murray Hill, NJ

Contents

List of Contributors

Henry S. Baird
Computer Science & Engineering Department
Lehigh University
Bethlehem, PA 18015, USA
baird@cse.lehigh.edu

Mitra Basu
National Science Foundation
4201 Wilson Blvd.
Arlington, VA 22230, USA
mbasu@nsf.gov

Richard Baumgartner
Institute for Biodiagnostics
National Research Council Canada
435 Ellice Avenue, Winnipeg
Manitoba, R3B 1Y6, Canada
Richard.Baumgartner@nrc-cnrc.gc.ca

Ester Bernadó-Mansilla
Computer Engineering Department
Enginyeria i Arquitectura La Salle
Ramon Llull Univerity
Quatre Camins, 2. 08022
Barcelona, Spain
esterb@salleurl.edu

Horst Bunke
University of Bern, CH-3012
Bern, Switzerland
bunke@iam.unibe.ch

Vladimir Cherkassky
Department of Electrical & Computer Engineering
University of Minnesota
Minneapolis, MN 55455, USA
cherkass@ece.umn.edu

Robert P. W. Duin
Information & Communication Theory Group
Faculty of Electrical Engineering,
Mathematics, and Computer Science
Delft University of Technology
Mekelweg 4, 2628 CD
Delft, The Netherlands
r.p.w.duin@ewi.tudelft.nl

Colin de la Higuera
EURISE, Facult des Sciences et Techniques
23 rue du Docteur Paul Michelon,
42023 Saint-Etienne Cedex 2
France
cdlh@univ-st-etienne.fr

Uwe Himmelreich
Institute for Magnetic Resonance Research
Department of Magnetic Resonance in Medicine
University of Sydney
Sydney NSW 2145, Australia
uwe@med.usyd.edu.au

Tin Kam Ho
Mathematical & Algorithmic Sciences Research Center
Bell Laboratories, Lucent Technologies
Murray Hill, NJ 07974-0636, USA
tkh@research.bell-labs.com

Abraham Kandel
University of South Florida
Tampa, FL 33620, USA
kandel@csee.usf.edu

Latifur Khan
Department of Computer Science
University of Texas at Dallas
Richardson, TX 75083, USA
lkhan@utdallas.edu

Mark Last
Ben-Gurion University of the Negev
Beer-Sheva 84105, Israel
mlast@bgu.ac.il

Martin H.C. Law
Department of Computer Science and Engineering
Michigan State University
East Lansing, MI 48824, USA
lawhiu@cse.msu.edu

Ping Wah Li
Hong Kong Observatory
134A, Nathan Road
Kowloon, Hong Kong
pwli@hko.gov.hk

Feng Luo
Computer Science Department
100 McAdams Hall
Clemson University,
Clemson, SC 29630, USA
luofeng@cs.clemson.edu

Yunqian Ma
Honeywell Labs
Honeywell International Inc.
3660 Technology Drive
Minneapolis, MN 55418,USA
yunqian.ma@honeywell.com

George Nagy
Electrical, Computer, & Systems Engineering
Rensselaer Polytechnic Institute
Troy, NY 12180, USA
nagy@ecse.rpi.edu

Albert Orriols
Computer Engineering Department
Enginyeria i Arquitectura La Salle
Ramon Llull Univerity
Quatre Camins, 2. 08022
Barcelona, Spain
aorriols@salleurl.edu

Elżbieta Pȩkalska
Information & Communication Theory group
Faculty of Electrical Engineering,
Mathematics, and Computer Science
Delft University of Technology
Mekelweg 4, 2628 CD
Delft, The Netherlands
e.m.pekalska@tudelft.nl

Šarūnas Raudys
Institute of Mathematics and Informatics
Akademijos 4
Vilnius 08663, Lithuania
raudys@ktlmii.lt

Adam Schenker
University of South Florida
Tampa, FL 33620, USA
aschenke@csee.usf.edu

Ray Somorjai
Institute for Biodiagnostics
National Research Council Canada
435 Ellice Avenue, Winnipeg
Manitoba, R3B 1Y6, Canada
Ray.Somorjai@nrc-crnc.gc.ca

Tania C. Sorrell
Centre for Infectious Diseases and Microbiology
University of Sydney at Westmead
Westmead, NSW 2145, Australia
Tanias@cidm.wh.su.edu

Ka Yan Wong
Department of Computer Science
The University of Hong Kong
Pokfulam, Hong Kong
kywong@cs.hku.hk

Chi Lap Yip
Department of Computer Science
The University of Hong Kong
Pokfulam, Hong Kong
clyip@cs.hku.hk

Xiaoli Zhang
DocLab
Rensselaer Polytechnic Institute
Troy, NY 12180, USA
zhangx@rpi.edu

Jie Zou
Electrical, Computer, & Systems Engineering
Rensselaer Polytechnic Institute
Troy, NY 12180, USA
zouj@alum.rpi.edu

Part I

Theory and Methodology

1

Measures of Geometrical Complexity in Classification Problems

Tin Kam Ho, Mitra Basu, and Martin Hiu Chung Law

Summary. When popular classifiers fail to perform to perfect accuracy in a practical application, possible causes can be deficiencies in the algorithms, intrinsic difficulties in the data, and a mismatch between methods and problems. We propose to address this mystery by developing measures of geometrical and topological characteristics of point sets in high-dimensional spaces. Such measures provide a basis for analyzing classifier behavior beyond estimates of error rates. We discuss several measures useful for this characterization, and their utility in analyzing data sets with known or controlled complexity. Our observations confirm their effectiveness and suggest several future directions.

1.1 Introduction

Research progress in supervised classification in the past several decades has produced a rich set of classifier technologies. But several fundamental questions remain unanswered: Given data from a new problem, can we determine whether there exists a clean decision boundary between the classes? To what extent can this boundary be inferred by the automatic algorithms? Which classifiers can do the best job?

In selecting a classifier methodology for a practical application, current approaches mostly follow a trial-and-error strategy. In benchmarking studies, one can often see many methods in close rivalry with similar levels of accuracy. Continuous attempts have been made on interpreting existing techniques, testing known methods on new applications, or mix-matching different approaches [6], but no revolutionary breakthrough appears to be in sight. It almost seems that a plateau has been reached in classification research, and questions like these begin to linger: (1) Have we reached the end of classifier development? (2) Have we exhausted what can be learned from a given set of data? (3) What else can be done?

But do we really need fundamental breakthroughs in classification research? Or are all remaining difficulties merely engineering problems that will eventually be solved with more machine power, or more likely, more human labor to find better feature extractors and fine-tune the classifier parameters?

To answer these questions we need to know whether there exists a limit in the knowledge that can be derived from a data set, and where this limit lies. That is, are the classes intrinsically distinguishable? And to what extent are they distinguishable, using each of our known methods? These questions are about the intrinsic complexity of a classification problem, and the match of a classifier's capability to a problem's intrinsic complexity. We believe that an understanding of these issues is the only way to find out about the current standing of classification research, and to obtain insights to guide further developments. In this chapter we describe our recent efforts along these lines, including a summary of the early studies reported in [7, 8].

1.2 Sources of Difficulty in Classification

We begin with an analysis of what makes classification difficult. Difficulties in classification can be traced to three sources: (1) class ambiguity, (2) boundary complexity, and (3) sample sparsity and feature space dimensionality.

Class Ambiguity

Class ambiguity refers to the situation when there are cases in a classification problem whose classes cannot be distinguished using the given features by *any* classification algorithm. It is often a consequence of the problem formulation. Classes can be ambiguous for two reasons. It could be that the class concepts are poorly defined and intrinsically inseparable. An example is that the shapes of the lower case letter "l" and the numeral "1" are the same in many fonts (Fig. 1.1a). Such ambiguity cannot be resolved at the classifier level, a solution has to involve the application context. Another way to say it is that the classes are not well defined; the two symbols should belong to the same shape class.

There is another situation where the classes are well defined, but the chosen features are not sufficient for indicating such differences (Fig. 1.1b). Again, there is no remedy at the classifier level. The samples need to be represented by other features that are more informative about the classes.

Class ambiguity can occur for only some input cases in a problem. Problems where the classes are ambiguous for at least some cases are said to have nonzero Bayes error, which sets a bound on the lowest achievable error rate.

(a) The shapes of the lower case letter "l" and the numeral "1" are the same in many fonts. They cannot be distinguished by shape alone. Which class a sample belongs to depends on context.

(b) There may be sufficient features for classifying the shells by shape, but not for classifying by the time of the day when they were collected, or by which hand they were picked up.

Fig. 1.1. Ambiguous classes due to (a) class definition; (b) insufficient features.

Boundary Complexity

Problems with the same Bayes erorr (such as zero) are not necessarily all alike because of their differences in boundary complexity (Fig. 1.2). Here we choose the class boundary to be the simplest (of minimum measure in the chosen feature space) decision boundary that minimizes Bayes error. With a complete sample, the class boundary can be characterized by its Kolmogorov complexity [12, 14], the length of the shortest program required to compute/describe it. A class boundary is complex if it requires a long description, possibly including a listing of all the points together with their class labels. This aspect of difficulty comes from the nature of the problem, and is unrelated to the sampling process. It exists even if a complete sample is given and if the classes are well defined. An example is a realization of a random labeling of all observable points in a feature space, where each point has a definite label, but points of the same label are scattered over the entire space with no obvious regularity. The only way to describe the classes could be an explicit listing of the positions of the points with the same label.

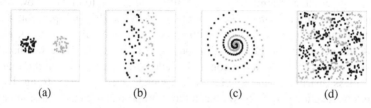

(a)   (b)   (c)   (d)

Fig. 1.2. Classification problems of different geometrical complexity: (a) linearly separable problem with wide margins and compact classes; (b) linearly separable problem with narrow margins and extended classes; (c) problem with nonlinear class boundary; (d) heavily interleaved classes following a checker board layout.

Kolmogorov complexity describes the absolute amount of information in a data set, and is known to be algorithmically incomputable [15]. Thus we resort to relative measures that depend on the chosen descriptors. Specifically, we can choose a number of geometrical descriptors that we believe to be relevant in the context of classification. We then describe the regularities and irregularities contained in the data set in terms of the chosen geometrical primitives. We refer to these descriptors as measures of the *geometrical complexity* of a data set. This would be sufficient for pattern recognition where most classifiers can also be characterized by geometrical descriptions of their decision regions.

Sample Sparsity and Feature Space Dimensionality

An incomplete or sparse sample adds another layer of difficulty to a discrimination problem. How an unseen point should share the class labels of the training samples in its vicinity depends on specific generalization rules. Without sufficient samples to constrain a classifier's generalization mechanism, the decisions on the unseen samples can be largely arbitrary. The difficulty is especially severe in high-dimensional spaces where the classifier's decision region, or the generalization rule, can vary with a large degree of freedom. The difficulty of working with sparse samples in high dimensional spaces has been addressed by many other researchers [3, 17, 20].

In practical applications, often a problem becomes difficult because of a mixture of boundary complexity and sample sparsity effects. Sampling density is more critical for an intrinsically complex problem (e.g., one with many isolated subclasses) than for an intrinsically simple problem (e.g., a linearly separable problem with wide margins), because longer boundaries need more samples to specify. If the sample is too sparse, an intrinsically complex problem may appear deceptively simple, for example, when representative samples are missing from many isolated subclasses. However, it can also happen that an intrinsically simple problem may appear deceptively complex. An example is a linearly separable problem that appears to have a nonlinear boundary when represented by a sparse training set. Thus, in lack of a complete sample, measures of problem complexity have to be qualified by the representativeness of the training set. We will refer to the boundary complexity computed from a fixed training set as the *apparent* complexity.

With a given, fixed training set, there is little one can do to find out how close the apparent complexity is to the "true" complexity. But this does not prevent one from inferring about the true complexity with some confidence, if some weak assumptions on the geometry of the class distributions can be made. Here we distinguish such assumptions from the more commonly adopted assumptions on the functional form of class distributions (e.g., Gaussians), which can be overly strong. By weak assumptions on class geometry, we mean those properties such as local compactness of the point sets, local continuity, and piecewise linearity of the boundaries, all to be constrained by parameters specifying a small neighborhood.

We believe that even with very conservative assumptions on the geometrical regularity, better uses of limited training samples can be made, and more useful error estimates can be obtained than those derived from purely combinatorial arguments emphasizing the worst cases. One should be able do these estimates without invoking strong assumptions on the functional form of the distributions.

1.3 Characterization of Geometrical Complexity

Among the different sources of classification difficulty, the geometrical complexity of class boundaries is probably most ready for detailed investigation. Thus in this chapter we focus on effective ways for characterizing the geometrical complexity of classification problems.

We assume that each problem is represented by a fixed set of training data consisting of points in a d-dimensional real space $\mathbf{R}^d$, and that each training point is associated with a class label. Furthermore, we assume that we have a sparse sample, i.e., there are unseen points from the same source that follow the same (unknown) probability distribution but are unavailable during classifier design. The finite and sparse sample limits our knowledge about the boundary complexity; thus we are addressing only the apparent geometrical complexity of a problem based on a given training set. We discuss only two-class problems, because most of the measures we use are defined only for two-class discrimination. For multiclass problems, one can either generalize the measure definitions as we will try later in this chapter, or produce a matrix of two-class values for each chosen measure. Summaries of the measure matrices can be made in many ways, possibly weighted with cost matrices. We acknowledge that the summary by itself is a nontrivial problem.

One natural measure of a problem's difficulty is the error rate of a chosen classifier. However, because our eventual goal is to study behavior of different classifiers, we want to find other measures that are less dependent on classifier choices. Moreover, measures other than classifier error rates may give hints on how the errors arise, which could lead to improvements in classifier design, and give guidance on collection of additional samples.

Early in our investigations it became clear that there are multiple aspects of a problem's geometrical complexity that cannot be easily described by a single known measure. Furthermore, while it is easy to construct many measures for various characteristics of a point set, an arbitrary measure does not necessarily give a complexity scale, such that values of the measure computed from easy problems are different from those computed from difficult problems. Such considerations led us to an evaluation of different types of measures using controlled or synthetic data with known levels of difficulty. We describe this early experiment as follows.

We constructed a complexity measurement space for classification problems where each feature dimension is a complexity measure. Each problem, specified by a labeled training set, is represented by a point in this space. Most of the individual measures came from the literature of both supervised and unsupervised learning, and a few others are defined by ourselves. All measures are normalized as far as possible for comparability across problems. The measures we investigated can be divided into several categories:

1. **Measures of overlaps in feature values from different classes.** These measures focus on the effectiveness of a single feature dimension in separating the classes, or the composite effects of a number of dimensions. They examine the range and spread of values in the data set within each class, and check for overlaps among different classes (Table 1.1).
2. **Measures of separability of classes.** These measures evaluate to what extent two classes are separable by examining the existence and shape of the class boundary. The contributions of individual feature dimensions are combined and *summarized* in a single score, usually a distance metric, rather than evaluated separately (Table 1.2).
3. **Measures of geometry, topology, and density of manifolds.** These measures give *indirect* characterizations of class separability. They assume that a class is made up of a single or multiple manifolds that form the support of the probability distribution of the given class. The shape, position, and interconnectedness of these manifolds give hints on how well two classes are separated, but they do not describe separability by design (Table 1.3).

Table 1.1. Measures of overlaps in feature values from different classes.

Complexity measure	Remarks
F1: maximum Fisher's discriminant ratio (`fisher`)	
Fisher's discriminant ratio for one feature dimension is defined as: $$f = \frac{(\mu_1 - \mu_2)^2}{\sigma_1^2 + \sigma_2^2}$$ where $\mu_1, \mu_2, \sigma_1^2, \sigma_2^2$ are the means and variances of the two classes respectively, in that feature dimension. We compute f for each feature and take the maximum as measure F1.	For a multidimensional problem, not all features have to contribute to class discrimination. The problem is easy as long as there exists one discriminating feature. Therefore, we can just take the maximum f over all feature dimensions in discussing class separability.
F2: volume of overlap region (`overlap`)	
Let the maximum and minimum values of each feature f_i in class c_j be $max(f_i, c_j)$ and $min(f_i, c_j)$, then the overlap measure F2 is defined to be $$\text{F2} = \prod_i \frac{\text{MINMAX}_i - \text{MAXMIN}_i}{\text{MAXMAX}_i - \text{MINMIN}_i}$$ where $i = 1, ..., d$ for a d-dimensional problem, and $$\text{MINMAX}_i = \text{MIN}(max(f_i, c_1), max(f_i, c_2))$$ $$\text{MAXMIN}_i = \text{MAX}(min(f_i, c_1), min(f_i, c_2))$$ $$\text{MAXMAX}_i = \text{MAX}(max(f_i, c_1), max(f_i, c_2))$$ $$\text{MINMIN}_i = \text{MIN}(min(f_i, c_1), min(f_i, c_2))$$	F2 measures the amount of overlap of the bounding boxes of two classes. It is the product of per-feature overlap ratios, each of which is the width of the overlap interval normalized by the width of the entire interval encompassing the two classes. The volume is zero as long as there is at least one dimension in which the value ranges of the two classes are disjoint.
F3: maximum (individual) feature efficiency (`maxfeaeff`)	
In a procedure that progressively removes unambiguous points falling outside the overlapping region in each chosen dimension [5], the *efficiency* of each feature is defined as the fraction of all remaining points separable by that feature. To represent the contribution of the feature most useful in this sense, we use the *maximum feature efficiency* (largest fraction of points distinguishable with only one feature) as a measure (F3).	This measure considers only separating hyperplanes perpendicular to the feature axes. Therefore, even for a linearly separable problem, F3 may be less than 1 if the optimal separating hyperplane is oblique.

Some of these measures have been used before, individually and sometimes implicitly, to characterize classification problems. But there have been few serious studies on their effectiveness. Some are known to be good only for certain types of data sets. For instance, Fisher's discriminant ratio is good for indicating the separation between two classes each following a Gaussian distribution, but not for two classes forming nonoverlapping concentric rings one inside the other. We believe that more measures used in combination can provide a better picture about class separation, which determines the difficulty of classification.

1.4 Data Sets for Validating Complexity Measures

Arbitrary functions can be constructed to measure characteristics of a point set, but the measures are useful for our purpose only if they can describe complexity relevant to classification, that is, they can distinguish easy classification problems from the difficult ones. The measures need to be validated first using problems known to be easy or difficult.

We evaluated the effectiveness of the complexity measures with two collections of classification problems, one from the real world and the other synthetic. The first collection includes all pairwise discrimination problems from 14 data sets in the University of California, Irvine (UCI) Machine Learning Depository [2]. The data sets are those that contain at least 500 points with no missing values: *abalone, car, german, kr-vs-kp, letter, lrs, nursery, pima, segmentation, splice, tic-tac-toe, vehicle, wdbc,* and *yeast*. Categorical features in some data sets are numerically coded. There are altogether 844 two-class discrimination problems, with training set sizes varying from 2 to 4648, and feature space dimensionality varying from 8 to 480. Using the linear programming procedure by Smith [18] (as given in the description of the L1 measure in Table 1.1), 452 out of the 844 problems are found to be linearly separable [1]. They are referred to as the UCI linearly separable group. The class boundary in each of these problems, as far as the training set is concerned, can be described entirely by the weight vector of the separating hyperplane, so by Kolmogorov's notion these are simple problems. Thus a valid complexity measure should place these problems at one end of its scale.

To nail the other end of a complexity scale, we need problems that are known to be difficult. These should be problems that are known to have no learnable structure. We created these problems artificially as the second collection. This collection consists of 100 artificial two-class problems each having 1000 points per class. Problem 1 has one feature dimension, problem 2 has two, and so forth, and the last problem contains 100 features. Each feature is a uniformly distributed pseudorandom number in $[0, 1]$. The points are randomly labeled, with equal probability, as one of two classes. Because the class label of a point cannot be used to predict the class of its neighbor, these problems have an intrinsically complex class boundary. They are expected to locate at the other end of any complexity scale.

We studied the complexity measures on the distribution of these three groups of problems: (1) UCI linearly separable, (2) UCI linearly nonseparable, and (3) random labelings. A single measure is considered useful for describing problem complexity if the three groups of problems are identifiable on its scale, and a set of measures are considered useful if the groups of problems are separable in the space spanned by the set.

1.5 Key Observations

The distribution of the three groups of classification problems in our chosen 12-dimensional complexity space displays many interesting characteristics. A detailed

Table 1.2. Measures of geometry, topology, and density of manifolds.

L3: nonlinearity of linear classifier by LP (nonlin-LP)	
Hoekstra and Duin [11] proposed a measure for the *nonlinearity* of a classifier with respect to a given data set. Given a training set, the method first creates a test set by linear interpolation (with random coefficients) between randomly drawn pairs of points from the same class. Then the error rate of the classifier (trained by the given training set) on this test set is measured. Here we use such a nonlinearity measure for the linear classifier defined for L1.	This measure is sensitive to the smoothness of the classifier's decision boundary as well as the overlap of the convex hulls of the classes. For linear classifiers and linearly separable problems, it measures the alignment of the decision surface with the class boundary. It carries the effects of the training procedure in addition to those of the class separation.
N4: nonlinearity of 1NN classifier (nonlin-NN)	
This is the nonlinearity measure, as defined for L3, calculated for a nearest neighbor classifier.	This measure is for the alignment of the nearest-neighbor boundary with the shape of the gap or overlap between the convex hulls of the classes.
T1: fraction of points with associated adherence subsets retained (pretop)	
This measure originated from a work on describing shapes of class manifolds using the notion of *adherence subsets* in pretopology [13]. Simply speaking, it counts the number of balls needed to cover each class, where each ball is centered at a training point and grown to the maximal size before it touches another class. Redundant balls lying completely in the interior of other balls are removed. We normalize the count by the total number of points.	A list of such balls is a composite description of the shape of the classes. The number and size of the balls indicate how much the points tend to cluster in hyperspheres or spread into elongated structures. In a problem where each point is closer to points of the other class than points of its own class, each point is covered by a distinctive ball of a small size, resulting in a high value of the measure.
T2: average number of points per dimension (npts-ndim)	
This is a simple ratio of the number of points in the data set over the number of feature dimensions.	This measure is included mostly for connection with prior studies on sample sizes. Because the volume of a region scales exponentially with the number of dimensions, a linear ratio between the two is not a good measure of sampling density.

Table 1.3. Measures of class separability.

L1: minimized sum of error distance by linear programming (`sumdist-LP`)	
Linear classifiers can be obtained by a linear programming formulation proposed by Smith [18]. The method minimizes the sum of distances of error points to the separating hyperplane (subtracting a constant margin): $$\text{minimize } \mathbf{a}^t\mathbf{t}$$ $$\text{subject to } \mathbf{Z}^t\mathbf{w} + \mathbf{t} \geq \mathbf{b}$$ $$\mathbf{t} \geq \mathbf{0}$$ where $\mathbf{a}$, $\mathbf{b}$ are arbitrary constant vectors (both chosen to be 1), $\mathbf{w}$ is the weight vector to be determined, $\mathbf{t}$ is an error vector, and $\mathbf{Z}$ is a matrix where each column $\mathbf{z}$ is defined on an input vector $\mathbf{x}$ (augmented by adding one dimension with a constant value 1) and its class c (with value c_1 or c_2) as follows: $$\begin{cases} \mathbf{z} = +\mathbf{x} \text{ if } c = c_1 \\ \mathbf{z} = -\mathbf{x} \text{ if } c = c_2. \end{cases}$$ The value of the objective function in this formulation is used as a measure (L1).	The measure has a zero value for a linearly separable problem. Its value can be heavily affected by outliers occurring on the wrong side of the optimal hyperplane. The measure is normalized by the number of points in the problem and also by the length of the diagonal of the hyperrectangular region enclosing all training points in the feature space.
L2: error rate of linear classifier by LP (`error-LP`)	
This measure is the error rate of the linear classifier defined for L1, measured with the training set.	With a small training set this can be a severe underestimate of the true error rate.
N1: fraction of points on class boundary (`boundary`)	
This method constructs a class-blind minimum spanning tree over the entire data set, and counts the number of points incident to an edge going across the two classes. The fraction of such points over all points in the data set is used as a measure.	For two heavily interleaved classes, a majority of points are located next to the class boundary. However, the same can be true for a sparsely sampled linearly separable problem with margins narrower than the distances between points of the same class.
N2: ratio of average intra/inter class NN distance (`intra-inter`)	
We first compute the Euclidean distance from each point to its nearest neighbor within the class, and also to its nearest neighbor outside the class. We then take the average (over all points) of all the distances to intraclass nearest neighbors, and the average of all the distances to interclass nearest neighbors. The ratio of the two averages is used as a measure.	This compares the within-class spread to the size of the gap between classes. It is sensitive to the classes of the closest neighbors to a point, and also to the difference in magnitude of the between-class distances and that of the within-class distances.
N3: error rate of 1NN classifier (`error-NN`)	
This is simply the error rate of a nearest-neighbor classifier measured with the training set.	The error rate is estimated by the leave-one-out method.

description of the observations in this study can be found elsewhere [8]. Here we summarize the main findings.

1.5.1 Continuum of Problem Locations in Complexity Space

The first remarkable observation in this study is that the data sets fall on a continuum of positions along many dimensions of the complexity space. Even though there have been no special selection criteria imposed on the naturally arising data sets, we find that the problems cover a large range of values in almost all the chosen complexity scales. This reminds us of the challenges in the practice of pattern recognition: to pursue a good match of methods to problems, we must make sure that the classifier methodology we choose is robust to variations in these problem characteristics, or we must understand the nature of the dependence of classifier behavior on such variations. Without accomplishing either, applications of arbitrary classifiers to a problem have little hope of ensuring highest success.

A more encouraging observation is that many of the real-world (UCI) data sets are located far away from the random labelings, suggesting that these practical problems do indeed contain some regularity or learnable structure.

Interestingly, there is substantial spread among the random labelings of different dimensionality. While there is no immediate explanation for how dimensionality affects their intrinsic difficulties, closer examination of the differences suggests that this is more an effect of differences in apparent complexity due to different sampling densities, because these data sets all have the same number of points while the volume of the space increases exponentially with dimensionality.

1.5.2 Effectiveness of Individual Measures in Separating Problems of Known Levels of Difficulty

The concentrations of the three groups of problems (UCI linearly separable, UCI linearly nonseparable, and random labelings) in different regions in the complexity space suggest that many of the chosen measures are able to reveal their differences. As a stand-alone scale of complexity, several measures (F1, F2, F3, L2, L3) are especially effective in separating at least two of the three groups, with the easiest set (UCI linearly separable) and the hardest set (random labelings) occupying two opposite ends of the scale. However, none of the measures can completely separate the three groups with no overlap. Some measures, such as N4 and T2, are especially weak when used in isolation.

The nearest-neighbor related measures (N1, N2, N3) have almost the same discriminating power for the three groups, except for a few peculiar cases where the training set consists of only two or three points. For those extremely sparse data sets, although the class boundary (for the training set) is linear, the nearest neighbors are almost always in a wrong class; thus the nearest-neighbor error rate becomes very high. This is an artifact of the leave-one-out estimate. However, it also suggests that a single error rate, even that of a simple and well-understood classifier, may tell a distorted story about the data complexity. This reinforces our belief that measures of data complexity should not be based entirely on classifier performances but should be on underlying problem characteristics.

1.6 Relationship among the Complexity Measures

1.6.1 Classifying the Measures

There are different ways to describe the measures. A complexity measure can be viewed as metric based or non–metric based. The fractions of points on class boundary (N1) and NN nonlinearity (N4) are examples of metric based measures, whereas the minimized sum of error distances by linear programming (L1) are example of a non–metric-based measure. The effectiveness of metric-based measures suffers when there are many noisy features in a classification problem, because in those cases the dissimilarity represented by the distance metric could be dominated by the noise and is no longer reliable. On the other hand, non–metric-based measures usually rely on some assumptions on the nature of the decision boundary, such as a linear separating hyperplane. The same is not true for metric-based measures.

1.6.2 Principal Components of the Complexity Space

A principal component analysis (PCA) using the distribution of the problems in the 12-dimensional space shows that there are six significant components each explaining more than 5% of the variance. Among these, the first component (PC1) explains over 50% of the variance, and comprises even contributions from F2, L2, L3, N1, N2, and N3. It is a combination of effects of linearity of class boundaries and proximity between opposite-class neighbors. The next three components explain 12%, 11% and 9% of the variance, respectively, and can be interpreted as the contrast between within-class and between-class scatter (PC2), the concentration and orientation of class overlaps (PC3), and within-class scatter (PC4). For a more detailed discussion of these components, as well as for the trajectory traced in the PC projection by an example series of problems with controlled class separation, we refer readers to our earlier work [8].

1.6.3 Pairwise Correlations Between the Complexity Measures

Bivariate plots of the distributions show that some pairs of measures, such as L2 and L3, or N1 and N3, are strongly correlated, whereas little correlation is seen between many other pairs. The correlation coefficients between each pair of measures are shown in Table 1.4. The existence of many uncorrelated pairs (as small values in the table) suggests that there are more than one independent factors affecting a problem's complexity.

An examination of the correlation between L2 (linear classifier error rate) and N3 (nearest neighbor error rate) and between each of these two measures and others suggests that these error rates are not perfectly correlated, nor are they always predictable by an arbitrary measure. This reconfirms the risk of relying on simple classifier error rates for complexity measurement. These two classifiers, operating on very different principles (linearity versus proximity), have difficulties caused by different characteristics of a problem (Fig. 1.3). More on these two classifiers will be discussed in a subsequent chapter in this book.

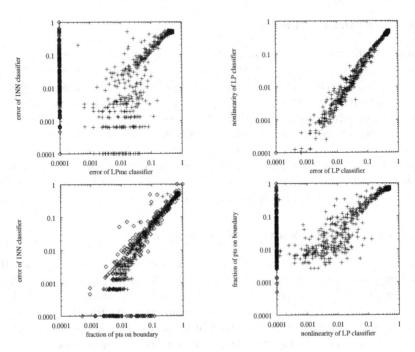

Fig. 1.3. Error rates of linear and nearest-neighbor classifiers, and the measures they are most strongly correlated with. (◇: UCI linearly separable problems; +: UCI linearly nonseparable problems; □: random labelings.)

Some measures, while on their own are very weak in separating all three groups of problems, can reveal between-group differences when used in combination with other measures (Fig. 1.4). This demonstrates the importance of a joint examination of multiple aspects of a problem's complexity.

The measure T1, while on its own being a strong separator of the three groups, characterizes a very different aspect of complexity from others as evidenced by its weak correlation with others. Inspection of the plots involving T1 and others suggests that while the shapes of the classes can vary a lot across different problems, it is less relevant to classification accuracy than the shapes of the class boundaries.

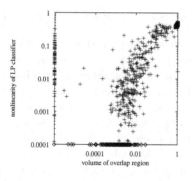 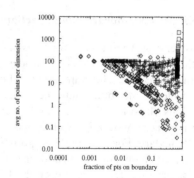

Fig. 1.4. Groups of problems that overlap heavily on an individual complexity scale may show clear separation in the interaction of the effects. (◇: UCI linearly separable problems; +: UCI linearly nonseparable problems; □: random labelings)

Table 1.4. Correlation coefficients between each pair of measures.

	F1	F2	F3	L1	L2	L3	N1	N2	N3	N4	T1	T2
F1	1.00	–0.02	0.06	–0.01	–0.02	–0.02	0.07	0.01	0.14	–0.02	0.03	–0.03
F2		1.00	–0.53	0.07	0.91	0.91	0.69	0.71	0.61	0.17	0.28	0.19
F3			1.00	–0.24	–0.65	–0.62	–0.39	–0.69	–0.29	–0.40	–0.68	–0.28
L1				1.00	0.33	0.32	0.37	0.37	0.28	0.53	0.18	–0.10
L2					1.00	1.00	0.78	0.81	0.67	0.47	0.37	0.16
L3						1.00	0.78	0.81	0.67	0.46	0.35	0.16
N1							1.00	0.76	0.96	0.49	0.39	–0.02
N2								1.00	0.68	0.51	0.55	0.12
N3									1.00	0.38	0.38	–0.04
N4										1.00	0.28	0.30
T1											1.00	0.17
T2												1.00

1.6.4 1NN Error Rates Are Equal to Or Less Than Fractions of Points on Boundary

Error rates of 1NN classifiers (N3) can be shown to relate closely with fractions of points on boundary (N1). If a point has its nearest neighbor in the opposite class, in the minimum spanning tree on which measure N1 is based, it is connected to the rest of the data set by an edge to that neighbor; thus it will always be a point on a cross-boundary edge. This point at the same time will contribute to nearest neighbor classification error. Thus the number of boundary points will be no less than the number of nearest neighbor errors. Note that there can be many boundary points that are not misclassified by 1NN. An extreme example is a configuration like this in one dimension:

xx   oo   xx   oo   xx   oo   xx   oo

1.6.5 1NN Nonlinearity and Fractions of Points on Boundary Are Unrelated

Another observation is that fractions of points on boundary (N1) have no relationship with 1NN nonlinearity (N4). Consider a data set made up of two concentric spirals as in Figure 1.2c. There are only two boundary points connecting the two classes at the center of the spirals; thus the value of N1 is small. However, the nonlinearity of the 1NN classifier (N4) is about 0.5, maximum for a classifier. In another scenario, the nonlinearity of a linear classifier (L3) can be small even if many points are on the boundary. For example, in a problem where points of the two classes form an elongated chain along a linear decision boundary with wide gaps between points in the same class, L3 is small even if all the data points are on a boundary causing a high value of N1.

1.6.6 Overlap Volume Versus Maximum Feature Efficiency

The volume of overlap (F2) is the product of the intervals in each dimension of the feature space that are occupied by points from both classes. Maximum feature efficiency (F3) is more related to the variation of density of data points. While it is usually the case that these two measures are anticorrelated (large overlap volume hints low feature efficiency), it is possible to come up with counterexamples of this rule as in the configuration below.

A one-dimensional example of large overlap volume and large feature efficiency is like this:

```
         x                          xxxxxxxxx
      o   o  o  o  o  o  o  o  o
```

Small overlap and small feature efficiency can also coexist if the points are dense within a small overlap region.

1.7 Extensions for More Complicated Classification Problems

The measures we used in the exploratory studies are shown to be useful for unambiguous two-class discrimination. There are many ways these can be extended to handle more complicated situations in classification. Here we describe four ways to do so, addressing issues caused by more than two classes, class ambiguity, differences between local and global data properties, and potential transformations on the data that may reduce their complexity.

1.7.1 Extension to Multiple Classes

We have discussed the complexity measures designed for two-class problems. Many of these measures are not directly applicable to a multiclass problem. An easy way out is to convert a multiclass problem to many instances of two-class problems by, say, one-versus-all-the-rest. Alternatively, we can extend the complexity measures to multiple classes according to their semantics. Examples include:

- **Fisher discriminant ratio.** Fisher's multiple discriminant ratio for C classes is defined to be

$$f = \frac{\sum_{i=1,j=1,i\neq j}^{C} p_i p_j (\mu_i - \mu_j)^2}{\sum_{i=1}^{C} p_i \sigma_i^2}$$

where μ_i, σ_i^2, and p_i are the mean, variance, and proportion of the ith class, respectively. In practice the inverse of the Fisher ratio is preferred, such that a small complexity value represents an easy problem.

- **Fractions of points on boundary.** To generalize to multiple classes, the count of boundary points can be changed to the count of edges with end points from different classes. The same applies to 1NN nonlinearly, LP nonlinearity, where misclassifications are now just points assigned to a wrong class. For the pretopological measure (T1), the adherence subsets around each point can be grown until touching any other point with a different class label.

- **Volume of overlap region.** This measure can be generalized to describe the overlap of the bounding boxes of any pair of classes. Let V_i be the hyperrectangular region spanned by the ith class. The overlapping volume can be defined as

$$f = \text{volume of } \bigcup_{i,j,i\neq j} V_i \cap V_j.$$

For computational efficiency one may approximate the above by

$$f = \sum_{i,j,i\neq j} \text{volume of } V_i \cap V_j.$$

For some complexity measure, extension to multiple classes is not straightforward. An example is the minimized sum of error distances by linear programming (L1) that is defined on a separating hyperplane between two classes. There are several possible generalizations. One can sum the values for all one-versus-all-the-rest problems, or one can consider the average value over different pairs of classes. Other ways include various proposed schemes to generalize the concept of margin to multiple classes [4].

1.7.2 Dealing with Intrinsic Ambiguity

Intrinsic ambiguity in the tails of class distributions can lead to deceptive values in some complexity measures, suggesting that the boundary is more complicated than that a dense sample would reveal. The ambiguity can be caused by inappropriate class definitions or a lack of class-discriminating power in the chosen features. It can also be caused by accidental errors in class labels in the training data. An illustrative example is given in Figure 1.5. There are two ways to interpret those "error" points. One can simply assume that those points are correct and estimate the complexity of the decision boundary as in Figure 1.5b. Alternatively, one can treat those "error" points as accidental and argue that the proper decision boundary is the straight line, as in Figure 1.5a. Without any prior information, it is difficult to choose between these two interpretations.

Labeling errors and intrinsic ambiguity can have a large impact on certain complexity measures. An example is the one-dimensional problem shown in Figure 1.6. The overlapping interval of the two classes in this feature is illustrated by the long arrow on top of the data points. However, if we interpret the leftmost point from class 2 as an erroneous data point and ignore it, the overlapping region shrinks significantly, as illustrated by the arrow at the bottom. Another way of saying this is that a complexity measure may depend too much on the details of the class boundary and is not robust.

As argued earlier, we cannot distinguish between an unambiguous, correctly labeled complex boundary and an ambiguous or erroneously labeled simple boundary. In practice, most classifiers do choose between these two by imposing assumptions on the decision boundary. For the study on measuring boundary complexity, however, such a choice can discard useful information and is undesirable. A modification of the measures can alleviate us of this choice. Instead of reporting a single complexity value, we can report a sequence of values, or a measure curve. If needed, the complexity measure curve can be summarized by, say, its average curvature or the area under the curve.

Formally, let $f(D)$ be a certain complexity measure applied on a data set D. Without loss of generality we shall assume that a small value of $f(.)$ corresponds to a simple classification problem. Let D^* be a perturbed version of D, and $h(D, D^*)$ be a distance metric that measures the difference between D and D^*. We define the complexity measure curve as

$$g_D(\epsilon) = \min_{D^*:h(D,D^*)\leq\epsilon} f(D^*)$$

where ϵ specifies an error level. The complexity measure curve consists of $g_D(.)$ evaluated at different values of ϵ. Note that the original complexity measure is a point in this complexity curve, namely the point $g_D(0)$.

Combinatorics may prohibit an exact calculation of the minimization which needs to find the best perturbation of D at each error level. A greedy algorithm may be preferable instead, which proceeds as follows. For each error level ϵ, we look for a good perturbation by trying to change the class labels of a sufficient number of points (depending on the error level) that individually cause the largest drop in the complexity value. There may be situations where no relabeling can decrease the complexity. In such cases the search can be made on omitting the points from the data set that cause the largest contribution to complexity.

1.7.3 Local Properties

The complexity measures we used describe global properties of a data set. However, sometimes local characteristics of the data may also be important. For example, a data set is often almost linearly separable when viewed locally but is not so globally.

Local characteristics like this can reveal themselves in a multiresolution study under reasonable choices of partitioning methods such as the grids used in Singh [19].

We propose using the neighborhood of a data point to define the local properties instead of grids, which make the values of the measures sensitive to grid boundaries. The drawback of using neighborhoods is that it is computationally more expensive. Let $N_{i,k}$ be the set of the k nearest neighbors of the point $\mathbf{x}_i$ in a data set D of size n, including $\mathbf{x}_i$ itself. We can then compute the complexity measure value at scale k by

$$\bar{f}(D, k) = \frac{1}{n} \sum_{i=1}^{n} f(N_{i,k}).$$

Implementation is straightforward for most of the measures we discussed, as one can simply recompute the measures at different locality levels. For some measures, such as those involving a minimum spanning tree, an incremental approach may be preferable for efficiency.

1.7.4 Nonlinear Boundaries

Some of the complexity measures implicitly assume a linear decision boundary. In particular, the calculation of measures L1, L2, and L3 starts with an optimal hyperplane for a linear classifier. Data with a nonlinear boundary will lead to a large value in those measures even if the class boundary can be fit with a simple, smooth (e.g., quadratic) surface with wide margin as in Figure 1.7b. In these cases, a kernel principal component transformation can be performed that projects the data to a linear feature space where the complexity can be evaluated (Fig. 1.7c).

The choice of the kernel function is based on what types of decision boundary characteristics one wants to use as references. For example, if we want to see how "quadratic"-like the decision boundary is, we should use the polynomial kernel of degree two. On the other hand, if we want to see how similar the decision boundary would be when compared to a spline, we should use a spline kernel.

1.8 Conclusion

We described some early investigation into the complexity of a classification problem, with emphasis on the geometrical characteristics that can be measured directly from a training set. We studied the validity of the chosen measures as a complexity scale using a collection of problems of known levels of difficulty. We found some interesting spread among different types of problems, and evidence of the existence of independent factors affecting a problem's difficulty. We believe that such descriptors of complexity are useful for identifying and comparing different types of problems, characterizing the domains of competence of a classifier [16], and in many ways guiding the development of a solution to a pattern recognition problem. We also investigated some relationship among these descriptors and potential generalizations of their definitions to more complicated classification problems.

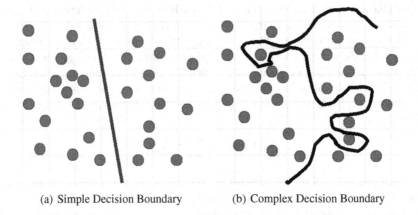

(a) Simple Decision Boundary   (b) Complex Decision Boundary

Fig. 1.5. An example illustrating the effect of intrinsic ambiguity. The erroneous data points can lead to an overly complex decision boundary, which is usually not optimal in practice because of overfitting.

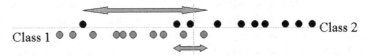

Fig. 1.6. An example illustrating that the overlap region can be severely affected by erroneous data points.

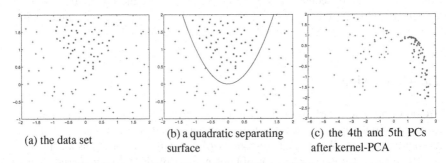

(a) the data set   (b) a quadratic separating surface   (c) the 4th and 5th PCs after kernel-PCA

Fig. 1.7. An example illustrating a nonlinear decision boundary.

A complexity measurement space like this has many potentially interesting uses. For a particular application, the measured levels of complexity can help determine the existence of any learnable structure and set expectations on potential gains by automatic learning algorithms. Within the context of the same application, the measures can be used to compare different problem formulations, including alternative class definitions, noise conditions and sampling strategies, choices of features, and potential feature transformations. They can be used to guide the selection of classifiers and classifier combination schemes, or control the process of classifier training. A use of these measures for comparing two methods for decision forest construction is reported in Ho[9].

For research in classification methods, the measures can be used to determine if a particular data set is suitable for evaluating different learning algorithms. Collection of benchmarking data sets can be tailored to span a large range in the complexity space to fully characterize the behavior of individual classifiers. Regions occupied by data sets on which classifiers display homogeneous performances can be used to outline the domain of competences of those classifiers, with the expectation that performances on new data sets falling in the same region can be predicted accordingly. Regions where no known classifiers can do well may be characterized in detail by the complexity measures, which could lead to new classifier designs covering those blind spots. In later chapters, we will report detailed characterizations of the domain of competence of XCS, a genetic algorithm-based classifier, as well as several other popular classifiers.

One may wish to study the distribution of all classification problems in this space. An empirical approach will be to seek a representation of the distribution by a much larger collection of synthetic or practical problems. A theoretical approach will be more challenging; it involves reasoning about regions in this space that are possible or impossible for any data set to occupy. The identification of such regions will require a better understanding of constraints in high-dimensional point set geometry and topology. The intrinsic dimensionality of the problem distribution will give more conclusive evidence on how many independent factors contribute to a problem's difficulty.

We have made some first steps towards developing elements of a mathematical language with which we can talk more precisely about properties of high-dimensional data sets, especially those aspects affecting classifier performances. We believe this is necessary for classification research to advance beyond the current plateau. Finally, we believe that such abstract studies are best accompanied by data generation facilities and software tools for interactive data visualization, so that an intuitive understanding may be obtained on how complexity arises from a particular problem [10].

References

[1] M. Basu, T.K. Ho. The learning behavior of single neuron classifiers on linearly separable or nonseparable input. *Proc. of the 1999 International Joint Confer-*

ence on Neural Networks, Washington, DC, July 1999.

[2] C.L. Blake, C.J. Merz. UCI Repository of machine learning databases. http://www.ics.uci.edu/ mlearn/MLRepository.html, University of California, Department of Information and Computer Science, Irvine, CA, 1998.

[3] L. Devroye. Automatic pattern recognition: A study of the probability of error. *IEEE Transactions on Pattern Analysis and Machine Intelligence*, 10(4), 530–543, 1988.

[4] A. Elisseeff, Y. Guermeur, H. Paugam-Moisy. Margin error and generalization capabilities of multiclass discriminant systems. *European Working Group NeuroCOLT 2*, Technical Report NC2-TR-1999-051, http://www.neurocolt.com/abs/1999/abs99051.html, 1999.

[5] T.K. Ho, H.S. Baird. Pattern classification with compact distribution maps. *Computer Vision and Image Understanding*, 70(1), 101–110, April 1998.

[6] T.K. Ho. Multiple classifier combination: lessons and next steps. In A. Kandel, H. Bunke, eds., *Hybrid Methods in Pattern Recognition*. Singapore:World Scientific, 2002.

[7] T.K. Ho, M. Basu. Measuring the complexity of classification problems. *Proc. of the 15th International Conference on Pattern Recognition*, Barcelona, Spain, September 3-8, 2000, 43–47.

[8] T.K. Ho, M. Basu. Complexity measures of supervised classification problems. *IEEE Transactions on Pattern Analysis and Machine Intelligence*, 24(3), 289–300, 2002.

[9] T.K. Ho. A data complexity analysis of comparative advantages of decision forest constructors, Pattern Analysis and Applications. 5, 102–112, 2002.

[10] T.K. Ho. Exploratory analysis of point proximity in subspaces. *Proc. of the 16th International Conference on Pattern Recognition*, Quebec City, Canada, August 11-15, 2002.

[11] A. Hoekstra, R.P.W. Duin. On the nonlinearity of pattern classifiers. *Proc. of the 13th International Conference on Pattern Recognition*, Vienna, August 1996, D271–275.

[12] A.N. Kolmogorov. Three approaches to the quantitative definition of information. *Problems of Information Transmission*, 1, 4–7, 1965.

[13] F. Lebourgeois, H. Emptoz. Pretopological approach for supervised learning. *Proc. of the 13th International Conference on Pattern Recognition*, Vienna, 256–260, 1996.

[14] M. Li, P. Vitanyi. *An Introduction to Kolmogorov Complexity and Its Applications*. New York:Springer-Verlag, 1993.

[15] J.M. Maciejowski. Model discrimination using an algorithmic information criterion. *Automatica*, 15, 579–593, 1979.

[16] E.B. Mansilla, T.K. Ho. Domain of competence of XCS classifier system in complexity measurement space. *IEEE Transactions on Evolutionary Computation*, 9(1), 82–104, February 2005.

[17] S. Raudys, A.K. Jain. Small sample size effects in statistical pattern recognition: recommendations for practitioners. *IEEE Transactions on Pattern Analysis and Machine Intelligence*, 13(3), 252–264, 1991.

[18] F.W. Smith. Pattern classifier design by linear programming. *IEEE Transactions on Computers*, C-17(4), 367–372, April 1968.
[19] S. Singh. Multiresolution estimates of classification complexity. *IEEE Transactions on Pattern Analysis and Machine Intelligence*, 25(12), 1534–1539, 2003.
[20] V. Vapnik. *Statistical Learning Theory*. New York:John Wiley & Sons, 1998.

2

Object Representation, Sample Size, and Data Set Complexity

Robert P.W. Duin and Elżbieta Pękalska

Summary. The complexity of a pattern recognition problem is determined by its representation. It is argued and illustrated by examples that the sampling density of a given data set and the resulting complexity of a learning problem are inherently connected. A number of criteria are constructed to judge this complexity for the chosen dissimilarity representation. Some nonlinear transformations of the original representation are also investigated to illustrate that such changes may affect the resulting complexity. If the initial sampling density is originally insufficient, this may result in a data set of a lower complexity and with a satisfactory sampling. On the other hand, if the number of samples is originally abundant, the representation may become more complex.

2.1 Introduction

To solve a particular problem, one will be interested in its complexity to find a short path to the solution. The analyst will face an easy and straightforward task if the solution follows directly from the way the problem is stated. The problem will be judged as complex if one needs to use a large set of tools and has to select the best procedure by a trial-and-error approach or if one has to integrate several partial solutions. A possible way to proceed is to simplify the initial problem, e.g., by removing its most weakly determined aspects. This chapter focuses on these two issues: judging the complexity of a problem from the way it is presented, and discussing some ways to simplify it if the complexity is judged as too large.

The complexity of pattern recognition problems has recently raised some interest [16, 17]. It is hoped that its study may contribute to the selection of appropriate methods to solve a given problem. As the concept of problem complexity is still ill-defined, we will start to clarify our approach, building on some earlier work [10].

Pattern recognition problems may have some intrinsic overlap. This does not contribute to the problem complexity, as an existing intrinsic overlap cannot be removed by any means. The complexity of the problem lies in difficulties one encounters in the above sketched sense, while approaching a classification performance related to the intrinsic class overlap. Because problems are numerically encoded by data sets representing the classes of objects for which either pattern classes have to be learned or classifiers have to be determined, the complexity of the recognition problem is the complexity of the representation as one observes through some data set. Such representations heavily influence the complexity of the learning problem.

An important aspect of the representation is the nature of numerical encoding used for the characterization of objects, as, for example, features or proximities between pairs of objects, or proximities of objects to class models. Even if objects are first represented in a structural form, such as relational graphs or strings, we will assume that a numerical representation (e.g., by dissimilarities) is derived from such an intermediate description. In addition, the number of objects in the data set, i.e., the sample size, and the way the objects are sampled from the problem (at random or by some systematic procedure) influence the complexity. As the exploration or classification problems have to be solved using a data set based on some representation, the complexity of the problem is reflected by the data set and the representation.

This chapter focuses on the influence of sample size on the complexity of data sets used for learning pattern classes. These classes are characterized by dissimilarity representations [22, 23], which are primarily identified by sample sizes and not yet by the dimensionality of some space, as feature vector representations are. Since the given problem, the chosen representation and the derived data set are essentially connected, we will use the word *complexity* interchangeably with respect to these three concepts.

To analyze complexity in learning, one needs to understand better what complexity is. In general, complexity is defined as "the quality of being intricate and compounded" [34]. Loosely speaking, this means that an entity, a problem, a task, or a system is complex if it consists of a number of elements (components) related such that it is hard to separate them or to follow their interrelations. Intuitively, an entity is more complex if more components and more interdependencies can be distinguished. So, complexity can be characterized by the levels and the kinds of distinction and dependency. The former is related to the variability, i.e., the number of elements,and their size and shape, while the latter refers to the dependency between the components. It will be a key issue of this chapter to make clear that the set of examples used to solve the pattern recognition problem should be sufficiently large in order to meet the complexity of the representation.

Reductionism treats an entity by the sum of its components or a collection of parts. Holism, on the other hand, treats an entity as a whole, hence it does not account for distinguishable parts. The complexity can be seen as an interplay between reductionism and holism: it needs to see distinct elements, but also their interrelations, in order to realize that they cannot be separated without losing a part of their meaning; see also the development of the science of complexity as sketched by Waldrop [31]. In fact, reductionism and holism can be seen on different, organizational levels. For instance, to understand the complexity of an ant colony (see Hofstadter's chapter on "Ant Fugue" [18]), one needs to observe the activities of individual ants as well as the colony as a whole. On the level of individuals, they may seem to move in random ways, yet on the level of specialized casts and the colony, clear patterns can be distinguished. These relate to a sequential (ants following other ants), parallel (groups of ants with a task), and simultaneous or emergent (the global movement) behavior of the colony. Therefore, complexity might be described by hierarchical systems, where the lowest, indivisible parts serve for building higher level structures with additional dependencies and abstraction (symbolism or meaning).

Complexity can also be placed between order and disorder (chaos). If all ants follow sequentially one another, then although the ant colony is composed of many individuals, its complexity is low because the pattern present there is simple and regular. In this sense, the colony possesses redundant information. A single ant and a direction of move will completely describe the entire colony. On the other hand, if individual ants move in different directions, but emerge into a number of groups with different tasks and following specified paths, the complexity of the ant colony becomes larger. Finally, if all ants move independently in random ways without any purpose and grouping behavior, no clear patterns can be identified. As a result, there is no complexity as it is just chaos. Therefore, complexity may be characterized by the surprise or unexpectedness on a low level that can be understood as following the structure observed from a higher point of view. In brief, following Waldrop's point of view [31], complexity arises at the edge of structure and chaos as it is pictorially illustrated in Figure 2.1.

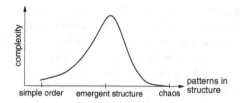

Fig. 2.1. Complexity vs. structure.

In pattern recognition one distinguishes the task of finding a classifier between some real-world classes of objects or phenomena. This task is defined on a high level. The classes may have some hidden structure that is partially reflected in the initial representation by which the problem is presented. For instance, this can be by features, dissimilarities, graphs, or other relations. Another part of the structure is implicitly available in the set of examples from which the pattern classifier has to be learned. The wholeness of the recognition problem is thereby available to us in its reduction to a set of examples by a chosen representation: the data set. The path from a pattern recognition problem to a data set determines the complexity we encounter if we try to solve the problem based on the given data set. The complexity of a pattern recognition problem (its intrinsic complexity) is simply not defined before a representation is chosen and a set of examples is collected. In the end, the data set depicts our problem.

The following example may illustrate this point. Imagine an automatic sorting of apples and pears on a moving conveyor. The complexity of this problem depends on a selection of a representative sample of apples and pears to learn from, initial measurements done by some sensors or other devices (images, spectral images, or simple characteristics such as weight, perimeter, or color) and the derived representation. In a chosen representation, the problem is complex if many examples are necessary to capture the variability and organization within the classes as well as the interrelations between the classes, leading to complicated decision functions. If one wishes to discriminate between apples and pears based on their weights only, such a problem will likely be simple. The reason is that a few suitably chosen examples will determine reliable thresholds on which such a decision relies, independently of whether this leads to frequent errors or not. On the other hand, if various Fourier coefficient and shape descriptors are computed on the images of apples and pears and treated as features, the resulting problem may become complex. Changes in light illumination or tilts of a camera may increase the variability of the (images of) apples and pears as perceived in their vector representations. This would require a large sample for a description. So, it is the representation that determines the complexity of the problem. We encounter this complexity through the data that are available.

Note, that the use of the data set as such is insufficient for solving the problem. It is just chaos if no additional background knowledge, such as the context, the way the examples are collected, or the way the numbers are measured, is given. This is very clearly shown by the "no free-lunch theorem" [33], which states that without additional knowledge, no learning algorithm is expected to be better than another. In particular, no learning algorithm outperforms a random assignment.

A very useful and often implicitly assumed type of knowledge used for a construction of the given data set is the compactness hypothesis [1, 8]. It states that similar real-world objects have similar representations. In practice, this hypothesis relies on some continuous mapping from an object to its (numerical) representation, because it is expected that a small change in an object will result in a small change in its representation. Still, the path from an object to its representation may be very nonlinear (and thereby attributing to the complexity of the problem), resulting in the violation of the reverse compactness hypothesis. This means that similar representations (e.g., feature vectors lying close in a feature vector space) may not necessarily refer to similar objects. This causes a class overlap (identical representations belong to essentially different objects as they differ in class membership) or complicates decision boundaries.

In a given data set of a limited cardinality the compactness might not be entirely realized if insufficient real-world objects are collected. Hence, it cannot be guaranteed that each object has at least one close companion. The complexity of the problem then demands a higher sampling density of (training) examples to make its characteristics apparent. As a result, the assumption needed for building classifiers on the data set is invalid and it is impossible to solve the pattern recognition problem with a sufficient accuracy. The data set resembles chaos (as patterns cannot be distinguished) and the structure of the problem cannot be determined.

The above discussion makes clear that complexity and sample size are interrelated. Complex problems (due to a complicated way they are represented by the data sets) need more samples. A question that arises now is: if the data set is insufficiently large, is it thereby less or more complex? We will return to this in the discussion section. In brief, the following issues are more explicitly studied by some examples:

- The influence of representation on the problem complexity
- The relation between the problem complexity and the necessary sample size
- The consequences of using too small sample sizes for solving complex problems

Our examples are based on a number of dissimilarity representations, which allow one to apply various modifications and transformations in a simple way. In section 2, the data sets and procedures are summarized. In section 3, various criteria are proposed and investigated to judge the sampling of single classes. Section 4 investigates and discusses the complexity issues in relation to classification. A final discussion is presented in section 2.5.

2.2 Data Sets

To limit the influence of dimensionality issues on the relations between the sample size and the complexity, we will focus on dissimilarity representations [22, 23, 26]. These are representations in which a collection of objects is encoded by their dissimilarities to a set of chosen examples, a so-called representation set. The reason we choose this name is twofold. First, the representation set is a set of examples that are not necessarily prototypical for the classes according to the usual understanding (on the contrary, some of them might be outliers). Second, this set serves for a construction of a representation space, in which both exploration and learning are performed. The representation set may be the training set itself, its randomly or selectively chosen subset or some other set. The representation set $R = \{p_1, p_2, \ldots, p_n\}$ of n examples, the (training) set $T = \{x_1, x_2, \ldots, x_N\}$ of N objects, and the dissimilarity measure d constitute together the representation $D(T, R)$. This is an $N \times n$ dissimilarity matrix, in which every entry $d(x_j, p_i)$ describes the difference between the object t_j and the representation object p_i.

Problems with various metric and nonmetric dissimilarity measures are chosen for the study. Six data sets are used in our experiments and are briefly summarized in Table 2.1. In addition to the given dissimilarity measures as listed in this table, two monotonic power transformations will be also investigated. Concerning the original representation $D = (d_{ij})$, the transformed representations are denoted as $D^{*2} = (d_{ij}^2)$ and $D^{*0.5} = (d_{ij}^{0.5})$, by taking the element-wise square or square root of the dissimilarities d_{ij}, respectively. Note that the metric properties of the measure d are preserved by a square root transformation, but not necessarily by a quadratic transformation [22]. By such modifications, it is expected that either large dissimilarities and, thereby, more global aspects of the data set are emphasized in D^{*2} or large dissimilarities are suppressed in $D^{*0.5}$, by which local aspects are strengthened. Remember that nondecreasing transformations like these do not affect the order of the given dissimilarities. Thereby, the nearest neighbor relations are preserved.

Digits-38. The data describe a set of scanned handwritten digits of the National Institute of Standards and Technology (NIST) data set [32], originally given as $128 \times$

Table 2.1. Data sets used in the experiments.

Data	Dissimilarity	Property	# classes	# objects per class
Digits-38	Euclidean	Euclidean	2	1000
Digits-all	Template-match	Nonmetric	10	200
Heart	Gower's	Euclidean	2	139/164
Polygon	Mod. Hausdorff	Nonmetric	2	2000
ProDom	Structural	Nonmetric	4	878/404/271/1051
Tumor-mucosa	$l_{0.8}$-distance	Nonmetric	2	132/856

128 binary images. Just two classes of digits, 3 and 8, are considered here. Each class consists of 1000 examples. The images are first smoothed by a Gaussian kernel with $\sigma = 8$ pixels and then the Euclidean distances between such blurred images are computed (summing up the squares of pixel-to-pixel gray value differences followed by the square root). The smoothing is done to make this distance representation more robust against tilting or shifting.

Digits-all. The data describe a set of scanned handwritten digits of the NIST data set [32], originally given as 128×128 binary images. The similarity measure, based on deformable template matching, as defined by Jain and Zongker [20], is used. Let $S = (s_{ij})$ denote the similarities. Since the similarity is asymmetric, the off-diagonal symmetric dissimilarities are computed as $d_{ij} = (s_{ii} + s_{jj} - s_{ij} - s_{ji})^{1/2}$ for $i \neq j$. D is significantly nonmetric [24].

Heart. This data set comes from the University of California, Irvine (UCI) Machine Learning Repository [2]. The goal is to detect the presence of heart disease in patients. There are 303 examples, of which 139 correspond to diseased patients. Various measurements are performed; however, only 13 attributes are used by other researchers for the analysis, as provided in Blake and Merz [2]. These attributes are age, sex (1/0), chest pain type (1-4), resting blood pressure, serum cholesterol, fasting blood sugar >120 mg/dl (1/0), resting electrocardiograph results, maximum heart rate achieved, exercise-induced angina (1/0), the slope of the peak exercise ST segment, ST depression induced by exercise relative to rest (1-3), number of major vessels colored by fluoroscopy (0-3), and heart condition (normal, fixed defect, and reversible defect). Hence, the data consist of mixed types: continuous, dichotomous, and categorical variables. There are also several missing values.

Gower's [14] dissimilarity is used for the representation. Assume m features and let x_{ik} be the kth feature value for the ith object. A similarity measure is defined as

$$s_{ij} = \frac{\sum_{k=1}^{m} w_k \, \delta_{ijk} \, s_{ijk}}{\sum_{k=1}^{m} w_k \, \delta_{ijk}}, \tag{2.1}$$

where s_{ijk} is the similarity between the ith and jth objects based on the kth feature f_k only, and $\delta_{ijk} = 1$, if the objects can legitimately be compared, and zero otherwise, as, for example, in the case of missing values. For dichotomous variables, $\delta_{ijk} = 0$ if $x_{ik} = x_{jk} = 0$ and $\delta_{ijk} = 1$ otherwise. The strength of feature contributions is determined by the weights w_k, which are omitted here as all $w_k = 1$. The similarity

s_{ijk}, $i,j = 1,\ldots,n$ and $k = 1,\ldots,m$ becomes then $s_{ijk} = 1 - \frac{|x_{ik} - x_{jk}|}{r_k}$ if f_k is quantitative, $s_{ijk} = \mathcal{I}((x_{ik} = x_{jk}) = 1)$ if f_k is dichotomous, $s_{ijk} = \mathcal{I}(x_{ik} = x_{jk})$ if f_k is categorical and $s_{ijk} = 1 - g(\frac{|x_{ik} - x_{jk}|}{r_k})$, where r_k is the range of f_k and g is a chosen monotonic transformation if f_k is ordinal. The Gower's dissimilarity between the ith and jth objects is defined as $d_{ij} = (1 - s_{ij})^{1/2}$.

Polygon. The data consist of two classes of randomly generated polygons, convex quadrilaterals and irregular heptagons [22, 24]. Each class consists of 2000 examples. First, the polygons are scaled such that their total contour lengths are equal. Next, the modified Hausdorff distances [7] are computed between their corners. Let A and B be two polygons. The modified Hausdorff distance is defined as $d_{MH}(A, B) = \max\{d^{\flat}_{avr}(A, B), d^{\flat}_{avr}(B, A)\}$, where $d^{\flat}_{avr}(A, B) = \frac{1}{|A|}\sum_{a \in A} \min_{b \in B} d(a, b)$, and it is evaluated at the polygon corners a and b. This measure is nonmetric [7, 22].

ProDom. ProDom is a comprehensive set of protein domain families [5]. A subset of 2604 protein domain sequences from the ProDom set [5] was selected by Roth et al. [28]. These examples are chosen based on a high similarity to at least one sequence contained in the first four folds of the Structural Classification of Proteins (SCOP) database. The pairwise structural alignments are computed by Roth using the FASTA software [12]. Each SCOP sequence belongs to a group as labeled by the experts [21]. We use the same set in our investigations. Originally, a structural symmetric similarity $S = (s_{ij})$ is derived first. Then, the nonmetric dissimilarities are obtained by $d_{ij} = (s_{ii} + s_{jj} - 2s_{ij})^{1/2}$ for $i \neq j$.

Tumor-mucosa. The data consist of the autofluorescence spectra acquired from healthy and diseased mucosa in the oral cavity [29]. The spectra were collected from 97 volunteers with no clinically observable lesions of the oral mucosa and 137 patients having lesions in oral cavity. The measurements were taken using the excitation wavelength of 365 nm. After preprocessing [30], each spectrum consists of 199 bins. In total, 856 spectra representing healthy tissue and 132 spectra representing diseased tissue were obtained. The spectra are normalized to a unit area. Here, we choose the nonmetric $l_{0.8}$-distances (l_p-distance is $d_p(\boldsymbol{x}, \boldsymbol{y}) = [\sum_k (x_k - y_k)^p]^{1/p}$) between the first-order Gaussian-smoothed ($\sigma = 3$ samples) derivatives of the spectra.[1] The zero-crossings of the derivatives indicate the peaks and valleys of the spectra, so they are informative. Moreover, the distances between smoothed derivatives contain some information of the order of bins. In this way, the property of a continuity of a spectrum is somewhat taken into account. This data set suffers from outliers, which are preserved here as we intend to illustrate their influence on the complexity.

---

[1] l_p-distances, $p \leq 1$, may be useful for problems characterized by the presence of a scattered and very heterogeneous class, such as the class of diseased people here. The effect of large absolute differences is diminished by $p < 1$. Indeed, this measure was found advantageous in our earlier experiments [22].

2.3 Criteria for Sampling Density

Consider an $n \times n$ dissimilarity matrix $D(R, R)$, where $R = \{p_1, p_2, \ldots, p_n\}$ is a representation set. In general, R may be a subset of a larger learning set T, but we assume here that $R = T$. Every object p_i is then represented by a vector of dissimilarities $D(p_i, R)$, $i = 1, 2, \ldots, n$, to the objects from R. The research question to be addressed is whether n, the cardinality of R, is sufficiently large for capturing the variability in the data or, in other words, whether it is to be expected that only little new information can be gained by increasing the number of representation objects. This can be further rephrased as judging whether new objects can be expressed in terms of the ones already present in R or not. Given the dissimilarity representations, some criteria are proposed to judge its sampling sufficiency, and their usefulness is experimentally evaluated on the data sets introduced in section 2. We focus here on a set of unlabeled objects forming a single class.

Some possible statistics that can be used are based on the compactness hypothesis [1, 8, 9], which was introduced in section 2.1. As it states that similar objects are also similar (close) in their representation, it constrains the dissimilarity measure d in the following way: d has to be such that $d(x, y)$ is small if the objects x and y are very similar; i.e., it should be much smaller for similar objects than for objects that are very different.

Assume that the dissimilarity measure d is definite, i.e., $d(x, y) = 0$ iff the objects x and y are identical. If the objects are identical, they belong to the same class. This reasoning can be extended by assuming that all objects z for which $d(x, z) < \varepsilon$, and the positive ε is sufficiently small, are so similar to x that they belong to the same class as x. Consequently, the dissimilarities of x and z to the representation objects should be close (or positively correlated, in fact). This means that $d(x, p_i) \approx d(z, p_i)$, implying that the representations $d(x, R)$ and $d(z, R)$ are also close. We conclude that for dissimilarity representations that satisfy the above continuity, the reverse compactness hypothesis holds, as objects that are similar in their representations are also similar in reality. Consequently, they belong to the same class.

A representation set R can be judged as sufficiently large if an arbitrary new object of the same class is not significantly different from all other objects of that class in the data set. This can be expected if R already contains many objects that are very similar, i.e., if they have a small dissimilarity to at least one other object. All the criteria studied below are based, in one way or another, on this observation. In pathological cases, the data set may contain just an optimal set of objects, but if there are no additional objects to validate this, it has to be considered as being too small.

We will illustrate the performance of our criteria on an artificial example and present also the results for some real data sets. The artificial example is chosen to be the $l_{0.8}$-distance representation between n normally distributed points in a k-dimensional vector space $\mathbb{R}^k$. Both n and k vary between 5 and 500. If $n < k$, then the generated vectors lie in an $(n-1)$-dimensional subspace, resulting in an undersampled and difficult problem. If $n \gg k$, then the data set may be judged as sufficiently sampled. Large values of k lead to difficult (complex) problems as they demand a large data cardinality n. The results are averaged over 20 experiments, each time based on a new, randomly generated data set. The criteria are presented and discussed below.

2.3.1 Specification of the Criteria

Sampling criteria for dissimilarity representations are directly or indirectly addressed in three different ways: by the dissimilarity values as given; in dissimilarity vector spaces, in which every dimension is defined by a dissimilarity to a representation object and in embedded vector spaces, which are determined such that the original dissimilarities are preserved; see [22, 23, 25] for more details. Each criterion is introduced and illustrated by a separate figure, e.g., Figure 2.2 refers to the first criterion. The results for artificially generated Gaussian data sets with the dimensionality k varying from 5 to 500 represented by a Euclidean distance matrix D are always shown on the top. Then, the results of other statistics are presented as applied to the six real data sets.

Skewness. This is a statistic that evaluates the dissimilarity values directly. A new object added to a set of objects that is still insufficiently well sampled will generate many large dissimilarities and just a few small ones. As a result, for unsatisfactory sampled data, the distribution of dissimilarities will peak for small values and will show a long tail in the direction of large dissimilarities. After the set becomes "saturated," however, adding new objects will cause the appearance of more and more small dissimilarities. Consequently, the skewness will grow with the increase of $|R|$. The value to which it grows depends on the problem.

Let the variable d denote now the dissimilarity value between two arbitrary objects. In practice the off-diagonal values d_{ij} from the dissimilarity matrix $D = (d_{ij})$ are used for his purpose. As a criterion, the skewness of the distribution of the dissimilarities d is considered as

$$J_{sk} = E \left[\frac{d - E[d]}{\sqrt{E[d - E[d]]^2}} \right]^3 , \tag{2.2}$$

where $E[\cdot]$ denotes the expectation. In Figure 2.2, top, the skewness of the Gaussian sets are shown. The cardinalities of small representation sets appear to be insufficient to represent the problem well, as it can be concluded from the noisy behavior of the graphs in that area. For large representation sets, the curves corresponding to the Gaussian samples of the chosen dimensionality "asymptotically" grow to some values of J_{sk}. The final values may be reached earlier for simpler problems in low dimensions, like $k = 5$ or 10. In general, the skewness curves for various k correspond to the expected pattern that the simplest problems (in low-dimensional spaces) reach the highest skewness values, whereas the most difficult problems are characterized by the smallest skewness values.

Mean rank. An element d_{ij} represents the dissimilarity between the objects p_i and p_j. The minimum of d_{ij} over all indices j points to the nearest neighbor of

p_i, say, p_z if $z = \operatorname{argmin}_{j \neq i}(d_{ij})$. So, in the representation set R, p_z is judged as the most similar to p_i. We now propose that a representation $D(p_i, R)$ describes the object p_i well if the representation of p_z, i.e., $D(p_z, R)$, is close to $D(p_i, R)$ in the dissimilarity space $D(\cdot, R)$. This can be measured by ordering the neighbors of the vectors $D(p_i, R)$ and determining the rank number r_i^{NN} of $D(p_z, R)$ in the list of neighbors of $D(p_i, R)$. By this we compare the nearest neighbor as found in the original dissimilarities with the neighbors in the dissimilarity space. For a well-described representation, the mean relative rank

$$J_{mr} = \frac{1}{n} \sum_{i=1}^{n} r_i^{NN} - 1 \tag{2.3}$$

is expected to be close to 0. In Figure 2.3, top, the results for the Gaussian example are shown. It can be concluded that the sizes of the representation set R larger than 100 are sufficient for Gaussian samples in 5 or in 10 dimensions.

PCA (principal component analysis) dimensionality. A sufficiently large representation set R tends to contain some objects that are very similar to each other. This means that their representations, the vectors of dissimilarities to R, are very similar. This suggests that the rank of D should be smaller than $|R|$, i.e., $\operatorname{rank}(D) < n$. In practice, this will not be true if the objects are not alike. A more robust criterion, therefore, may be based on the principal component analysis applied to the dissimilarity matrix D. Basically, the set is sufficiently sampled if n_α, the number of eigenvectors of D for which the sum of the corresponding eigenvalues equals a fixed fraction α, such as 0.95 of the total sum of eigenvalues (hence α is the explained fraction of the variance), is small in comparison to n. So, for well-represented sets, the ratio of n_α / n is expected to be smaller than some small constant (the faster the criterion curve drops with a growing R, the smaller intrinsic dimensionality of the dissimilarity space representation). Our criterion is then defined as

$$J_{\text{pca},\alpha} = \frac{n_\alpha}{n}, \tag{2.4}$$

with n_α such that $\alpha = \sum_{i=1}^{n_\alpha} \lambda_i / \sum_{i=1}^{n} \lambda_i$. There is usually no integer n_α for which the above holds exactly, so it would be found by interpolation. Note that this criterion relies on an intrinsic dimensionality[2] in a dissimilarity space $D(\cdot, R)$.

---

[2] If a certain phenomenon can be described (or if it is generated) by m independent variables, then its intrinsic dimensionality is m. In practice, however, due to noise and imprecision in measurements or some other uncontrolled factors, such a phenomenon may seem to be generated by more variables. If all these factors are not too dominant such that they completely disturb the original phenomenon, one should be able to rediscover the proper number of significant variables. Hence, the intrinsic dimensionality is the minimum number of variables that explains the phenomenon in a satisfactory way. In pattern recognition, one usually discusses the intrinsic dimensionality with respect to a collection of data vectors in the feature space. Then, for classification, the intrinsic dimensionality can be defined as the minimum number of features needed to obtain a similar classification performance as by using all features. In a geometrical sense, the intrinsic dimensionality can be defined as the

In the experiments, in Figure 2.4, top, the value of $J_{\text{pca},0.95}$ is shown for the artificial Gaussian example as a function of $|R|$. The Gaussian data are studied as generated in spaces of a growing dimensionality k. It can be concluded that the data sets consisting of more than 100 objects may be sufficiently well sampled for small dimensionalities such as $k=5$ or $k=10$ as just a small fraction of the eigenvectors is needed (about 10% or less). On the other hand, the considered number of objects is too small for the Gaussian sets of a larger dimensionality. These generate problems of a too high complexity for the given data-set size.

Correlation. Correlations between objects in a dissimilarity space are also studied. Similar objects show similar dissimilarities to other objects and, thereby, are positively correlated. As a consequence, the ratio of the average of positive correlations $\rho_+(D(p_i,R),D(p_j,R))$ to the average of absolute values of negative correlations $\rho_-(D(p_i,R),D(p_j,R))$, given as

$$J_\rho = \frac{\frac{1}{n^2-n}\sum_{i,j\neq i}^{n}\rho_+(D(p_i,R),D(p_j,R))}{1+\frac{1}{n^2-n}\sum_{i,j\neq i}^{n}|\rho_-(D(p_i,R),D(p_j,R))|} \tag{2.5}$$

will increase for large sample sizes. The constant added in the denominator prevents J_ρ from becoming very large if only small negative correlations appear. For a well-sampled representation set, J_ρ will be large and it will increase only slightly when new objects are added (new objects should not significantly influence the averages of either positive or negative correlations). Figure 2.5, top, shows that this criterion works well for the artificial Gaussian example. For the lower dimensional data sets (apparently less complex) J_ρ reaches higher values and exhibits a flattening behavior for sets consisting of at least 100 objects.

Intrinsic embedding dimensionality. For the study of dissimilarity representations, one may perform dimensionality reduction of a dissimilarity space (as the PCA criterion, described above, does) or choose an embedding method. Consequently, the judgment about whether R is sufficiently sampled relies on the estimate of the intrinsic dimensionality of an underlying vector space determined such that the original dissimilarities are preserved. This can be achieved by a linear embedding of the original objects (provided that D is symmetric) into a (pseudo-)Euclidean space. A pseudo-Euclidean space[3] is needed if D does not exhibit the Euclidean behavior, as, for example, the l_1-distance or max-norm distance measures do [22, 23]. In this way, a vector space is found in spite of the fact that one starts from a dissimilarity matrix D. The representation X of $m \leq n$ dimensions is determined such that it is centered at the origin and the derived features are uncorrelated [13, 26].

---

dimension of a manifold that approximately (due to noise) embeds the data. In practice, the estimated intrinsic dimensionality of a sample depends on the chosen criterion. Thereby, it is relative for the task.

[3] A pseudo-Euclidean space $\mathcal{E} := \mathbb{R}^{(p,q)}$ is a $(p+q)$-dimensional nondegenerate indefinite inner product space such that the inner product $\langle \cdot,\cdot\rangle_\mathcal{E}$ is positive definite (pd) on $\mathbb{R}^p$ and negative definite on $\mathbb{R}^q$. Therefore, $\langle \boldsymbol{x},\boldsymbol{y}\rangle_\mathcal{E} = \sum_{i=1}^{q} x_i y_i - \sum_{i=p+1}^{p+q} x_i y_i = \boldsymbol{x}^T \mathcal{J}_{pq}\boldsymbol{y}$, where $\mathcal{J}_{pq} = \text{diag}(I_{p\times p}; -I_{q\times q})$ and I is the identity matrix. Consequently, the square pseudo-Euclidean distance is $d_\mathcal{E}^2(\boldsymbol{x},\boldsymbol{y}) = \langle \boldsymbol{x}-\boldsymbol{y},\boldsymbol{x}-\boldsymbol{y}\rangle_\mathcal{E} = d_{\mathbb{R}^p}^2(\boldsymbol{x},\boldsymbol{y}) - d_{\mathbb{R}^q}^2(\boldsymbol{x},\boldsymbol{y})$.

The embedding relies on linear operations. The inner product (Gram) matrix G of the underlying configuration X is expressed by the square dissimilarities $D^{*2} = (d_{ij}^2)$ as $G = -\frac{1}{2}JD^{*2}J$, where $J = I - \frac{1}{n}11^T$ is the centering matrix [13, 22, 26]. X is determined by the eigen-decomposition of $G = Q\Lambda Q^T = Q|\Lambda|^{1/2}\text{diag}(\mathcal{J}_{p'q'}; 0)|\Lambda|^{1/2}Q^T$, where $\mathcal{J}_{p'q'} = (I_{p' \times p'}; -I_{q' \times q'})$ and I is the identity matrix, $|\Lambda|$ is a diagonal matrix of first decreasing p' positive eigenvalues, then decreasing magnitudes of q' negative eigenvalues, followed by zeros. Q is a matrix of the corresponding eigenvectors. The sought configuration is first represented in $\mathbb{R}^k$, $k = p' + q'$, as $Q_k|\Lambda_k|^{1/2}$. Because only some eigenvalues are large (in magnitude), the remaining ones can be disregarded as noninformative. This corresponds to the determination of intrinsic dimensionality. The final representation $X = Q_m|\Lambda_m|^{1/2}$, $m = p + q < k$, is defined by the largest p positive and the smallest q negative eigenvalues, since the features are uncorrelated.

This means that the number of dominant eigenvalues (describing the variances) should reveal the intrinsic dimensionality (small variances are expected to show just noise). (Note, however, that when all variances are similar, the intrinsic dimensionality is approximately n.) Let n_α^{emb} be the number of significant variances for which the sum of the corresponding magnitudes equals a specified fraction α, such as 0.95, of the total sum. Because n_α^{emb} determines the intrinsic dimensionality, the following criterion is proposed:

$$J_{emb,\alpha} = \frac{n_\alpha^{emb}}{n}. \tag{2.6}$$

For low intrinsic dimensionalities, smaller representation sets are needed to describe the data characteristics. Figure 2.6, top, presents the behavior of this criterion as a function of $|R|$ for the Gaussian data sets. The criterion curves clearly reveal different intrinsic embedding dimensionalities. If R is sufficiently large, then the intrinsic dimensionality estimate remains constant. Because the number of objects is growing, the criterion should then decrease and reach a relatively constant small value in the end (for very large sets). From the plot it can be concluded that data sets with more than 100 objects are satisfactorily sampled for Gaussian data of an originally low dimensionality such as $k \leq 20$. In other cases, the data set is too complex.

Compactness. As mentioned above, a symmetric distance matrix D can be embedded in a Euclidean or a pseudo-Euclidean space $\mathcal{E}$, depending on the Euclidean behavior of D. When the representation set is sufficiently large, the intrinsic embedding dimensionality is expected to remain constant during a further enlargement. Consequently, the mean of the data should remain approximately the same and the average distance to this mean should decrease (as new objects do not surprise anymore) or be constant. The larger the average distance, the less compact the class is, requiring more samples for its description. Therefore, a simple compactness criterion can be investigated. It is estimated in the leave-one-out approach as the average square distance to the mean vector in the embedded space $\mathcal{E}$:

$$J_{comp} = \frac{1}{n^2 - n}\sum_{j=1}^{n}\sum_{i \neq j} d_\mathcal{E}^2(x_i^{-j}, m^{-j}), \tag{2.7}$$

where x_i^{-j} is a vector representation of the ith object in the pseudo-Euclidean space found by $D(R^{-j}, R^{-j})$ and R^{-j} is a representation set of all the objects, except the jth one. m^{-j} is the mean of such a configuration. This can be computed from the dissimilarities directly without the necessity of finding the embedded configuration; see [26]. Figure 2.7, top, shows the behavior of this criterion, clearly indicating a high degree of compactness of the low-dimensional Gaussian data. The case of $k = 500$ is judged as not having a very compact description.

Gaussian intrinsic dimensionality. If the data points come from a spherical normal distribution in an m-dimensional Euclidean space, then m can be estimated from the χ_m^2 distributed variable d^2 denoting the pairwise square Euclidean distances as $m = 2 \frac{(E[d^2])^2}{E[d^4] - (E[d^2])^2}$, where $E[\cdot]$ denotes the expectation; see [22]. If the data points come from any other normal distribution, still some sort of an intrinsic dimensionality estimate can be found by the above formula. The judgement will be influenced by the largest variances in the data. Basically, the volume of the hyper-ellipsoidal normally distributed data is captured in the given distances. They are then treated as if computed from a spherically symmetric Gaussian distribution. Hence, the derived intrinsic dimensionality will reflect the dimensionality of a space to which the original data sample is made to fit isotropically (in simple words, one can imagine the original hyper-ellipsoidal Gaussian sample reshaped in space and "squeezed" in the dimensions to make it largest hyper-spherical Gaussian sample, the dimensionality of the latter is then estimated). Since the above formula makes use of the distances only, it can be applied to any dissimilarity measure. The criterion is then defined as

$$J_{Gid} = 2 \frac{(E[d^2])^2}{E[d^4] - (E[d^2])^2}, \tag{2.8}$$

where d^2 is realized by the off-diagonal square dissimilarity values d_{ij}^2.

Boundary descriptor. A class descriptor (a one-class classifier) in a dissimilarity space was proposed in Pekalska et al. [27]. It is designed as a hyperplane $H: w^T D(x, R) = \rho$ in a dissimilarity space that bounds the target data from above (it assumed that d is bounded) and for which some particular distance to the origin is minimized. Non-negative dissimilarities impose both $\rho \geq 0$ and $w_i \geq 0$. This is achieved by minimizing $\rho/\|w\|_1$, which is the max-norm distance of the hyperplane H to the origin in the dissimilarity space. Therefore, H can be determined by minimizing $\rho - \|w\|_1$. Normalizing such that $\|w\|_1 = 1$ (to avoid any arbitrary scaling of w), H is found by the optimization of ρ only. A (target) class is then characterized by a linear proximity function on dissimilarities with the weights w and the threshold ρ. It is defined as $\mathcal{I}(\sum_{w_j \neq 0} w_j D(x, p_j) \leq \rho)$, where $\mathcal{I}$ is the indentificator (characteristic) function (it takes the value of 1 if the condition is true and zero otherwise), w_j are found as the solution to a soft-margin linear programming formulation (the hard-margin case is then straightforward) with $\nu \in (0, 1]$ being the upper bound on the target rejection fraction in training [27]:

Minimize $\rho + \frac{1}{\nu n} \sum_{i=1}^{n} \xi_i$

such that, $\boldsymbol{w}^T D(p_i, R) \le \rho + \xi_i, \quad \sum_j w_j = 1, \quad w_j \ge 0,$ (2.9)

$\rho \ge 0, \ \xi_i \ge 0, \quad i = 1, \ldots, n.$

As a result, a sparse solution is obtained. This means that many weights w_i become zero and only some are positive. The objects $R_{so} \subseteq R$ for which the corresponding weights are positive are called *support objects* (SO). Our criterion then becomes the number of support objects:

$$J_{so} = |R_{so}|. \qquad (2.10)$$

In the experiments we suffered from numerical problems for large representation set sizes. For that reason, the solutions were found for all but one of the dimensionalities, i.e., except for the case $|R| = 500$.

2.3.2 Discussion on Sampling Density Experiments

While studying the results presented in Figures 2.2 to 2.8, one should recall that the height of the curve is a measure of the complexity and that a flat curve may indicate that the given data set is sufficiently sampled. For the skewness, mean rank and correlation statistics, it holds that lower values are related to a higher complexity. For the other criteria, it is the other way around: lower values are related to a lower complexity. An exception is the compactness, as defined here, since its behavior is scale dependent.

For all data sets and all criteria, it can be observed that the complexity of the original data set D (continuous lines) increases by the square root transformation (dashed lines) and decreases by the quadratic transformation (dotted lines). This implies that the $D^{*0.5}$ data sets tend to be undersampled in most cases. For the original data sets, this just holds for some of the classes of the Digits-all, the Heart, and the ProDom problems. The diseased class of the Tumor-mucosa problem shows a very irregular behavior, due to some large outliers. This is in fact useful as a number of very different outliers is a sign of undersampling. Most D^{*2} data sets may be judged as well sampled. Exceptions are the Heart data set and, again, the diseased class of the Tumor-mucosa problem.

It is interesting to observe the differences between various data sets, e.g., that the curves of the boundary descriptor sometimes start with a linear increase or that the correlation curve is usually an increasing function with some exceptions in the case of the Polygon data. The high increase of the PCA dimensionality criterion for the artificial Gaussian data set (Fig. 2.4) and for a large dimensionality k can nowhere be observed, with an exception of the Heart data set. A global comparison of all figures shows that the characteristics of high-dimensional Gaussian distributions cannot be found in real-world problems. This may indicate that various methods for data analysis and classification, based on the Gaussian assumption, need to be either improved before they can be used in practice or avoided.

In general, the flattened behavior of a criterion curve implies a sufficient sampling. All criteria, except for mean rank, are very sensitive to data modifications, indicating that quadratic transformations decrease the original data-set complexity, whereas square root transformation increase it. Concerning specific approaches, the following can be summarized:

- Skewness is informative to judge the distribution of dissimilarities. Negative skewness denotes a tail of small dissimilarities, whereas positive skewness describes a tail of large dissimilarities. Large positive values indicate outliers in the class (the Tumor-mucosa data), whereas large negative values indicate heterogeneous characteristics of the class (the Heart data) or a class of possible clusters having various spreads (the ProDom data). Skewness can be noisy for very small sample sizes.

- Mean rank is a criterion judging the consistency between the nearest neighbors directly applied to the given dissimilarities and the nearest neighbor in a dissimilarity space. For an increasing number of objects, this should approach zero. As original nearest neighbor relations do not change after nondecreasing transformations (although they are affected in a dissimilarity space), this criterion is not very indicative for such modifications. Except for the artificial Gaussian examples, the curves exhibit a similar behavior.

- PCA dimensionality describes the fraction of significant eigenvalues in a dissimilarity space of a growing dimensionality. If the data set is "saturated," then the criterion curve approaches a value close to zero since the intrinsic dimensionality should stay constant. If the criterion does not approach zero, the problem is characterized by many relatively similar eigenvalues, hence many similar intrinsic variables. In such cases, the problem is judged as complex, for instance for the Heart and the Digits-all problems.

- The correlation criterion indicates the amount of positive correlations versus negative correlations in a dissimilarity space. Positive values > 0.5 may suggest the presence of outliers in the data as observed in the case of the ProDom and Tumor-mucosa problems.

- Intrinsic embedding dimensionality is judged by the fraction of dominant dimensions determined by the number of dominant eigenvalues in a linear embedding. In contrast to the PCA dimensionality, it is not likely to observe the criterion curve approaching zero. Large dissimilarities determine the embedded space and considerably affect the presence of large eigenvalues. Therefore, the criterion curve may be close to zero if many eigenvalues tend to be so or if there are some notable outliers (as the diseased class of the Tumor-mucosa problem). In this case, a flat behavior of the curve may give evidence of an acceptable sampling. However, the larger the final value of the criterion curve, the more complex the class description (there is a larger variability in the class).

- Compactness indicates how compact a set of objects is as judged by the distances to the mean in an embedded space. In this case, the flattened behavior of the curve is not very indicative, as all our problems for small sample sizes would be judged as well sampled. What is more important is the value that the criterion curve attains – the smaller the value the more compact the description.

- Similarly to the criterion above, the smaller the final value to which the Gaussian intrinsic dimensionality criterion curve converges, the less complex the problem.

- The boundary descriptor indicates the number of boundary objects necessary to characterize the class. A large number of objects with respect to $|R|$ indicates a complex problem, as, for example, the Heart data set is. The criterion curves may be noisy for small samples, as observed for the ProDom and Tumor-mucosa cases, possibly indicating the presence of outliers.

In brief, the most indicative and insightful criteria are skewness, PCA dimensionality, correlation, and boundary description. Intrinsic embedding dimensionality may be also informative; however, a good understanding of the embedding procedure is needed to judge it well. The remaining criteria have less impact, but they still bring some additional information.

2.4 Classification Experiments

2.4.1 Introduction

Complexity should be studied with respect to a given task such as class description, clustering, or classification. Hence, the complexity of the data set should describe some of its characteristics or of an assumed model, relative to the chosen representation. In the previous section, some criteria for the complexity of unlabeled data (data geometry and class descriptions) were studied. This section is concerned with supervised learning.

As data-set complexity is a different issue than class overlap, its relation to classifier performance is not straightforward. We argued in the introduction that more complex problems may need more complex tools, or more training samples, which will be our focus here. Therefore, we will study the influence of data-set complexity on the classifier performance. The original representation will be transformed by the same power transformations as in section 2.3. As has been already observed, D^{*2} representations decrease, while $D^{*0.5}$ representations increase the data set complexity of the individual classes.

As we indicated in the chapter introduction, an intrinsic problem complexity, as such, does not exist. Its complexity is entirely determined by the representation and observed through the data set. If the data-set complexity is decreased by some transformation simplifying the problem, as a result simpler classifiers may be used. Note that no monotonic transformation of the data can either reduce or increase the intrinsic class overlap. Transformations are applied to enable one to train classifiers that reach a performance, which is closer to this intrinsic overlap. If the problem becomes less complex, smaller training sets probably will be sufficient. If it was originally abundant, the decreased complexity may yield a better classification performance. If the training set size was initially sufficient, the decreased complexity may decrease the performance (due to perceived higher class overlap). An increased problem complexity may open a way for constructing more complex classifiers. If the sample size permits, these classifiers will reach an increased performance. If the sample size is insufficient, such classifiers will be overtrained, resulting in a decrease of the performance.

In addition to these effects, there is a direct relation between data-set complexity and a desirable size of the representation set. Remember that this desirable size is indicated by the stability of the measures or the observed asymptotic behavior of the criteria identified to be useful in the preceding analysis. More complex problems need a larger representation set. The other way around also holds: a larger representation set used for the description may indicate more complex aspects of the problem.

The above effects will be illustrated by a set of classification experiments. Assume that a training set of N examples is provided. First, a suitable representation set $R \subset T$ has to be determined. We will proceed in two ways, starting from a full representation $D(T, T)$. The representation set will be chosen either as a condensed set found by the editing-and-condensing [condensed nearest neighbor (CNN)] procedure [6] or as the set of support objects determined in the process of constructing a sparse linear programming classifier (LPC). In the resulting dissimilarity space, a Fisher classifier on $D(T, R)$ is trained.

2.4.2 Classifiers

The following classifiers are used in our experiments:

1-Nearest neighbor rule (1-NN). This classifier operates directly on the dissimilarities computed for a test object. It assigns a test object to the class of the training object that is the most similar as judged by the smallest dissimilarity. Because no training is required, the values in $D(T, T)$ are not used for the construction of this rule.

k-Nearest neighbor rule (k-NN). Here, the test object is assigned to the most frequent class in the set of the k-nearest neighbors. The value of k is optimized over the original representation $D(T, T)$ using a leave-one-out procedure. In this way, the training set T is somewhat used in the learning process.

Editing and condensing (CNN). An editing and condensing algorithm is applied to the entire dissimilarity representation $D(T, T)$, resulting in a condensed set (CS) R_{CS}. Editing takes care that the noisy objects are first removed so that the prototypes can be chosen to guarantee a good performance of the 1-NN rule, which is used afterward.

Linear programming classifier (LPC). By training a properly formulated linear classifier $f(D(x, T)) = \sum_{j=1}^{N} w_j \, d(x, p_j) + w_0 = \boldsymbol{w}^T D(x, R) + w_0$ in a dissimilarity space $D(T, T)$, one may select objects from T necessary for the construction of the classifier. The separating hyperplane is obtained by solving a linear programming problem, where a sparse solution on R is imposed by minimizing the l_1-norm of the weight vector $\boldsymbol{w}$, $||\boldsymbol{w}||_1 = \sum_{j=1}^{r} |w_j|$; see [4, 11] on the sparseness issues. As a result, only some weights become nonzero. The corresponding objects define the representation set.

A flexible formulation of a classification problem is proposed in Graepel et al. [15]. The problem is to minimize $||\boldsymbol{w}||_1 - \mu \, \rho$, which means that the margin ρ becomes a variable of the optimization problem. To formulate such a minimization task properly, the absolute values $|w_j|$ should be eliminated from the objective function. Therefore, the weights w_j are expressed by nonnegative variables α_j and β_j as $w_j = \alpha_j - \beta_j$. (When the pairs (α_j, β_j) are determined, then at least one of them is zero.) Nonnegative slack variables ξ_i, accounting for possible classification errors are additionally introduced. Let $y_i = +1/-1$ indicate the class membership. By imposing $||w||_1$ to be constant, the minimization problem for $x_i \in T$ then becomes

$$\text{Minimize } \tfrac{1}{N} \sum_{i=1}^{N} \xi_i - \mu \rho$$
$$\text{such that, } \sum_{i=1}^{N} (\alpha_i + \beta_i) = 1 \tag{2.11}$$
$$y_i f(D(x_i, T)) \geq 1 - \xi_i, \; i = 1, \ldots, N$$
$$\xi_i, \; \alpha_i, \; \beta_i, \; \rho \geq 0.$$

A sparse solution w is obtained, which means that important objects are selected (by nonzero weights) from the training set T, resulting in a representation set R_{so}. The solution depends on the choice of the parameter $\mu \in (0, 1)$, which is related to a possible class overlap [15]. To select it automatically, the following values are found (as rough estimates based on the 1-NN error computed over a number of representations $D(T, T)$ for various sizes of T). These are 0.2 for the Heart data, 0.1 for the Digits-all and Tumor-mucosa data, and 0.05 for the remaining sets.

The selection of objects described above is similar to the selection of features by linear programming in a standard classification task; see [3, 4] . The important point to realize is that we do not have control over the number of selected support objects. This can be somewhat influenced by varying the constant μ (hence influencing the trade-off between the classifier norm and the training classification errors).

Fisher classifier (FC). This linear classifier minimizes the mean square error on the training set $D(T, R)$ with respect to the desired labels $y_i = +1/-1$. It finds the minimal mean square error solution of $\sum_{j=1}^{N} w_j \, d(x_i, x_j) + w_0 = y_i$. Note that the common opinion that this classifier assumes Gaussian class densities is wrong. The truth is that in the case of Gaussian densities with equal covariance matrices, the corresponding Bayes classifier is found (in the case of equal class priors). The Fisher classifier, however, is neither based on a density assumption nor does it try to minimize the probability of misclassification in a Bayesian sense. It follows a mean square error approach. As a consequence, it does suffer from multimodality in class distributions.

Multiclass problems are solved for the LPC and the FC in a one-against-all-others strategy using the classifier conditional posterior probability estimates [10]. Objects are assigned to the class that receives the highest confidence as the "one" in this one-against-all-others scheme.

2.4.3 Discussion on the Classification Experiments

The classification results for the six data sets are presented in Figures 2.9 to 2.14. In each figure, the first plot shows the results of the LPC as a function of the training set size. The averaged classification errors for the three modifications of the dissimilarity measures are presented. For comparison also the results of the 1-NN, the k-NN, and the CNN rules are shown. Note that these are independent of the nondecreasing transformations. The CNN curves are often outside the shown interval.

The resulting reduced object sets selected by the CNN, the condensed set CS, are used as a representation set R. Then, the Fisher classifier FC is constructed on the dissimilarity representation $D(T, R)$. This will be denoted as FC-CS. The averaged errors of this classifier are, again, together with the results for the 1-NN, the k-NN, and the CNN rules (these are the same as in the first graph), shown in the second plot. All experiments are averaged over 30 repetitions in which independent training and test sets are generated from the original set of objects.

The third plot illustrates the sizes of the reduced training sets found by the LPC and the CNN. For most data sets, the CNN reduces the training set further than the LPC. The resulting sample sizes of the CNN set are approximately a linear function of the training size $|T|$. In all cases, the sets of support objects found by the LPC are for the D^{*2} representations smaller than for the original one, D, which are, in turn, smaller than for the $D^{*0.5}$ representations. This is in agreement with our expectation (see section 2.2) and with the results of section 2.3, that the data-set complexity of D^{*2} is lower and the data-set complexity of $D^{*0.5}$ is higher than it is of D.

The first two plots can be considered as learning curves (note, however, that the determined representation set R increases with a growing training set T). The dissimilarity-based classifiers, the LPC and the FC-CS, perform globally better than the nearest neighbor rules, which is in agreement with our earlier findings; see [22, 23, 25]. The LPC and the FC-CS are comparable. The LPC is often better than the FC-CS for smaller sample sizes, whereas the FC-CS is sometimes somewhat better than the LPC for larger sample sizes. This might be understood from the fact that the LPC, like the support vector machine, focuses on the decision boundary, whereas the FC uses the information of all objects in the training set. Where this is profitable, the FC will reach a higher accuracy.

Learning curves usually show a monotonic decreasing behavior. For simple data sets they will decrease fast, whereas for complex data sets they will decrease slowly. The complexity is understood here in relation to single class descriptions and to the intricateness of the decision boundary between the classes (hence their geometrical position in a dissimilarity space). The asymptotic behavior will be similar if a more complex representation does not reveal any additional details that are useful for the class separation. If it does, however, a more complex representation will show a higher asymptotic accuracy, provided that the classifier is able to use the extra information.

Following this reasoning, it is to be expected that the learning curves for D^{*2} representations decrease fast, but may have worse asymptotic values. This appears to be true with a few exceptions. For the Tumor-mucosa problem (Fig. 2.15), the expectation is definitely wrong. This is caused by the outliers as the quadratic transformation strengthens their influence. The global behavior, expected from this transformation, is overshadowed by a few outliers that are not representative for the problem. A second exception can be observed in the Digits-all results (see Fig. 2.11), especially for the FC. In this multiclass problem the use of the FC suffers from the multimodality caused by the one-against-all-others strategy.

The learning curves for the $D^{*0.5}$ data sets change in most cases, as expected, slower than those for the original data sets. The FC-CS for the Digits-all case (Fig. 2.11), is again an exception. In some cases, these two learning curves are almost on top of each other; in some other cases, they are very different, as for the FC-CS and the ProDom data set (Fig. 2.14). This may indicate that the data set complexity increased by the square root transformation is really significant.

There are a few situations for which crossing points of the learning curves can be observed after which a more complex representation ($D^{*0.5}$ or D) enables the classifiers to reach a higher performance than a simpler one (D or D^{*2}, respectively) due to a sufficient sample size. Examples are the LPC classification of the Digits-all data (Fig. 2.11) and the Polygon data (Fig. 2.13).

Finally, we observe that for the undersampled Heart data set (see section 2.3), the k-NN does relatively very well. This is the only case where the dissimilarity-based classifiers LPC and FC-CS perform worse than the straightforward use of the nearest neighbor rule.

2.5 Discussion

A real-world pattern recognition problem may have an inherent complexity: objects of different classes may be similar; classes may consist of dissimilar subgroups; and essential class differences may be hidden, distributed over various attributes or may be context dependent. All that matters, however, is how the problem is represented using object models, features, or dissimilarity measures. The problem has to be solved from a given representation, and its complexity should be judged from that. It is the representation that is explicitly available, and it may be such that seemingly simple problems are shown as complex or the other way around.

In this chapter we argued that the complexity of a recognition problem is determined by the given representation and observed through a data set and may be judged from a sample size analysis. If for a given representation, a problem is sampled sufficiently well, then it is simpler than for a representation for which it appears to be too low. In section 2.3, a number of tools are presented to judge the sample size for a given unlabeled dissimilarity representation. It has been shown that these tools are consistent with modifications of the representation that make it either more or less complex. All the considered criteria are useful when judged as complementary to each other. The most indicative ones, however, are skewness, PCA dimensionality, correlation, embedding intrinsic dimensionality, and boundary descriptor.

In section 2.4, the same observations concerning the power transformations have been confirmed by classification experiments. By putting emphasis on remote objects (hence considering D^{*2} representations), a problem becomes simpler as local class differences become less apparent. As a result, this simpler problem will have a higher class overlap, but may be solved by a simpler classifier. By emphasizing small distances between objects (hence considering $D^{*0.5}$ representations), on the contrary, local class distances may be used better. The problem may now be solved by a more complex classifier, requiring more samples, but resulting in a lower error rate.

It can be understood from this study that data-set complexity is related to sampling density if the data set has to be used for generalization like the training of classifiers. A more complex data set needs a higher sampling density, and, consequently, better classifiers may be found. If the training set is not sufficiently large, representations having a lower complexity may perform better. This conclusion is consistent with the earlier insights in the cause of the peaking phenomenon and the curse of dimensionality [19]. The concepts of representation complexity and data-set complexity, however, are more general than the dimensionality of a feature space.

In conclusion, we see a perspective for using the sample density to build a criterion judging the complexity of a representation as given by a data set. If sufficient samples are available, the representation may be changed such that local details become highlighted. If not, then the representation should be simplified by emphasizing its more global aspects.

Acknowledgments

This work is supported by the Dutch Technology Foundation (STW), grant RRN 5699, as well as the Dutch Organization for Scientific Research (NWO). The authors thank Douglas Zongker, Anil Jain, and Volker Roth for some of the data sets used in this study.

References

[1] A.G. Arkadev, E.M. Braverman. *Computers , Pattern Recognition.* Washington, DC: Thompson, 1966.

[2] C.L. Blake, C.J. Merz. UCI repository of machine learning databases. University of California, Irvine, Department of Information and Computer Sciences, 1998.

[3] P.S. Bradley, O.L. Mangasarian. Feature selection via concave minimization and support vector machines. In *International Conference on Machine Learning*, pages 82–90. San Francisco: Morgan Kaufmann, 1998.

[4] P.S. Bradley, O.L. Mangasarian, W.N. Street. Feature selection via mathematical programming. *INFORMS Journal on Computing*, 10, 209–217, 1998.

[5] F. Corpet, F. Servant, J. Gouzy, D. Kahn. Prodom and prodom-cg: tools for protein domain analysis and whole genome comparisons. *Nucleic Acids Research*, 28, 267–269, 2000.

[6] P.A. Devijver, J. Kittler. *Pattern Recognition, A Statistical Approach.* Englewood Cliffs, NJ: Prentice Hall, 1982.

[7] M.P. Dubuisson, A.K. Jain. Modified Hausdorff distance for object matching. In *International Conference on Pattern Recognition*, volume 1, pages 566–568, 1994.

[8] R.P.W. Duin. Compactness and complexity of pattern recognition problems. In *International Symposium on Pattern Recognition 'In Memoriam Pierre Devijver'*, pages 124–128. Brussels: Royal Military Academy, 1999.

[9] R.P.W. Duin, E. Pękalska. Complexity of dissimilarity based pattern classes. In *Scandinavian Conference on Image Analysis*. pages 663–670, Bergen, Norway, 2001.

[10] R.P.W. Duin, D.M.J. Tax. Classifier conditional posterior probabilities. In A. Amin, D. Dori, P. Pudil, H. Freeman, eds. *Advances in Pattern Recognition, LNCS*, volume 1451, pages 611–619. New York: Springer Verlag, 1998.

[11] R.P.W. Duin, D.M.J. Tax. Combining support vector and mathematical programming methods for classification. In B. Schoelkopf, C. Burges, A. Smola, eds. *Advances in Kernel Methods — Support Vector Machines*, pages 307–326. Cambridge, MA: MIT Press, 1999.

[12] Fasta. http://www.ebi.ac.uk/fasta/index.html.

[13] L. Goldfarb. A new approach to pattern recognition. In L.N. Kanal, A. Rosenfeld, eds. *Progress in Pattern Recognition*, volume 2, pages 241–402. Amsterdam: Elsevier Science Publishers BV, 1985.

[14] J.C. Gower. A general coefficient of similarity and some of its properties. *Biometrics*, 27, 25–33, 1971.

[15] T. Graepel, B. Schölkopf, et al. Classification on proximity data with LP-machines. In *International Conference on Artificial Neural Networks*, pages 304–309, 1999.

[16] T.K. Ho, M. Basu. Measuring the complexity of classification problems. In *International Conference on Pattern Recognition*, volume 2, pages 43–47, Barcelona, Spain, 2000.

[17] T.K. Ho, M. Basu. Complexity measures of supervised classification problems. *IEEE Transactions on Pattern Analysis and Machine Intelligence*, 24(3), 289–300, 2002.

[18] D. Hofstadter. *Gödel, Escher, Bach — an Eternal Golden Braid*. New York: Basic Books, 1979.

[19] A.K. Jain, B. Chandrasekaran. Dimensionality and sample size considerations in pattern recognition practice. In P.R. Krishnaiah, L.N. Kanal, eds. *Handbook of Statistics*, volume 2, pages 835–855. Amsterdam: North-Holland, 1987.

[20] A.K. Jain, D. Zongker. Representation and recognition of handwritten digits using deformable templates. *IEEE Transactions on Pattern Analysis and Machine Intelligence*, 19(12), 1386–1391, 1997.

[21] A.G. Murzin, S.E. Brenner, T. Hubbard, C. Chothia. SCOP: a structural classification of proteins database for the investigation of sequences and structures. *Jornal of Molecular Biology*, 247, 536–540, 1995.

[22] E. Pękalska. *Dissimilarity representations in pattern recognition. Concepts, theory and applications*. Ph.D. thesis, Delft University of Technology, Delft, The Netherlands, January 2005.

[23] E. Pękalska, R.P.W. Duin. Dissimilarity representations allow for building good classifiers. *Pattern Recognition Letters*, 23(8), 943–956, 2002.

[24] E. Pękalska, R.P.W. Duin. On not making dissimilarities euclidean. In T. Caelli, A. Amin, R.P.W. Duin, M. Kamel, de D. Ridder, eds. *Joint IAPR International Workshops on SSPR and SPR, LNCS*, pages 1143–1151. New York: Springer-Verlag, 2004.

[25] E. Pękalska, R.P.W. Duin, and P. Paclík. Prototype selection for dissimilarity-based classifiers. *Pattern Recognition*, 39(2), 189–208, 2006.

[26] E. Pękalska, P. Paclík, R.P.W. Duin. A generalized kernel approach to dissimilarity based classification. *Journal of Machine Learning Research*, 2, 175–211, 2001.

[27] E. Pękalska, D.M.J. Tax, R.P.W. Duin. One-class LP classifier for dissimilarity representations. In S. Thrun S. Becker, K. Obermayer, eds. *Advances in Neural Information Processing Systems 15*, pages 761–768. Cambridge, MA: MIT Press, 2003.

[28] V. Roth, J. Laub, J.M. Buhmann, K.-R. Müller. Going metric: Denoising pairwise data. In *Advances in Neural Information Processing Systems*, pages 841–856. Cambridge, MA: MIT Press, 2003.

[29] M. Skurichina, R.P.W. Duin. Combining different normalizations in lesion diagnostics. In O. Kaynak, E. Alpaydin, E. Oja, L. Xu, eds. *Artificial Neural Networks and Information Processing, Supplementary Proceedings ICANN/ICONIP*, pages 227–230, Istanbul, Turkey, 2003.

[30] D.C.G. de Veld, M. Skurichina, M.J.H. Witjes, et al. Autofluorescence characteristics of healthy oral mucosa at different anatomical sites. *Lasers in Surgery and Medicine*, 23, 367–376, 2003.

[31] M.M. Waldrop. *Complexity, the Emerging Science at the Edge of Order and Chaos*. New York: Simon & Schuster, 1992.

[32] C.L. Wilson, M.D. Garris. Handprinted character database 3. Technical report, National Institute of Standards and Technology, February 1992.

[33] D. Wolpert. *The Mathematics of Generalization*. New York: Addison-Wesley, 1995.

[34] Wordnet dictionary. http://www.cogsci.princeton.edu/ wn/.

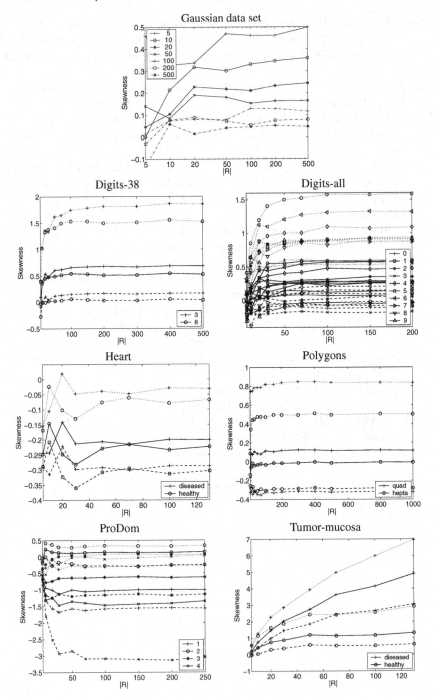

Fig. 2.2. Skewness criterion applied to dissimilarity representations $D^{*p}(R, R)$, $p = 0.5, 1, 2$, per class. Continuous curves refer to the original representation, while the dashed and dotted curves correspond to D^{*05} and D^{*2} representations, respectively. Note scale differences.

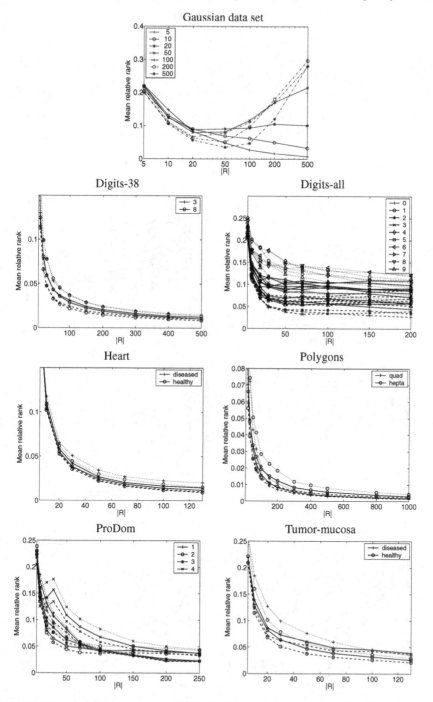

Fig. 2.3. Mean rank criterion applied to dissimilarity representations $D^{*p}(R, R)$, $p = 0.5, 1, 2$, per class. Continuous curves refer to the original representation, while the dashed and dotted curves correspond to D^{*05} and D^{*2} representations, respectively. Note scale differences.

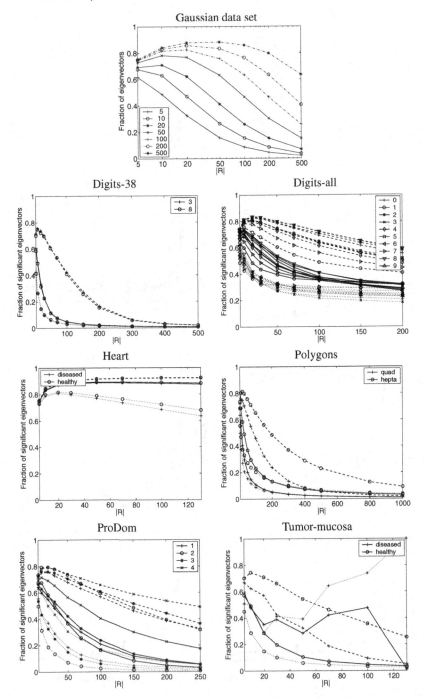

Fig. 2.4. PCA dimensionality criterion applied to dissimilarity representations $D^{*p}(R, R)$, $p = 0.5, 1, 2$, per class. Continuous curves refer to the original representation, while the dashed and dotted curves correspond to D^{*05} and D^{*2} representations, respectively.

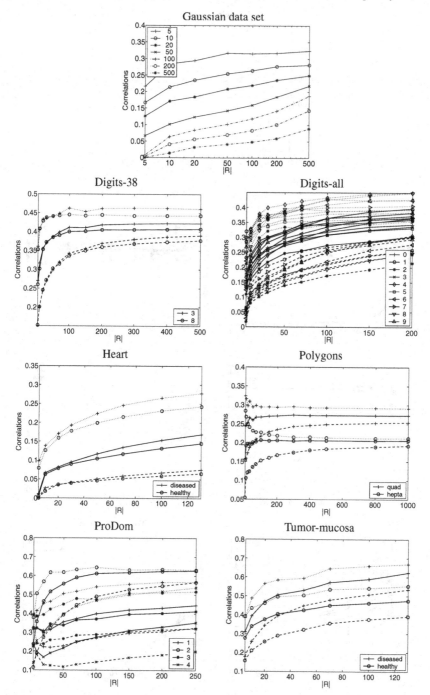

Fig. 2.5. Correlation criterion applied to dissimilarity representations $D^{*p}(R, R)$, $p = 0.5, 1, 2$, per class. Continuous curves refer to the original representation, while the dashed and dotted curves correspond to D^{*05} and D^{*2} representations, respectively. Note scale differences.

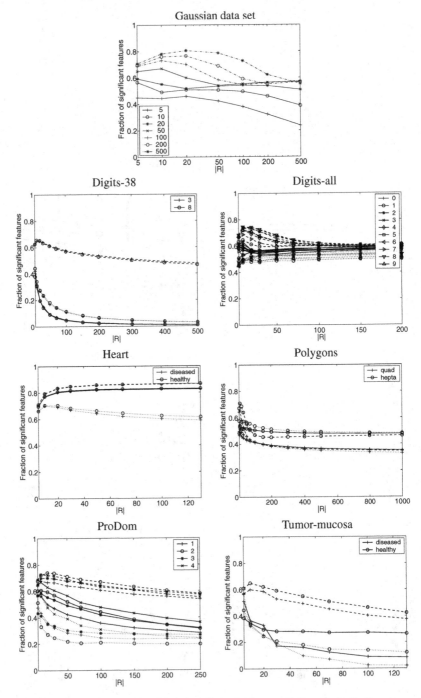

Fig. 2.6. Intrinsic embedding dimensionality criterion applied to dissimilarity representations $D^{*p}(R, R)$, $p = 0.5, 1, 2$, per class. Continuous curves refer to the original representation, while the dashed and dotted curves correspond to D^{*05} and D^{*2} representations, respectively.

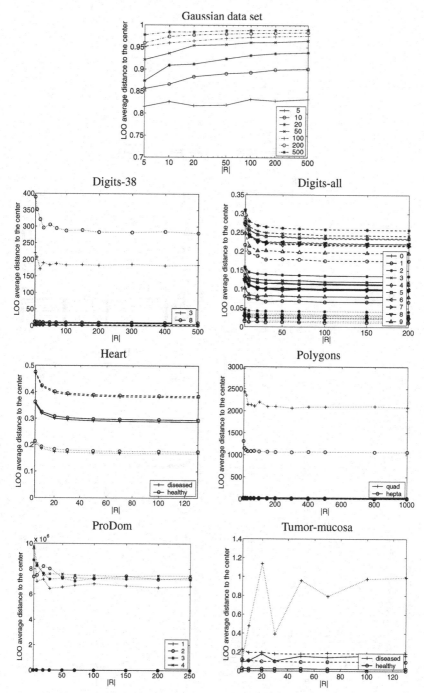

Fig. 2.7. Compactness criterion applied to dissimilarity representations $D^{*p}(R, R)$, $p =$ 0.5, 1, 2, per class. Continuous curves refer to the original representation, while the dashed and dotted curves correspond to D^{*05} and D^{*2} representations, respectively. Note scale differences.

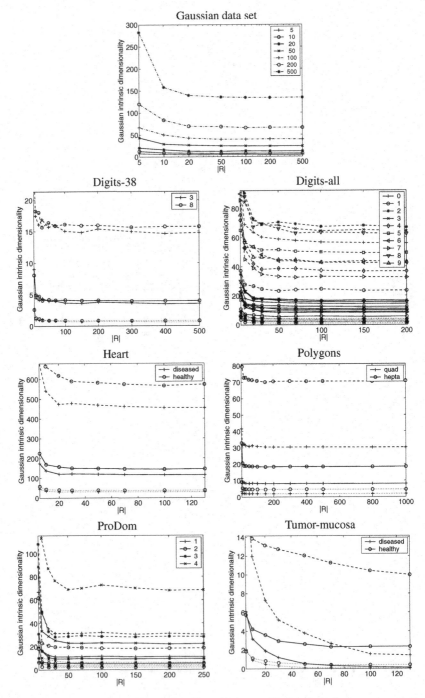

Fig. 2.8. Gaussian intrinsic dimensionality criterion applied to dissimilarity representations $D^{*p}(R, R)$, $p = 0.5, 1, 2$, per class. Continuous curves refer to the original representation, while the dashed and dotted curves correspond to D^{*05} and D^{*2} representations, respectively. Note scale differences.

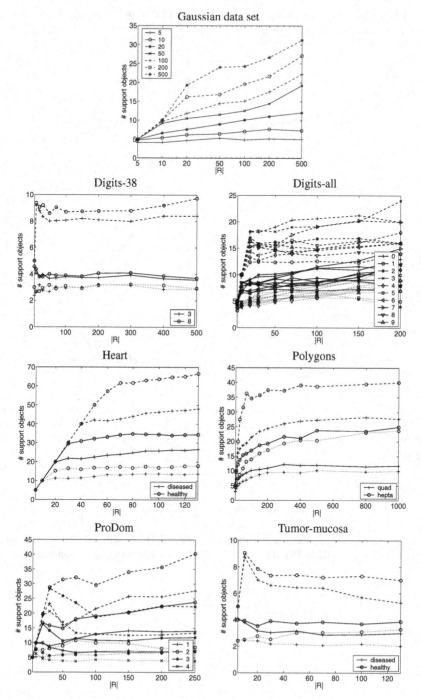

Fig. 2.9. Boundary descriptor criterion applied to dissimilarity representations $D^{*p}(R, R)$, $p = 0.5, 1, 2$, per class. Continuous curves refer to the original representation, while the dashed and dotted curves correspond to D^{*05} and D^{*2} representations, respectively. Note scale differences.

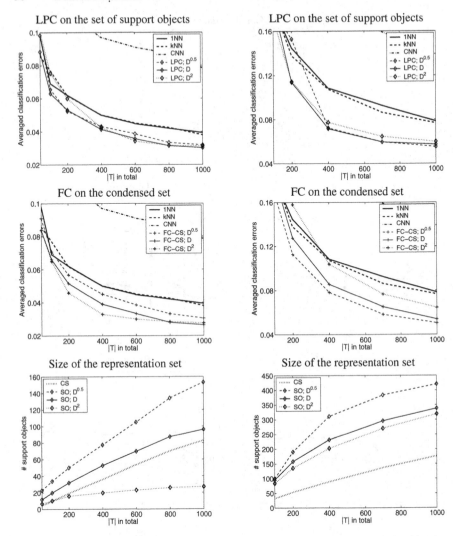

Fig. 2.10. Results of the classification experiments on the **Digits-38 data**.

Fig. 2.11. Results of the classification experiments on the **Digits-all data**.

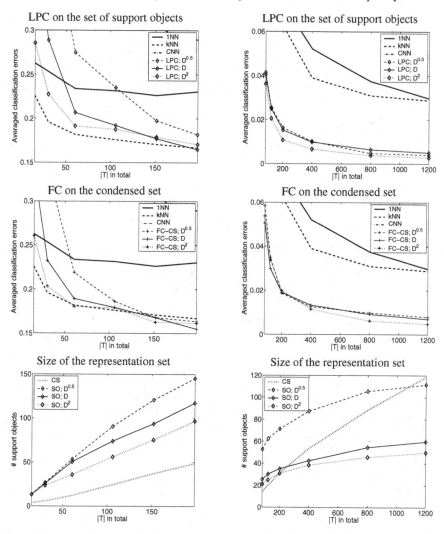

Fig. 2.12. Results of the classification experiments on the **Heart data**.

Fig. 2.13. Results of the classification experiments on the **Polygon data**.

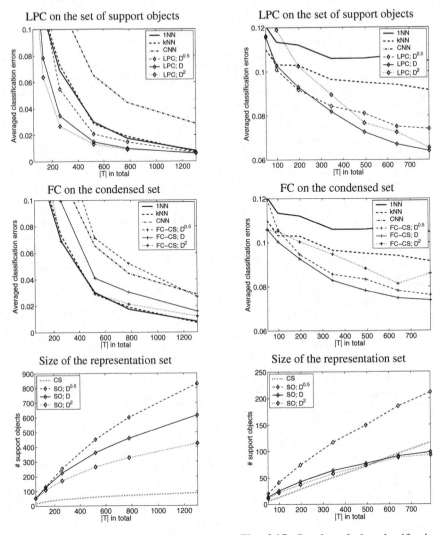

Fig. 2.14. Results of the classification experiments on the **ProDom data**.

Fig. 2.15. Results of the classification experiments on the **Tumor-mucosa data**.

3

Measures of Data and Classifier Complexity and the Training Sample Size

Šarūnas Raudys

Summary. The size of the training set is important in characterizing data complexity. If a standard Fisher linear discriminant function or an Euclidean distance classifier is used to classify two multivariate Gaussian populations sharing a common covariance matrix, several measures of data complexity play an important role. The types of potential classification rules cannot be ignored while determining the data complexity. The three factors — sample size, data complexity, and classifier complexity — are mutually dependent. In situations where many classifiers are potentially useful, exact characterization of the data complexity requires a greater number of characteristics.

3.1 Introduction

Today it is generally recognized that the complexity of a pattern recognition algorithm should be chosen in accordance with the training sample size. The more complex the classifier is, the more data are required for estimating its parameters reliably. Conversely, if the sample size is small, one is obliged to use the simplest classification algorithms (e.g., [9]). In addition, the complexity of the most suitable classifier depends also on the complexity of the data.

Theory shows that the difference between generalization and asymptotic errors of sample-based classifiers depends on both the sample size and the data configuration. Consequently, data complexity affects both the sensitivity of the classifier to training-set size and the complexity of the resultant decision boundary. For that reason, there is no wonder that numerous attempts to introduce general measures of data and classifier complexity that satisfy a majority of researchers did not lead to definite success (see, e.g., comments in [6, 8]).

We believe that *the concept "complexity of the data" does not exist without reference to a concrete pattern recognition problem and a concrete decision-making method.* The measure of the data complexity depends on the purpose for which this measure will be used. Three factors — the sample size, data complexity, and classifier complexity — are mutually related. An objective of this chapter is to examine the complexity of the classification rule and that of the data from the point of view of the sample size necessary to train the classifier.

The study of data complexity is a complicated issue, and we do not expect to obtain immediate success. For that reason, we restrict our main analysis to very simple data models and two standard statistical classification algorithms. We will consider linear decision boundaries and multivariate Gaussian distribution with a common covariance matrix for two pattern classes.

3.2 Generalization Errors of Two Statistical Classifiers

In this section we present definitions of distinct types of classification errors: the Bayes error, which is the asymptotic, conditional, and expected probabilities of misclassifications (PMC). We also present expressions of expected PMC (generalization error) for two typical statistical classifiers frequently used in applications: the standard Fisher linear discriminant function and the Euclidean distance classifier.

Suppose one knows probability density functions (PDF) of the input vectors and the prior probabilities of the pattern classes C_1 and C_2. One can then design the optimal Bayes classifier B, which, in classifying all possible vectors from C_1 and C_2, results in a minimal probability of misclassification. This PMC is called the *Bayes error* and is denoted by P_B. The probability of misclassification of a classifier designed from one particular training set using the classifier training algorithm A is conditioned on this specific algorithm and on this particular training set. The error rate for classifying the pattern vectors from the general population is called the *conditional probability of misclassification* and is denoted by P_N^A, where the index A indicates that the classifier training algorithm A is utilized and the index N symbolizes that the training set size is fixed. In the equation below, I assume $N = N_1 = N_2$, *where N_1 and N_2 are the sample sizes of the two classes.* In theoretical analysis, vectors of the training set may be considered as random ones; however, the sample size (N_1 and N_2) is fixed. Then the conditional PMC, P_N^A, may be considered as a random variable too.

Let $f(P_N^A)$ be the probability density function of the random variable P_N^A and let $\bar{P}_N^A$ be its expectation over all possible randomly formed training sets of size N_1 and N_2 for each of the two classes, respectively. This expectation is called an *expected probability of misclassification.* The limit $P_\infty^A = \lim_{N_1 \to \infty, N_2 \to \infty} \bar{P}_N^A$ is called an *asymptotic probability of misclassification.* In the neural network literature, both the conditional and expected PMC frequently are called *generalization error*, often without mentioning a proper distinction between the two notions.

The mathematical model of the data to be considered below are two multivariate Gaussian distributions with different means, μ_1, μ_2, and a common covariance matrix for both classes, Σ (the GCCM data model). The linear discriminant function (DF)

$$g(\mathbf{X}) = \boldsymbol{W}^T \mathbf{X} + w_0 \tag{3.1}$$

is an asymptotically optimal (when $N_1 \to \infty, N_2 \to \infty$) decision rule for this data model. In equation (3.1) $\boldsymbol{W} = \boldsymbol{\Sigma}^{-1}(\boldsymbol{\mu}_1 - \boldsymbol{\mu}_2)$, $w_0 = \boldsymbol{W}^T \boldsymbol{\mu}$, $\boldsymbol{\mu} = -\frac{1}{2}(\boldsymbol{\mu}_1 + \boldsymbol{\mu}_2)$, and ^{T} denotes a transpose operation. The Bayes error rate can be expressed as

$$P_B = \Phi\{-\frac{\delta}{2}\} = P_\infty^A, \tag{3.2}$$

where $\Phi(c)$ is the cumulative distribution function of a standard N(0,1) Gaussian random variable and δ is the Mahalanobis distance, $\delta^2 = (\mu_1 - \mu_2)^T \Sigma^{-1} (\mu_1 - \mu_2)$.

In sample-based classifiers, the true values of the parameters μ_1, μ_2, and Σ are unknown and are substituted by sample-based estimates. If one makes use of maximum likelihood estimates, $\hat{\mu}_1, \hat{\mu}_2, \hat{\Sigma}$, one obtains the standard Fisher discriminant function, F, with $W^F = \hat{\Sigma}^{-1}(\hat{\mu}_1 - \hat{\mu}_2), w_0 = W^T \hat{\mu}$, and $\hat{\mu} = -1/2(\hat{\mu}_1 + \hat{\mu}_2)$. The Fisher DF was proposed 70 years ago; however, up to this day it remains one of the most often used classification rules [4, 5, 12]. Approximately two dozen alternative ways have been suggested to estimate the unknown coefficients of the linear discriminant function in situations where either the data is non-Gaussian or the number of training vectors is too small to estimate the covariance matrix reliably (see references in [2, 3, 10, 11, 12]).

One easy way to develop a simple linear discriminant function is to ignore the covariance matrix. Then one obtains the Euclidean distance (nearest mean) classifier E. Here only the mean vectors are used to calculate the weights: $W^E = \hat{\mu}_1 - \hat{\mu}_2, w_0 = W^T \hat{\mu}$. Therefore, it is less sensitive to sample size.

The expected (generalization) error of Fisher DF can be approximated by a rather simple expression (see, e.g., [12, 14] and references therein)

$$\bar{P}_N^F \approx \Phi\left\{ -\frac{\delta}{2} \frac{1}{\sqrt{T_M T_{\Sigma}}} \right\} \tag{3.3}$$

where the term $T_M = 1 + \frac{4p}{\delta^2 n}$ arises due to the inexact sample estimation of the mean vectors of the classes and the term $T_{\bar{\Sigma}} = 1 + \frac{p}{n-p}$ arises due to the inexact sample estimation of the covariance matrix, p denotes the number of input variables (the dimensionality of the feature vector), and n is the sample size: $n = N_1 + N_2$. In equation (3.3) we assume $N_1 = N_2 = N$. An asymptotic error of Fisher linear classifier, $\bar{P}_\infty^F$, can be computed when $N_1 \to \infty$, $N_2 \to \infty$, and thus $\bar{P}_N^F \to \bar{P}_\infty^F$. Note, for GCCM data model, the Bays error is $\bar{P}_\infty^F = P_B$.

In an analogous expression for the Euclidean distance classifier (EDC) we have to skip the term $T_{\bar{\Sigma}}$. This analytical expression for the generalization error of EDC is valid if the data distribution is spherically symmetric Gaussian, i.e.,

$$\Sigma = \sigma^2 \begin{bmatrix} 1 & 0 & & 0 \\ 0 & 1 & & 0 \\ & & \cdots & \\ 0 & 0 & & 1 \end{bmatrix} = \sigma^2 I,$$

where I is the identity matrix and σ^2 is a positive scalar constant.

In real-world applications, the input variables are often correlated. In those cases the asymptotic errors differ:

$$P_\infty^E = \Phi\{-\frac{\delta^*}{2}\} \geq \bar{P}_\infty^F = P_B, \tag{3.4}$$

where P_∞^E is the asymptotic error of EDC, and δ^* is an effective distance between pattern classes,

$$\delta^* = \frac{(\mu_1-\mu_2)^T(\mu_1-\mu_2)}{\sqrt{(\mu_1-\mu_2)^T \bar{\Sigma}(\mu_1-\mu_2)}}. \tag{3.5}$$

The expected PMC of EDC is also affected by an effective number of features p^*,

$$\bar{P}_N^E \approx \Phi\left\{ -\frac{\delta^*}{2}\frac{1}{\sqrt{1+\frac{4p^*}{n(\delta^*)^2}}}\right\}, \tag{3.6}$$

where

$$1 \leq p^* = \frac{((\mu_1-\mu_2)^T(\mu_1-\mu_2))^2\mathrm{tr}(\Sigma^2)}{((\mu_1-\mu_2)^T\Sigma(\mu_1-\mu_2)^T)^2} \leq \infty. \tag{3.7}$$

3.3 Complexities of the Classifiers and the Data

Perhaps the least complicated theoretical data model in pattern recognition is the spherically symmetric Gaussian distribution. Here all variables are uncorrelated and have identical variances. In such a situation, $P_\infty^E = P_\infty^F = P_B$, $p^* = p$, and $\delta^* = \delta$. Only two parameters are needed to describe the data distribution: the dimensionality p and the Mahalanobis distance δ. This data model is illustrated with the pair of classes C1, C2 in Figure 3.1.

In a majority of known generalization error studies, the complexity of the data is characterized by the dimensionality only (see, e.g., [1, 17]). The equations presented in the previous section advocate that, from the point of view of statistical pattern recognition, a difference between the asymptotic and expected probabilities of misclassification also is inducing the complexity of the data. The situation becomes much more complicated in the case where input variables are mutually correlated. Then it may happen that $\delta^* < \delta$ or even $\delta^* << \delta$ (for illustration see the pair of classes C6, C7 in Fig. 3.1). It may also happen that the effective dimensionality p^* is close to 1 (the pair of classes C4, C5 in Fig. 3.1). In this case, for EDC the actual dimensionality of the data is one. Thus, looking from a perspective of a difference between expected and asymptotic error rates, the pair of classes C4, C5 is very simple for EDC; however, it becomes more complex for the Fisher classifier. In another extreme case, p^* tends to infinity (the pair of classes C3, C4 in Fig. 3.1). In the latter case, the distribution of pattern classes is much more "complicated" for the EDC. For the Fisher classifier, however, the complexity of the data remains the same.

The following measures of complexity could be useful in characterizing the complexity of the data from the point of view of classification error:

$$\bar{P}_N^F/\bar{P}_N^E, \quad \bar{P}_N^F/P_\infty^F, \quad \bar{P}_N^E/\bar{P}_\infty^E,$$

$$\min(\bar{P}_N^F, \bar{P}_N^E)/P_B, \quad P_\infty^E/P_B, \quad P_\infty^F/P_B, \quad P_\infty^E/P_\infty^F, p/p^*. \tag{3.8}$$

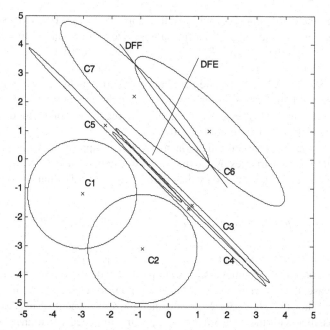

Fig. 3.1. Effect of the covariance matrix and the difference between the mean vectors, $\hat{\mu}_1 - \hat{\mu}_2$, on the effective dimensionality p^* and the effective distance δ^*: for classes C1 and C2, $p^* = p = 2, \delta^* = \delta$; for C3 and C4, $p^* >> p$, $\delta^* = \delta$; for C4 and C5, $p^* << p, \delta^* = \delta$. For classes C6 and C7, $\delta^* << \delta$, $p^* = 1.8$ (DFE and DFF are the decision boundaries of the EDC and the Fisher classifiers, respectively).

Instead of the ratios, absolute differences between each pair of quantities could be utilized too. At first sight, in terms of these measures, the simplest data model is the spherically symmetric Gaussian distribution where $P_\infty^E/P_\infty^F = 1$ and $p^* = p$. From this viewpoint, it seems that the measure $\gamma^{EF\infty} = P_\infty^E/P_\infty^F$ is quite reasonable. Condition $\gamma^{EF\infty} = 1$ indicates that the data set is simple enough and the simple classifier EDC can be used instead of the more complex Fisher classifier. It is true only if one does not take into account the fact that the training sample size is finite. A deeper examination reveals, however, that the situation could exist where $p^* >> p$. In such cases, instead of EDC, the Fisher classifier could become more useful.

If $P_\infty^E/P_\infty^F = 1$ and p^* is close to 1, one prefers to use EDC. In those cases, the intrinsic dimensionality for the data is equal to 1, and such data models should be considered as very simple. For that reason, the parameter $\gamma^{EF\infty}$ alone is insufficient to characterize the data complexity. In fact *all four parameters, p, δ, and p^*, δ^*, jointly determine the complexity of a pattern recognition task* if the data distribution is Gaussian with a common covariance matrix for the two classes, such that either EDC or Fisher potentially could be used for classification.

The data complexity problem becomes even more complicated if more types of classification rules are considered as potential candidates for decision making. Consider the GCCM data model. Let $p = 200, N_1 = N_2 = 100$, and $\delta = 3.76$ ($P_\infty^F =$

0.03). Then the Fisher classifier will result in approximately 11% error. Such a high generalization error rate means that the sample size is too small. If the features are correlated, it could happen that $P_\infty^E / P_\infty^F \gg 1$. Therefore, EDC will be an inappropriate classifier too.

A number of ways could be attempted in order to design the classifier given small sample size and high feature dimensionality. Examples are dimensionality reduction by feature selection or feature extraction, different regularization methods, and structuralization of the covariance matrix with a small number of parameters [12, 16].

A rather universal structuralization method is to approximate the dependence structure among the variables by the first-order tree dependence. Here the probability density function is approximated by the product of $p-1$ conditional and one marginal density:

$$p(x_1, x_2, ..., x_p) = \prod_{j=1}^{n} f(x_j | x_{mj})(1 \leq m_j \leq p). \tag{3.9}$$

In representation equation (3.9) the sequence $m_1, m_2, ..., m_p$ constitutes an unknown permutation of the integers, and $f(x_1 | m_1)$, by definition, is equal to $p(x_1)$. In a general case, the covariance matrix has $p \times p$ nonzero elements. An inverse of this matrix Σ^{-1}, however, has only $2p - 1$ distinct nonzero elements. Thus, to design the Fisher classifier with the first-order tree type structuralized covariance matrix (denoted by FT_1), we estimate $2p$ parameters that are different in the opposite pattern classes and $2p - 1$ parameters that are common for both classes. In addition, we need to know the permutation $m_1, m_2, ..., m_p$.

In practice, unknown permutations have to be found from the sample covariance matrix. The theory shows that the expected PMC of this classifier is expressed by equation (3.3) with $T_{\bar{\Sigma}} = 1$ [12, 18]. Experiments with a dozen real-world data sets indicated that in a majority of cases, such a decision-making rule outperforms both the Euclidean distance and the Fisher classifiers [13].

For a layman, it seems that such a data model is very complex; we have to understand the permutation structure and know how to estimate it and the coefficients of the structuralized covariance matrix. For an expert in pattern recognition equipped with well-organized software, such a model (the case where the dependencies between p input variables are determined by the first-order tree dependence model, so that the asymptotic errors $P_\infty^{FT_1} \approx P_\infty^F$) implies that the classifier FT_1 has very favorable small sample properties: $\bar{P}_N^{FT_1} / P_\infty^{FT_1} \approx \bar{P}_N^E / \bar{P}_\infty^E$. For him or her the data set for classifier FT_1 is rather simple. In contrast, for the Euclidean distance and the Fisher classifiers this data set is complex. The above considerations about the first-order tree dependence model advocate that the complexity of data depends also on the researcher's knowledge about this model and on the presence of the software for estimating the structuralized covariance matrix.

3.4 Other Classifiers and Concluding Remarks

Our main concern in this chapter is to show that the complexity of data should be evaluated from the standpoint of the classifier utilized for decision making. In sections 3.2 and 3.3 we considered the unimodal GCCM model where a linear decision rule is asymptotically optimal. Even in such a simple data model, we have found that a number of issues are important while evaluating the data complexity.

If the covariance matrices of the classes are different, i.e., $\Sigma_2 \neq \Sigma_1$, the asymptotically optimal classifier is a quadratic disriminant function (DF). A good alternative in the two-class case is a linear classifier suggested by Anderson-Bahadur (known as the AB procedure) where the weight vector is expressed as (see, e.g., [12])

$$w_{AB} = (\Sigma_1 \alpha + \Sigma_2)^{-1} (\mu_1 - \mu_2) \tag{3.10}$$

The unknown coefficients α_1 and threshold weight w_0 have to be found to minimize certain selected classification performance criteria. If $\Sigma_2 \neq \Sigma_1$, the differences among the asymptotic errors of the quadratic DF, the AB procedure, and the Fisher linear DF will affect the evaluation of the data complexity. If the sample size is taken into account, one needs to remember that the quadratic DF is very sensitive to sample size if the dimensionality of the input feature space is high. In a relatively small region of a multidimensional feature space where the pattern classes overlap, the quadratic DF can be approximated by a hyperplane. In the remaining space, we will have relatively few overlapping vectors. Therefore, in a major part of the multivariate feature space, an exact position of the decision boundary is not important. Simulations show that small sample properties of the AB procedure are much more favorable than that of the quadratic DF. Therefore, in many real-world two-class problems, the AB procedure works as well as or even better than the quadratic classifier [12, 14].

A very important concern in considering the quadratic DF is the fact that the expected classification error depends on the sample sizes of both classes, i.e., N_1 and N_2. Such a situation is characteristic of nonoptimal statistical classifiers trained with the plug-in design principle [5]. Another example where both sample sizes N_1 and N_2 are affecting the generalization error is a multinomial classifier, such as the one used in the behavior knowledge space method (see, e.g.. [7, 12]). In certain situations, an increase in the number of training vectors of one pattern class increases the generalization error instead of decreasing it! [12, 15]. Therefore, while characterizing data complexity; both sample sizes N_1 and N_2 are important.

In addition to statistical pattern recognition and heuristics based methods, linear classifiers can be obtained by other procedures, such as by training a single layer perceptron (SLP). In this way, one may obtain the EDC, regularized and robust discriminant analysis, the standard Fisher rule and that with covariance matrix pseudo-inversion, the minimum empirical error classifier, as well as the support vector machine [11, 12]. Which classifier will be obtained depends on the training parameters and, most importantly, on stopping moment. Thus, the SLP is not a single classification rule. It is a set of different rules of diverse complexity. Here the classifier's complexity is measured in terms of a number and a type of parameter of distribution density function if statistical methods would be utilized to estimate the weights of the linear classifier. Some data sets could be very difficult for SLP training at the very beginning; however, it becomes "easier" later. For example, the GCCM data with low p and very high p^* could become very difficult for the classical SLP training procedure [12].

In difficult pattern classification problems, we deal with multimodal distribution densities of input pattern vectors. In such situations nonparametric (local) classification rules (k-NN, Parzen window, decision trees, etc.) have to be applied [5]. Complexities of the local classification rules could be characterized by values of smoothing parameters like the number of nearest neighbors, k, in the k-NN rule or the kernel width in the Parzen window classifier. Optimal values of these parameters have to be chosen according to the sizes of the training set (N_1 and N_2). Consequently, we have a vicious circle: the complexity of the data depends on the complexity of the optimal local classifier. Optimal parameters of these classifiers depend on training sample size and data complexity.

Generally speaking, each new pattern classifier that potentially could be utilized for classification introduces one or several measures of complexity. Yet *a large number of characteristics is impractical* to determine data complexity in concrete work. As a compromise, a question arises: could some of the measures be clustered into a smaller number of groups? The question remains unanswered. Factors similar to that presented in equation (3.8) should be taken into account while trying to taxonomize the data sets obtained in real experiments — comparative measures of asymptotic errors of distinct classifiers, and the small sample properties of them.

In this chapter we discussed the possibilities and difficulties in estimating data complexity assuming some simple data models, such as the spherically symmetric Gaussian, where certain simple classifiers are known to be suitable. Based on the behavior of several popular classifiers, a number of possible measures for the difficulty of a classification task were given, each representing the perspective of some specific classifiers. Examples were shown where the same problem may appear easy or difficult depending on the classifier being used, through the influences of the density parameters and the sample sizes on the relevant measures such as the effective dimensionality and the effective Mahalanobis distance.

Returning to the GCCM data model, it is worth mentioning also that the estimation of complexity parameters from experimental data may become very problematic. For example, in estimating the effective number of features p^* [equation (3.7)], we have to estimate the means and the covariance matrix. The confidence interval in estimating parameter p^* is too wide to be practically useful. Thus, the estimation of parameter p^* is more difficult and less reliable than training the linear Fisher classifier. This fact suggests once more that the estimation of data complexity measures is not necessarily easier than training a classifier for the task.

References

[1] S. Amari, N. Fujita, S. Shinomoto. Four types of learning curves. *Neural Computation*, 4, 605–618, 1992.

[2] M. Basu, T.K. Ho. The learning behavior of single neuron classifiers on linearly separable or nonseparable input. *Proc. of IEEE Intl. Joint Conf. on Neural Networks*, July 10-16, 1999, Washington, DC.

[3] J. Cid-Sueiro, J.L. Sancho-Gomez. Saturated perceptrons for maximum margin and minimum misclassification error. *Neural Processing Letters*, 14, 217–226, 2001.

[4] R.O. Duda, P.E. Hart, D.G. Stork. *Pattern Classification and Scene Analysis*. 2nd ed. New York: John Wiley, 2000.

[5] K. Fukunaga. *Introduction to Statistical Pattern Recognition*. 2nd ed. New York: Academic Press, 1990.

[6] T.K. Ho, M. Basu. Complexity measures of supervised classification problems. *IEEE Transactions on Pattern Analysis and Machine Intelligence*, 24, 289–300, 2002.

[7] Y.S. Huang, C.Y. Suen. A method of combining multiple experts for the recognition of unconstrained handwritten numerals. *IEEE Transactions on Pattern Analysis and Machine Intelligence*, 17(1), 90–94, 1995.

[8] M. Li, P. Vitanyi. *An Introduction to Kolmogorov Complexity and its Applications*. New York: Springer, 1993.

[9] S. Raudys. On the problems of sample size in pattern recognition. In V. S. Pugatchiov, ed. *Detection, Pattern Recognition and Experiment Design*, volume 2, pages 64–76. Proc. of the 2nd All-Union Conference Statistical Methods in Control Theory. Moscow: Nauka, 1970 (in Russian).

[10] S. Raudys. On dimensionality, sample size and classification error of nonparametric linear classification algorithms. *IEEE Transactions on Pattern Analysis and Machine Intelligence*, 19, 669–671, 1997.

[11] S. Raudys. Evolution and generalization of a single neuron. I. SLP as seven statistical classifiers. *Neural Networks*, 11, 283–296, 1998.

[12] S. Raudys. *Statistical and Neural Classifiers: An Integrated Approach to Design*. New York: Springer-Verlag, 2001.

[13] S. Raudys, A. Saudargiene. Tree type dependency model and sample size - dimensionality properties. *IEEE Transaction on Pattern Analysis and Machine Intelligence*, 23, 233–239, 2001.

[14] S. Raudys. Integration of statistical and neural methods to design classifiers in case of unequal covariance matrices. *Lecture Notes in Computer Science*, New York: Springer, 3238, 270–280, 2004.

[15] S. Raudys, D. Young. Results in statistical discriminant analysis: A review of the former Soviet Union literature. *Journal of Multivariate Analysis*, 89, 1–35, 2004.

[16] A. Saudargiene. Structurization of the covariance matrix by process type and block diagonal models in the classifier design. *Informatica* 10(2), 245–269, 1999.

[17] V. N. Vapnik. *The Nature of Statistical Learning Theory*. New York: Springer, 1995.

[18] V.I. Zarudskij. The use of models of simple dependence problems of classification. In S. Raudys, ed. *Statistical Problems of Control*, volume 38, pages 33–75, Vilnius: Institute of Mathematics and Informatics, 1979 (in Russian).

4

Linear Separability in Descent Procedures for Linear Classifiers

Mitra Basu and Tin Kam Ho

Summary. Determining linear separability is an important way to understand structures present in data. We review the behavior of several classical descent procedures for determining linear separability and training linear classifiers in the presence of linearly nonseparable input. We compare the adaptive procedures to linear programming methods using many pairwise discrimination problems from a public database. We found that the adaptive procedures have serious implementational problems that make them less preferable than linear programming.

4.1 Introduction

Usually classification approaches in pattern recognition appear to fall into two broad types: the parametric methods that often rely on an assumption that each class of vectors follows certain known forms of probability distribution, and the nonparametric methods that do not make any assumptions about the class distributions. When there are indications from the observations that the assumption of Gaussian distributions has to be abandoned, there are few alternatives left, so that one has to resort to non-parametric methods. We believe that if some knowledge about the class boundaries can be derived from the data, there are advantages in using a recognition method suited to such boundaries.

In practice, a classification problem is often presented with a finite training set assumed to be representative of the expected input. Important clues about the complexity of the problem can be obtained by studying the geometrical structures present in such a training set. Extracting important information from small amount of data is also the focus of a recent trend in statistical learning theory [32].

A geometrical property that is of fundamental importance is linear separability of the classes. Based on this property, a number of descriptors of the point set geometry can be constructed. Whether the input is linearly separable or nonseparable, in constructing a classifier, deriving a linear discriminant that is optimal in some sense is a useful first step. Linear discriminants can serve as building blocks for piecewise linear classifiers, or be used to separate points transformed into a higher dimensional space where they may become linearly separable.

The need to study the structures in data also arises from the study of neural networks. One of the most promising attributes of a neural network is its ability to learn by interacting with an information source. Learning in a neural network is achieved through an adaptive procedure, known as a *learning rule or algorithm*, whereby the weights of the network are incrementally adjusted so as to improve a predefined performance measure over time. There is usually an assumed architecture of the network and a desired mapping. Very often, the outputs of the mapping are specified only for some subset of the possible inputs, namely, the training set. One of the main issues in learning is the design of efficient learning algorithms with good generalization properties. Although generalization is not a mathematically well-defined term, it usually refers to the capability of the network to produce desirable responses to inputs that are not included in the training set. The existing learning rules can be broadly categorized into three main groups: (1) *supervised*, (2) *unsupervised*, and (3) *reinforced*. We focus our attention on *Supervised* learning where the network architecture consists of a single layer of neurons, which can represent all linear classifiers. The rules in this category can be viewed as *error-correction* or *gradient-descent* types. Gradient descent is an iterative method commonly used to search for a solution (the global minima) in a high-dimensional space that has a number of local minima. Specifically, given a criterion function, the search point can be incrementally improved at each iteration by moving in the direction of the negative of the gradient on the surface defined by this criterion function in the appropriate parameter space. It has been shown that all these rules can be derived as minimizers of a suitable criterion function [6], and the corresponding algorithms, also appropriately known as *descent algorithms*, for implementation are based on gradient-descent method.

Notations

Consider a two-class (ω_1, ω_2) problem. Let us assume that there are m sets of training pairs, namely, $(\mathbf{x}^1, d^1)$, $(\mathbf{x}^2, d^2)$,..., where $\mathbf{x}^j \in R^n$ is the jth input vector and $d^j \in \{-1, +1\}$, $j = 1, 2, ..., m$ is the desired output for the jth input vector. In a single unit neural network, the output y^j for an input vector $\mathbf{x}^j$ is computed as $y^j = sgn(\mathbf{w}^t\mathbf{x}^j - \theta)$, where $\mathbf{w}^t$ denotes the transpose of the (column) weight vector $\mathbf{w}$. Such a network is referred to as a *single-layer perceptron* or a linear classifier.

Remark 1: Without loss of generality we include the threshold value θ in the weight vector as its last element and increase the dimension of every input vector by augmenting it with an entry that equals 1. Thus the weight vector is $\mathbf{w}^t = [w_1, ..., w_n, \theta]$ and the input vector is $\mathbf{x}^{j^t} = [x_1^j, ..., x_n^j, 1]$, and the output of the perceptron can be written as $y^j = sgn(\sum_{k=1}^{n+1} w_k x_k^j) = sgn(\mathbf{w}^t\mathbf{x}^j)$.

From now on let us assume that the input and the weight vectors are already augmented, and let n be the augmented dimension; then the problem of learning can be defined as follows:

Proposition 4.1.1 *Given a set of input vectors* $(\mathbf{x}^1, ..., \mathbf{x}^m)$, $\mathbf{x}^i \in R^n$, *and a set of desired output values* $\{d^1, ..., d^m\}$, $d^i \in \{1, -1\}$, *find a weight vector* $\mathbf{w} \in R^n$ *such that* $sgn(\mathbf{w}^t\mathbf{x}^j) = y^j = d^j$ *for* $j = 1, ..., m$.

The goal is to determine a weight vector $\mathbf{w}$ such that the following conditions are satisfied:

$$\mathbf{w}^t\mathbf{x}^j > 0 \text{ if } d^j = +1,$$
$$\mathbf{w}^t\mathbf{x}^j < 0 \text{ if } d^j = -1. \tag{4.1}$$

The equation $\mathbf{w}^{*t}\mathbf{x} = 0$ defines a hyperplane in R^n. Therefore finding a solution vector $\mathbf{w}^*$ to this equation is equivalent to finding a separating hyperplane that correctly classifies all vectors $\mathbf{x}^j$, j=1,2,...,m. In other words, an algorithm must be designed to find a hyperplane $\mathbf{w}^{*t}\mathbf{x} = 0$ that partitions the input space into two distinct half-spaces, one containing all points $\mathbf{x}^j$ for which the desired output is +1 and the other containing all points $\mathbf{x}^j$ for which the desired output is -1. We reformulate this condition (4.1) to adopt the convention usually followed in the literature.

Remark 2: Define a vector $\mathbf{z}^j$:

$$\begin{cases} \mathbf{z}^j = +\mathbf{x}^j \text{ if } d^j = +1, \\ \mathbf{z}^j = -\mathbf{x}^j \text{ if } d^j = -1. \end{cases}$$

The data matrix $\mathbf{Z}$ is defined to be $[\mathbf{z}^1, \mathbf{z}^2, ..., \mathbf{z}^m]$. The output y^j for the modified input vector $\mathbf{z}^j$ is computed as $y^j = sgn(\mathbf{w}^t\mathbf{z}^j)$. The goal is to determine a weight vector $\mathbf{w}$ such that the following condition is satisfied:

$$\mathbf{w}^t\mathbf{z}^j > 0 \quad \text{for all } j. \tag{4.2}$$

Note that this simplification aids only in theoretical analysis. As far as the implementation is concerned, this does not alter the actual computation in a significant manner.

All learning algorithms[1] for neural networks are guaranteed to find a separating surface in a finite number of steps for *linearly separable classes*. A comprehensive review of standard learning algorithms and analysis of their behavior for linearly separable classes can be found in reference [34]. However, when it comes to *linearly nonseparable* cases, the behavior of these algorithms is not usually explored. In practice, most real-world problems are *assumed* to be nonlinear without any concrete evidence, and multilayer neural networks are used to address these problems. However, the use of a multilayer network is overkill for a problem that is linear. Moreover, effective use of a multilayer neural net involves a proper choice of the network architecture.

Backpropagation, the standard learning algorithm, is used to train a fixed topology multilayer neural net. In general, this approach works well only when the network architecture is chosen correctly. Too small a network may not be able to capture the characteristics of the training samples, and too large a size may lead to overfitting and poor generalization performance. Results are available to determine the *correct* size of a network. It has been shown that a single hidden-layer neural network with $N-1$ hidden units can give any N input-target relationship exactly [14, 25], whereas a network with two hidden layers can do the same with negligible error using $N/2+3$

---

[1] The only exceptions are the Widrow-Hoff and other linear regression-based algorithms.

hidden units [28]. Note that these results provide only an upper bound on the number of hidden neurons needed. For a specific problem one may be able to do far better by exploiting the structure in the data.

Recently, some researchers have investigated methods that alter network architecture as learning proceeds. These can be grouped into two categories, namely, (1) *pruning* algorithms, where one starts with a larger than needed network that iteratively removes inactive hidden neurons and associated connections until an acceptable solution is found; and (2) *constructive* algorithms, where one starts with a small network and adds hidden units and weights until a satisfactory solution is obtained. Each of the two methods has distinct advantages and disadvantages. For an overview on pruning algorithms, see [22]. Discussion on constructive approaches can be found in [15].

This chapter presents a review of standard learning algorithms for single-neuron/two-class problems where the set of input vectors is not linearly separable. We begin in section 4.2 with a review of the concepts of linear separability and its relationship to linear independence. In section 4.3 we categorize all such learning algorithms into two broad classes, and discuss representative algorithms from each class. In section 4.4 we choose a set of examples where the input data are not necessarily linearly separable and study the performance of each of these algorithms. The chapter concludes with a brief discussion in section 4.5.

In our analysis of performance of various learning algorithms we will draw from reference [26], which presents a detailed study on linearly nonseparable sets of input in general. It also includes specifically an analysis of the perceptron algorithm. In the rest of this chapter, we assume that the vectors are modified to satisfy the properties mentioned in remarks 1 and 2 above.

4.2 Linear Separability and Linear Independence

Let us explore the geometrical interpretation of equation (4.2) for a better understanding of the structure of the data set. For a linearly separable set of vectors, a separating hyperplane can be determined such that all vectors lie on one side of it. The normal to this hyperplane is the solution weight vector w^*. In other words, placing a hyperplane such that all vectors lie on one side of this plane implies that the angle between any pair of vectors from the set must be less than π. Equivalently, the angle between the weight vector and any vector from the set must be less than $\pi/2$. This observation agrees with the fact presented in Nilsson [21] that input vectors that are almost perpendicular to the weight vectors are most difficult to train. Next, we explore the interesting relationship between linear separability and the more general concept of linear dependence/independence of a set of vectors.

The following theorems and definitions are taken from Siu et al. [26].

Proposition 4.2.1 *A set of vectors* $\{z^1, z^2, ..., z^m\}$ *is linearly nonseparable if and only if there exists a positive linear combination of the vectors that equals* 0, *i.e., there exists* $q_i \geq 0, 1 \leq i \leq m$, *such that* $\sum_{i=1}^{m} q_i z^i = 0$ *and* $q_j > 0$ *for some* j, $1 \leq j \leq m$.

Note the similarity with the definition of a set of vectors that are linearly dependent. We provide definitions of linear dependence and linear independence for easy reference.

Proposition 4.2.2 *A set of vectors* $\{z^1, z^2, ..., z^m\}$ *in vector space Z are linearly dependent if there exists numbers* q_1, q_2, ..., q_m *not all equal to zero [the key difference with (4.2.1) is that here* $q_i s$ *may take negative values] such that* $\sum_{i=1}^{m} q_i z^i = 0$.

We use geometry to present an alternative interpretation. The convention for measuring the angle between a pair of vectors is specified in the following remark:

Remark 3: The angle between any pair of vectors is the angle subtended on that side of the hyperplane for which the desired responses of the original set of vectors are +1.

A set of vectors is linearly dependent if one can construct a closed figure[2] using a subset (possibly the whole set) of the vectors. It is permissible to change the magnitude as well as the orientation of the vectors (change in orientation in this context means that one may either include the vector **a** or include −**a**). On the other hand, a set of vectors is linearly nonseparable (that is, they cannot be made to lie on the same side of a hyperplane) if one can construct a closed figure using a subset (possibly the whole set) of the vectors. Here it is permissible to change the magnitude of the vectors but not their orientations. One may easily deduce that linear nonseparability implies linear dependence. However, linear dependence may or may not lead to linear nonseparability since if in constructing the closed figure one is required to change orientations of vectors, that would violate the restrictions imposed by linear nonseparability. Intuitively, it is more likely that one may be able to construct a closed figure (without changing the orientations) if the vectors do not lie on one side of a plane.

Proposition 4.2.3 *A set of vectors* $\{z^1, z^2, ..., z^m\}$ *in vector space Z is linearly independent if and only if the following condition is satisfied: Whenever* q_1, q_2, ..., q_m *are numbers such that* $\sum_{i=1}^{m} q_i z^i = 0$, *then* $q_i = 0 \ \forall i$.

Note that linear independence implies linear separability, but the converse is not true. That is, linear separability may or may not lead to linear independence (Fig. 4.1), since all we need to show for a set of vectors to be linearly separable is that no positive q can be found. If some negative q's (multiplication by $-q$ amounts to changing the direction of the vector) are found, then the set of vectors is linearly dependent as well as linearly separable. Intuitively, if all vectors are lying on the same side of a plane (the set is linearly separable), then it is highly unlikely that one can construct a closed figure with these vectors without changing their directions.[3] Here, we present a more general definition of linear nonseparability than one that is found in Siu et al.[26].

---

[2] We plot a set of n vectors by joining the head of the ith to the tail of the $(i+1)$th. A closed figure is formed if the head of the nth vector touches the tail of the 1st vector.

[3] It is rather conceivable that, for all vectors lying on one side of a hyperplane, a mixture of positive and negative q's can be found that satisfies linear dependence.

Proposition 4.2.4 *A set of vectors* $\{z^1, z^2, ..., z^m\}$ *is linearly nonseparable if and only if there exists a linear combination of the vectors that equals* $\mathbf{0}$, *i.e., there exists* $q_i, 1 \le i \le m$, *such that* $\sum_{i=1}^{m} q_i z^i = \mathbf{0}$ *and* $q_j \ne 0$ *for some* j, $1 \le j \le m$ *and all nonzero* q_j*'s have the same sign.*

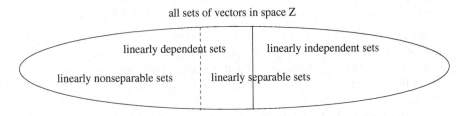

Fig. 4.1. Illustration of the relationship between linear dependence and linear separability. The dashed line divides between the linearly separable and nonseparable vector sets, and the solid line divides between the linearly dependent and independent vector sets. Linearly nonseparable sets are in a proper subset of linearly dependent sets.

In other words, a set of vectors can be (1) linearly nonseparable and dependent, (2) linearly separable and dependent, and (3) linearly separable and independent, but not (4) linearly nonseparable and independent.

Example 1: Linearly nonseparable and linearly dependent set

Consider a linearly nonseparable set **A** (XOR problem)

$$A_1 = [-1 - 1\, 1]^t; \quad A_2 = [1\, 1\, 1]^t; \quad A_3 = [-1\, 1 - 1]^t; \quad A_4 = [1 - 1 - 1]^t.$$

One solution to the equation $q_1 A_1 + q_2 A_2 + q_3 A_3 + q_4 A_4 = \mathbf{0}$ is

$$q_1 = q_2 = q_3 = q_4 = a,$$

where a can be any real number. The vectors in set **A** are linearly nonseparable since they satisfy proposition (4.2.1) and more generally proposition (4.2.4). Note that these vectors are linearly dependent since they satisfy proposition (4.2.2).

Example 2: Linearly separable and linearly dependent set

Consider a linearly separable set **B**

$$B_1 = [1\, 1\, 1]^t; \quad B_2 = [1 - 1\, 1]^t; \quad B_3 = [1 - 1 - 1]^t; \quad B_4 = [1\, 1 - 1]^t.$$

A linear combination with either **all** positive or **all** negative coefficients that equals to zero cannot be found for the vectors in set **B**.

The only possible solution, with all q's bearing the same sign, to $q_1 B_1 + q_2 B_2 + q_3 B_3 + q_4 B_4 = \mathbf{0}$ is

$$q_1 = q_2 = q_3 = q_4 = 0.$$

Thus we conclude that vectors in this set are linearly separable. Note that these vectors are linearly dependent, since the equation can be satisfied with $q_1 = 1, q_2 = -1, q_3 = 1, q_4 = -1$.

Example 3: Linearly separable and linearly independent set

The following example illustrates that a set of linearly separable vectors can be linearly independent.

$$C_1 = [1\,1\,1]^t; \quad C_2 = [1 - 1\,1]^t; \quad C_3 = [1 - 1 - 1]^t.$$

The only values of coefficients that satisfy $q_1 C_1 + q_2 C_2 + q_3 C_3 = \mathbf{0}$ are $q_1 = q_2 = q_3 = 0$.

In discussions of linear separability, one usually refers to a set of vectors of different classes. However, if the input vectors have been modified to carry the class membership as in remark 2, discussion on linear separability can be extended to single vectors. Such a discussion turns out to be helpful for characterization of the detailed structure of a data set.

Definition: A vector $\mathbf{z}^i$ is defined to be separable if it never participates in a positive linear combination that equals 0, i.e., $\sum_{j=1}^m q_j \mathbf{z}^j = \mathbf{0}; q_j \geq 0$ implies that $q_i = 0$.

Definition: A vector $\mathbf{z}^i$ is defined to be nonseparable if it participates in a positive linear combination that equals 0, i.e., $\sum_{j=1}^m q_j \mathbf{z}^j = \mathbf{0}; q_j \geq 0$ implies that there is some $q_i \neq 0$.

Two properties are noted on a set of nonseparable vectors [26]:

1. If the set of nonseparable vectors is nonempty, then it must consist of at least two vectors.
2. There exists a hyperplane passing through the origin, such that all the nonseparable vectors lie on the plane, and all the separable vectors lie on one side of it.

Geometrically, any given set of vectors are in one of the three configurations [17] (as shown in Fig. 4.2):

(a) there exists a vector x that makes a strict acute angle ($< \pi/2$) with all the vectors in A;
(b) there exists a vector x that makes an acute angle ($\leq \pi/2$) with all the vectors in A, and the origin 0 can be expressed as a nonnegative linear combination of vectors in A with positive weights assigned to those vectors in A that are orthogonal to x; and
(c) the origin can be expressed as a positive linear combination of all the vectors in A.

The proof is from Tucker's [30] first existence theorem, which states:
For any given $p \times n$ matrix A, the systems

$$Ax \geq 0 \text{ and } A'y = 0, y \geq 0$$

possess solutions x and y satisfying

$$Ax + y > 0.$$

The set of vectors is linearly separable in case (a), and nonseparable in cases (b) and (c). The nonseparability is caused by all the vectors in case (c), but only some of the vectors in case (b).

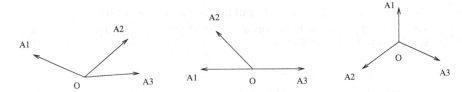

Fig. 4.2. Any given set of vectors A must be in one of these three configurations [17] shown by examples of three vectors in a two-dimensional space

Roychowdhury et al. [24] give a simple procedure to determine the set of separable and nonseparable vectors using a linear programming (LP) formulation. Let e_i be a column vector with component i being 1 and all other components being zero. Vector z_i is nonseparable if the objective function of the linear program

$$
\begin{aligned}
\text{minimize} \quad & e_i{}^t\mathbf{q} \\
\text{subject to } & \mathbf{Z}^t\mathbf{q} = \mathbf{0} \\
& \mathbf{q} \geq \mathbf{0}
\end{aligned}
\tag{4.3}
$$

is unbounded. This happens if and only if vector z_i participates, with a nonzero coefficient, in a positive linear combination of the input vectors that equals zero. Hence, the set of separable and nonseparable vectors can be determined by solving one such LP problem for each input vector, i.e., a total of m LP problems.

4.3 Analysis of Representative Learning Algorithms

Descent procedures are those that modify the weight vector as the algorithms examine the input vectors one by one. There are non–descent- based methods for obtaining linear classifiers such as Fisher's linear discriminant analysis. In this chapter we focus on descent procedures. We broadly categorize them into two groups, namely, (A) error correction procedures and (B) error minimization procedures. However, it should be noted that the term *error* is defined differently in each context. In group A it refers to an instance of misclassification, and in group B it refers to a measure of distance of a point from a hyperplane. The remainder of this section discusses representative methods from each group.

4.3.1 Group A: Error Correction Procedures

Fixed-Increment Perceptron Training Rule: Among the adaptive procedures, the fixed-increment perceptron training rule (from now on called the perceptron rule) is the most well known. We discuss the performance of the classic perceptron rule and its several variations for the nonseparable case. The perceptron weight update rule [23] can be stated as

$$\mathbf{w}^0 \qquad\qquad \text{arbitrary}$$
$$\mathbf{w}^{j+1} = \mathbf{w}^j + \alpha \mathbf{z}^j \text{ if } \mathbf{z}^{j^t} \mathbf{w}^j \leq 0 \qquad\qquad (4.4)$$
$$\mathbf{w}^{j+1} = \qquad \mathbf{w}^j \qquad \text{otherwise.}$$

The learning coefficient $\alpha > 0$ and the length of the input vector control the magnitude of change. It can be shown [23] that if the vectors are linearly separable, this rule will produce a solution vector $\mathbf{w}^*$ in a finite number of steps. However, for input vectors that are not linearly separable the perceptron algorithm does not converge, since, if the input vectors are nonseparable, then for any set of weights $\mathbf{w}$, there will exist at least one input vector, $\mathbf{z}$, such that $\mathbf{w}$ misclassifies $\mathbf{z}$. In other words, the algorithm will continue to make weight changes indefinitely. The following theorem, however, states that even if the algorithm iterates indefinitely, the length of the weight vector will remain bounded.

Proposition 4.3.1 The perceptron cycling theorem:[4] *Given a finite set of linearly nonseparable training samples* $\{\mathbf{z}^1, \mathbf{z}^2, ..., \mathbf{z}^m\}$, *there exists a number N such that if the perceptron learning rule is applied to this set, then the weight vector $\mathbf{w}^l$ at any iteration l remains bounded, i.e.,* $|\mathbf{w}^l| \leq N$.

Instead of formally proving this theorem (interested readers can find the proof in [3]), for intuitive purposes we explore the geometric aspect of the perceptron updating rule to see why the perceptron cycling theorem holds. Let $\mathbf{z}^n$ be the training sample that is misclassified by the current weight vector $\mathbf{w}^n$. Therefore, the angle between the two vectors must satisfy

$$\pi/2 < \theta(\mathbf{z}^n, \mathbf{w}^n) < 3\pi/2 \qquad\qquad (4.5)$$

in order for the inner product to be negative. We observe that, maintaining the satisfiability of the criterion $|\mathbf{w}^n|^2 < |\mathbf{w}^{n+1}|^2 < (|\mathbf{w}^n|^2 + |\mathbf{z}^n|^2)$, with $|\mathbf{z}^n|$ remaining fixed, becomes increasingly difficult as $|\mathbf{w}^n|$ grows. Ultimately, the above criterion becomes unsatisfiable at some point as $|\mathbf{w}^n|$ becomes larger than certain limiting value. Therefore, $|\mathbf{w}^n|$ cannot grow without bound.

In cases where the input vectors are integer-valued, the bounded weight vectors cycle through a finite set of values [19]. An observation of such cycling is an indication that the input is linearly nonseparable, though there are no known time bounds for this to become observable. Therefore, this theorem is of little use for practical applications.

Gallant [8] has proposed a modification of the perceptron rule, the pocket algorithm, so that it finds the optimal weight vector, i.e., a weight vector that will classify as many training samples as possible. The idea is to keep a separate set of weights, $\mathbf{w}^{pocket}$, along with the number of consecutive training samples that it has classified correctly. Whenever the current perceptron weight, $\mathbf{w}^n$, has a longer run of correct classification, the pocket weight $\mathbf{w}^{pocket}$ is replaced by $\mathbf{w}^n$. Unfortunately, there is no known bound on the number of iterations required to guarantee optimal weight.

---

[4] This theorem is also true for separable classes.

Usually suboptimal weight is achieved by this algorithm. A further revised version, the pocket algorithm with ratchet, is proposed [8] to ensure that the pocket weight strictly improves as it gets replaced by the current weight. This is implemented by checking whether the current weight $\mathbf{w}^n$ classifies more training examples than the current $\mathbf{w}^{pocket}$. Only then $\mathbf{w}^{pocket}$ is replaced by $\mathbf{w}^n$. Note that this improvement comes with increased computational burden, especially when there are many training samples.

In a much earlier and rarely cited reference, we find that Butz [5] has proposed to modify the perceptron update rule to address nonseparable data. A small positive *reinforcement* factor $\mu, \mu \leq \mu_0 < 1$ is introduced, with μ_0 being a certain constant, so that in place of (4.4) one has

$$
\begin{aligned}
\mathbf{w}^0 & \qquad \text{arbitrary} \\
\mathbf{w}^{j+1} &= \mathbf{w}^j + \alpha \mathbf{z}^j \text{ if } {\mathbf{z}^j}^t \mathbf{w}^j \leq 0 \qquad (4.6)\\
\mathbf{w}^{j+1} &= \mathbf{w}^j + \mu \mathbf{z}^j \text{ otherwise.}
\end{aligned}
$$

Note the similarity in the underlying concept in (4.6) and the pocket algorithm. Both attempt to reward the weight vector that correctly classifies the training samples. This approach moves the weight vector closer to the sample that is correctly classified, unlike the perceptron rule (and most others) where no action is taken in such cases. Let $\mathbf{z}^j$ and $\mathbf{z}^{j+1}$ be two consecutive training samples from the same class. Let us assume that $\mathbf{z}^j$ gets correctly classified by the current weight vector $\mathbf{w}^j$. The next weight vector is $\mathbf{w}^{j+1} = \mathbf{w}^j + \mu \mathbf{z}^j$. Let us assume that the next sample $\mathbf{z}^{j+1}$ is misclassified by the weight vector $\mathbf{w}^{j+1}$. The resulting weight vector $\mathbf{w}^{j+2}$ is more likely to keep $\mathbf{z}^j$ correctly classified in the current procedure than in that of the perceptron update procedure. Butz has shown that the error rate $k(n)/n$ decreases considerably with the introduction of a small reinforcement factor where n is the number of samples and $k(n)$ is the number of misclassifications.[5] The author goes on to show that

- A $\mu_0 < 1$ exists.
- If $\{\mathbf{z}^n\}$ is a sequence of mutually independent sample vectors, then $k(n)/n \leq G(\mu)$ with probability 1 as $n \to \infty$. $G(\mu)$ is a continuous and monotone nonincreasing function of μ, with $G(0) < 1$ and $G(\mu_0) = p_0$. The quantity p_0 is the lower limit of the error probabilities associated with the weight vector set.

In other words, with the choice of *right* $\mu \leq \mu_0$, one can find a weight vector $\mathbf{w}'$ such that the rate of misclassification decreases.

However, the quantity μ_0 (thus μ) rarely is known or can be estimated with reasonable accuracy. Successful application of this rule depends on a good value of μ

---

[5] The comparison between Butz's result and the perceptron behavior is not quite appropriate. With nonlinear input (i.e., linearly nonseparable input) the weight vectors produced by the perceptron rule may go from the best possible to the worst possible classification result in one iteration. It is almost impossible to pick the best weight vector from the perceptron procedure to make comparisons on misclassification especially for a large data set.

which has to be searched for, and the search may be computationally expensive. The other major concern is the stopping criterion, which is not discussed in this chapter.

It has been shown in [26] that perceptron learning algorithm can be used to learn the set of separable vectors and identify the set of nonseparable vectors. The definitions of separable and nonseparable vectors are given at the end of section 4.2. The major results related to the perceptron algorithm with nonlinear input are as follows:

Proposition 4.3.2 *The perceptron algorithm can separate a set of given vectors into (i) a set of separable vectors and (ii) a set of nonseparable vectors in a finite number of steps.*

A note of caution is in order. The proof of this theorem establishes the finiteness of the number of steps by showing that the upper bound for the number of steps is the constant N, which appears in the perceptron cycling theorem. With no concrete information on the upper bound and no stopping criterion, the usefulness of the above theorem in practical applications is questionable.

Proposition 4.3.3 *Given a set of vectors, the perceptron algorithm can be used to determine a linearly separable subset of maximum cardinality.*

Proposition 4.3.2 can be implemented in polynomial time using linear programming formulation (not the perceptron algorithm). This yields a set of separable vectors that may not lead to the best possible classification result. Proposition 4.3.3 is much more useful because it can be used to produce a weight vector that gives the least number of misclassifications. In this sense it is a more powerful result than the least-square methods (Widrow-Hoff, since there is no problem with local minima), Gallant's pocket algorithm, and Butz's reinforcement approach. Unfortunately, the authors show that an algorithm for this proposition is NP-complete. They propose a heuristic approach to solve proposition 4.3.3, which does not guarantee optimal results.

Projection Learning Rule (Alias fractional correction rule:) The projection learning rule [1] (more commonly known as the fractional correction rule), a variation of the perceptron rule, is also based on the error correcting principle. However, its behavior with nonlinear input is quite different from that of the perceptron rule. The weights are updated in the following manner:

$$\mathbf{w}^0 \qquad\qquad\qquad \text{arbitrary}$$
$$\mathbf{w}^{j+1} = \mathbf{w}^j - \alpha \frac{(\mathbf{w}^{j\,t}\mathbf{z}^j)\mathbf{z}^j}{|\mathbf{z}^j|^2} \text{ if } \mathbf{z}^{j\,t}\mathbf{w}^j \leq 0. \qquad (4.7)$$

It can be shown that this algorithm converges for linearly separable input. The result pertaining to nonlinear input can be stated as follows [1]:

Proposition 4.3.4 *If the pattern set is not linearly separable, then the projection learning rule converges to a 0 solution for $0 < \alpha < 2$.*

Proof: Since no hyperplane can separate the input, the weight vector has to be updated at least once in each cycle. From equation 4.7 one can derive that

$$\|\mathbf{w}^{j+1}\|^2 - \|\mathbf{w}^j\|^2 = \frac{\alpha(\alpha-2)(\mathbf{z}^{j^t}\mathbf{w}^j)^2}{\|\mathbf{z}^j\|^2}.$$

Note that $\forall\ \alpha, 0 < \alpha < 2, \|\mathbf{w}^{j+1}\|^2 < \|\mathbf{w}^j\|^2$. This indicates that the sequence $\|\mathbf{w}^0\|, \|\mathbf{w}^1\|, ...$ is a strictly monotonically decreasing sequence with the lower bound 0. Therefore, $\|\mathbf{w}^j\|$ approaches zero as j approaches infinity. This proves that the projection learning rule converges to the only solution (i.e., $\mathbf{w} = \mathbf{0}$) in the linearly nonseparable case for $0 < \alpha < 2$.

For one-dimensional linearly nonseparable input, one can show that $\|w\|$ falls within a small distance ϵ from zero in a number of steps that can be expressed as a function of the initial weight vector, α, ϵ, and the angles between the input vectors [1]. However, no similar expression has been known for higher dimensional input.

A link can be established between this result and the concept of linear independence. From the given set of m n-dimensional vectors $\{\mathbf{z}^1, \mathbf{z}^2, ..., \mathbf{z}^m\}$, construct a set of n m-dimensional vectors $\{\hat{\mathbf{z}}^1, \hat{\mathbf{z}}^2, ..., \hat{\mathbf{z}}^n\}$ in the following manner:

$$\hat{\mathbf{z}}^j = \{z_j^1, z_j^2, ...z_j^m\}$$

where z_j^i is the jth component of the $\mathbf{z}^i$ vector. If the original set of vectors is not linearly separable, the weight update rule converges to the only solution, which is $\mathbf{w} = \mathbf{0}$. This leads to the fact that the constructed set of vectors will be a linearly independent set in m-dimensional space.

4.3.2 Group B: Error Minimization Procedures

The error correction procedure focuses on misclassified samples. Other procedures modify the weight vector using all samples at each iteration. Moreover, thus far a weight vector $\mathbf{w}$ is sought such that $\mathbf{w}^t\mathbf{z}^j\ \forall j$ is positive. Next, we discuss attempts to reformulate the problem of finding the solution to a set of linear inequalities as a problem of finding a solution to a set of linear equations. Let $\mathbf{b} = (b^1, b^2, ..., b^m)^t$ be a column vector. The decision equation (4.2) can be restated as

$$\mathbf{Z}^t\mathbf{w} = \mathbf{b}. \tag{4.8}$$

The solution vector $\mathbf{w}$ is overdetermined since $\mathbf{Z}^t$ is rectangular with more rows than columns, assuming $m > n$. The idea is to search for a weight vector that minimizes some function of the error between the left and the right sides of equation (4.8). The usual choice of a function to be minimized is the one that represents the sum-of-squared error:

$$J = |\mathbf{Z}^t\mathbf{w} - \mathbf{b}|^2.$$

The central theme in both the Widrow-Hoff and the Ho-Kashyap procedures is to minimize J, though the difference in the details of the algorithms leads to drastically different results.

Widrow-Hoff delta rule: The α-Least-Mean-Square (α-LMS) algorithm or Widrow-Hoff delta rule embodies the minimal disturbance principle[6] [33]. It is designed to handle both linearly separable and linearly nonseparable input. The criterion function is minimized with respect to the weight vector $\mathbf{w}$ using the gradient decent method. The unknown vector $\mathbf{b}$ is chosen arbitrarily and held constant throughout the computation. See [35] for derivation of the weight update equation using the gradient decent method. The iterative version of the weight update equation can be written as follows [35]:

$$\mathbf{w}^0 \qquad\qquad\qquad \text{arbitrary}$$
$$\mathbf{w}^{j+1} = \mathbf{w}^j + \alpha \frac{(b^j - \mathbf{w}^{j^t}\mathbf{z}^j)\mathbf{z}^j}{|\mathbf{z}^j|^2}. \tag{4.9}$$

Note that the class labels (or desired output for all input samples) d^j, which are the output after the nonlinearity, are known. Since the error $\epsilon_l^j = (b^j - \mathbf{w}^{j^t}\mathbf{z}^j)$ is measured at the linear output, not after the nonlinearity, as in the case of the perceptron rule, one must choose the magnitude as well as the sign of b^j (arbitrarily) to continue. It has been shown [35] that, in both linearly separable as well as linearly nonseparable cases, this rule converges in the mean square sense to the solution $\mathbf{w}^*$ that corresponds to the least mean square output error if all input vectors are of the same length. It is known that in some cases this rule may fail to separate training vectors that are linearly separable [18]. This is not surprising, since the mean square error (MSE) solution depends on the margin vector $\mathbf{b}$. Different choices for $\mathbf{b}$ give the solution different properties. Hence, when one does not have any clue about the distribution of the input data and arbitrarily fixes a margin vector, it is very likely that the resulting weight vector may not classify all vectors correctly even for a linearly separable problem.

Ho-Kashyap algorithm: Ho and Kashyap [13] modified the Widrow-Hoff procedure to obtain a weight vector $\mathbf{w}$ as well as a margin vector $\mathbf{b}$. They imposed the restriction that the m-dimensional margin vector must be positive-valued, i.e., $\mathbf{b} > 0$, ($b_k > 0, \ \forall \ k$). The problem is equivalent to finding $\mathbf{w}$ and $\mathbf{b} > 0$ such that $J = |\mathbf{Z}^t\mathbf{w} - \mathbf{b}|^2$ is minimized with respect to both $\mathbf{w}$ and $\mathbf{b}$. Note that since both $\mathbf{w}$ and $\mathbf{b}$ (subject to the imposed constraint) are allowed to play a role in the minimization process, the minimum value (i.e., 0) for J can be achieved in this case. Thus the $\mathbf{w}$ that achieves that minimum is the separating vector in the linearly separable case. The weight update rule is (for detailed derivation see [13])

---

[6] The rule aims at making minimum possible change in the weight vector during the update process such that the output for as many of the previously correctly classified samples as possible remains unperturbed.

$$\mathbf{b}^0 \quad > 0 \quad \text{otherwise arbitrary}$$
$$\mathbf{w}^0 \quad = (\mathbf{Z}^t)^\dagger \mathbf{b}^0$$
$$\epsilon^j \quad = \mathbf{Z}^t \mathbf{w}^j - \mathbf{b}^j$$
$$\mathbf{b}^{j+1} \quad = \mathbf{b}^j + \alpha(|\epsilon^j| + \epsilon^j)$$
$$\mathbf{w}^{j+1} = \mathbf{w}^j + \alpha(\mathbf{Z}^t)^\dagger(|\epsilon^j| + \epsilon^j) \tag{4.10}$$

where $(\mathbf{Z}^t)^\dagger = (\mathbf{Z}\mathbf{Z}^t)^{-1}\mathbf{Z}$ is the pseudoinverse of $\mathbf{Z}^t$. Computation of the pseudoinverse may be avoided by using the following alternate procedure [12]:

$$\epsilon_k^j \quad = \mathbf{z}^{k^t} \mathbf{w}^j - b_k{}^j$$
$$b_k{}^{j+1} = b_k{}^j + \rho_1/2(|\epsilon_k^j| + \epsilon_k^j)$$
$$\mathbf{w}^{j+1} = \mathbf{w}^j - \rho_2 \mathbf{z}^k(\mathbf{z}^{kt}\mathbf{w}^j - b_k^{j+1}). \tag{4.11}$$

This algorithm yields a solution vector in the case of linearly separable samples in a finite number of steps if $0 < \rho_1 < 2$, and $0 < \rho_2 < 2/\|\mathbf{z}^k\|^2$. Since the focus of this chapter is on data that are not separable, let us examine the behavior of this algorithm under nonseparable situation.

Note the following two facts for nonseparable case: **fact 1**, $\epsilon^j \neq 0$ for any j; and **fact 2**, $|\epsilon^{j+1}|^2 < |\epsilon^j|^2$, i.e., the sequence $|\epsilon^1|^2, |\epsilon^2|^2, \dots$ is a strictly monotonically decreasing sequence and must converge to the limiting value $|\epsilon|^2$, though the limiting value cannot be zero. It can be shown that $(\epsilon^j + |\epsilon^j|)$ converges to zero, suggesting a termination of the procedure. Now consider the following two cases:

- Suppose the error vector has no positive component for some finite j, then $|\epsilon^j| + \epsilon^j = 0$. In that case the correction will cease and neither the weight vector nor the margin vector will change [see (4.10)]. Thus an error vector with no positive components conclusively points to the nonlinear nature of the data.[7]
- Suppose $\epsilon_j{}^+ = (\epsilon^j + |\epsilon^j|)$ is never zero for finite j. We can derive from **fact 2** that $|\epsilon_{j+1}{}^+|^2 < |\epsilon_j{}^+|^2$. Therefore, $|\epsilon_j{}^+|$ must converge to zero. However, its distance from zero is unknown for any fixed j.

In summary, the Ho-Kashyap algorithm indicates nonseparability, but there is no bound on the number of steps.

Hassoun and Song [12] propose a variation of the Ho-Kashyap algorithm equipped to produce an *optimal* separating surface for linearly nonseparable data. The authors claim that it can identify and discard nonseparable samples to make the data linearly separable with increased convergence speed. Again we notice similarity with the heuristic approach proposed in Siu et al. [26]. However, the authors do not provide any theoretical basis to their claim. The algorithm is tested only on simple toy problems. We have no knowledge of any extensive testing on real-world problems.

---

[7] It can be shown that for linearly separable data, it is impossible for all components of the error vector to be negative at any given iteration.

linear programming: In searching for a linear classifier, the input vectors give a system of linear inequalities constraining the location and orientation of the optimal separating hyperplane. With a properly defined objective function, a separating hyperplane can be obtained by solving a linear programming problem. Several alternative formulations have been proposed in the past ([4, 9, 16, 24, 27]) employing different objective functions. An early survey of these methods is given in Grinold [11]. Here we mention a few representative formulations.

In a very simple formulation described in [24], the objective function is trivial, so that it is simply a test of linear separability by finding a feasible solution to the LP problem

$$\text{minimize} \quad \mathbf{0}^t \mathbf{w}$$
$$\text{subject to } \mathbf{Z}^t \mathbf{w} \geq \mathbf{1} \tag{4.12}$$

where $\mathbf{w}$ is the weight vector of a separating hyperplane, $\mathbf{Z} = [\mathbf{z}^1, \mathbf{z}^2, ..., \mathbf{z}^m]$ is a matrix of column vectors $\mathbf{z}^j$ $(j = 1, ..., m)$, the m augmented input vectors are as defined before, and $\mathbf{0}$ and $\mathbf{1}$ are vectors of zero's and one's, respectively. The constraint requires that all training samples must fall on the same side of the hyperplane (the linear classifier to be found). This is possible only if the points are linearly separable. $\mathbf{1}$ is an arbitrarily chosen nonzero constant vector that specifies a margin, so that the points do not lie on the hyperplane.

This formulation gives only a test for linear separability (whether the constraints give a feasible region) but does not lead to any useful solution if the data are not linearly separable [24]. Another formulation suggested by Smith ([27]; see also [10]) minimizes an error function:

$$\text{minimize} \quad \mathbf{a}^t \mathbf{t}$$
$$\text{subject to } \mathbf{Z}^t \mathbf{w} + \mathbf{t} \geq \mathbf{b}$$
$$\mathbf{t} \geq \mathbf{0} \tag{4.13}$$

where $\mathbf{Z}$ is the augmented data matrix as before, $\mathbf{a}$ is a positive vector of weights, $\mathbf{b}$ is a positive margin vector chosen arbitrarily (e.g., $\mathbf{b} = \mathbf{1}$), and $\mathbf{t}$ and $\mathbf{w}$ are the error and weight vectors, which are also decision variables for the LP problem. In [27] each component of $\mathbf{a}$ was set to be $1/m$. The variable error vector $\mathbf{t}$ allows that some points locate on the other side of the hyperplane. $\mathbf{t}$ is required to be positive so it will decrease the fixed margin specified by $\mathbf{b}$. Using this formulation, the error function will be minimized at zero with linearly separable data, and at a nonzero value with linearly nonseparable data.

Bennett and Mangasarian [4] modified this formulation to use different weights for input vectors belonging to each of the two classes. Let m_1, m_{-1} be the number of vectors belonging to the two classes, respectively, $\mathbf{a} = (a_1, a_2, ..., a_m)^t$, for $j = 1, ..., m$,

$$a_j = 1/m_1 \ \text{ if } \ d^j = 1,$$
$$a_j = 1/m_{-1} \ \text{ if } \ d^j = -1.$$

It is argued that this formulation is more robust in the sense that it can guarantee a nontrivial solution **w** even if the centroids of the two classes happen to coincide.

Instead of minimizing an error function that depends on distances of all input points to the separating hyperplane, Vapnik and Chervonenkis [31] proposed maximizing the distances of only those points that are closest to the hyperplane. This approach of maximal margin hyperplanes led to the development of support vector machines [32], which optimize the same objective function for points transformed to a different space.

Though arguably algorithms for solving LP problems are more sophisticated than the previously discussed iterative procedures, an important advantage of finding **w** by solving an LP problem is that if the feasible region is nonempty, the solution can be determined in a finite number of steps.

The number of steps it takes to arrive at the solution, however, is dependent on the geometrical configuration of the data points. If the LP is solved by the simplex method, in the worst case the algorithm may have to visit every vertex formed by the intersections of the constraining hyperplanes before reaching an optimum. Empirical evidence shows that in practice this rarely happens. More recently, interior-point methods [36], such as Karmarkar's, are shown to have a better worst-case time complexity. Still, the comparative advantages of such methods for an arbitrary problem remain unclear, partly because there has not been a good way to characterize the structure of a particular problem and relate that to the detailed operations of the algorithms.

4.4 Experimental Results

In this section we present some experimental results on applying several representative learning algorithms to data sets that are not necessarily linearly separable. The purpose of these experiments is more for assessing the practicality of the methods than for a comprehensive evaluation and comparison.

4.4.1 Algorithms for Determining Linear Separability

We applied the three procedures [Ho-Kashyap (HK), fractional correction rule (FCR), and linear programming (LP)] that are claimed to indicate linear nonseparability to a collection of two-class discrimination problems. The original Ho-Kashyap rule involves computing a pseudoinverse matrix, which turned out to be overly expensive for large problems. So the adaptive algorithm (4.11) was used instead. With LP, we used the simple formulation (4.12) to test for linear separability (referred to as LPtest), and also Smith's formulation (4.13) to derive a minimum error separating hyperplane (referred to as LPme). We included the perceptron training rule too for comparison purpose (denoted by PER for PERceptron), although it is understood that it does not converge for nonseparable input.

Recall that as reviewed in previous sections, LPtest determines linearly separability by checking whether the constraints give a feasible region, and LPme by checking whether the optimal value for the objective function is zero. HK reports linear separability by arriving at an error vector with zero norm, and linear nonseparability by that the error vector has only negative components, or the norm of the positive part of the error is very close to zero. FCR determines separability by arriving at a solution, or the norm vector as well as the difference in subsequent norm vectors are very close to zero; and PER determines separability by arriving at a solution. Experimentally, a solution is not pursued further after some fixed time, and no solution indicates that the programs do not stop within that time.

The problem was discrimination between all pairs of classes in each of 14 data sets from the University of Californa, Irvine (UCI) Machine Learning Depository [2]: abalone, car, german, kr-vs-kp, letter, lrs, nursery, pima, segmentation, splice, tic-tac-toe, vehicle, wdbc, and yeast. The data sets were chosen so that each set has at least 500 input vectors and no missing values in the features. For those sets containing categorical features, the values were numerically coded. There are a total of 844 two-class discrimination problems. Outcomes from the algorithms may be a conclusion of whether the problem is linearly separable or not, or inconclusive after a chosen number of iterations. We compared such outcomes from all three procedures and the relative time it took for them to derive the results.

Table 4.1 shows the number of problems reported by each algorithm as separable, nonseparable, or inconclusive. Since LPtest always gives a definite answer, conclusions of other algorithms are compared to its results.

Table 4.1. Conclusion on linear separability by each algorithm (entries are number of problems; sep: separable, non: nonseparable, inc: inconclusive).

	LPtest	HK			FCR			PER		
		sep	non	inc	sep	non	inc	sep	non	inc
separable	452	272	31	149	449	0	3	428	0	24
nonseparable	392	0	1	391	0	4	388	0	0	392

We found that within similar, affordable run-time limits, linear programming always arrived at a definite conclusion, while HK and FCR often ended the runs inconclusively (100,000 iterations were used for HK, FCR, and PER). Of the 844 problems, LPtest reported that 452 are linearly separable and 392 are not. For 54% (453/844) of these problems, FCR arrived at a conclusion, but the fraction is only 36% (304/844) for HK. For the separable problems, FCR arrived at the conclusion generally sooner than HK. For the nonseparable problems, both algorithms have a problem fulfilling the claim of giving an indication; within the affordable time, only one problem was reported to be nonseparable by HK, and only four by FCR.

We also found that the results were very sensitive to the choices of the learning coefficient and convergence thresholds for the Ho-Kashyap rule. Other than affect-

Table 4.2. Correlation coefficients of number of iterations for each pair of algorithms to converge to a separating hyperplane.

	LPme	HK	FCR	PER
LPtest	0.6974	0.0164	0.1930	0.1256
LPme		−0.0275	0.1586	0.1341
HK			0.7306	0.5723
FCR				0.5421

Table 4.3. Correlation coefficients of problem size measures and number of iterations for each algorithm to converge to a separating hyperplane. n: no. of dimensions; m: no. of input vectors.

	LPme	LPtest	HK	FCR	PER
n	0.1970	0.5749	−0.0928	−0.0746	−0.0555
m	0.8856	0.4056	−0.0067	−0.0704	−0.0768
nm	0.4778	0.7636	−0.0429	−0.0388	−0.0287

ing the speed of convergence, they can change the conclusion on separability; for 31 separable problems HK reported that they were nonseparable. An improper learning coefficient may cause overly large correction steps. The tolerance threshold determines when a number is considered zero, which leads to a conclusion. Of those 31 problems falsely reported to be nonseparable by HK, 26 contain only one vector in the smaller class. The other five problems have two vectors in the smaller class. With a change in the learning coefficient (to 10% of original value), six were reported separable, nine remained nonseparable, and the other 16 became inconclusive.

Table 4.2 shows, for the separable problems, the correlation coefficients of the number of iterations it took for each pair of algorithms to converge to a hyperplane, computed over only those cases where both algorithms converged. In LP each iteration involves an input vector, but in the adaptive algorithm each iteration involves a loop through all relevant vectors in the entire set. For this reason, significant correlation exists only between the adaptive algorithms or the two LP formulations, but not between any of the adaptive algorithms and LP. The correlation is stronger between HK and FCR than between each of them and PER.

Correlation coefficients were also calculated between measures of the problem size and the number of iterations before convergence for each algorithm (Table 4.3). For the adaptive procedures, the absence of significant correlation suggests that the difficulty of a problem does not necessarily depend on the problem size.

4.4.2 Analysis of the Linearly Nonseparable Cases

For each of the 392 problems that LPtest reported to be linearly nonseparable, we applied procedure (4.3) to determine the set of separable and nonseparable vectors. Several of those problems can be considered nearly linearly separable, since only a small fraction of vectors are found responsible for nonseparability. However, for the majority (332) of those problems, the LP procedure found no separable vectors. That is to say, every point in those problems is (jointly) responsible for linear nonseparability. This is a rather surprising result. It suggests a need to further examine the difference between these problems and those with some separable points.

We attempted to relate the fraction of separable vectors to the number of steps taken for the three algorithms (LPtest, HK, FCR) to reach the conclusion of linear separability. However, since HK and FCR arrived at the conclusion for only a few of these nonseparable cases, we studied only the run time of LPtest. It appears that for most of the problems with no separable vectors and for almost all problems with many separable vectors, LPtest determined nonseparability fairly quickly. However, occasionally it did take many iterations for LPtest to arrive at that conclusion. This suggests a need for a more detailed examination of the locations of the separable and nonseparable vectors to understand the implications.

4.4.3 Discussion

Our experiments show that linear programming, although long neglected in classification studies, generally yields more affordable and dependable results. In contrast, the Ho-Kashyap and the fractional correction rules frequently do not converge within affordable time limits. The Ho-Kashyap rule may even lead to the wrong conclusions. It is very difficult to choose the learning coefficients and error tolerance thresholds to get all the conclusions right. This reinforces the theoretical results that there is no known proof of convergence for HK and FCR in a predictable number of steps, and that linear programming has known, predictable time bounds for convergence on both linearly separable and nonseparable cases. The implementation difficulties raise doubts about the practicality of these adaptive algorithms.

The only reservation we have about this conclusion is related to the efficiency of the implementations. For linear programming we used the MINOS solver [20] through the AMPL interface [7], which was a highly optimized commercial code, whereas the adaptive procedures were run with simple implementations in C written by ourselves. So, affordable (elapsed) time may not mean the same thing for the two groups. Also, we have not tested the dependence of the run time on the order in which the input vectors were presented to the adaptive procedures, and we have not investigated the dual problems that can be formulated for a given problem and solved by any of these procedures [24]. Nevertheless, we advocate that linear programming methods warrant more serious attention in classification studies. Without more sophisticated derivatives such as simultaneous primal-dual algorithms, the only apparent advantages of the adaptive procedures such as HK and FCR rules seem to be that (1) they can be implemented on very simple machines; and (2) their adaptive nature permits easier inclusion of new input that may become available during the training process, and thus they are better suited for online learning.

4.5 Conclusion

We reviewed a set of representative descent procedures for constructing linear classifiers, and experimented, using a public database, with three of those procedures that are claimed to detect linear nonseparability. We found that both the fractional correction rule and the adaptive Ho-Kashyap algorithm are not delivering on their promises, and that linear programming is the only reliable and efficient method. We suggest that linear programming methods can play a more significant role in classification studies. Moreover, we tested a linear programming formulation that reveals how close a problem is to linear separability by identifying vectors that are responsible for nonseparability. We believe further investigations along this line will lead to better understanding of the complexity of a given data set.

Acknowledgments

We thank Ken Clarkson, David Gay, Linda Kaufman, George Nagy, and Margaret Wright for helpful discussions and suggestions of references. Mitra Basu thanks Bell Labs for summer support in 1998.

References

[1] M. Basu, Q. Liang. The fractional correction rule: a new perspective. *Neural Network,* 11, 1027–1039, 1998.

[2] C. Blake, E. Keogh, C.J. Merz. UCI repository of machine learning databases [http://www.ics.uci.edu/~mlearn/MLRepository.html]. Irvine, CA: University of California, Department of Information and Computer Science, 1998.

[3] H.D. Block, S.A. Levin. On the boundedness of an iterative procedure for solving a system of linear inequalities. *Proc. AMS,* 26, 229–235, 1970.

[4] K.P. Bennett, O.L. Mangasarian. Robust linear programming discrimination of two linearly inseparable sets. *Optimization Methods and Software,* 1, 23–24, 1992.

[5] A.R. Butz. Perceptron type learning algorithms in nonseparable situations. *Journal of Mathematical Analysis and Applications,* 17, 560–576, 1967.

[6] R.O. Duda, P.E. Hart. *Pattern Classification and Scene Analysis.* New York:Wiley, 1973.

[7] R. Fourer, D.M. Gay, B.W. Kernighan. *AMPL: A Modeling Language for Mathematical Programming.* South San Francisco:The Scientific Press, 1993.

[8] S.I. Gallant. *Neural Network Learning & Expert Systems.* Cambridge, MA: MIT Press, 1993.

[9] F. Glover. Improved linear programming models for discriminant analysis. *Decision Sciences,* 21(4), 771–785, 1990.

[10] R.G. Grinold. Comment on "Pattern Classification Design by Linear Programming". *IEEE Transactions on Computers,* C-18(4), 378–379, April 1969.

[11] R.G. Grinold. Mathematical programming methods of pattern classification. *Management Science,* 19(3), 272–289, 1972.

[12] M.H. Hassoun, J. Song. Adaptive Ho-Kashyap rules for perceptron training. *IEEE Transactions on Neural Networks,* 3, 51–61, 1992.

[13] Y.C. Ho, R.L. Kashyap. An algorithm for linear inequalities and its applications. *IEEE Transactions on Electronic Computers,* 14, 683–688, 1965.

[14] S.-C. Huang, Y.-F. Huang. Bounds on the number of hidden neurons in multilayer perceptrons. *IEEE Transactions on Neural Networks*, 2, 47–55, 1991.

[15] T.Y. Kwok, D.Y. Yeung. Objective functions for training new hidden units in constructive neural networks. *IEEE Transactions on Neural Networks*, 8(5), 1131–1148, 1997.

[16] O.L. Mangasarian. Linear and nonlinear separation of patterns by linear programming. *Operations Research*, 13, 444–452, 1965.

[17] O.L. Mangasarian. *Nonlinear Programming*, New York:McGraw-Hill, 1969.

[18] C.H. Mays. *Adaptive Threshold Logic*. Ph.D. thesis, Stanford Electronics Labs, Stanford, CA, 1963.

[19] M. Minsky, S. Papert. *Perceptrons*, expanded edition. Cambridge, MA:MIT Press, 1988.

[20] B.A. Murtagh, M.A. Saunders. Large-scale linearly constrained optimization. *Mathematical Programming*, 14, 41–72, 1978.

[21] N.J. Nilsson. *The Mathematical Foundations of Learning Machines*. San Mateo, CA: Morgan Kaufmann, 1990.

[22] R. Reed. Pruning algorithms—a survey. *IEEE Transactions on Neural Networks*, 4, 740–747, 1993.

[23] F. Rosenblatt. *Principles of Neurodynamics: Perceptron and the Theory of Brain Mechanism*. Washington, D.C.: Spartan Press, 1962.

[24] V.P. Roychowdhury, K.Y. Siu, T. Kailath. Classification of linearly nonseparable patterns by linear threshold elements. *IEEE Transactions on Neural Networks*, 6(2), 318–331, March 1995.

[25] M.A. Sartori, P.J. Antsaklis, A simple method to derive bounds on the size and to train multilayer neural networks. *IEEE Transactions on Neural Networks*, 2, 467–471, 1991.

[26] K.Y. Siu, V.P. Roychowdhury, T. Kailath. *Discrete Neural Computation*. Englewood Cliffs, NJ: Prentice Hall, 1995.

[27] F.W. Smith. Pattern classifier design by linear programming. *IEEE Transactions on Computers*, C-17(4), 367–372, April 1968.

[28] S. Tamura, T. Masahiko. Capabilities of a four-layered feedforward neural network: four layer versus three. *IEEE Transactions on Neural Networks*, 8, 251–255, 1997.

[29] J.T. Tou, R.C. Gonzalez. *Pattern Recognition Principles*. Reading, MA:Addison-Wesley, 1974.

[30] A.W. Tucker. Dual systems of homogeneous linear relations. In H.W. Kuhn, A.W. Tucker, eds., *Linear Inequalities and Related Systems*. Annals of Mathematics Studies Number 38, Princeton, NJ: Princeton University Press, pages 3–18, 1956.

[31] V.N. Vapnik, A.J. Chervonenkis. *Theory of Pattern Recognition* (in Russian). Nauka, Moscow, 1974; German translation: W.N. Wapnik, A.J. Tschervonenkis. *Theorie der Zeichenerkennung*. Berlin: Akademia, 1979.

[32] V.N. Vapnik. *Statistical Learning Theory*. New York: Wiley, 1998.

[33] B. Widrow, M.E. Hoff, Jr. *Adaptive switching circuits*. Tech. Report 1553-1, Stanford Electronics Labs, Stanford, CA, 1960.

[34] B. Widrow, M.A. Lehr. 30 years of adaptive neural networks: perceptron, made-line, and backpropagation. *Proceedings of the IEEE*, 78, 1415–1442, 1990.

[35] B. Widrow, S.D. Stearns. *Adaptive Signal Processing*. Englewood Cliffs, NJ: Prentice Hall, 1985.

[36] M.H. Wright, Interior methods for constrained optimization. In A. Iserles, ed. *Acta Numerica*, pages 341–407, Cambridge:Cambridge University Press, 1992.

5

Data Complexity, Margin-Based Learning, and Popper's Philosophy of Inductive Learning

Vladimir Cherkassky and Yunqian Ma

Summary. This chapter provides a characterization of data complexity using the framework of Vapnik's learning theory and Karl Popper's philosophical ideas that can be readily interpreted in the context of empirical learning of inductive models from finite data. We approach the notion of data complexity under the setting of predictive learning, where this notion is directly related to the flexibility of a set of possible models used to describe available data. Hence, any characterization of data complexity is related to model complexity control. Recent learning methods [such as support vector machines (SVM), aka kernel methods] introduced the concept of margin to control model complexity. This chapter describes the characterization of data complexity for such margin-based methods. We provide a general philosophical motivation for margin-based estimators by interpreting the concept of margin as the degree of a model's falsifiability. This leads to a better understanding of two distinct approaches to controlling model complexity: *margin-based*, where complexity is controlled by the size of the margin (or adaptive empirical loss function); and *model-based*, where complexity is controlled by the parameterization of admissible models. We describe SVM methods that combine margin-based and model-based complexity control, and show the effectiveness of the SVM strategy via empirical comparisons using synthetic data sets. Our comparisons clarify the difference between SVM methods and regularization methods. Finally, we introduce a new index of data complexity for margin-based classifiers. This new index effectively measures the degree of separation between the two classes achieved by margin-based methods (such as SVMs). The data sets with a high degree of separation (hence, good generalization) are characterized as *simple, as opposed to complex data sets with heavily overlapping class distributions*.

5.1 Introduction and Motivation

The task of estimating (learning) a useful model from available data arises in many applications ranging from financial engineering to genomics and signal processing. In many cases, the parametric form of the "true" model is unknown, and estimating a "good" model involves a trade-off between the model complexity and the accuracy of fitting the available data. Since learning problems with finite data are inherently ill-posed, one can only expect to obtain reasonably good (but not perfect) models.

Hence, it is important to understand the assumptions and inherent limitations of a particular methodological framework underlying various learning algorithms.

There are two distinct goals of learning [1, 2], leading to different interpretations of what constitutes a good model:

- *Understanding/interpretation* of a given data set
- *Prediction (generalization)*, where the goal is to estimate models providing good prediction (for future data)

In an ideal world, one may attempt to achieve both goals at the same time; however, for many applications accurate *prediction* does not require good *understanding* of an underlying (physical or social) system generating the training data. Likewise, good understanding (of past data) does not necessarily guarantee good prediction. Interpretation is usually subjective, and it is heavily influenced by the personal bias (belief system) of an observer. In contrast, predictive modeling is more objective, because the generalization performance can, in principle, be empirically evaluated. Frequently, the distinction between the two goals (understanding vs. generalization) is rather blurred, because most constructive learning methods (for both approaches) implement the idea of fitting a model to the empirical data. Moreover, many practical applications are difficult to formalize, so practitioners tend to apply existing learning algorithms developed under the predictive learning setting, in order to perform exploratory data analysis.

This chapter assumes the setting of predictive learning, following the framework of statistical learning theory or Vapnik-Chervonenkis (VC) theory. This theory is concerned with establishing general conditions and developing methods for estimating (learning) good predictive models from past (or training) data. Under this framework, any discussion of data complexity should be related to predictive capabilities of models (estimated from data).

The problem of predictive learning (with finite data) has a natural connection to the philosophy of science, as explained next. All scientific theories are obtained from and/or corroborated by empirical data. However, not every theory explaining the data is scientific. Truly scientific theories can be used to explain new observations, i.e., in a predictive way. Hence we can see the similarity between the central problem in predictive learning (i.e., formulating conditions for good generalization) and the central problem in the philosophy of science known as the criterion for demarcation between "true" scientific theories and metaphysical theories (or beliefs). This demarcation criterion can be interpreted as a general requirement under which a method can learn good predictive models (i.e., can generalize). Karl Popper proposed his famous criterion for demarcation, stating that the necessary condition for a theory to be true is its testability or falsifiability. In other words, a genuine theory cannot explain every possible fact (in its domain), and there are facts (observations) that such a theory cannot explain. In predictive learning, this can be interpreted as the condition that a "good" learning method cannot explain (fit) some data samples. The fundamental result in VC theory, stating that any learning method should have limited capacity (finite VC dimension) in order to be able to generalize [3], can be viewed as a mathematical formulation of Popper's demarcation criterion in predictive learning [1, 3]. Moreover, Popper's criterion implies that all true theories should be predictive (rather than explanatory), because falsifiability refers to the inability of making correct predictions for all possible future samples.

This chapter extends Popper's ideas to the analysis of data complexity and model complexity. In particular, we provide an interpretation of the concept of margin as the degree of a model's falsifiability. This leads to a better understanding of two distinct approaches to model complexity control: *margin-based*, where complexity is controlled by the size of the margin (or adaptive empirical loss function), and *model-based*, where complexity is controlled by the parameterization of admissible models. The proposed approach provides a very general framework for understanding many recent methods inspired by SVM methodology (such as kernel-based methods, regularization networks, etc.).

The chapter is organized as follows. Section 5.2 reviews the general setting for predictive learning, following Vapnik's terminology. Section 5.3 provides an interpretation of Popper's ideas in the context of predictive learning with finite samples. This interpretation leads naturally to margin-based learning formulations for various learning problems (such as inductive classification, inductive regression, and transduction). Section 5.4 contrasts margin-based methods and regularization approaches (implementing model-based complexity control). We include several empirical comparisons illustrating the role of margin for model complexity control in classification (pattern recognition) problems. Based on these comparisons, we argue that for small-sample settings, margin-based complexity control tends to be more effective than traditional model-based complexity control. This helps to explain the practical success of SVMs and other related methods. Conclusions and discussion are presented in Section 5.5.

5.2 General Setting for Predictive Learning

This section briefly reviews the general setting for predictive learning and three major methodological frameworks for estimating predictive models from data. A learning system shown in Figure 5.1 describes so-called supervised learning problems such as regression and classification [1, 3], also known as statistical inference problems [2]. This system has three components: a generator of input samples (according to some unknown but fixed distribution); a system that produces a (scalar) output y for each input vector $\mathbf{x}$, and a learning machine (or learning algorithm) that tries to approximate the system's output. Estimation (or learning) is based on a given (finite) number of samples called training data $\mathbf{Z} = (\mathbf{x}_i, y_i), (i = 1, \ldots, n)$, and the goal of learning is to estimate the unknown mapping $f : \mathbf{x} \mapsto y$ in order to predict future samples. More formally, the learning machine implements a set of possible models (aka approximating functions) $f(\mathbf{x}, \boldsymbol{\omega}), \boldsymbol{\omega} \in \Omega$ parameterized by a set of parameters $\boldsymbol{\omega}$, and the goal of learning is to select the function (model) $f(\mathbf{x}, \boldsymbol{\omega}^*)$ providing the best *generalization* for future samples. This (generic) setting describes many types of learning problems, i.e., the regression learning formulation, where the system's output is real-valued $y \in R$, and the classification formulation, where the system's output is binary indicator function $y \in (+1, -1)$ [1, 2, 3].

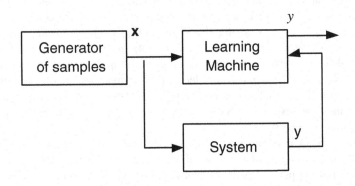

Fig. 5.1. Generic system for supervised learning.

Depending on specific assumptions about the "true" model of the system, several different learning methodologies (for estimating predictive models from data) have been developed:

1. *Parametric estimation.* This classical statistical inference approach (attributed to R. Fisher) assumes that the form of the unknown dependency (or true model) is *known*, up to the value of its parameters. So the goal of statistical inference is *accurate parameter estimation* using the available data. It can be easily shown, however, that the parametric setting does not yield accurate generalization with *finite samples*, even when the true parametric model is known [1].
2. *Model identification or function approximation.* This is an extension of the classical approach (1) where the assumption of knowledge about the parametric form is relaxed. Under the function approximation framework, the true model (aka target function) is unknown, and the goal of learning is *accurate approximation of the target function* via a set of known basis functions. Classical approaches consider representations linear in parameters (i.e., polynomials, harmonic functions), whereas recent nonlinear methods include nonlinear parameterizations (such as multilayer perceptron networks, projection pursuit, multivariate adaptive regression splines, etc.). Many references extend the classical statistical and function approximation approach to developing flexible (adaptive) learning algorithms [2, 4, 5, 6].
3. *Risk minimization approach,* aka *predictive learning.* Under this framework, the goal of learning is generalization, i.e., obtaining models providing minimal prediction risk (for future samples). This approach has been developed by practitioners in the field of artificial neural networks in the late 1980s (with no particu-

lar theoretical justification). The theoretical framework for predictive learning is known as statistical learning theory or VC theory [7]. VC theory investigates the conditions for generalization for methods based on fitting a set of possible models (or approximating functions) $f(\mathbf{x}, \omega)$ to the training data. In this sense, the VC theory describes the generalization properties of the other two approaches (parametric estimation and model identification), which are also based on the idea of fitting the model to available data.

Unfortunately, an important distinction between approaches (2) and (3) is not clearly understood in the current research literature. Effectively, the goal of approach (2) is accurate *identification* of the unknown system, whereas the goal of (3) is accurate *imitation* (of the unknown system). Clearly, achieving the more ambitious goal (2) is not necessary for achieving good generalization in the sense of (3). As pointed out by Vapnik [8], the goal of learning under the model identification/ function approximation approach is to estimate the true model of observed random events (presumed to exist), whereas under the predictive learning approach the goal is just to find a "good" model (in the sense of generalization). This distinction is critical for learning with finite samples, for the following reasons:

- One can easily show examples where a good model (in the sense of generalization) provides very inaccurate (poor) approximation of the true model.
- One can easily show examples where attempting to use the true parametric form of unknown dependency leads to poor generalization [1].
- Classical statistics and function approximation frameworks rely on the notion of the true model (for describing available data). This is clearly an additional (restrictive) assumption imposed on the learning problem. In many applications, the goal is to find a good model (in the sense of generalization), and the notion of the true model (target function) is simply a theoretical construct (i.e., a by-product of a theoretical framework) that cannot be observed (i.e., measured). In contrast, the VC theoretical formulation is based only on the concept of risk minimization, and it does not rely on the notion of the true model.

Likewise, the *characterization of data complexity* has different flavors under each learning framework. Under the model identification approach, data complexity is usually expressed in terms of the *properties of a true model* (being estimated from data), i.e., the properties of the unknown distributions, or the complexity of the Bayesian decision boundary. Under the predictive learning (system imitation) setting, data complexity is directly related to the *properties of a set of possible models* (aka approximating functions). More specifically, the well-known trade-off between the accuracy of fitting the data and the complexity (capacity) of the approximating functions affects the generalization performance [3]. Hence, under the predictive learning (system imitation) framework used in this chapter, characterization of data complexity can be discussed only in the context of this trade-off.

5.3 Margin-Based Methods and Popper's Concept of Falsifiability

In the philosophy of science, the central question is the problem of demarcation, that is, determining under what conditions an inductive theory (based on experimental data or past observations) is true or scientific, as opposed to nonscientific or meta-physical theories (such as alchemy or astrology, which also can be used to "explain" experimental data). In the field of predictive learning, one can interpret "true" inductive theories as predictive models with good generalization (for future data). Karl Popper formulated his famous criterion for distinguishing between scientific (true) and nonscientific theories [9], according to which the necessary condition for true theory is the possibility of its falsification by certain observations (facts, data samples) that cannot be explained by this theory. Quoting Popper [10]:

It must be possible for an empirical theory to be refuted by experience ... Every "good" scientific theory is a prohibition; it forbids certain things to happen. The more a theory forbids, the better it is.

Of course, general philosophical ideas can be interpreted (in the context of learning) in many different ways. For example, the main result of VC theory (the finiteness of VC dimension as a condition for generalization) can be interpreted as the possibility of falsification [3]. Next we propose another specific interpretation of Popper's ideas in the context of predictive learning from finite samples. The goal of learning is to select a good empirical model from a set of possible models or approximating functions $f(\mathbf{x}, \boldsymbol{\omega})$, based on a finite number of training samples $(\mathbf{x}_i, y_i), (i = 1, \ldots, n)$. Next we interpret several notions in Popper's criterion, and relate them to predictive learning:

- In Popper's quotation, empirical theory seems to refer to a single model (function). However the VC theoretical setting considers a set of functions $f(\mathbf{x}, \omega)$ as possible models. We interpret Popper's notion of empirical theory as a predictive model $f(\mathbf{x}, \omega^*)$ estimated from training data.
- Experimental facts or empirical observations can be interpreted as data samples in predictive learning. However, there seems to be no clear distinction between the training and test data in Popper's writings.
- The notion of falsifiability is qualitative and rather vague. We propose to interpret falsifiability via an empirical loss function. That is, a model is falsified by a data sample if the empirical loss (for this sample) is large (nonzero). On the other hand, if a model explains the data well, then the corresponding loss is small (or zero).

An inductive model should explain past observations (i.e., training data) but also be easily falsified by additional observations (new data). In other words, a good model should have maximum ambiguity with respect to future data ("the more a theory forbids, the better it is"). Under standard inductive learning formulations, we only have the training data. During learning, the training data are actually used as a proxy for future (test) data, as in resampling techniques. So a good predictive model should strive to achieve two (conflicting) goals:

1. Explain the training data, i.e., minimize the empirical risk.
2. Achieve maximum ambiguity with respect to other possible data, i.e., the model should be refuted (or falsified) by other unlabeled data.

A possible way to achieve both goals is to introduce a loss function such that a (large) *portion of the training data* can be explained by a model perfectly well (i.e., achieve zero empirical loss), and the rest of the data can only be explained with some uncertainty (i.e., nonzero loss). Such an approach effectively partitions the sample space into two regions, where the training data can be explained by the model with perfect certainty (i.e., zero loss) or not (i.e., nonzero loss). For classification problems, the region with nonzero loss specifies the band separating the two classes, called the *margin*. Moreover, such a loss function should have an *adjustable parameter* that controls the partitioning (the size of margin, for classification problems), and effectively controls the trade-off between the two conflicting goals of learning. The idea of margin-based loss is illustrated in Figure 5.2 for the (nonseparable) binary classification problem, where a model $D(\mathbf{x}) = sign(f(\mathbf{x}, \boldsymbol{\omega}))$ is the decision boundary separating an input space into a positive class region where $f(\mathbf{x}, \boldsymbol{\omega}) > 0$, and a negative class region where $f(\mathbf{x}, \boldsymbol{\omega}) < 0$. In this case, training samples that are correctly classified by the model *and* lie far away from the decision boundary $f(\mathbf{x}, \boldsymbol{\omega}) = 0$, are assigned zero loss. On the other hand, samples that are incorrectly classified by the model *and /or* lie close to the decision boundary have nonzero (positive) loss (see Fig. 5.2). Then a good decision boundary achieves an optimal balance between

- minimizing the total empirical loss for samples that lie inside the margin, and
- achieving maximum separation (margin) between training samples that are correctly classified (or explained) by the model.

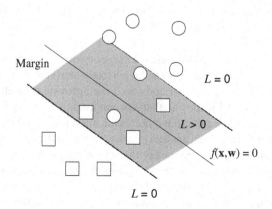

Fig. 5.2. Margin-based loss for classification (nonseparable case).

Clearly, these two goals are contradictory, since a larger margin (or greater falsifiability) implies larger empirical risk. So in order to obtain good generalization, one chooses the appropriate margin size (or the degree of falsifiability, according to Popper's interpretation).

Next we show several examples of margin-based formulations for specific learning problems. All examples assume a linear parameterization of approximating functions, i.e., linear models $f(\mathbf{x}, \boldsymbol{\omega}) = (\mathbf{x} \cdot \mathbf{w}) + b$

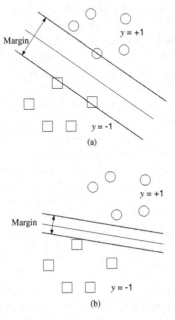

Fig. 5.3. Binary classification for separable data, where $\bigcirc$ denotes samples from one class, and $\square$ denote samples from another class. The margin describes the region where the data cannot be unambiguously explained (classified) by the model. (a) Linear model with margin size Δ_1. (b) Linear model with margin size Δ_2.

Classification inductive formulation. First, consider a case of linearly separable data when the first goal of learning can be perfectly satisfied. That is, a set of linear models can fit the training data perfectly well (i.e., provide separation with zero error). Then the best model is the one that has maximum ambiguity for other possible data. For example, consider the (binary) classification problem with linearly separable data shown in Figure 5.3a. Instead of using a single decision boundary, a band (called the *margin*) is used to represent the region where the output is ambiguous, dividing the input space into two regions (Fig. 5.3a). That is, new unlabeled data points falling on the "correct" side of the margin can be always correctly classified, whereas data points falling inside the margin cannot be unambiguously classified. The size of the margin (denoted as Δ_1 in Fig. 5.3a) plays an important role in controlling the flexibility (complexity) of the decision boundary. Even though there are many linear decision boundaries that separate (explain) this training data perfectly well, such models differ in the degree of separation (or *margin*) between the two classes. For example, Figure 5.3b shows another possible linear decision boundary, for the same data set, which has a smaller margin Δ_2. Then, according to our interpretation of Popper's philosophy, the better classification model should have the largest margin (i.e., maximum possibility of falsification by the future data). The mathematical formulation for this setting, known as the optimal hyperplane, is introduced below following Vapnik [3]. First note that the distance between a separating hyperplane $f(\mathbf{x}, \boldsymbol{\omega}) = (\mathbf{x} \cdot \mathbf{w}) + b = 0$ and a sample $\mathbf{x}_k$ is $\frac{|(\mathbf{w} \cdot \mathbf{x}_k) + b|}{||\mathbf{w}||}$. Hence for the linearly separable data (with separation margin 2Δ) all samples obey this inequality:

$$\frac{y_k((\mathbf{w} \cdot \mathbf{x}_k) + b)}{||\mathbf{w}||} \geq \Delta \text{ where } k = 1, \ldots, n \text{ and } y_k \in (+1, -1) \qquad (5.1)$$

This inequality implies that maximizing the margin Δ is equivalent to minimization of $||\mathbf{w}||$. Rescaling parameters $\mathbf{w}$ and b by fixing the scale $\Delta||\mathbf{w}|| = 1$ leads to the canonical form representation for the separating hyperplane:

$$y_k((\mathbf{w} \cdot \mathbf{x}_k + b)) \geq 1 \text{ where } k = 1, \ldots, n \text{ and } y_k \in (+1, -1) \qquad (5.2)$$

The optimal separating hyperplane satisfies the above constraints and also minimizes $||\mathbf{w}||^2$, with respect to both $\mathbf{w}$ and b.

The optimal separating hyperplane formulation makes a strong assumption that the data can be explained perfectly well by a set of admissible models, i.e., the training data are linearly separable. In most cases, however, the empirical risk cannot be minimized to zero. In this case, a good inductive model attempts to strike a balance between the goal of minimization of empirical risk (i.e., fitting the training data) and maximizing the margin (or model's falsifiability). In the case of classification with nonseparable training data, this is accomplished by allowing some training samples to fall inside the margin, and quantifying the empirical risk (for these samples) as deviation from the margin borders, i.e., the sum of slack variables ξ_i corresponding to the deviation from the margin borders (Fig. 5.4). In this case, again, the notion of ambiguity or falsifiability can be directly related to the margin. More precisely, for classification problems the *degree* of falsifiability can be naturally measured as the *size* of the margin. For the nonseparable case, the optimization formulation known as "soft margin" hyperplane is

$$\text{minimize } \frac{1}{2}||\mathbf{w}||^2 + C \sum_{i=1}^{n} \xi_i \qquad (5.3)$$

$$\text{subject to } y_i(\mathbf{w} \cdot \mathbf{x}_i + b) \geq 1 - \xi_i, i = 1, \ldots, n$$

Note that soft margin formulation (5.3) attempts to maximize the margin (via minimization of $||\mathbf{w}||^2$) and minimize the total empirical loss for incorrectly classified samples (inside the margin). The trade-off between these two goals is controlled by (positive) parameter C. The appropriate value of C is usually determined via resampling. A given C value implicitly specifies the size of margin Δ via formulation (5.3), so the optimal soft margin hyperplane $\mathbf{w}^*$ defined by (5.3) is the Δ-margin hyperplane with $\Delta = 1/||\mathbf{w}^*||$. Alternatively, one can think of an equivalent soft

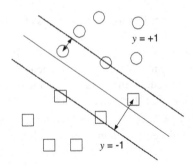

Fig. 5.4. Binary classification for nonseparable data involves both goals: (1) minimizing the total error for samples inside the margin, usually quantified as a sum of slack variables ξ_i corresponding to deviation from margin borders; (2) maximizing the size of the margin.

margin formulation where the size of the margin is used explicitly as a user-defined parameter controlling generalization. This interpretation leads to an adaptive loss function that effectively partitions the input space into two regions, one where the training data can be explained by the model (zero loss) and the margin band (where the data are falsified or cannot be explained by the model). Such a loss function [aka support vector machine (SVM) loss] can be defined for classification problems as

$$L_{\Delta}(y, f(\mathbf{x}, \boldsymbol{\omega})) = \max(\Delta - yf(\mathbf{x}, \boldsymbol{\omega}), 0) \qquad (5.4)$$

Our notation for SVM loss uses explicitly margin Δ, in order to emphasize its importance, in contrast to traditional representation for SVM loss [2]:

$$L(y, f(\mathbf{x}, \boldsymbol{\omega})) = \max(1 - yf(\mathbf{x}, \boldsymbol{\omega}), 0) \qquad (5.5)$$

Both representations (5.4) and (5.5) are, of course, equivalent and differ only in scaling of $f(\mathbf{x}, \boldsymbol{\omega}) = (\mathbf{x} \cdot \mathbf{w}) + b$. The soft margin SVM formulation (5.3) is sometimes described as a special case of regularization formulation with a "particular SVM loss function". The interpretation of margin-based loss proposed in this chapter takes a different view. That is, we argue that the special form of SVM loss is, in fact, responsible for generalization. Later in section 5.4 we elaborate on the resemblance between SVM and classical regularization formulations, and present several empirical comparisons.

Regression inductive formulation. Even though the interpretation of margin in the sense of Popper's "possibility of falsification" for classification is fairly natural, such an interpretation for other types of learning problems is not quite straightforward. For example, for real-valued function estimation (aka regression), an appropriate interpretation of falsifiability is not obvious. In this case we will formalize the interpretation of the two goals of learning according to Popper's philosophy, as explained next. A good model should be able to

- explain well the majority of the training data (i.e., achieve zero empirical loss); and

- maximize the region in the $(\mathbf{x}, y)$ space where the data cannot be explained by the model, i.e., where the loss is nonzero.

Formally, achieving these two (conflicting) goals can be achieved via specification of a new empirical loss function, which equals zero when the discrepancy between the model and the data is small (below a certain threshold) and nonzero when the discrepancy is large (above this threshold). The first goal favors a large threshold, so that the empirical risk for the majority of training data is zero, whereas the second goal favors a small threshold, so that the ambiguity of the model with respect to available data is maximized. The optimal threshold value is selected typically based on a priori knowledge or using resampling methods in order to achieve optimal generalization performance.

In the case of regression, an appropriate margin-based loss function called ε-insensitive loss [3] is defined as

$$L_\epsilon(y, f(\mathbf{x}, \boldsymbol{\omega})) = \max(|f(\mathbf{x}, \boldsymbol{\omega})| - \varepsilon, 0) \qquad (5.6)$$

where parameter ε controls the margin size. This loss function is shown in Figure 5.5, illustrating the partitioning of the $(\mathbf{x}, y)$ space for linear parameterization of $f(\mathbf{x}, \boldsymbol{\omega})$.

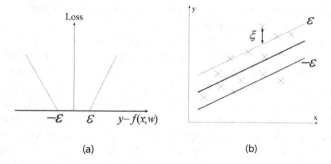

(a)   (b)

Fig. 5.5. ε-insensitive loss function: (a) ε-insensitive loss for SVM regression; (b) slack variable ξ for linear SVM regression formulation.

This loss function is used in the SVM regression formulation [3, 8]. For linear regression problems $f(\mathbf{x}, \boldsymbol{\omega}) = \mathbf{w} \cdot \mathbf{x} + b$, SVM regression amounts to (simultaneous) minimization of ε-insensitive loss (5.6) and minimization of the norm of linear parameters $||\mathbf{w}||^2$. Minimization of the ε-insensitive loss function can be formally described by introducing (nonnegative) slack variables $\xi_i, \xi_i^*, i = 1, \ldots, n$, to measure the deviation of training samples outside ε-insensitive zone (see Fig. 5.5). Thus SVM regression can be formulated as minimization of the following functional:

$$\text{minimize } \frac{1}{2}||\mathbf{w}||^2 + C \sum_{i=1}^{n} (\xi_i + \xi_i^*) \qquad (5.7)$$

$$\text{subject to} \begin{cases} y_i - \mathbf{w} \cdot \mathbf{x}_i - b \leq \varepsilon + \xi_i \\ \mathbf{w} \cdot \mathbf{x}_i + b - y_i \leq \varepsilon + \xi_i^* \\ \xi_i, \xi_i^* \geq 0, i = 1, \ldots, n \end{cases}$$

For such a loss function (5.6), the model is falsified by samples outside the ε-insensitive zone around the model $f(\mathbf{x}, \boldsymbol{\omega})$. Note that small ε-values correspond to a small margin (for classification formulation), so that a model can explain well just a small portion of available (training) data. On the other hand, larger ε-values correspond to a larger margin, when the model can explain well most (or all) of the data, so it cannot be easily falsified. We also point out the conceptual similarity between the SVM loss for classification (5.4) and regression (5.6). In fact, many other SVM-inspired formulations, such as single-class learning [17], can be described using a similar margin-based loss.

The loss function (5.6) effectively partitions the $(\mathbf{x}, y)$ space into two regions – one where the model explains the data perfectly well (zero loss) and another where the loss is nonzero. The relative size of these two regions is effectively controlled by the value of ε. Since the proper choice of ε-value controls the model's degree of falsification, it is critical for generalization. It depends mainly on the standard deviation of the additive noise and the number of samples [12]. An important point here is that such margin-based loss functions are *adaptive*, in the sense that the size of the margin (for classification problems) or the value of ε (for regression) should be optimally selected for a given data set.

We point out that for inductive learning problems (such as classification and regression, discussed above), the concept of margin describes partitioning of the sample space into regions where the model can or cannot be falsified by the data. This approach can be naturally extended to other inductive learning problems, and to other (noninductive) types of learning. In this sense, Popper's idea of falsification can be used as a general philosophical principle for introducing margin-based methods (such as SVMs). For example, consider the problem of local learning for binary classification, where the goal is to predict the class label of a given (unlabeled) input, given a set of labeled examples $(\mathbf{x}_i, y_i)$. Let us assume (for simplicity) that the training data $(\mathbf{x}_i, y_i), i = 1, \ldots, n$ is linearly separable, so we can use linear approximating functions. Then one can consider two possible class labels for the unlabeled input, yielding two possible labeled data sets. For each possible data set, we estimate the maximum-margin linear model, resulting in two candidate models (Fig. 5.6). Note that each of the maximum-margin models explains its training data set perfectly well, so we choose the model that is easier to falsify, i.e., has the largest margin, in accordance with Popper's principle. This model predicts a class label of $y = -1$ for the unlabeled input. It is also worth noting that margin-based approaches may yield different solutions than standard learning methods. For example, for the data set shown in Figure 5.6, the standard nearest neighbor classification method would assign class label $y = +1$ to the unknown input.

The previous discussion suggests that margin-based methods introduce new loss functions that can be naturally interpreted using Popper's notion of falsifiability. So next we elaborate on the differences between margin-based loss functions and the traditional loss functions used in statistics. The main distinction is that statistical

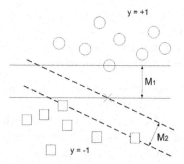

Fig. 5.6. Example of margin-based local learning for classification. Unknown input X can be classified as $y = -1$, resulting in a linear decision boundary with margin M_1, or it can be classified as $y = +1$, resulting in another linear decision boundary with margin M_2. Since $M_1 > M_2$, unknown input is classified as negative class.

loss functions have been introduced for parametric estimation under large sample settings. For example, the squared loss (in regression problems) is statistically optimal when the true parametric form of a model is known, the noise model is known (Gaussian), and the number of samples is large. In contrast, margin-based loss functions are appropriate under sparse (or finite) sample settings when the noise model is unknown and the true parametric model is unknown. For finite sample problems, the use of squared loss is difficult to justify even for linear regression with Gaussian noise. Further, it can be shown that the width of the margin effectively controls the model complexity or the VC dimension [3]. This means that with margin-based loss functions, model selection (complexity control) can be achieved via the loss function itself. In terms of VC theory, the structure of margin-based methods is defined via an (adaptive) loss function. This is in contrast to classical statistical methods, where the empirical loss function is given (fixed) a priori, and the structure is usually defined via the parameterization of approximating functions $f(\mathbf{x}, \boldsymbol{\omega})$, i.e., by the number of basis functions in dictionary methods [1].

Similarly, we can also contrast the two philosophical interpretations of inductive learning, one originating from the classical statistical framework (related to Occam's razor principle) and another based on Popper's philosophy appropriate for finite sample estimation. The statistical framework is based on the idea of function approximation appropriate for low-dimensional problems with large number of training samples. Under this framework, the goal of learning is accurate estimation of an unknown (target) function $t(\mathbf{x}) = E(y/\mathbf{x})$. This naturally leads to the minimization of risk based on the squared loss functional. Here the trade-off is between the accuracy of function approximation (i.e., mean squared error) and the model complexity (quantified as the number of basis functions or the number of free parameters). This trade-off is usually described as Occam's razor principle, which prescribes the selection of a model with lowest complexity that explains (fits) the training data. There are two important points implicit in this classical approach:

1. The measure of function approximation accuracy (empirical loss) is given (fixed) a priori (i.e., squared loss).
2. Model complexity is quantified as the number of free parameters (number of entities in the original Occam's razor formulation).

In contrast, the VC theoretical approach is based on the notion of prediction risk minimization. This goal is less demanding than the goal of function approximation/density estimation. Since the VC theory has been developed for finite sample settings where accurate model (function) estimation is intrinsically difficult (or impossible, due to the curse of dimensionality), we adopt Popper's idea of falsifiability as a guiding principle. That is, we seek a trade-off between the model's accuracy and the possibility of its falsification. This leads naturally to margin-based loss functions that are adaptable and can be tuned for a given data set (via some parameter controlling the size of margin). For such (margin-based) methods, the model complexity [of the structural risk minimization (SRM) structure] is indirectly controlled by the size of the margin, rather than directly by the number of free parameters.

Based on the above discussion, we can identify two distinct approaches for controlling model complexity with finite samples:

(a) Use an *adaptive* parameterization of the approximating functions $f(\mathbf{x}, \boldsymbol{\omega})$, along with *fixed* empirical loss to fit the training data. This approach leads to types of structures used in classical statistical methods such as dictionary methods, penalization, and subset selection.
(b) Use an *adaptive* loss function (margin-based) along with a *fixed* parameterization of approximating functions $f(\mathbf{x}, \boldsymbol{\omega})$. This leads to margin-based methods introduced in this section (see examples in Figs.5.2-5.5).

Note that both types of structures (a) and (b) originate from the same SRM inductive principle, where one jointly minimizes empirical risk and complexity (VC dimension), in order to achieve the minimal value of the upper bound on risk. In adaptive parameterization methods the VC dimension is controlled by the chosen parameterization of $f(\mathbf{x}, \boldsymbol{\omega})$, whereas in margin-based methods the VC-dimension is (implicitly) controlled via an adaptive empirical loss function.

In this section, we used the notion of falsifiability to motivate margin-based estimators (structures), but the original motivation attributed to Vapnik [3, 7] is based on the general SRM inductive principle. For example, the VC generalization bound for classification has the form

$$R(\boldsymbol{\omega}) \leq R_{emp}(\boldsymbol{\omega}) + \Phi\left(R_{emp}(\boldsymbol{\omega}), \frac{n}{h}\right) \qquad (5.8)$$

Here the first term is the empirical risk (i.e., classification error), and the second term is called the confidence interval (its analytical form is provided in VC theory). Since the empirical risk decreases with h (VC dimension) whereas the confidence interval increases with h, there is an optimal VC dimension providing the minimum bound (5.8) on prediction risk. The usual strategy for minimizing this bound is to minimize the first term (empirical risk) using a set of functions (an element of a structure) of fixed complexity. Under this strategy for implementing SRM (used in dictionary methods), the value of the confidence interval is fixed while the empirical risk is minimized. In contrast, under the margin-based approach, the confidence interval is minimized (by maximizing the margin) while the empirical risk is kept zero. Pure implementation of such a strategy is only possible for restricted data sets, i.e., linearly separable data as shown in Figure 5.2. For more realistic (nonseparable) data sets, implementation of the margin-based approach requires a trade-off between the two terms in the bound (5.8). This leads to the soft margin SVM formulation (5.3), where the optimal margin size is adaptively selected for a given data set.

5.4 Support Vector Machines and Regularization

The distinction between margin-based methods and adaptive parameterization methods presented in section 5.3 leads to two obvious questions: First, under what conditions do margin-based methods provide better (or worse) generalization than adaptive parameterization methods? Second, is it possible to combine both approaches? It is difficult to answer the first question, since both types of structures may provide comparable performance, depending on a number of factors, such as the noise level, number of samples, type of noise (in regression problems), etc. Empirical evidence suggests that under sparse sample settings, margin-based methods are generally more robust than methods implementing classical structures. In response to the second question, the two approaches can be easily combined into a single formulation. Effectively, this is done under the SVM framework, where the model complexity is controlled (simultaneously) via adaptive parameterization of approximating functions (kernel selection) and adaptive loss function (margin selection). Nonlinear SVM loss functions effectively combine

- margin-based loss in order to control the complexity (VC-dimension) of a learning method, and
- nonlinear (adaptive) parameterization of possible models via selection of the so-called kernel functions.

Let us consider learning problems where (for simplicity) admissible models have linear parameterization $f(\mathbf{x}, \omega) = \mathbf{w} \cdot \mathbf{x} + b$. Then the generic SVM risk functional has the following form:

$$R_{SVM}(\mathbf{Z}, \mathbf{w}, b) = \frac{1}{2}||\mathbf{w}||^2 + C \sum_{i=1}^{n} L(y_i, f(\mathbf{x}_i, \omega)) \qquad (5.9)$$

where the specific form of the loss function depends on a learning problem formulation. For regression problems, the loss $L_\varepsilon(y, f(\mathbf{x}, \omega))$ is specified by (5.6), and for classification problems the loss is given by (5.5).

Nonlinear or kernel-based methods extend the SVM approach to estimating nonlinear models [3]. By using flexible parameterizations (more complex models), one can significantly increase the degree of falsifiability, by effectively using "curved margin" boundaries (Fig. 5.7). SVM provides the mathematical framework for generating such nonlinear models with curved margin boundaries, via the use of kernels [3]. Such nonlinear SVM methods achieve improved generalization by effectively combining flexible nonlinear (kernel) parameterizations with margin-based loss.

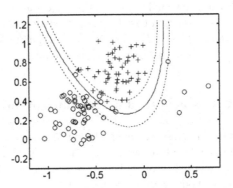

Fig. 5.7. Example of nonlinear SVM decision boundary (curved margin).

In this chapter, however, we only focus on *linear* SVMs, i.e., use linear parameterization of $f(\mathbf{x}, \omega)$, in order to explain the role of margin. Since the SVM risk functional (5.9) has an obvious similarity to standard regularization (penalization) loss, many recent references [2, 6] describe SVMs as a special case of the regularization formulation. For example, consider the standard formulation for ridge regression:

$$R_{reg}(\mathbf{Z}, \mathbf{w}, b) = \sum_{i=1}^{n} (y_i - f(\mathbf{x}_i, \omega))^2 + \lambda \|\mathbf{w}\|^2 \qquad (5.10)$$

Hence, we can obtain the SVM formulation (5.9) by using ε-insensitive loss and substituting the regularization parameter $\lambda \sim 1/C$ in formulation (5.10). The difference, however, is that the SVM formulation includes an *adaptive* (margin-based) loss that controls the model complexity, in addition to the penalization term. So the SVM functional (5.9) depends on two hyperparameters: the regularization parameter C (which controls the trade-off between the smoothness of approximating functions) and the parameter controlling the margin [i.e., the value of ε-parameter in SVM loss (5.6)]. So interpretations of SVMs as a "special case of the regularization formulation" simply ignore an important role of the margin-based loss. In fact, all classical regularization formulations use a fixed (nonadaptive) loss term (i.e., squared loss), so that the model complexity is controlled exclusively by the regularization parameter.

Similarly, for classification problems, the soft margin SVM formulation (5.3) is sometimes contrasted to the penalized linear least squares formulation that minimizes

$$R_{reg}(\mathbf{Z}, \mathbf{w}, b) = \sum_{i=1}^{n} (\xi_i)^2 + \lambda ||\mathbf{w}||^2 \tag{5.11}$$

subject to $\xi_i = y_i - (\mathbf{w} \cdot \mathbf{x}_i + b), i = 1, \ldots, n$

It can be shown that the least squares regression to the class labels (5.11) is equivalent to (penalized) linear discriminant analysis LDA [2, 11]. The nonlinear version of formulation (5.11) has been introduced under the names least squares SVM classifiers [13] and Fisher kernel discriminants [16].

Next we show empirical comparisons between the SVM formulation (5.3) and the penalized least squares classifier (5.11), aka penalized LDA for binary classification. Such comparisons are fair, in the sense that both formulations have a single parameter for complexity control. Since both formulations use the same (linear) parameterization, such comparisons clarify the importance of margin vs. standard regularization approach. The first toy data set is shown in Figure 5.8 and described next. Each class is a two-dimensional ellipsoid, with a long-to-short axis variance ratio of 4:1. The long axes of the two ellipsoids are perpendicular to each other. More specifically,

- the positive class data is centered at $(1.2, 1.2)$, with the short axis's variance 0.02, and the long axis's variance 0.08; and
- The negative class data is centered at $(0, 0)$, with the short axis's variance 0.02, and the long axis's variance 0.08.

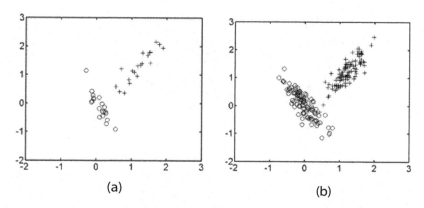

(a)   (b)

Fig. 5.8. Training data for empirical comparisons: (a) small data set; (b) large data set.

Both classes have equal prior probabilities, and we used a small training set (40 samples, 20 per class), and large training set (200 samples, 100 per class), for comparisons. A test set of 1000 samples was used to estimate the prediction error, i.e., the classification error rate. The effect of each method's tuning parameter on the prediction error is shown in Tables 5.1 and 5.2, for the small training set. Likewise, the effect of each method's tuning parameter on the prediction error for the large data set is shown in Tables 5.3 and 5.4.

Table 5.1. Prediction error for linear SVM: small sample size.

C	0.13	0.37	1	2.7	7.3	256
Margin	1.57	1.14	0.97	0.64	0.56	0.56
Prediction error	2.45%	1.1%	1.1%	0.5%	0.9%	0.9%

Table 5.2. Prediction error for penalized LDA: small sample size.

	LDA	Penalized Linear Discriminant				
λ		$\lambda = 0.01$	$\lambda = 0.1$	$\lambda = 1$	$\lambda = 10$	$\lambda = 100$
Prediction error	2.8%	2.8%	2.8%	2.9%	3%	3.8%

Table 5.3. Prediction error for linear SVM: large sample size.

C	0.37	1	2.7	20	54	148	1096
Margin	0.94	0.75	0.62	0.45	0.35	0.19	0.16
Prediction error	1.5%	1.4%	1.1%	0.6%	0.5%	0.4%	0.5%

Table 5.4. Prediction error for penalized LDA: large sample size.

	LDA	Penalized Linear Discriminant				
λ		$\lambda = 0.01$	$\lambda = 0.1$	$\lambda = 1$	$\lambda = 10$	$\lambda = 100$
Prediction error	2.8%	2.8%	2.8%	2.9%	3%	3.8%

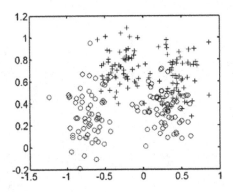

Fig. 5.9. Training data for classification problem generated according to a mixture of Gaussians [15].

These comparisons suggest that margin-based complexity control is more effective than standard regularization. In particular, penalized LDA is rather ineffective when the number of samples is large (see results in Table 5.4 and Table 5.6), whereas margin-based complexity control is very effective for both small and large sample settings. Optimal selection of parameter C ($\sim$margin) for SVM formulation, and regularization parameter λ for the least squares classifier can be performed using standard resampling techniques. However, our empirical comparisons suggest that for these data sets even the best choice of λ for penalized LDA would yield inferior generalization performance than crude tuning of the margin in the SVM classifier.

The next data set is a mixture of Gaussians proposed by Ripley [15], and used in many empirical comparisons [4]. In this example, the training data (250 samples) are generated according to a mixture of Gaussian distributions as shown in Figure 5.9. The positive class data have centers $(0.3, 0.7)$ and $(0.4, 0.7)$, and the negative class data have centers $(-0.7, 0.3)$ and $(0.3, 0.3)$. All Gaussian clusters have the same variance 0.03. A test set of 1000 samples is used to estimate the prediction error, shown in Tables 5.5 and 5.6. For this data set, there is no significant difference in the prediction performance of a (linear) SVM vs. LDA classifier. This can be explained by the nonlinear nature of an optimal decision boundary, which cannot be captured by the linear parameterization. Hence, in this case, the prediction accuracy suffers due to a mismatch between a complex (nonlinear) optimal decision boundary and a too simple (linear) class of possible models, assumed for both LDA and SVM. This example shows that in practice *margin-based* complexity control should be used in combination with *model-based* complexity control, i.e., adaptive parameterization of admissible models. This combination is implemented in nonlinear SVMs, via the choice of a kernel [8]. In fact, the distinction between model-based and margin-based approaches naturally leads to two complementary measures of data complexity, as discussed later in section 5.5.

Table 5.5. Prediction error for linear SVM: mixture of Gaussians data set.

C	1	2.7	7.3	54	256
Margin	0.37	0.31	0.27	0.24	0.23
Prediction error	11.5%	10.2%	10.4%	10.5%	10.5%

Also, it should be clear that the notion of margin has a very distinct meaning for different learning problem formulations (i.e., classification vs. regression). This implies different strategies for margin-based complexity control, specific to each formulation. For instance, there exist simple analytic prescriptions for selecting good values of the ε-parameter in regression problems [12].

Finally, the proposed distinction between margin-based and model-based approaches to complexity control leads to a simple quantitative characterization of data complexity with respect to a given (fixed) model parameterization. The basic idea is to compare the generalization (prediction risk) of an SVM model with optimally tuned margin vs. the prediction risk of a model with a smallest possible margin. Then if margin-based complexity control can achieve significant improvement in the

Table 5.6. Prediction error for penalized LDA: mixture of Gaussians data set.

	LDA	Penalized Linear Discriminant				
λ		$\lambda = 0.01$	$\lambda = 0.1$	$\lambda = 1$	$\lambda = 10$	$\lambda = 1000$
Prediction error	10.8%	10.8%	10.8%	10.8%	10.8%	11.9%

prediction risk, the data set is "simple." We emphasize that the proposed data complexity measure is defined with respect to a given parameterization, say linear SVM $f(\mathbf{x}, \omega) = \mathbf{w} \cdot \mathbf{x} + b$, or radial basis function (RBF) kernels with a given (fixed) width parameter. Using formal notation, the proposed data complexity index is defined as

$$\rho(\mathbf{Z}, f(\mathbf{x}, \omega)) = \frac{R(opt\_margin)}{R(small\_margin)} \qquad (5.12)$$

That is, the complexity index ρ of a data set $\mathbf{Z}$ is a ratio of the prediction risk achieved by an SVM model with optimally selected margin, to the prediction risk of a model with a "small" margin. Then index ρ is a positive number between 0 and 1, such that small values of ρ (closer to zero) indicate low data complexity, and large values (close to 1) suggest high complexity. For example, for a data set with totally random class labeling, this index equals 1, indicating that all SVM classifiers (irrespective of tuning the margin) provide the same prediction risk (i.e., about 50% error).

Technically, this index can be evaluated by applying standard SVM implementations to the data, and estimating the prediction risk using standard resampling approaches. The model with small margin is obtained by an appropriate setting of the SVM hyperparameters, i.e., setting the value of C very large (in the classification formulation), or setting the ε-value to zero (in the regression formulation). The proposed measure of data complexity is quite different from many existing criteria, such as the shape (complexity) of the decision boundary, the shape of class distributions, the amount of overlap between classes, etc., in that such traditional criteria do not account for the role of margin.

Next we show a few examples of calculating this index for synthetic data sets introduced earlier in this chapter. For the first data set (two ellipsoids), the complexity index obtained with linear SVM is

- for the small data set,

$$\rho(\mathbf{Z}, f(\mathbf{x}, \omega)) = \frac{R(opt\_margin)}{R(small\_margin)} = \frac{0.5\%}{0.9\%} = 0.56$$

- for the large data set,

$$\rho(\mathbf{Z}, f(\mathbf{x}, \omega)) = \frac{R(opt\_margin)}{R(small\_margin)} = \frac{0.4\%}{0.5\%} = 0.8$$

Note that the complexity index has lower value for the small data set, indicating that this data set is "simpler" than the large data set. This is consistent with our intuitive interpretation (see Fig. 5.8) since the small data set is linearly separable. Also, the complexity index clearly depends on the number of samples (since both data sets originate from the same distribution).

For the data set from Ripley [15], the index obtained using linear SVM is

$$\rho(\mathbf{Z}, f(\mathbf{x}, \omega)) = \frac{R(opt\_margin)}{R(small\_margin)} = \frac{10.2\%}{10.5\%} = 0.97$$

This high value suggests that linear parameterization is not a good choice for this data, since the decision boundary should be nonlinear (see Fig. 5.9). However, for the same data set using nonlinear SVM with RBF kernel, the complexity index becomes

$$\rho(\mathbf{Z}, f(\mathbf{x}, \omega)) = \frac{R(opt\_margin)}{R(small\_margin)} = \frac{8.7\%}{14.6\%} = 0.6$$

The low value of index ρ suggests that the nonlinear SVM classifier is a very good choice for this data set. Note that margin-based complexity control is very effective in combination with flexible RBF kernel parameterization, in achieving an error rate of 8.7%, quite close to the Bayes-optimal error rate of 8% [15].

5.5 Discussion and Conclusion

The empirical success of SVM-based methods has motivated the development of various conceptual interpretations of SVM such as the regularization framework, Bayesian formulations, and fuzzy logic. This could be expected since the SVM approach combines several powerful ideas from statistical learning ("margin"), functional analysis ("kernels"), and optimization theory. This chapter provides a novel philosophical motivation for the notion of margin, which is central to the success of all SVM-based approaches. The idea of margin is introduced as a general philosophical concept related to Karl Popper's notion of falsifiability. This view enables better understanding of many different SVM formulations. On a technical level, improved understanding of the role of margin leads to an important distinction between margin-based methods (such as SVM) and classical regularization methods. We elaborate on this distinction and show empirical comparisons between the two approaches. Our comparisons intentionally apply linear estimators to simple data sets, in order to demonstrate the importance of margin-based complexity control, as opposed to standard regularization. It may be interesting to note that our findings (regarding superiority of linear SVM over penalized LDA) contradict several empirical comparison studies, suggesting similar generalization performance of nonlinear SVMs and nonlinear penalized least squares classifiers [6, 14, 16]. The reasons for this disagreement are likely due to many additional factors arising in application of flexible nonlinear classifiers to real-life data sets, such as a methods tuning, data preprocessing and encoding, kernel selection, etc. These considerations are very important for practical applications, but they have nothing to do with the role of the margin. In contrast, our (arguably simple) comparison setup has a single tunable parameter for each method, so one can clearly see the effect of margin on the generalization performance.

Finally, we introduced a new index for data complexity, designed for margin-based methods, and showed its application for pattern recognition problems. Whereas most existing data complexity measures aim at evaluating the complexity of the decision boundary itself, the proposed index measures the benefits of using the margin for a given model parameterization. The index effectively measures the degree of separation between the two classes that can be achieved by margin-based methods (such as SVM). This index provides discrimination of simple data sets that can achieve a high degree of separation (hence, good generalization) vs. complex data sets that cannot achieve high separation. A high value of the data complexity index may be due to a large amount of overlap between the two classes and/or poorly chosen model parameterization (as in the case of a linear decision boundary for Ripley's data set in Fig. 5.9).

However, the proposed data complexity index does not provide information about the nature of the decision boundary itself. In a way, the margin-based complexity index is complementary to many traditional complexity measures describing the complexity of the decision boundary (i.e., linear, piecewise linear, second-order polynomial, etc.). The distinction between model-based and margin-based complexity control, introduced in this chapter, appears quite useful for understanding these two complementary measures of data complexity and their effect on the generalization performance. For traditional model-based classifiers, the choice of the correct parameterization is critical for achieving good generalization. In contrast, SVM methods combine both the margin-based and the model-based complexity control (where the latter is performed by the choice of a kernel).

For SVM classifiers with noisy real-life data, correct model parameterization (kernel selection) is less important than for traditional classifiers, in the sense that the overfitting due to (too complex) kernel selection can be usually compensated by margin-based complexity control. This robustness with respect to a wide range of kernel specifications may help to explain the practical success of SVM methods. These points are clarified next using toy data sets in Figures 5.8 and 5.9. For example, for both data sets in Figure 5.8, we can apply *nonlinear* SVM (e.g., with polynomial kernels of second or third degree) and achieve an optimal prediction accuracy very similar to the best error of a linear SVM (reported in Tables 5.1 and 5.3, for the small and large data set, respectively). As an aside, note that for the distributions used to generate data sets in Figure 5.8, the theoretically optimal decision boundary is known to be a second-order polynomial. However, it does not mean that estimating a second-order polynomial model from *finite data* is a good idea. In fact, with finite data it is often better to estimate an LDA model even when the optimal decision boundary is known to be nonlinear [1]. Likewise, for the nonlinear data set in Figure 5.9, we can apply nonlinear SVM with different kernels (i.e., linear spline, higher-order polynomials etc.) and achieve the prediction accuracy very similar to optimal results obtained with RBF kernels (in section 5.4). In all of these cases, kernels provide very flexible model parameterization, and the problem of overfitting is effectively controlled by using the margin. The same effect can be seen in the results used to calculate the complexity index for the Ripley's data set using nonlinear SVM with RBF kernel (see the last paragraph in section 5.4). These results show that such an SVM classifier (with a small margin) has a high error rate (14.6%), indicating the problem of overfitting. However, the same RBF parameterization yields excellent performance (error rate of 8.7%) with an optimally tuned margin. Even though SVM complexity control is arguably similar to traditional regularization approaches (such as penalized LDA, ridge regression, etc.), this chapter underscores an important role of margin for complexity control and for the characterization of data complexity in predictive methods.

Acknowledgments

The authors thank Dr. S. Mika from IMA, Germany, for providing Matlab implementation of the penalized LDA used for empirical comparisons presented in this chapter. We also acknowledge several insightful comments and suggestions of anonymous reviewers. This work was supported, in part, by National Science Foundation grant ECS-0099906.

References

[1] V. Cherkassky, F. Mulier. *Learning from Data: Concepts, Theory, and Methods*. New York: John Wiley & Sons, 1998.

[2] T. Hastie, R. Tibshirani, J. Friedman. *The Elements of Statistical Learning: Data Mining, Inference and Prediction*. New York: Springer, 2001.

[3] V. Vapnik. *The Nature of Statistical Learning Theory*. New York: Springer, 1995.

[4] B.D. Ripley. *Pattern Recognition and Neural Networks*. Cambridge: Cambridge University Press, 1996.

[5] A. Barron, L. Birge, P. Massart. Risk bounds for model selection via penalization. *Probability Theory and Related Fields*, 113, 301–413, 1999.

[6] T. Poggio, S. Smale. The Mathematics of Learning: Dealing with Data. *Notices American Mathematical Society*, 50, 537–544, 2003.

[7] V. Vapnik. *Estimation of Dependences Based on Empirical Data*. Berlin: Springer Verleg, 1982.

[8] V. Vapnik. *Statistical Learning Theory*. New York: Wiley, 1998.

[9] K. Popper. *The Logic of Scientific Discovery*. New York: Harper Torch Books, 1968.

[10] K. Popper. *Conjectures and Refutations: The Growth of Scientific Knowledge*. London and New York: Routledge, 2000.

[11] R. Duda, P. Hart, D. Stork. *Pattern Classification*. 2nd. ed., New York: Wiley, 2000.

[12] V. Cherkassky, Y. Ma. Practical selection of SVM parameters and noise estimation for SVM regression. *Neural Networks*, 17(1), 113–126, 2004.

[13] J. Suykens, J. Vanderwalle. Least squares support vector machine classifiers. *Neural Processing Letters*, 9(3), 293–300, 1999.

[14] J. Suykens, T. Van Gestel, et al. *Least Squares Support Vector Machines*. Singapore: World Scientific, 2002.

[15] B.D. Ripley. Neural networks and related methods for classification (with discussion). *J. Royal Stat. Soc.*, B56, 409–456, 1994.

[16] S. Mika. *Kernel Fisher discriminants*, Ph.D. thesis, Technical University of Berlin, 2002.

[17] B. Schölkopf, A. Smola. *Learning with Kernels: Support Vector Machines, Regularization, Optimization and Beyond.* Cambridge, MA: MIT Press, 2002.

6

Data Complexity and Evolutionary Learning

Ester Bernadó-Mansilla, Tin Kam Ho, and Albert Orriols

Summary. We study the behavior of XCS, a classifier based on genetic algorithms. XCS summarizes the state of the art of the evolutionary learning field and benefits from the long experience and research in the area. We describe the XCS learning mechanisms by which a set of rules describing the class boundaries is evolved. We study XCS's behavior and its relationship to data complexity. We find that the difficult cases for XCS are those with long boundaries, high class interleaving, and high nonlinearities. Comparison with other classifiers in the complexity space enables identifying domains of competence for XCS as well as domains of poor performance. The study lays the basis to further apply the same methodology to analyze the domains of competence of other classifiers.

6.1 Introduction

Genetic algorithms (GAs) are search algorithms based on the mechanisms of natural selection and genetics [14, 15, 18]. They have been applied to search, optimization, and machine learning problems with great success. GAs explore the search space by using a population of solutions instead of a single point. This population is evaluated and then developed with potential improvements by the mechanisms of selection, crossover, and mutation. One of the abilities of GAs is to keep a good balance between exploration of the search space and exploitation of the best found solutions. This equilibrium facilitates exploring large search spaces efficiently, tending to avoid local minima. GAs can also be applied to a wide range of applications, because it does not require many assumptions on the data model. They can also work with different representations, allowing even wider applicability.

The GAs' capability to use different types of representations has resulted in their usage in many learning scenarios that are as diverse as induction of decision trees [12], instance sets [21], rule sets [6, 10], evolution of neural networks [23, 29], etc. Particularly, the evolution of rule sets has attracted growing interest in the last decades. Since the first proposal developed by Holland [18] in 1975, the field has benefited from much active research and development, which have resulted in effective classifiers such as XCS [26]. Currently, XCS is mature enough to be considered as a competitive classifier, supported by experimental studies demonstrating its efficiency in real problems [3, 6], as well as theoretical studies giving insight in the functioning of their mechanisms and providing guidelines to exploit its potential by the use of appropriate parameter settings [10]. XCS has also been improved from its first version, with the inclusion of generalization mechanisms [27], new representations [19, 20, 25, 28], improved components [10], etc.

At this stage of XCS's maturity, researchers have started to analyze its domain of competence to understand where XCS is applicable and whether it is better or worse than other classifiers for certain types of problems. Several studies have approached this subject by comparing XCS's performance to that of other classifiers in a varied range of classification problems [3, 4, 6]. These studies draw their conclusions from observable measures of the data sets, such as the number or types of attributes or the number of classes. But this approach is insufficient for relating XCS's performance, and relative performances between classifiers, to the data-set complexity. A more recent approach [5] started to analyze XCS's performance related to data complexity, building on previous proposals of complexity metrics for classification problems [17]. The aim of this chapter is to summarize this study and enhance the investigation on the domain of competence of XCS.

First, we introduce XCS and its learning mechanisms, showing how XCS evolves rules approximating the class boundaries. The study by Bernadó-Mansilla and Ho [5] included an extended analysis on XCS's performance related to data complexity, and introduced an analysis on relative performances by making pairwise comparisons of XCS with other classifiers. In this chapter, we briefly summarize this study by showing how XCS adapts to data complexity. Then, we extend it by showing the best and worst domain of XCS with comparison to several other representative classifiers.

The chapter is structured as follows. Section 6.2 gives a brief introduction to genetic algorithms and evolutionary learning classifier systems. It sets the framework and defines the basic GA's terminology that is used here. Section 6.3 describes the learning mechanisms of XCS, and section 6.4 introduces the available knowledge representations, focusing on the hyperrectangle representation , which is the approach taken in this chapter. Next, we study XCS's behavior in two classification problems designed artificially, and we show graphically how classification problems may imply different degrees of difficulty to different types of classifiers (section 6.5). Then, we evaluate XCS's performance on data complexity and identify the complexity measures most relevant to XCS (section 6.6). We also aim at identifying problems to which XCS is best suited among a set of competing classifiers. Although there are other types of classifiers based on GAs, we focus our study on XCS because it is one of the best representatives of evolutionary learning classifier systems (LCSs). Section 6.7 outlines how this study can be extended to other types of evolutionary learning classifier systems and summarizes the main conclusions.

6.2 Genetic Algorithms for Classification

6.2.1 GA Basics

Genetic algorithms (GAs) [14, 15, 18] are defined as search algorithms inspired by natural selection and genetics. GAs explore the search space by means of a *population* of candidate solutions to the problem. Each solution is called an *individual* and is codified in a *chromosome*, a data structure that keeps the genetic information of the solution in a representative way so that it can be manipulated by the genetic operators.

The population may be initialized at random and then incrementally evaluated and improved through *selection*, *crossover*, and *mutation*. Evaluation of each solution is performed by the *fitness* function, which provides the quality of the solution for the given problem. Fitness guides the evolution toward the desired areas of the search space. Individuals with higher fitness have higher chances to be selected and to participate in recombination (crossover) and mutation. Crossover combines the genetic material of two parent individuals to form new offspring. Thus, it exploits good solutions to potentially move the population toward even better solutions. Mutation is applied to single individuals, performing slight changes into their chromosomes. Its aim is to introduce diversity in the population. The new solutions thus obtained are evaluated and the cycle of selection, crossover, and mutation is repeated until a satisfactory solution is found or a predefined time limit expires.

6.2.2 Evolutionary Learning Classifier Systems

Although GAs are primarily defined as search algorithms, they can be applied to learning problems where learning is expressed as a search in a space of models representing the target concept. In this sense, GAs must codify a model and evolve it by means of selection, recombination, and mutation. The so-called *learning classifier systems* (LCSs) approach searches for a set of rules describing the target concept. In this context, there are two different approaches, called Pittsburgh and Michigan, respectively, which differ mainly in their representation.

The Pittsburgh approach [2, 13] codifies each individual as a rule set. Then the GA evolves a population of rule sets. Once convergence is achieved, the best individual is selected and their rule set used as the result of learning. Evaluation of each individual (rule set) is performed independently against the training set of examples, considering different aspects as the classification accuracy, the number of required rules, etc.

The Michigan approach [18, 26] codifies each individual as a single rule. Thus each individual represents a partial solution, and the whole population is needed to codify a rule set. Evaluation differs from the Pittsburgh approach in that each individual's relative contribution to the whole target concept must be measured. Also the GA takes a different approach so that at convergence a set of diverse solutions are present that jointly codify a rule set. The XCS classifier system, where we base the current study, takes this approach. The next section describes it in more detail.

6.3 The XCS Classifier System

XCS evolves a set of rules, by means of interacting with the environment through a *reinforcement learning* scheme and a search mechanism based on a GA. Although XCS can be applied to both single-step and multistep tasks, we restrict this analysis to XCS acting only as a classifier system. For more details, the reader is referred elsewhere for an introduction of XCS [26, 27], and for an algorithmic description [11].

6.3.1 Representation

XCS evolves a population [P] of classifiers. In the XCS context, a classifier[1] consists of a rule and a set of associated parameters. Each rule has a condition part and a class part: *condition* → *class*. The condition specifies the set of input states where the rule can be

---

[1] In XCS, the term *classifier* is used to refer to a rule and a set of associated parameters. In the machine learning and pattern recognition fields, a *classifier* refers to the whole system that classifies. In this section, we use this term in the sense of a rule and a set of associated parameters. The remaining sections use the term *classifier* as the whole system.

applied. The class part specifies the classification that the rule proposes when its condition is satisfied.

The condition of each rule is a conjunction of tests over the features. If an example satisfies these tests, then it is classified with the class codified in the rule. The representation of these tests depends on the types of the features. It also depends on the particular setting of XCS, since several representations are available for a particular type of attribute. Section 6.4 gives an introduction to the most commonly used representations.

Each classifier has a set of associated parameters that estimate the quality of the rule for the given problem:

- Payoff prediction (p): an estimate of the payoff that the classifier will receive if its condition matches the input and its action is selected.
- Prediction error (ϵ): an estimate of the average error between the classifier's prediction and the payoff received from the environment.
- Fitness (F): an estimate of the accuracy of the payoff prediction.
- Experience (exp): the number of times that the classifier has participated in a classification.
- Action set size (as): the average number of classifiers of the action sets where the classifier has participated.
- Time-step (ts): time-step of the last application of the genetic algorithm.
- Numerosity (num): the number of actual *microclassifiers* this *macroclassifier* represents.[2]

These parameters are incrementally evaluated each time the classifier participates in the classification of an example. Their values serve as the basis to guide the search mechanisms.

6.3.2 Performance Component

At each time step, an input example coming from the training data set is selected randomly and presented to XCS. The system finds the matching classifiers and proposes a classification. Then, the environment returns a reward that is used by XCS to update the parameters of the contributing rules. In the following discussion we give the details.

At each time step, an input example x is presented to XCS. Given x, the system builds a match set [M], which is formed by all the classifiers in [P] whose conditions are satisfied by the example.

An XCS's run may be started with an empty or incomplete rule set. Therefore, an input example may not find any matching classifier. In this case the covering operator is triggered, creating new classifiers that match the current sample. Covering may also trigger if the number of actions represented in [M] is less than a threshold θ_{mna}. Then new classifiers are generated with conditions matching the example and classes selected randomly from those not present in [M].

From the resulting match set, a class must be selected and sent to the environment. In exploration mode (i.e., during training), the class is selected randomly so that the system can learn the consequences of all possible classes for each input. The chosen class is used to form the action set [A], which consists of all the classifiers proposing that class. Then, the parameters of these classifiers are updated as described in the next section.

In exploitation mode (i.e., during test) the best class, from those present in [M], is selected to maximize performance. This selection is based on a measure of quality for each class,

---

[2] Classifiers in XCS are in fact *macroclassifiers* i.e., each classifier represents *num microclassifiers* having the same conditions and actions [11].

$P(a)$, which is computed as a fitness-weighted average of the predictions of all classifiers proposing that class. In fact, $P(a)$ estimates the payoff that the system will receive if class a is chosen. The selected class determines the action set [A] as in the case of exploration mode. The difference here is that the classifier's parameters are not updated.

6.3.3 Reinforcement Component

In exploration mode, the class is sent to the environment, which returns a reward r that is used to update the parameters of the classifiers in [A]. First, the prediction of each classifier is updated:

$$p \leftarrow p + \beta(r - p) \tag{6.1}$$

where β $(0 \leq \beta \leq 1)$ is the learning rate. Next, the prediction error:

$$\epsilon \leftarrow \epsilon + \beta(|r - p| - \epsilon) \tag{6.2}$$

Then, the accuracy of the classifier is computed as an inverse function of its prediction error:

$$k = \begin{cases} \alpha(\epsilon/\epsilon_0)^{-\nu} & \epsilon \geq \epsilon_0 \\ 1 & \text{otherwise} \end{cases} \tag{6.3}$$

where ϵ_0 $(\epsilon_0 > 0)$ determines the threshold error under which a classifier is considered to be accurate. α $(0 < \alpha < 1)$ and ν $(\nu > 0)$ control the degree of decline in accuracy if the classifier is inaccurate [9]. Then, XCS computes the classifier's accuracy relative to the accuracies of the classifiers in the action set:

$$k' = \frac{k}{\sum_{cl \in [A]} k_{cl}} \tag{6.4}$$

This value is then used to update the fitness F as follows:

$$F \leftarrow F + \beta(k' - F) \tag{6.5}$$

Thus, fitness estimates the accuracy of the classifier's prediction relative to the accuracies of the classifiers belonging to the same action sets.

The experience parameter exp counts the number of times that a classifier is updated. It is increased by 1 each time the classifier participates in an action set. It is a measure of the confidence on the classifier's parameters. The action set size parameter as averages the number of classifiers of the action sets where the classifier participates. It is updated whenever the classifier belongs to an action set.

6.3.4 Search Component

The search component in XCS tries to improve the rule set, by means of a GA. The GA is triggered eventually and takes place in [A]. The GA's trigger mechanism is designed to give balanced resources to the different action sets. That is, the GA is activated when the average time since the last occurrence of the GA in the action set (computed from the classifiers' parameter ts) exceeds a threshold θ_{GA}. If the GA is triggered, then it is applied locally into the current [A]. It selects two parents from [A] with probability proportional to fitness, and gets two offspring by applying crossover with probability χ and mutation with probability μ per allele.

The resulting offspring are introduced into the population. First, the offspring are checked for subsumption with their parents. If one of the parents is experienced, accurate, and more general that the offspring, then the offspring is subsumed by its parent. This tends to condense the population toward maximally general classifiers.

If an offspring classifier cannot be subsumed by its parents, it is inserted into the population, deleting another classifier if the population is full. Deletion is the mechanism by which useless classifiers are discarded from the population, leaving its place to promising solutions. The classifiers with higher probabilities of being deleted are those that participate in large action sets. Also those classifiers with enough experience and low fitness have higher probabilities of being removed from the population. This biases the search toward highly fit classifiers, and at the same time balances the distribution of classifiers through the feature space.

6.3.5 How XCS Learns the Target Concept

When XCS operates as a pure classifier system, it receives training instances from the data set, performs classifications, and gets feedback from the environment in the form of rewards. The environment is designed to give a maximum reward if the system predicts the correct class and a minimum reward (usually zero) otherwise. XCS's goal is to maximize rewards, which is internally translated to the compound goal of evolving a *complete, consistent, and minimal representation* of the target concept.

XCS learns incrementally. Usually, it starts from an empty population and performs generalizations (in the form of rules) of the input examples to cover the empty regions of the feature space. These rules are incrementally evaluated by the reinforcement component and revised by the search mechanism.

The reinforcement component evaluates the current classifiers so that highly fit classifiers correspond to consistent (accurate) descriptions of the target concept. The fitness of each classifier is based on the accuracy of the reward prediction. Highly fit classifiers are those that accurately predict the environmental reward in all the situations where they match.

The search component is based on a genetic algorithm. The GA is guided by fitness, and since fitness is based on accuracy, the GA will tend to evolve accurate rules. The GA should also favor the maintenance of a diverse set of rules that jointly represent the target concept. This is enforced by the use of niching mechanisms, which try to balance the classifiers' allocation in the different regions of the search space. Niching is implicit in different parts of the GA: (a) the GA's triggering mechanism, which tries to balance the application of the GA among all the action sets; (b) selection, applied locally to the action sets; (c) crossover, performing a kind of restricted mating; and (d) the deletion algorithm, which tends to delete resources from the more numerous action sets. The GA also enforces the evolution of maximally general rules, which allow more compact representations. This generalization pressure is explained by Wilson's generalization hypothesis [26], which can be summarized as follows: if two classifiers are equally accurate but have different generalizations, then the most general one will participate in more action sets, having more reproductive opportunities and finally displacing the specific classifier. Through the interaction of these components, the GA tries to evolve consistent, complete, and minimal representations. For more details, see Butz [10].

6.4 Knowledge Representation

A rule in XCS takes the form: *condition* → *class*. The condition is a conjunction of tests over the problem features: $t_1 \wedge t_2 \wedge \cdots \wedge t_n$. The representation of each test depends on the type of attribute. Even for some types of attributes, several representations are available. In fact, this is a particularity of the codification of solutions in GAs. GAs are not tied to any specific representation, so that they can be applied to many domains. The only restriction is to adapt the genetic operators to the particular representation so that the search algorithm can explore efficiently.

If the feature is binary (or belongs only to two categories), the test over this feature is usually codified in the ternary representation, which consists of the symbols $\{0,1,\#\}$. 0 and 1 codify the two categories, respectively, while the symbol # codifies the "don't care" case, which belongs to the case where the feature is found to be irrelevant.

If the feature is categorical, several encodings are available. The enumeration encoding maps an attribute with c possible categories into a binary string of length c, where each bit tests membership to a distinct category. The test is then a disjunction of the membership tests over each category. An irrelevant feature is codified by a string with all bits set to 1. The nominal encoding codifies the test with a single symbol, which can take values from $\{0,1,2,...,c-1,\#\}$, where c is the number of categories. Again the "don't care" symbol makes the attribute irrelevant.

In the case of continuous-valued features, a possibility is to discretize the real values into nominal ranges, and then proceed as in the categorical case. However, this can limit the accuracy of the rule since the nominal ranges must be fixed a priori. Another approach is to let the GA find the necessary ranges, by codifying an interval of type $[l_i, u_i]$, where $l_i \leq u_i$. A set of such intervals describes a hyperrectangle in the feature space. For simplicity, the attributes of the data set examples are usually normalized to the range [0,1].

Other representations have been proposed for XCS, such as messy coding [19] and S-expressions [20]. Focusing on real features within the scope of this chapter, we use the hyperrectangle representation, one of the most used and successful representations (see [4]). The class is codified as an integer.

Genetic Operators

Once the representation is designed, the genetic operators that manipulate representations must be adapted. This affects covering, mutation, and crossover. Covering must be designed to cover training points that are not covered by the current pool of rules. Crossover exploits the potentially good solutions by recombining parts of them. Mutation should give randomness to explore new regions of the rule space.

Covering initializes new rules that cover empty regions of the search space. Given a training example described by its features $x = (x_1, x_2, ..., x_n)$, covering obtains a rule by means of generalizing each attribute with a matching interval. For each attribute x_i, covering creates an interval $[l_i, u_i]$, where $l_i = x_i - rand(r_0)$ and $u_i = x_i + rand(r_0)$. $rand(r_0)$ gives a random value between 0 and r_0, where r_0 is a parameter set by the user. Figure 6.1(a) gives two examples of rules obtained by covering.

Mutation introduces randomness into the exploration process. It is applied with probability μ per allele, where an allele is each of the hyperrectangle bounds. To mutate an allele, its valued is changed by an amount $\pm rand(m_0)$, where the sign is selected randomly and m_0 is a parameter set by the user (a typical value is 0.1). Figure 6.1(b) shows the effect of mutation

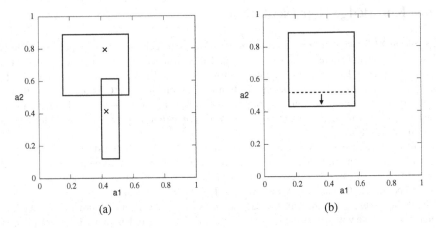

(a)   (b)

Fig. 6.1. Example of covering and mutation on the hyperrectangle representation. (a) The covering operator is applied to two training points (plotted by a cross) and two rules are obtained. (b) Mutation alters one of dimensions of the hyperrectangle rule.

over an individual in a two-feature space. The individual, with interval ranges defined by $([l_1, u_1], [l_2, u_2])$, suffers mutation on l_2, which is decreased by 0.09.

Crossover takes two parent solutions and produces two offspring. Usually two-point crossover is applied. It computes two random cut points on the rule, and the subsequences defined by them are interchanged into the offspring. The cut points can occur between intervals as well as within intervals. Figure 6.2 shows an example of crossover. On the left, there are two parents selected for crossover. On the right, two offspring are obtained by their recombination. This case corresponds to a cut point among the first and the second dimension. Observe that each offspring gets respectively the first interval (i.e., that of the first attribute) from one parent and the second interval from the other parent.

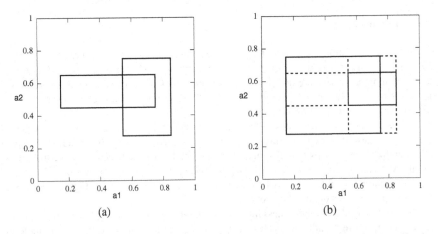

(a)   (b)

Fig. 6.2. A crossover example: (a) plots for two parent individuals; (b) plots for the offspring resulting from a cut point occurring between the first and the second interval.

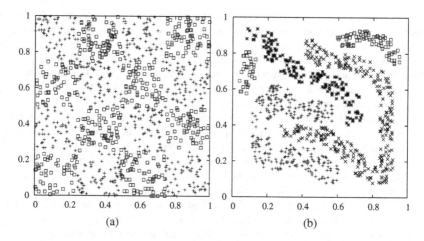

Fig. 6.3. Distribution of training points in the checkerboard problem (a) and the four-class problem (b).

If the recombination operators result in an invalid interval, either exceeding the [0,1] range or violating the condition $l_i \leq u_i$, then a repair process is applied so that the interval is restricted to a valid one.

6.5 Evolving Class Boundaries: Two Case Studies

We study XCS's behavior in two artificial problems: the checkerboard problem (depicted in Fig. 6.3a) and the four-class problem (Fig. 6.3b). The checkerboard problem is designed to test XCS on a case of multiple distributed classification regions. It has two classes alternating as in a checkerboard. The four-class problem is designed to test XCS in problems with multiple classes and curved boundaries. Figure 6.3 shows the distribution of the training points in each problem. Each point is plotted with a different symbol depending on the class to which it belongs. We analyze XCS's behavior in these problems, and compare its performance with a nearest neighbor (NN) classifier. We aim to show that classification problems may present different degrees of difficulty to different classifiers. We restrict the analysis to two-feature problems so that we can have a graphical representation of the results of each classifier.

To analyze the classification boundaries evolved by each classifier, we train a classifier with the training points depicted in Figure 6.3. Then we test the classifier with a dense data set that samples the feature space with 10,000 points distributed uniformly. XCS is run with the following parameter settings (see [11] for the terminology): $reward = 1000/0$, $N = 6400$, explore trials $= 200,000$, $\theta_{mna} =$ number of actions, $\beta = 0.2$, $\epsilon_0 = 1.0$, $\alpha = 0.1$, $\nu = 5$, $\theta_{GA} = 25$, $\chi = 0.8$, $\mu = 0.04$, $\theta_{del} = 20$, $\delta = 0.1$, $doGASubsumption = yes$, $doActionSetSubsumption = no$, $\theta_{sub} = 30$, $r_0 = 0.6$, and $m_0 = 0.1$. The NN is designed with neighborhood 1 and Euclidian distance.

Figure 6.4a,c shows the classification boundaries obtained by XCS. In the checkerboard problem, XCS has evolved an accurate representation of the feature space. The boundaries almost correspond to the true boundaries of the problem. This is a case where the hyperrectangle representation fits very well, which coupled with the learning mechanisms of XCS, allows

XCS to extract a good knowledge representation. In the four-class problem, XCS approximates the curved boundaries by partially overlapping several hyperrectangles. The resulting boundaries are less natural than the original training set, due to this knowledge representation. The generalization mechanisms of XCS result in complete coverage of the feature space, although there are no representative training points in all the feature space. This means that rules tend to expand as much as possible until they reach the boundaries with points belonging to different classes. Figure 6.4b,d shows the same test performed on a nearest neighbor classifier, whose representation based on the Voronoi cells is more suitable to the four-class problem but less appropriate for the checkerboard problem. The result is that classification accuracy in both classifiers is different; in the checkerboard problem, XCS's error is 0.6%, while NN's error is 0.7%; in the four-class problem, XCS's error is 1.9% and NN's error is 0.06%.

The classifier's behavior depends on the geometrical complexity of boundaries and the capability of the knowledge representation to approximate these boundaries. In XCS, as also happens with most of the classifiers, the error rate depends on both the knowledge representation and the ability of the search mechanisms to evolve it. Although a knowledge representation may fit perfectly, the algorithms of XCS may not find the appropriate rules. This especially tends to happen with imbalanced problems, i.e., when there are regions of the search space with very few examples. The generalization algorithms of XCS may mask these regions by overgeneral rules (see [4]).

We emphasize the need to characterize XCS's behavior on computable measures of problem complexity and relate the differences between classifiers to these measures. The study performed in the next section takes this approach. The study is tied to XCS using the hyperrectangle representation, so we include the limitations of the search algorithms coupled with the hyperrectangle constraints.

6.6 How XCS Adapts to Data Complexity

We study how XCS's behavior depends on data complexity. First, we aim to relate XCS's performance to measures of problem complexity and identify easy and difficult domains for XCS. Such an study could serve to give an expectation of accuracy for XCS given a classification problem with computed complexity measures. We also want to establish the relation between XCS's performance and that of other classifiers in the complexity measurement space. The final aim is to identify areas of the measurement space where XCS excels among other classifiers. Thus, given a problem with its complexity characterization, we could either recommend XCS as a suitable classifier or discard XCS in favor of other better approaches.

6.6.1 Analysis Procedure

We characterize the complexity of a classification problem by a set of measures that describe different aspects of boundary complexity. We rely on the study by Ho and Basu [17] where a suite of metrics is proposed and analyzed as measurements of problem complexity. These metrics are found to quantify the complexity of problems so that easy problems (such as linearly separable problems) and difficult problems (such as random labeling problems) represent two extremes of the complexity space, with different problems spanning through these extremes. From this study, we select seven metrics representative of the most relevant aspects of complexity. These are enumerated in Table 6.1. They describe different geometrical distributions of class boundaries, such as boundary, intra-inter, nonlin-NN, nonlin-LP, and

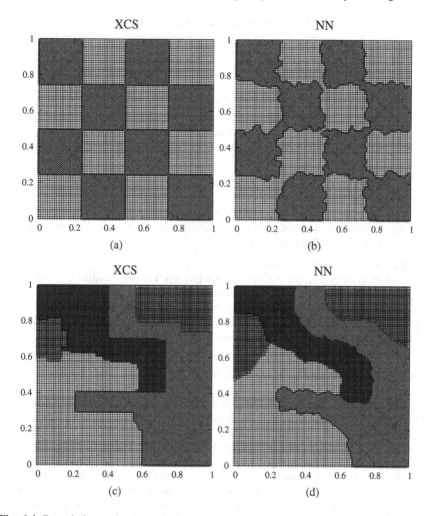

Fig. 6.4. Boundaries evolved by (a) XCS and (b) NN in the checkerboard problem, and (c) XCS and (d) NN in the four-class problem.

pretop, as well as the discriminant power of attributes (fisher). We include the ratio of the number of points to the number of dimensions (npts-ndim) as an estimation of sparsity. All these metrics are computed from the available training sets, so that they give measurements of the apparent complexity of problems.

We evaluate XCS on a set of 392 two-class problems. These problems are generated from pairwise comparisons of 14 problems from the University of California, Irvine (UCI) repository [7] containing at least 500 points with no missing values. These are *abalone*, *car*, *german*, *kr-vs-kp*, *letter*, *lrs*, *nursery*, *pima*, *segmentation*, *splice*, *tic-tac-toe*, *vehicle*, *wdbc*, and *yeast*. Their pairwise comparisons result in 844 two-class problems, 452 of which are discarded for being linearly separable problems. The remaining 392 are used as our test-bed. All the

Table 6.1. Complexity metrics used in this study

Measure	Description
boundary	Percentage of points on boundary estimated by an MST
intra-inter	Ratio of average intra-inter class nearest neighbor distances
nonlin-NN	Nonlinearity of nearest neighbor
nonlin-LP	Nonlinearity of linear classifier
pretop	Percentage of points with maximal adherence subset retained
fisher	Maximum Fisher's discriminant ratio
npts-ndim	Ratio of the number of points to the number of dimensions

categorical values are translated into numerical values. Therefore, XCS is using only the hyperrectangle representation.

We measure the relation between XCS's error and data complexity, which is characterized by a set of seven metrics. To estimate the classifier's error, we use a ten-pass twofold cross-validation test. The detailed steps are as follows:

1. Each data set is randomly permuted ten times.
2. Each time, the data set is divided in two disjoints sets. Then the classifier is trained in each of these two sets and tested on the other one. The error rate for this particular permutation is estimated as the sum of the errors on each half, divided by the data set size.
3. Thus, for each data set there are ten error estimates, one for each permutation. The final XCS's error on the data set is the average of these ten error rates.

6.6.2 XCS's Error and Data Complexity

Figure 6.5 plots XCS's error related to each of the complexity measures. The y axis depicts the error of XCS for a given problem, while the x axis is one of the complexity metrics.

We observe a clear dependency (almost a linear correlation) of XCS's error rate with respect to the percentage of points in boundary. Since this behavior is also observed in other classifiers (not shown, for brevity), it seems that the percentage of points of boundary is a good measure for data complexity. Nevertheless, there are some exceptions to this behavior where XCS performs reasonably well despite a high number of points in boundary. These cases are *car (acc vs. good)*, *kr-vs.-kp (no-win vs. won)*, *nursery (priority vs. spec_prior)*, and *tic-tac-toe (neg vs. pos)*. As shown in Table 6.2, these cases belong to very low nonlinearities. This suggests that the combined effect of different measures may be necessary to explain data complexity.

Other metrics are also relevant for XCS's performance. These are the intra-interclass NN distances ratio and the nonlinearities. A high value of intra-interclass ratio means that the classes are very dispersed with respect to the class groupings. Also the nonlinearities impose a degree of difficulty for XCS. If the nonlinearity is high, it probably means that the classes are very interleaved. In both cases, the complex distribution of class groupings makes XCS evolve a high number of small rules, i.e., specialized rules with few possible generalizations, producing higher classification errors.

The remaining metrics do not influence XCS's error in the same way as before. For example, the highest XCS's error rates correspond to high percentages of retained adherence subsets (pretop), but the converse is not true; a high pretop value does not imply necessarily a high error. On the contrary, low values on the pretop measure always give low XCS's error rates.

Table 6.2. Four easy problems for XCS despite having moderate boundary values. The table shows the values of the complexity measures for each of the problems.

	car acc-good	kr-vs.-kp nowin-won	nursery pr-sp	tic-tac-toe neg-pos
boundary	33.11	20.49	22.90	32.99
intra-inter	0.87	0.71	0.96	0.96
nonlin-NN	0.00	0.00	0.00	0.00
nonlin-LP	0.93	0.79	5.14	1.67
pretop	100.00	100.00	100.00	100.00
fisher	0.47	0.54	0.38	0.28
npts	453	3196	8310	958
ndim	21	73	27	27
npts-ndim	21.57	43.78	307.78	35.48
XCS's error	1.96	4.82	1.19	2.00

The error rate of XCS depends neither directly on the ratio between the number of points nor the number of dimensions of the data set. We can observe only that there are some problems where the XCS's error rate is high (greater than 40%), which corresponds to a ratio npts-ndim below 50%. In fact, the ratio of the number of points to the number of dimensions is a rough estimate of the sparsity of the training set, so it is difficult to relate XCS's error to the training set sparsity.

High values of the maximum Fisher's discriminant ratio indicate that there is an attribute discriminating fairly well. The higher this value, the easier the problem. This is consistent with our results with XCS. Observe that high values of this metric (greater than 3) always correspond to low error rates. The converse is not necessarily true. A low value of fisher does not lead necessarily to high error rates. However, note that the highest error rates all belong to low fisher values.

Trying to identify easy and difficult domains for XCS, we have classified our current set of problems in four types: the most difficult problems (XCS's error ≥45%), difficult problems (XCS's error ≥40%), easy problems (XCS's error ≤10%), and the easiest problems (XCS's error ≤5%). Table 6.3 gives the mean and standard deviation of the complexity metrics for these types of problems. Note that if we move from difficult problems to easy problems, the percentage of points in the boundary decreases dramatically, as well as the nonlinearities. Also the intra-interclass NN distances decrease in the easy problems. The maximum Fisher's discriminant ratio tends to be higher for low error rates. Similarly, the ratio of the number of points to the number of dimensions is higher for the easiest problems. The percentage of retained adherence subsets is very similar in the three types of problems, although a bit higher for the most difficult problems.

In summary, the highest error rates correspond to problems with a high percentage of points in the boundary between classes, a high percentage of retained adherence subsets, high training set sparsity, high values of intra-interclass distances, high nonlinearities of NN and LP, and low Fisher values. The easiest problems correspond to a small percentage of points in the boundary, low nonlinearities (both NN and LP), low values of intra-interclass NN distances, and a varied range over percentage of adherence subsets, fisher, and npts-ndim values.

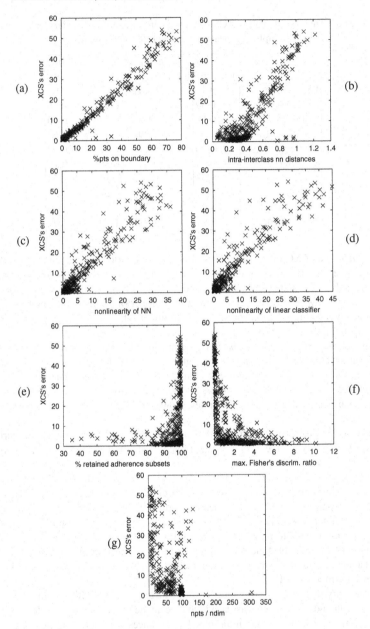

Fig. 6.5. Relation between XCS's error and data complexity. The y axis shows the error of XCS, and the x axis shows, respectively, the following complexity metrics: (a) the percentage of points in the boundary, (b) the ratio of intra-interclass nearest neighbor distances, (c) the nonlinearity of the nearest neighbor, (d) the nonlinearity of the linear classifier, (e) the percentage of retained adherence subsets, (f) the maximum Fisher's discriminant ratio, and (g) the ratio of the number of points to the number of dimensions.

Table 6.3. Four groups of problems, classified according to XCS's error rates. For each group, we show the mean and standard deviation of each complexity metric.

| | $error \geq 45\%$ | | $error \geq 40\%$ | | $error \leq 10\%$ | | $error \leq 5\%$ | |
	mean	std	mean	std	mean	std	mean	std
boundary	67.13	7.29	65.01	6.72	4.03	5.12	2.56	3.94
intra-inter	0.99	0.11	0.98	0.097	0.30	0.12	0.30	0.12
nonlin-NN	27.78	3.48	27.80	4.23	1.88	1.80	1.48	1.21
nonlin-LP	34.38	7.00	32.14	7.65	1.42	1.80	1.02	1.45
pretop	99.62	0.57	99.51	0.72	92.05	10.32	92.69	9.49
fisher	0.06	0.089	0.06	0.075	2.69	1.90	2.82	1.92
npts	213.31	240.79	288.86	347.36	1268.57	685.80	1411.58	642.56
ndim	10.88	3.50	10.79	2.99	14.56	4.78	15.42	4.65
npts-ndim	17.69	13.43	26.12	31.79	83.10	27.81	89.26	24.09
No. of data sets	16		28		281		238	

6.6.3 On the Domain of Competence of XCS

The previous section identified easy and difficult domains for XCS. Here we want to analyze whether other classifiers can perform better or worse than XCS in the current set of problems and identify where these cases are located in the complexity measurement space.

We have chosen an initial set of five classifiers:

- A nearest neighbor classifier (nn), with neighborhood set to 1 and Euclidian distance [1].
- A linear classifier (lc) computed by linear programming using the AMPL software [24]. It separates the classes by linear boundaries.
- A decision tree (odt) using oblique hyperplanes [22]. The hyperplanes are derived using a simplified Fisher's method, as described in [16].
- A subspace decision forest (pdfc), which trains oblique trees on sampled feature subsets and combines them by averaging the posterior leaf probabilities [16].
- A subsample decision forest (bdfc), also known as bagged decision trees, which trains oblique trees on sampled training subsets and then combines the result by averaging the posterior leaf probabilities [8].

Decision forests belong to the category of classifier ensemble methods. They are known to outperform decision trees in a varied range of domains. Their comparison with XCS aims to identify the relation between the behavior of classifier combination methods and XCS.

In reference [5], pairwise comparisons of XCS with each classifier enabled identifying regions of the measurement space where XCS was better, equivalent, or worse than each particular classifier. Here we take a different approach; we analyze for each problem which is the best classifier and the worst classifier (from those mentioned above including XCS) and compare XCS with their results. This tells us where XCS excels among the classifiers and where XCS is the worst method. The results are tied to the particular set of classifiers; as a future effort, we plan to add other well-known classifiers, such as neural networks, support vector machines, boosting ensembles, and stochastic discrimination.

The methodology is the following:

1. For each problem and each method, we estimate the error rate by a ten-pass twofold cross-validation test, as explained in section 6.2.

Table 6.4. Mean and standard deviation of complexity metrics for problems where XCS performs as the best classifier, as an "average" classifier, and as the worst classifier. Last row shows the percentage of problems in each case.

Metric	Best		Average		Worst	
	mean	*std*	*mean*	*std*	*mean*	*std*
boundary	17.53	19.17	9.21	16.30	33.79	22.72
intra-inter	0.40	0.28	0.37	0.18	0.60	0.29
nonlin-NN	6.14	8.50	4.36	7.04	13.64	10.03
nonlin-LP	6.26	10.02	4.07	7.83	14.89	12.10
pretop	89.90	14.76	94.85	6.12	94.12	10.40
fisher	2.11	2.45	2.39	1.69	0.86	1.64
npts-ndim	57.66	45.16	84.88	25.16	33.38	25.22
Problems (%)	19%		64%		17%	

2. For each problem, we consider the classifier with the lowest mean error. Then, we span the ten error estimates of the best method, and compare all other classifiers with these values by means of a paired t-test with a 95% confidence level.
3. The same procedure is used to find the *worst* method of each problem and test the remaining methods against it.

Figure 6.6 shows where XCS performs equivalently to the best classifier (marked by a circle), equivalently to the worst classifier (marked by a cross), and the remaining cases (denoted by a small plus sign). The plots show XCS's error against selected projections of the measurement space. Figure 6.6a shows XCS's error against the percentage of points in the boundary, plotted in a logarithmic scale. Observe that for very low boundary values, XCS is in the average methods. For larger values, a range of problems correspond to a higher proportion of XCS performing as the best classifier. And while the boundary metric is increasing, the percentage of problems where XCS is best diminishes while the problems where XCS is worst increase. The problems where XCS is best also correspond to low nonlinearities (Fig. 6.6c) and low ratio of intra-interclass NN distances (Fig. 6.6b). The fisher metric is higher where XCS is best (Fig. 6.6d), while the sparsity of the training set (npts-ndim) tends to be smaller (Fig. 6.6e). Figure 6.6f shows XCS's performance in a projection of two combined metrics: the percentage of points in boundary vs. the percentage of retained adherence subsets. This plot separates more clearly the three types of problems: problems where XCS performs in the average are located in boundary values under 2% and high pretop values. In these cases, the nearest neighbor was shown to perform better than XCS [5]. There is another range of problems for which XCS is the best method that are mainly located in boundary values between 2% and 20%, with a varied range of pretop. Finally, for boundary values higher than 20% and high pretop values, XCS is the worst method or equivalent to the worst. The plot also reveals gaps in the measurement space. We are currently investigating if they correspond to constraints imposed by the current pool of data sets or they reflect some geometrical and topological constraints tied to our complexity measurement space. Table 6.4 complements these observations by averaging the complexity measurements in the three types of problems.

6.7 Conclusion

XCS is an evolutionary learning classifier system that evolves a set of rules describing the target concept. Rules are incrementally evaluated by means of a reinforcement learning scheme

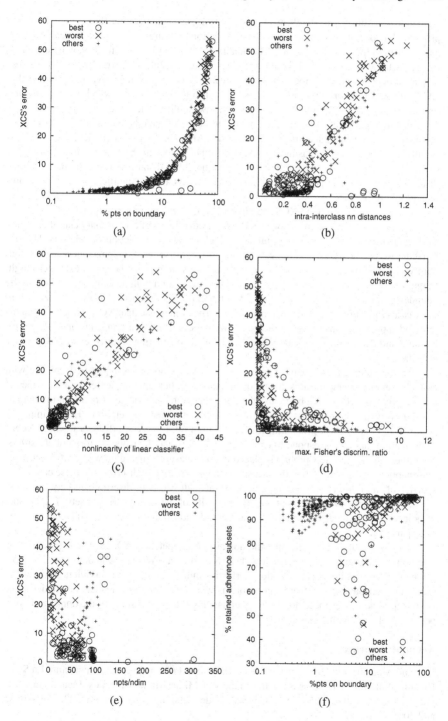

Fig. 6.6. Distribution of problems where XCS is the best method (plotted with a ⊙), the worst method (plotted with a ×), and the remaining problems (plotted with a small +).

and improved through a search mechanism based on a genetic algorithm. Through an appropriate balance of generalization and specialization pressures, rules cover the feature space approximating the class boundaries. The quality of the rule set approximation will depend on the geometrical distribution of these boundaries. Thus we studied to what degree XCS's performance depends on it. Using computable measures of data complexity, we identified that XCS's error is low for very compact classes, with little interleaving, which is characterized by a low percentage of points in the boundary, low nonlinearities, and low nearest neighbor distances with points of the same class related to points of the other classes. Problems with a dominant discriminating feature tend to be easier. Moving along the complexity axis, XCS's performance becomes increasingly worse for higher points in the class boundaries, higher nonlinearities, and higher intra-interclass nearest neighbor distances. The maximum Fisher's discriminating ratio and percentage of adherence subsets are not significant in setting a complex problem for XCS.

We centered our study on XCS, because it is one of the best representatives of evolutionary learning classifier systems. However, there are other types of evolutionary classifiers, such as those based on the Pittsburgh approach, which evolve a population of rule sets. Usually Pittsburgh-type classifiers tend to evolve a low number of rules. Problems that require a high number of rules will be difficult for them, since the search space becomes extremely high. Large rule sets will be needed for dispersed classes, i.e., for a high percentage of points in the boundary, high nonlinearities, and high intra-interclass NN distances. We hypothesize that in these cases Pittsburgh classifiers will perform poorly, even worse than XCS, while they can offer good approximations for easier problems. We believe that the current study on evolutionary learning and data complexity can be much enhanced considering other types of evolutionary classifiers.

We also studied the domain of competence of XCS, by comparing its performance with that of other classifiers: a nearest neighbor, a linear classifier, an oblique tree, and two types of decision forests. XCS is the best classifier for a moderate percentage of points in the boundary. For very low boundaries, XCS is overcome by the nearest neighbor. High number of points in the boundary, high nonlinearities, and high intra-interclass distances, where XCS's error is high, mainly correspond to cases where XCS is one the worst performing classifiers. Nevertheless, there are few problems placed in this measurement region where XCS performs reasonably well, indicating that the measures may not suffice to discriminate these cases. The sparsity of the training set may be an important factor to help discriminate between these cases, although we cannot compute the true sparsity of the real-world data sets. The number of points to the number of dimensions has been demonstrated to be a rough estimate of the true sparsity.

The current study has estimated the domain of competence of XCS, leaving many open questions related to the other classifiers' behavior, such as: What are the domains of competence of other classifiers? Do classifiers perform similarly or are some classifiers significantly dominant over others? Are there any problems where several classifiers can be applied? The next chapter addresses these questions by enhancing the current study to the domain of competence of the remaining classifiers.

Acknowledgments

Bernadó-Mansilla and Orriols acknowledge the support of Enginyeria i Arquitectura La Salle, Ramon Llull University, as well as the support of Ministerio de Ciencia y Tecnología under grant TIC2002-04036-C05-03 and Generalitat de Catalunya under grants 2002SGR-00155 and 2005FI-00252.

References

[1] D.W. Aha, D. Kibler, M.K. Albert. Instance-based learning algorithms. *Machine Learning*, 6, 37–66, 1991.

[2] J. Bacardit. *Pittsburgh genetic-based machine learning in the data mining era: representations, generalization and run-time*. Ph.D. thesis, Enginyeria i Arquitectura La Salle, Ramon Llull University, Barcelona, Spain, 2004.

[3] J. Bacardit, M.V. Butz. Data mining in learning classifier systems: comparing XCS with GAssist. In *Seventh International Workshop on Learning Classifier Systems (IWLCS-2004)*, Seattle, WA, June 26, 2004.

[4] E. Bernadó-Mansilla, J.M. Garrell Guiu. Accuracy-based learning classifier systems: models, analysis and applications to classification tasks. *Evolutionary Computation*, 11(3), 209–238, 2003.

[5] E. Bernadó-Mansilla, T.K. Ho. Domain of competence of XCS classifier system in complexity measurement space. *IEEE Transactions on Evolutionary Computation*, 9(1), 82–104, 2005.

[6] E. Bernadó-Mansilla, X. L. Fàbrega, J.M. Garrell Guiu. XCS and GALE: a comparative study of two learning classifier systems on data mining. In P.L. Lanzi, W. Stolzmann, S.W. Wilson, eds. *Advances in Learning Classifier Systems, 4th International Workshop*, volume 2321 of *Lecture Notes in Computer Science*, pages 115–132. New York:Springer, 2002.

[7] C.L. Blake, C.J. Merz. UCI Repository of machine learning databases, [http://www.ics.uci.edu/~mlearn/MLRepository.html]. University of California, Irvine, Department of Information and Computer Sciences, 1998.

[8] L. Breiman. Bagging predictors. *Machine Learning*, 24, 123–140, 1996.

[9] M.V. Butz, M. Pelikan. Analyzing the Evolutionary Pressures in XCS. In L. Spector, E.D. Goodman, A. Wu, et al., eds. *Proceedings of the Genetic and Evolutionary Computation Conference (GECCO'2001)*, pages 935–942. San Francisco: Morgan Kaufmann, 2001.

[10] M.V. Butz. *Rule-based evolutionary online learning systems: learning bounds, classification, and prediction*. Ph.D. thesis, University of Illinois, 2004.

[11] M.V. Butz, S.W. Wilson. An algorithmic description of XCS. In P.L. Lanzi, W. Stolzmann, S.W. Wilson, eds. *Advances in Learning Classifier Systems: Proceedings of the Third International Workshop*, volume 1996 of *Lecture Notes in Artificial Intelligence*, pages 253–272. Berlin, Heidelberg:Springer-Verlag, 2001.

[12] E. Cantú-Paz, C. Kamath. Inducing oblique decision trees with evolutionary algorithms. *IEEE Transactions on Evolutionary Computation*, 7(1), 54–68, 2003.

[13] K.A. De Jong, W.M. Spears, D.F. Gordon. Using genetic algorithms for concept learning. *Genetic Algorithms for Machine Learning (John J. Grefenstette ed.), A Special Issue of Machine Learning*, 13,2-3, 161–188, 1993.

[14] D.E. Goldberg. *Genetic Algorithms in Search, Optimization and Machine Learning*. New York, Addison-Wesley, 1989.

[15] D.E. Goldberg. *The Design of Innovation. Lessons from and for Competent Genetic Algorithms*. Kluwer Academic Publishers, 2002.

[16] T.K. Ho. The random subspace method for constructing decision forests. *IEEE Transactions on Pattern Analysis and Machine Intelligence*, 20(8), 832–844, 1998.

[17] T.K. Ho, M. Basu. Complexity measures of supervised classification problems. *IEEE Transactions on Pattern Analysis and Machine Intelligence*, 24(3), 289–300, 2002.

[18] J.H. Holland. *Adaptation in Natural and Artificial Systems*. Ann Arbor:University of Michigan Press, 1975.

[19] P.L. Lanzi. Extending the representation of classifier conditions. Part I: from binary to messy coding. In W. Banzhaf, J. Daida, A.E. Eiben, et al., eds. *Proceedings of the Genetic and Evolutionary Computation Conference, (GECCO-99)*, pages 337–344. San Francisco:Morgan Kaufmann, 1999.

[20] P.L. Lanzi. Extending the representation of classifier conditions. Part II: from messy coding to S-expressions. In W. Banzhaf, J. Daida, A.E. Eiben, et al., eds. *Proceedings of the Genetic and Evolutionary Computation Conference, (GECCO-99)*, pages 345–352. San Francisco:Morgan Kaufmann, 1999.

[21] X. Llorà, J.M. Garrell Guiu. Co-evolving different knowledge representations with fine-grained parallel learning classifier systems. In *Proceedings of the Genetic and Evolutionary Computation Conference (GECCO2002)*, pages 934–941. San Francisco:Morgan Kaufmann, 2002.

[22] S. Murthy, S. Kasif, S. Salzberg. A system for induction of oblique decision trees. *Journal of Artificial Intelligence Research*, 2(1), 1–32, 1994.

[23] J.D. Schaffer. Combinations of genetic algorithms with neural netwoks or fuzzy systems. In J.M. Zurada, R.J. Marks, J. Marks, II, C.J. Robinson, eds. *Computational Intelligence Imitating Life*, pages 371–382. New York: IEEE Press, 1994.

[24] F.W. Smith. Pattern classifier design by linear programming. *IEEE Transactions on Computers*, C-17, 367–372, 1968.

[25] C. Stone, L. Bull. For real! XCS with continuous-valued inputs. *Evolutionary Computation*, 11(3), 299–336, 2003.

[26] S.W. Wilson. Classifier fitness based on accuracy. *Evolutionary Computation*, 3(2), 149–175, 1995.

[27] S.W. Wilson. Generalization in the XCS classifier system. In J.R. Koza, W. Banzhaf, K. Chellapilla, et al., eds. *Genetic Programming: Proceedings of the Third Annual Conference*. San Francisco: Morgan Kaufmann, 1998.

[28] S.W. Wilson. Get real! XCS with continuous-valued inputs. In L. Booker, S. Forrest, M. Mitchell, R. Riolo, eds. *Festschrift in Honor of John H. Holland*, pages 111–121. Center for the Study of Complex Systems, University of Michigan, 1999.

[29] X. Yao. Evolving artificial neural networks. *Proceedings of the IEEE*, 87(9), 1423–1447, 1999.

7

Classifier Domains of Competence in Data Complexity Space

Tin Kam Ho and Ester Bernadó-Mansilla

Summary. We study the domain of competence of a set of popular classifiers, by means of a methodology that relates the classifier's behavior to problem complexity. We find that the simplest classifiers—the nearest neighbor and the linear classifier—have extreme behavior in the sense that they mostly behave either as the best approach for certain types of problems or as the worst approach for other types of problems. We also identify that the domain of competence of the nearest neighbor is almost opposed to that of the linear classifier. Ensemble methods such as decision forests are not outstanding in any particular set of problems but perform more robustly in general. A by-product of this study is the identification of the features of a classification task that are most relevant in optimal classifier selection.

7.1 Introduction

Research in pattern recognition and machine learning has yielded many competent classifiers from different families, including decision trees, decision forests, support vector machines, neural networks, and genetic algorithms, in addition to traditional methods like Bayesian and nearest neighbor classifiers. Researchers have often demonstrated the competence and robustness of such classifiers across different domains. Nevertheless, the practitioner may find it difficult to choose a particular classifier for a given problem, due to the great variability of classifiers and a lack of knowledge on the optimal classifier family for the given problem. Many classifiers appear in close rivalry in benchmark problems. Which one can be selected? Many seem applicable to a wide range of problems, but will they also be suitable to the given problem?

The analysis of data complexity sets a framework to characterize the problem and identify domains of competence of classifiers. In Ho and Basu [8] a methodology is introduced by which classification problems are characterized by a set of complexity measures. This characterization facilitates identifying easy problems (close to linearly separable problems) and difficult problems (close to random labeling) in the complexity measurement space. Derivations of this study led to relating the behavior of classifiers to problem complexity. The first attempt is made in Ho [7], where two decision forests are compared to identify for which problems each is preferable. Chapter 6 studied the behavior of a particular classifier based on genetic algorithms called XCS. The study identifies the domain of competence of XCS compared with a set of other classifiers. In this chapter, we extend this analysis to study the domain of competence of different classifiers.

We investigate the domain of competence of six popular classifiers in the complexity measurement space, and compare these domains to identify which classifiers are optimal for certain classes of problems. We include classifiers as diverse as a nearest neighbor, a linear classifier, an oblique decision tree, two types of decision forests, and XCS. We also analyze whether different classifiers have opposed domains of applicability or some of them perform similarly. Ensemble methods are shown to outperform single classifiers, but we aim to establish if single classifiers are still suitable to certain types of problems. Along this analysis we will validate the current measurement space and identify the set of complexity metrics most relevant for the identification of optimal classifiers.

This chapter is structured as follows. First, we describe the methodology that we use to analyze the domain of competence of classifiers. Although this methodology is essentially the same as that described in the last chapter, we summarize it here to make the chapter self-contained. Section 7.3 analyzes where each classifier performs optimally and poorly. Section 7.4 takes a different view and analyzes the problems with a single dominant classifier and a single worst classifier. Section 7.5 discusses the limitations of the current study and directions to overcome them. Section 7.6 gives the main conclusions.

7.2 Analysis Methodology

We characterize a classification problem by a set of complexity metrics. Table 7.1 summarizes the set of metrics used in our study. They are selected from Ho and Basu [8] for being the best representatives of problem complexity. They describe different geometrical distributions of class boundaries, such as `boundary`, `intra-inter`, `nonlin-NN`, `nonlin-LP`, `pretop`, as well as the discriminant power of attributes (`fisher`, `max-eff`, and `volume-overlap`). We include the ratio of the number of points to the number of dimensions (`npts-ndim`) as an estimation of sparsity. All these metrics are computed from the available training sets; therefore, they give measurements of the apparent complexity of problems.

Table 7.1. Complexity metrics used in this study

Measure	Description
boundary	Percentage of points on boundary estimated by an MST (minimum spanning tree)
intra-inter	Ratio of average intra-interclass nearest neighbor distances
nonlin-NN	Nonlinearity of nearest neighbor
nonlin-LP	Nonlinearity of linear classifier
pretop	Percentage of points with maximal adherence subset retained
fisher	Maximum Fisher's discriminant ratio
max-eff	Maximum individual feature efficiency
volume-overlap	Volume of overlap region of class bounding boxes
npts-ndim	Ratio of the number of points to the number of dimensions

We study the domain of competence of six classifiers:

- A nearest neighbor classifier (nn), with neighborhood set to 1 and Euclidian distance [1]

- A linear classifier (lc) computed by linear programming using the AMPL software [10]
- A decision tree (odt) using oblique hyperplanes [9]; the hyperplanes are derived using a simplified Fisher's method, as described in Ho [6]
- A subspace decision forest (pdfc), which trains oblique trees on sampled feature subsets and combines them by averaging the posterior leaf probabilities [6]
- A subsample decision forest (bdfc), also known as bagged decision trees, which trains oblique trees on sampled training subsets and then combines the result by averaging the posterior leaf probabilities [5]
- XCS, an evolutionary learning classifier [11, 12]

They have been selected for representing different families of classifiers. The nearest neighbor, the linear classifier, and the single tree are traditional well-known classifiers. The forests belong to the category of classifier combination. They train several decision trees by subsampling either the training points (bdfc) or the features (pdfc). They are known to outperform single trees. XCS evolves a set of rules by means of a genetic algorithm. This particular selection facilitates studying whether ensemble methods are always preferable to individual classifiers or, on the contrary, whether there are still cases where single classifiers can be applied, and if so, where these cases are located in the measurement space. We do not pretend to have a fully representative set of classifiers. Rather, we want to try the methodology with an initial subset of classifiers and expand this study to other popular classifiers once the methodology becomes mature.

We evaluate each classifier in a set of 392 two-class problems, extracted from the University of California, Irvine (UCI) repository [4], as explained in the previous chapter. For each problem, we estimate its complexity by computing each of the complexity metrics on the whole available data set. We run each classifier using a ten-pass, twofold cross-validation test and identify the best and worst classifier for each problem. Then, we compare each classifier against them respectively. Details are as follows:

1. Each data set is randomly permuted ten times.
2. Each time, the data set is divided in two disjoints sets. Then each classifier is trained in each of these two sets and tested on the other one. The classifier's error rate for this particular permutation is estimated as the sum of the errors on each test set, divided by the data-set size.
3. Thus, for each data set there are ten error estimates, one for each permutation. The final classifier's error on the data set is the average of its ten error rates.
4. For each problem, we identify the classifier with the lowest mean error. Then, we use its ten error estimates as the basis for comparison with the other classifiers, using a paired t-test with a 95% confidence level. Thus, we identify which classifiers are equivalent to the best method or worse than the best method.
5. The same procedure is used to identify the worst classifier for each problem and test the remaining classifiers against it, so that we identify classifiers equivalent to the worst method or better than the worst method.

We approach the domains of competence of classifiers from two different views. The first one, taken in section 7.3, estimates the domain of competence of each classifier. We analyze where each classifier performs as the best method, and as the worst method, trying to identify types of problems where the classifier is well suited and poorly suited. The second approach, taken in section 7.4, analyzes, for each problem, the set of classifiers that are well suited and poorly suited. Although the views are similar, here we distinguish the problems where there is a single dominant best classifier from problems where more than one classifier is optimal. Thus, we try to determine if there are differences between these types of problems. We also study the problems where a single classifier performs significantly worse and those problems where several classifiers are equivalently poor. This approach was already taken in Bernadó-Mansilla and Ho [3], where the domains of dominant competence were succinctly identified. This study is enhanced here with the addition of the first approach. Both views are necessary to help choose an optimal classifier, given a problem with computed complexity metrics. The results obtained herein are tied to the particular choice of classifiers, so other choices or the inclusion of new classifiers may lead to different results.

7.3 On the Domains of Competence of Classifiers

We analyze where each classifier performs as one of the best methods and as one of the worst methods. We try to relate this to the complexity measurement space so that we can identify domains of competence of classifiers.

We show different projections of the complexity measurement space and plot the classifier's membership to three categories: best, worst, or none of them. We use a circle when the classifier is equivalent to the best method (i.e., it is the best method or its performance is equivalent to the best method on a paired t-test with a 95% confidence level). We use a cross when the classifier is equivalent to the worst method (which means it is the worst classifier or its performance is found to be equivalent to that of the worst classifier). The rest of the problems, where the classifier is neither best nor worst, are shown with a small plus sign.

Nearest Neighbor

Figure 7.1 shows the domain of competence of the nearest neighbor classifier. We find that most of the problems where nn performs optimally belong to very low percentage of points in boundary and low nonlinearities (see Fig. 7.1a). They also tend to be placed in low intra-interclass nearest neighbor distances, as shown in Figure 7.1b, although other problems with low values in this metric do not correspond to an optimal nn's behavior. The remaining metrics do not influence the classifier's behavior significantly. The pretopological measure on the percentage of retained adherence subsets is not very significant to set the nn's behavior, as shown in Figure 7.1c. The discriminant power of the attributes is not significant for determining the nn's behavior; see, for example, the maximum's Fisher discriminant ratio in Figure 7.1b. Analyzing npts-ndim, it seems that almost all the problems where the nn is optimal correspond to high ratios of npts-ndim (about 100, Figure 7.1d). But this is just a coincidence because almost all problems located in this value belong to the letter problem, which all have the same relation of the number of points over the number of dimensions. The problems do not present a uniform distribution over this metric, so it is difficult to extrapolate observations from it. We note that the nn is optimal for the easiest problems; observe that in these cases, the nn's error is very low. We also verified that these problems also correspond to low errors from the remaining classifiers.

Table 7.2 summarizes the number of problems where each classifier is best, worst, and average. We identify that the nearest neighbor has the extreme behavior of either behaving mostly like the best classifier (54% of the problems) or like the worst classifier (34% of the problems). There is a greater tendency to behave optimally, although this may be biased by the current selection of problems. Only in 12% of the problems is the nn an average classifier.

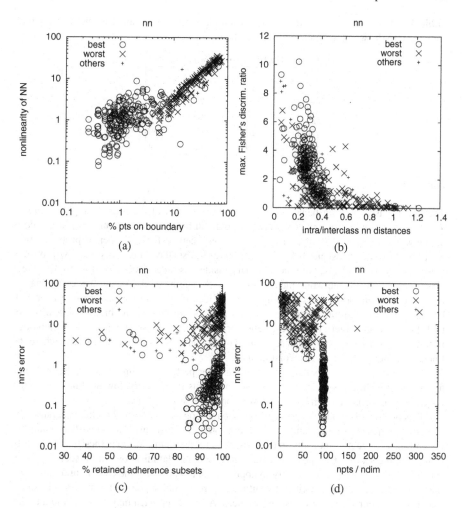

Fig. 7.1. Problems where the nearest neighbor (nn) performs best (⊙), worst (×), and average (+), shown in selected projections of the complexity measurement space: (a) percentage of points in boundary vs. nonlinearity of nn, both in logarithmic scale; (b) intra-interclass nearest neighbor distances vs. maximum Fisher's discriminant ratio; (c) percentage of retained adherence subsets vs. nn's error (in logarithmic scale); and (d) ratio of the number of points to the number of dimensions vs. nn's error (in logarithmic scale).

Table 7.2. Percentage of problems where each classifier is equivalent to the best method, equivalent to the worst method, and none of them.

	Best(%)	Worst (%)	Avg. (%)
nn	54	34	12
lc	33	40	27
odt	3	70	27
pdfc	12	10	78
bdfc	20	11	69
xcs	19	17	64

Linear Classifier

The linear classifier has a behavior almost contrary to that of the nearest neighbor. Figure 7.2 shows that for a very low percentage of points in boundary (less than 10%), it performs as the worst method, while it performs as the best method for a number of problems with boundary values between 10% and 70%. Nevertheless, there are also some few problems with the percentage of points in the boundary inside this range (10%–70%) where the linear classifier performs as the worst method or as an average method. Tracing the lc's behavior along the different projections of complexity, we identify that the lc performs best for high boundary values, high intra-interclass nearest neighbor distances, and high nonlinearities of both the linear classifier and nearest neighbor. But there are also some problems (although in fewer proportions) that are placed in similar regions of the measurement space, where the linear classifier performs as the worst method.

The general tendency is that the linear classifier performs optimally when the problems are more difficult. For very easy problems (few points in boundary, low nonlinearities, etc.) the linear classifier, although having a low error, is the worst method.

This behavior is in fact surprising; one can question how a linear classifier separating the class boundaries by a hyperplane can overcome other more sophisticated classifiers as the decision forests or XCS, especially in the most difficult problems. We hypothesize that sparsity of the training set may be a possible cause, making other classifiers overfit. In sparse training sets, sophisticated classifiers may try to approximate too precisely the class boundaries when these boundaries are not described by sufficient representative points. Then, these classifiers may perform poorly with new unseen instances. A linear approach may be well suited to this type of problem, having less tendency to overfit. The number of points to the number of dimensions tries to approximate the sparsity of the training set. But we find no clear relation between the lc's behavior and this metric, which may indicate that the metric is a rough estimation of the training set sparsity. In fact, the metric can only consider the apparent sparsity of the training set, which may be uncorrelated from the true sparsity. The distribution of points in the available training set might be very different from the original distribution of the problem. As we do not have the original sources of the data sets, we cannot compute the true sparsity for the current set of problems.

Since we find that the linear classifier tends to behave optimally for the most complex problems, where the classifiers' errors are very high, we may also hypothesize that this condition can be due to the presence of noise, i.e., the presence of mislabeled points in these data sets. For these types of problems, a linear classifier may be more robust than other classifiers that try to evolve more complex boundaries, which result in being too overfitted.

The current measurement space is insufficient to distinguish clearly the problems where the linear classifier is best and worst. Although the reasons may be justified by the two previous hypotheses, they may also be due to a lack of metrics describing more precisely the complexity of the problem.

The lc's behavior is somehow extreme too, as found in the case of the nn classifier. Observe that lc is optimal in 33% of cases, and worst in 40% of cases, as shown in Table 7.2.

Decision Tree

The decision tree performs optimally in very few problems; to be exact, in only 12 problems out of 392, which corresponds to a percentage of 3%. In 70% of the problems, the single tree performs as the worst method, while it performs in the average in 27% of the problems, as shown in Table 7.2.

It is difficult to determine for what kind of problems the single tree is best suited. It performs optimally in only 12 problems, which is not sufficient to extrapolate general observations. Moreover, these problems are not compacted in the same area of the measurement space, as can be observed from Figure 7.3. It is also difficult to discriminate between the problems where the single tree performs worst and the problems where the single tree is an average performer.

Subspace Decision Forest

The subspace decision forest improves the behavior of the single tree, in the sense that the forest is more robust in a high proportion of problems. Table 7.2 shows that the subspace forest is an average method in 307 problems (78%), and is best and worst in fewer proportions (12% and 10%, respectively).

Figure 7.4 shows the pdfc's behavior on selected projections of the complexity measurement space. The plots do not show very compact areas of the measurement space to distinguish clearly among the best, average, and worst problems for the subspace decision forest. But the general trend is that a higher percentage of problems where the pdfc performs optimally belong to a small percentage of points in the boundary, and also small nonlinearities and intra-interclass nearest neighbor distances. However, observe that for very few points in boundary and small nonlinearities, the best classifier is the nearest neighbor, as shown in Figure 7.3. For boundary values higher than 30%, there are cases where the pdfc is best and also other cases where the pdfc is worst or average. Other projections of the complexity measurement space do not show any significant discrimination between these three cases.

Subsample Decision Forest

Comparing the subsample forest with the single tree, we find that the subsample forest has more robustness across a high range of problems. In almost 69% of the problems, the subsample decision forest is in the average, being the best method in 20% of problems and the worst in the remaining 11% (see Table 7.2). A similar behavior in terms of robustness is observed with the subspace decision forest.

Nevertheless, it seems that the subspace decision forest and the subsample decision forest do have differences in their domains of competence. Comparing Figure 7.4 with Figure 7.5, we note that the subsample forest is able to be optimal in problems with higher boundary values than the subspace forest. In fact, the average percentage of points in boundary is 14.38% for the problems where the subspace forest is best, and 30.37% for the problems where the subsample forest is best. The same behavior is observed with the nonlinearities. While the

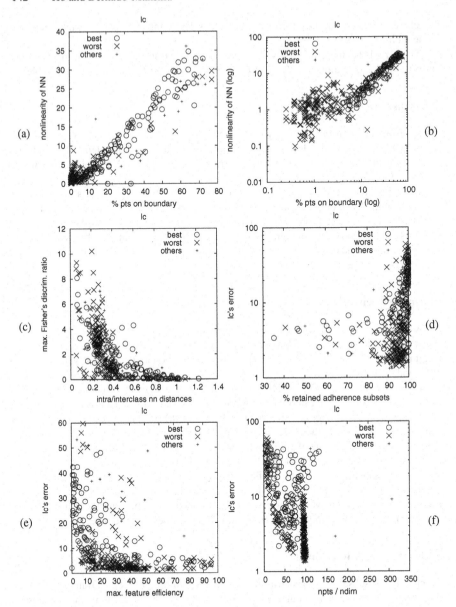

Fig. 7.2. Problems where the linear classifier (lc) performs best (⊙), worst (×), and average (+), shown in selected projections of the complexity measurement space: (a) percentage of points in boundary vs. nonlinearity of nn; (b) percentage of points in boundary vs. nonlinearity of nn, in logarithmic scale; (c) intra-interclass nn distances vs. maximum Fisher's discriminant ratio; (d) percentage of retained adherence subsets vs. lc's error; (e) maximum individual feature efficiency vs. lc's error; and (f) ratio of the number of points to the number of dimensions vs. lc's error.

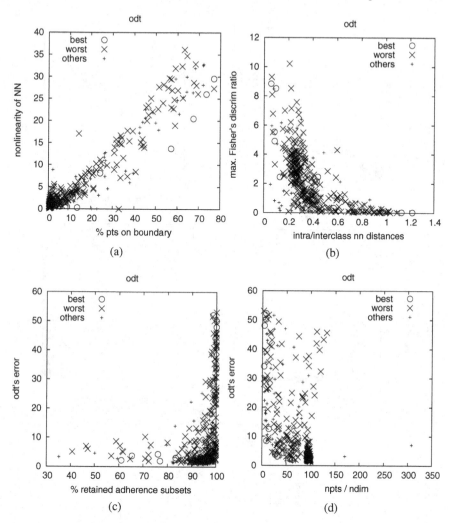

Fig. 7.3. Problems where the single tree (odt) performs best (⊙), worst (×), and average (+), shown in selected projections of the complexity measurement space: (a) percentage of points in boundary vs. nonlinearity of nn; (b) intra-interclass nearest neighbor distances vs. maximum Fisher's discriminant ratio; (c) percentage of retained adherence subsets vs. odt's error; and (d) ratio of the number of points to the number of dimensions vs. odt's error.

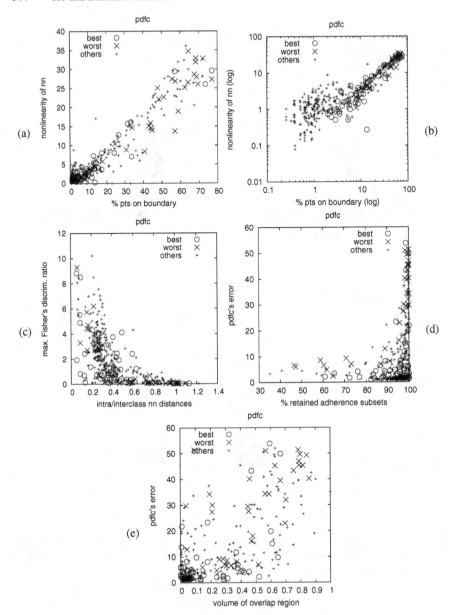

Fig. 7.4. Problems where the subspace decision forest (`pdfc`) performs best (⊙), worst (×), and average (+), shown in selected projections of the complexity measurement space: (a) percentage of points in boundary vs. nonlinearity of `nn`; (b) percentage of points in boundary vs. nonlinearity of `nn` in logarithmic scale; (c) intra-interclass nearest neighbor distances vs. maximum Fisher's discriminant ratio; (d) percentage of retained adherence subsets vs. `pdfc`'s error; and (e) volume of overlap region vs. `pdfc`'s error.

subspace forests work best for low nonlinearities, the subsample forests work best for higher values. This also happens with the ratio of intra-interclass nearest neighbor distances. These results are consistent with previous experiments in the literature [7], where subspace decision forests are compared with subsample decision forests.

XCS

The domain of competence of XCS was analyzed in the previous chapter. Summarizing our results, we found that XCS performs best for low points in boundary. For the lowest percentages of points in boundary, XCS is in the average methods (in these cases, the best classifier is the nearest neighbor). XCS also tends to be optimal for low nonlinearities and low ratios of intra-interclass nn distances. The maximum's Fisher discriminant ratio and the number of points to the number of dimensions tend also to be higher for the problems where XCS is best.

The domain of competence of XCS appears to have similarities with that of the subspace decision forest (see [2]). In fact, we can view XCS as a type of classifier ensemble method, where each classifier contains a rule with generalizations in some attributes, having an effect similar to that of sampling over the feature space.

Comparative Analysis

Figure 7.6 compares jointly the domains of competence of each classifier against some selected metrics. Each column refers to a classifier; from left to right these are the nn, lc, pdfc, bdfc, and XCS. The single tree is omitted because of its scarce contribution as an optimal classifier. Each row plots a particular complexity metric. Each figure shows three box plots summarizing the complexity distribution of each classifier when it performs best (1), worst (2), or average (3). The box plot has a box with lines at the lower quartile, the median, and the upper quartile. Whiskers extend to 1.5 times the box length, and the remaining points are considered as outliers and are plotted with points. The box plot is useful to analyze the ·distribution of each type of problems succinctly, because the ranges and the spread of data can be easily observed. Nevertheless, the number of points in each box plot remains hidden so that this number must be coupled with the previous figures.

Note that the comparison of complexity distributions between the nn and the lc emphasizes again that these classifiers have opposed domains of competence, as seen especially in measures such as boundary, nonlin-NN, intra-inter, and volume-overlap. The fisher metric is not as relevant, although we also observe a tendency for higher discriminant attributes in problems where the nn is best. The decision forests have different domains of competence, being the measures related with class distributions; boundary, nonlin-NN, and intra-inter are the most discriminant ones. XCS's domain of competence appears again very similar to that of the subspace decision forest. Again the three metrics boundary, nonlinNN, and intra-inter show high correlations for the domains where XCS and the subspace decision forests are best and worst.

7.4 Dominant Competence of Classifiers

So far we have studied the problems where each classifier performs best and worst. The approach taken was that of analyzing each classifier separately and relating the results to the

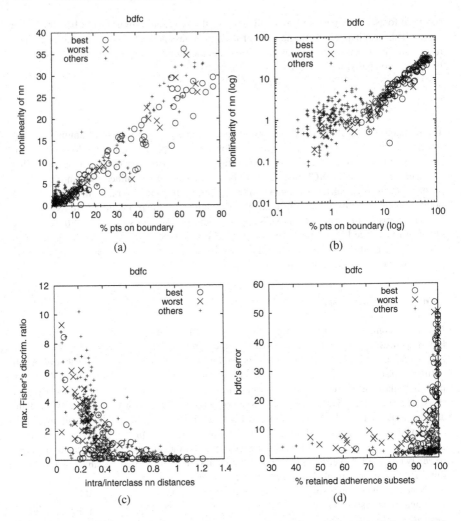

Fig. 7.5. Problems where the subsample decision forest (bdfc) performs best (⊙), worst (×), and average (+), shown in selected projections of the complexity measurement space: (a) percentage of points in boundary vs. nonlinearity of nn; (b) percentage of points in boundary vs. nonlinearity of nn, in logarithmic scale; (c) intra-interclass nearest neighbor distances vs. maximum Fisher's discriminant ratio; and (d) percentage of retained adherence subsets vs. bdfc's error.

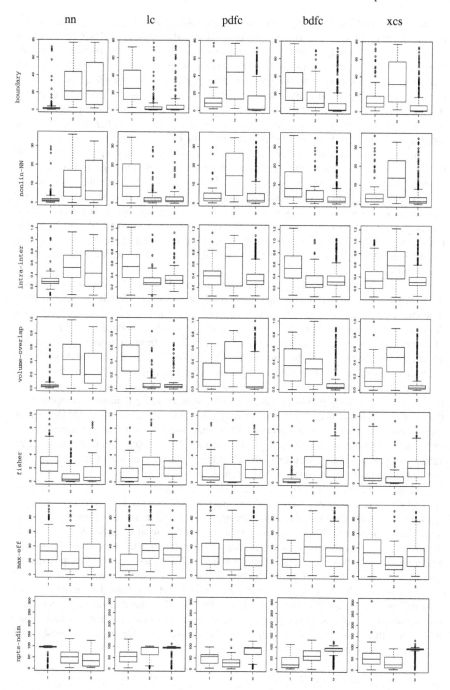

Fig. 7.6. Box plot distributions of best (1), worst (2), and average (3) domains for each classifier, shown in individual projections of the complexity measurement space.

complexity measurement space. In this section, we take a different point of view. We analyze, for each problem, which is the best and worst classifier solving it. Doing this, we have observed that some problems are solved by only one dominant method. In contrast, other problems have more than one outstanding methods. These are problems where several classifiers can obtain good results and therefore their study is less important. Therefore, we will focus on the first types of problems, that is, problems that are solved by only one dominant method. A similar behavior is observed for the worst methods of each problem. Some problems have only one worst classifier, while others have more than one worst classifier. We also analyze which kinds of problems present only one worst classifier.

There are 270 problems that have a dominant best classifier. This represents 69% of all the data sets. Figure 7.7 shows these problems, plotted against selected projections of the measurement space. We use a different symbol for each classifier, as indicated in the legend of each plot. We also show with small dots the location of the problems with more than one optimal classifiers. Note that there are only four methods that are dominant out of six methods. These are the nearest neighbor, the linear classifier, the subsample decision forest, and XCS. The rest of the classifiers (the single tree and the subspace decision forest) are not outstanding in any problem. When they perform as the best method, there are also other methods performing equivalently.

Moreover, it is also interesting to note that almost all these problems are solved predominantly by the nearest neighbor or the linear classifier. Table 7.3 details the proportion of problems where each method is predominantly best and worst. See that the nn classifier is dominantly best in 69% of problems, and worst in 11%. The lc is dominantly best in 23% of problems and worst in 30%. This is significantly different from the forests and XCS; they are almost neither dominantly best nor worst. We can conclude that the nearest neighbor and the linear classifier are very specialized methods, being successful only for specific types of problems. On the other hand, the ensemble methods and XCS are more robust but they are not outstanding in many problems. Figure 7.7 also shows that the domain of competence of the nearest neighbor is placed in a low percentage of points in the boundary, and low nonlinearities. For increasing boundary values, XCS seems to be the best classifier, although for a small range of problems (in boundary values between 2% and 10%). For higher boundary values, there is a range of problems where the linear classifier mostly stands out, but also sometimes, and with less frequency, the subsample forest and XCS stand out.

It is also interesting to compare Figure 7.7a–c with Figure 7.7d–f, which show the problems where there is only one method performing poorly. There are 157 problems with a single worst classifier. Note that the single tree appears very often as the dominant worst classifier, mainly located in low boundary values. Also the linear classifier is worst for low boundary values and low nonlinearities. The nearest neighbor tends to be worst for percentage of points in the boundary greater than 10% and nonlinearities greater than approximately 4%. XCS appears as the worst method for high boundaries and nonlinearities.

We also note that there is no compact area where problems solved by more than one outstanding (best or worst) methods are placed. They are distributed along all projections of the complexity measurement space, so we cannot give any apparent reason to discriminate problems with a dominant method from those with several applicable methods, at least for the current measurement space.

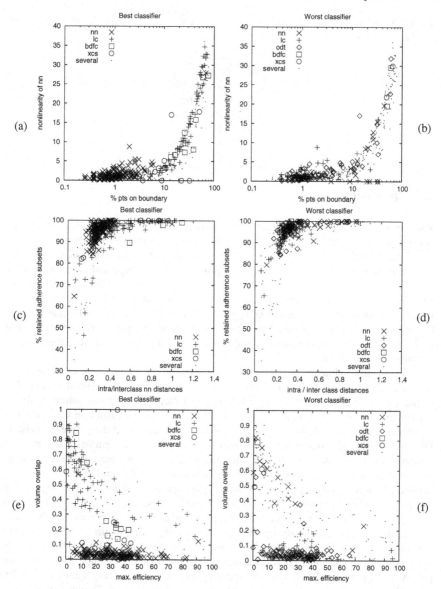

Fig. 7.7. Dominant competence of classifiers. Problems with a dominant best classifier (a, c, and e), and problems with a dominant worst classifier (b, d, and f), shown in selected projections of the complexity measurement space: percentage of points in boundary vs. nonlinearity of nn (a and b), intra-interclass nearest neighbor distances vs. percentage of retained adherence subsets (c and d), and maximum feature efficiency vs. volume of overlap region (e and f).

Table 7.3. Distribution of classifiers for problems with a best dominant classifier and a worst dominant classifier.

	Best	Worst
nn	69%	11%
lc	23%	30%
odt	0%	56%
pdfc	0%	0%
bdfc	4%	1%
xcs	4%	1%
total	270	157

7.5 Discussion

The current study facilitates also identifying the most relevant metrics for discriminating between domains of competence of classifiers. These are the percentage of points in the boundary, the nonlinearities, and the ratio of intra-interclass nearest neighbor distances. These metrics are more related to the geometry of the problem and the shape and distribution of the class boundaries. The metrics describing the discriminative power of the attributes, like the maximum Fisher's discriminant ratio and the maximum feature efficiency, seem to be less important in identifying domains of competence. Although they influence the complexity of the problem, they are not as useful as the other metrics to discriminate between two classifiers. This means that the domains of competence of classifiers are mostly determined by the geometry of the problem.

Some metrics, although also describing the geometry of the problem, are able to give particular explanations of some classifier's behavior, but they are not general enough. One of the reasons for their narrower applicability is that they are not spread uniformly for the current set of problems. This is the case of the pretopological measure on the percentage of retained adherence subsets. It presents high values for almost all the problems (between 80% and 100%). Although small values may indicate that the problem has a less complex geometry, there are insufficient problems located in these cases to extract useful conclusions. Moreover, there are empty regions in the measurement space. The problems are not evenly distributed along all dimensions of the measurement space; i.e., there are some regions that are not covered by any problem. We still do not know if these empty regions are induced by some geometrical constraints or are due to the particular choice of classification problems.

Another source of difficulty for the current study, which limits the extraction of more conclusive results, is the estimation of the complexity of the problems. Recall that all metrics are computed from the available training sets, and therefore they represent the apparent complexity of the problem. The measure of sparsity seems to be particularly sensitive to it. The estimation of the sparsity of the training set by the ratio of the number of points to the number of dimensions on the available training set may be uncorrelated with the real distribution of points in the original problem. This leads us to inconclusive results when we try to explain the domain of competence of the linear classifier related to the sparsity of the training set.

On the other hand, there are also some correlations between the metrics themselves. For example, the percentage of points in the boundary is fairly related to the nonlinearities, and to the intra-interclass nearest neighbor distances to some extent. Although this correlation is reasonable, it is not necessary. For example, a problem can have a high percentage of points in the boundary but present low nonlinearities. The correlation between these metrics in the current set of problems may lead to conclusions too overfitted for these problems.

The lack of uniformity, the apparent estimation of metrics and the correlation between metrics are some of the sources of difficulty found in the present study. Also the current choice of problems may bias the results and lead to conclusions that may not be directly extrapolated to other types of problems. The use of problems designed artificially may overcome these difficulties.

7.6 Conclusion

We propose a methodology based on the analysis of data complexity to study the domains of competence of classifiers. We find that the simplest methods, i.e., the linear classifier and the nearest neighbor, have *extreme* behaviors. They perform optimally in a number of problems (1/3 and 1/2 of all the problems, respectively), but also perform as the worst method in almost the same percentages of problems. This means that they are very specialized methods. When the conditions are favorable for these particular methods, they perform optimally. The key issue is to detect which conditions these are and whether they apply given a certain problem. The single decision tree is almost biased toward performing as the worst method or as an average method. On the other hand, the most elaborate classifiers tend to have a more robust behavior. They are mostly placed between the best and the worst method. They are not very specific to behave optimally in a particular set of problems, nor to behave poorly in another type of problems, but to behave in the average for a high proportion of problems. These types of classifiers are more general methods. They are applicable to a higher range of problems, where we can expect a moderately good result. This happens with the subsample decision forest, the subspace decision forest, and XCS.

The key issue is to identify which type of problems are suitable and not suitable for each classifier. This is more important for the most specialized classifiers, since their behavior can change dramatically depending on the problem. The domain of competence of the nearest neighbor classifier is located in problems with compact classes and little interleaving. Particularly for problems with less than 10% of points in the boundary, intra-interclass nearest neighbor distances less than 0.4, and nonlinearities less than 5%, the nearest neighbor classifier has good applicability. For problems outside this region, the nearest neighbor classifier is hardly recommended. The identification of the domain of competence of the linear classifier is more difficult. We effectively identify that the linear classifier is not well suited for problems with compact classes. In these cases, other classifiers perform better. But to what kind of problems the linear classifier is best suited is not conclusive enough, at least for the current measurement space. A possible hypothesis points out the problems with sparse training sets, but this is also difficult to determine since we do not know the original distribution of the problems. The decision tree is almost always outperformed by the other classifiers. Nevertheless, the ensemble classifiers based on the same tree, the subspace decision forest, and the subsample decision forest are much more applicable. In fact, the ensemble classifiers and XCS are average methods for a wide range of problems. In cases of uncertainty, so that there is no guarantee that a simple classifier will perform best, ensemble methods can offer a reasonable result. In these cases, XCS seems to perform better when the classes are more compact, similarly to the subspace decision forest. In contrast, the subsample decision forest works better for higher percentage of points in boundary and higher nonlinearities.

Limitations of the current study are identified, such as biases due to the current choice of problems, uneven distribution of problems along the measurement space, and apparent estimation of complexity. The study is also biased by the current pool of classifiers. Further studies are needed to provide higher understanding on the relationship among class distributions, complexity, and classifier's behavior. Also adding in synthetic data sets may be useful to control the apparent estimation of complexity and its influence on data complexity.

Acknowledgments

Bernadó-Mansilla thanks the support of *Enginyeria i Arquitectura La Salle*, Ramon Llull University, as well as the support of *Ministerio de Ciencia y Tecnología* under project TIC2002-04036-C05-03, and *Generalitat de Catalunya* under grant 2002SGR-00155.

References

[1] D.W. Aha, D. Kibler, M.K. Albert. Instance-based learning algorithms. *Machine Learning*, 6, 37–66, 1991.

[2] E. Bernadó-Mansilla, T.K. Ho. Domain of competence of XCS classifier system in complexity measurement space. *IEEE Transactions on Evolutionary Computation*, 9(1), 82–104, 2005.

[3] E. Bernadó-Mansilla, T.K. Ho. On classifier domains of competence. In *Proceedings of the 17th International Conference on Pattern Recognition*, 1, pages 136–139, 2004.

[4] C.L. Blake, C.J. Merz. UCI Repository of machine learning databases, [http://www.ics.uci.edu/~mlearn/MLRepository.html]. University of California, Irvine, Department of Information and Computer Sciences, 1998.

[5] L. Breiman. Bagging predictors. *Machine Learning*, 24, 123–140, 1996.

[6] T.K. Ho. The random subspace method for constructing decision forests. *IEEE Transcations on Pattern Analysis and Machine Intelligence*, 20(8), 832–844, 1998.

[7] T.K. Ho. A data complexity analysis of comparative adavantages of decision forest constructors. *Pattern Analysis and Applications*, 5, 102–112, 2002.

[8] T.K. Ho, M. Basu. Complexity measures of supervised classification problems. *IEEE Transactions on Pattern Analysis and Machine Intelligence*, 24(3), 289–300, 2002.

[9] S. Murthy, S. Kasif, S. Salzberg. A system for induction of oblique decision trees. *Journal of Artificial Intelligence Research*, 2(1), 1–32, 1994.

[10] F.W. Smith. Pattern classifier design by linear programming. *IEEE Transactions on Computers*, C-17, 367–372, 1968.

[11] S.W. Wilson. Classifier fitness based on accuracy. *Evolutionary Computation*, 3(2), 149–175, 1995.

[12] S.W. Wilson. Generalization in the XCS classifier system.. In J.R. Koza, W. Banzhaf, K. Chellapilla, et al., eds. *Genetic Programming: Proceedings of the Third Annual Conference*. San Francisco: Morgan Kaufmann, 1998.

8

Data Complexity Issues in Grammatical Inference

Colin de la Higuera

Summary. Grammatical inference (also known as grammar induction) is a field transversal to a number of research areas including machine learning, formal language theory, syntactic and structural pattern recognition, computational linguistics, computational biology, and speech recognition. Specificities of the problems that are studied include those related to data complexity. We argue that there are three levels at which data complexity for grammatical inference can be studied: at the first (inner) level the data can be strings, trees, or graphs; these are nontrivial objects on which topologies may not always be easy to manage. A second level is concerned with the classes and the representations of the classes used for classification; formal language theory provides us with an elegant setting based on rewriting systems and recursivity, but which is not easy to work with for classification or learning tasks. The combinatoric problems usually attached to these tasks prove to be indeed difficult. The third level relates the objects to the classes. Membership may be problematic, and this is even more the case when approximations (of the strings or the languages) are used, for instance in a noisy setting. We argue that the main difficulties arise from the fact that the structural definitions of the languages and the topological measures do not match.

8.1 Introduction

8.1.1 The Field

Grammatical inference is transversal to various fields including machine learning, formal language theory, structural and syntactic pattern recognition, computational linguistics, computational biology, and speech recognition.

In a very broad sense, a learner has access to some data that are sequential or structured (strings, words, trees, terms, or even limited forms of graphs) and is asked to return a grammar that should in some way explain these data. The grammar is supposed to be able to generate the data, or recognize it. The learner is at least partially automatic, and is therefore sometimes called an inference machine, or a learning algorithm. The induced (or inferred) grammar can then be used to classify unseen data, compress this data, or provide some suitable model for this data. Typical features of the problem are:

- The data, composed from a finite alphabet; is thus usually discrete, as opposed to numerical; but on the other hand the unbounded length of strings makes the classification tasks harder than with the usual symbolic data.

- The sort of result: a grammar or an automaton, traditional objects from formal language theory studied in computer science. The advantage of these objects is that they are understandable. The classes that are learned are described in an intelligible and sometimes even graphical way, which may not always be the case in pattern recognition or classification. In fields where human experts need to be able to derive new knowledge from what the computer provides, this is undoubtedly a key feature.
- The hardness of even the easiest of problems: Grammatical inference is a field where there are only a few positive theoretical results. Most learning problems are considered intractable and are even used as examples of hard tasks in machine learning.
- The variety of potential applications: Data in many fields is today more and more complex and structured, and therefore, techniques that concentrate on structural data are of increasing importance.

There are a number of ways of addressing the different problems in grammatical inference: searching for new algorithms, broadening the class of data for which existing techniques work, better understanding the boundaries between those problems that one can solve and those that correspond to classes that are not learnable, and the application of known techniques to new problems.

8.1.2 The Literature and the Community

Grammatical inference scientists belong to a number of larger communities: machine learning (with special emphasis on inductive inference), computational linguistics, and pattern recognition (within the structural and syntactic subgroup). There is a specific conference the *International Colloquium on Grammatical Inference* (ICGI) devoted to the subject, within whose proceedings it is possible to find a number of technical papers. These conferences have been held at Alicante, Spain [13], Montpellier, France [59], Ames, Iowa [37], Lisbon [24], and Amsterdam [1]. The web page of the grammatical inference community [85], and those of related communities can be used to find most of the papers in the field. The *Computational Learning Theory* (COLT) web page [46] or the *Algorithmic Learning Theory* (ALT) web page [92] can provide good lists of papers with the machine learning perspective. Important key papers setting the first definitions and providing important heuristics are those by Fu [27] and Fu and Booth [28]. The structural and syntactic pattern recognition approaches can be found, for instance, in Miclet's book [57] and in the survey by Bunke and Sanfeliu [10], with special interest in Miclet's chapter [58].

Surveys or introductions to the subject have been published by Lee [51], Sakakibara [76], Honavar and de la Higuera [36], and de la Higuera [20].

Books on formal languages by Harrison [35] and by Hopcroft and Ullman [38] give most of the elementary definitions and results needed for the language theoretical background to grammatical inference. Parsing issues are discussed in Aho and Ullman's textbook [2]. On machine learning the books by Mitchell [60], Natarajan [63], and Kearns and Vazirani [42] all give elements that are of use to derive grammar induction results. Another place where structural pattern recognition issues are discussed is Gonzalez and Thomason's book [33]. An early book with many important mathematical results on the subject of automata inference is that by Trakhtenbrot and Barzdin [84].

8.1.3 Organization of This Chapter

The question under study is, What are the *data complexity* issues involved in grammatical inference? The first problem is to discuss the different meanings that can be linked with these terms. The first idea is that the actual data (strings and trees) have a specific complexity, independently of the concept classes that are involved. A second point of view may be that it concerns the classes themselves (languages) which are non trivial mathematical objects when dealing with grammatical inference: languages defined by grammars and automata. And a third point of view appears when we consider simultaneously the strings and the languages.

Before discussing these issues, we will survey some of the main definitions and results concerning grammar induction.

In section 8.2 we define the objects we intend to learn from. These are especially strings and trees, but other more complex objects have sometimes been studied, such as infinite strings or graphs. We also visit (section 8.3) the concept classes that are used in typical classification tasks. In grammatical inference these are languages that are defined by automata or grammars in the case of languages as sets of strings (section 8.3.1) or distributions (section 8.3.2). In section 8.4 we survey the topological issues regarding both strings (8.4.1) and languages (8.4.2). We deal in section 8.5 with the problems that arise from these definitions and that concern what can be grouped under the heading of "data complexity problems" for grammatical inference: problems concerning the data from which one wants to learn (section 8.5.1), problems relating to language theory and the specificity of grammatical definitions (section 8.5.2) and questions arising from the specific relationship between the data and the classes, i.e., between the strings and the languages (section 8.5.3). We draw conclusions in section 8.6.

8.2 Strings and Trees: from Which We Learn

Let Σ be a finite alphabet and Σ^* the (infinite) set of all strings that can be built from Σ, including the empty string denoted by λ.

By convention, symbols in Σ are denoted by letters from the beginning of the alphabet $(a, b, c, ...)$, and strings in Σ^* are denoted by the end of the alphabet letters $(..., x, y, z)$. The length of a string $x \in \Sigma^*$ is written $|x|$. The set of all strings of length n (less than, at most n) is denoted by Σ^n ($\Sigma^{<n}$, $\Sigma^{\leq n}$). A substring of x from position i to position j is denoted as $x_i \ldots x_j$. A substring $x_i \ldots x_j$ with $j < i$ is the empty string λ.

Strings are totally ordered according to the hierarchical order, i.e., if x and y belong to Σ^*, $x \leq y \Leftrightarrow |x| < |y|$ or $|x| = |y| \wedge x \leq_{\text{lex}} y$. The first strings, according to the hierarchical order (also sometimes called the length-lexicographic or length-lex order), with $\Sigma = \{a, b\}$ are $\{\lambda, a, b, aa, ab, ba, bb, aaa, \ldots\}$.

Extensions of strings include:

- Trees or terms that are recursively defined from a given ranked alphabet $F = F_0 \cup F_1 ... F_k$ as $\forall c \in F_0, c \in T$ and $t_1, ..t_k \in T, f \in F_k \implies f(t_1, .., t_k) \in T$. Alternative definitions exist where the trees are unranked (the same symbol may belong to various alphabets), or unordered (the order on the subtrees is not important). Learning tree automata and grammars are of increasing importance due to the interest in tasks involving structured information (for instance XML files).
- Graphs and hypergraphs are even more complex to define by generative means, and grammars that produce them have been studied in specific fields only. No positive learning result is known, at least for nontrivial classes.
- Infinite strings are used to model situations in reactive systems. Grammatical inference has been used on such data [18, 55, 79].

8.3 Languages: What We Want to Learn

When considering languages, two points of view leading to two different settings have been studied:

- A *language* is a subset of Σ^*. In this case problems are those of membership (Does a string belong or not to a language?) and the related issue of parsing strings, or that of the equivalence of grammars (Do they define or generate the same language?).
- A (stochastic) language can also be a distribution of probabilities over Σ^*. In this setting the question is to use automata or grammars that assign a higher probability to the more probable strings and a lower (or null) one to the others.

8.3.1 Languages

Formal language theory has been studied consistently over the past 50 years. The usual definitions and results can be found in references [35, 38]. Languages are sets of strings defined through generative (grammars) or recognition (automata) processes. We recall here two of the simpler but also more important definitions.

Regular Languages

Definition 1. *A deterministic finite automaton (DFA) is a quintuple* $A = \langle Q, \Sigma, \delta, F, q_0 \rangle$ *where* Σ *is an alphabet,* Q *is a finite set of states,* $q_0 \in Q$ *is the initial state,* $\delta : Q \times \Sigma \to Q$ *is a transition function, and* $F \subseteq Q$ *is a set of marked states, called the final states.*

It is usual to recursively extend δ to Σ^*: $\delta(q, \lambda) = q$ and $\delta(q, a.w) = \delta(\delta(q, a), w)$ for all $q \in Q, a \in \Sigma, w \in \Sigma^*$. Let $\mathcal{L}(A)$ denote the language recognized by automaton A:

$$\mathcal{L}(A) = \{w \in \Sigma^* \mid \delta(q_0, w) \in F\}$$

An alternative definition considers that the automaton may be nondeterministic [$\delta(q, a)$ may have various values]. It is well known that the languages recognized by DFA form the family of regular languages. This class is considered as a borderline case for grammatical inference [19] in the sense that DFA are learnable (in different senses), whereas slightly more complex objects are not. Also, because the class is known to be the first level of the Chomsky hierarchy, considerable attention has been given to the problem of learning it [23, 65, 66, 68].

There are alternative ways of defining regular languages; rational expressions, regular grammars, or nondeterministic finite automata are some of these, but they all lead to learning problems that are more complex than when considering DFA.

Context-Free Languages

The second level of the Chomsky hierarchy is concerned with context-free languages and grammars:

Definition 2 (Context-Free Grammar). *A Context-Free Grammar (CFG)* $G = (\Sigma, V, P, S)$ *is a quadruple where* Σ *is a finite alphabet (of terminal symbols),* V *is a finite alphabet (of variables or nonterminals),* $P \subset V \times (\Sigma \cup V)^*$ *is a finite set of production rules, and* $S \in V$ *is the axiom (start symbol).*

We denote $uTv \rightarrow uwv$ when $(T, w) \in P$. $\overset{*}{\rightarrow}$ is the reflexive and transitive closure of $\rightarrow$. If there exists $u_0, \ldots, u_k$ such that $u_0 \rightarrow \cdots \rightarrow u_k$, we write $u_0 \overset{k}{\rightarrow} u_k$. We denote by $L_G(T)$ the language $\{w \in \Sigma^* : T \overset{*}{\rightarrow} w\}$. Two grammars are equivalent if they generate the same language. A language is context-free if it can be generated by a context-free grammar.

Learning context-free grammars has proved to be a much harder task than learning DFA. Serious efforts in the past few years have included the following approaches:

- Subclasses of linear languages: linearity is considered by several authors to be a necessary condition for learning to be possible. There has been active and successful research of even linear grammars [44, 54, 80, 81, 82].
- Learning from structured data: learning tree automata [26, 34, 43], or context-free grammars from bracketed data [74, 75], allows to obtain better results, either with queries, regular distributions [15, 45, 72], or negative information [29]. This has also led to different studies concerning the probability estimation of such grammars [11, 50].
- Heuristics based on genetic algorithms [40, 77, 78], lattice exploring [31, 86], or simplicity bias [49].

Membership Issues

The problem of deciding if a given string belongs or not to a language is the first problem one has to deal with. In both cases (for regular languages defined by DFA and context-free languages defined by CFG) the problem is tractable: parsing can take place in linear time with a DFA and in cubic time with a CFG.

Other language formalisms may exist where parsing is not an easy problem. For instance, parsing with pattern languages [5, 25] is an intractable problem.

Equivalence Issues

Two grammars or automata are equivalent if they generate or recognize the same language. If equivalence of DFA is easy to check (thanks to the existence of a nice canonical minimal form), this is not the case if the regular languages are defined by other formalisms such as regular expressions of nondeterministic finite automata. In the case of context-free grammars the same holds: equivalence is undecidable.

This has direct consequences for the learning tasks, as is proved in [19].

8.3.2 Stochastic Languages

Stochastic languages and mechanisms allowing their generation are described in a number of articles and books [39, 50, 51, 56, 64, 67, 71, 87, 88]. We describe only the key ideas of stochastic languages and automata here.

A *stochastic language* $\mathcal{D}$ is a probability distribution over Σ^*.

The probability of a string $x \in \Sigma^*$ under the distribution $\mathcal{D}$ is denoted as $Pr_{\mathcal{D}}(x)$ and must verify $\sum_{x \in \Sigma^*} Pr_{\mathcal{D}}(x) = 1$. If the distribution is modeled by some syntactic machine $\mathcal{A}$, the probability of x according to the probability distribution defined by $\mathcal{A}$ is denoted $Pr_{\mathcal{A}}(x)$. The distribution modeled by a machine $\mathcal{A}$ will be denoted $\mathcal{D}_{\mathcal{A}}$ and simplified to $\mathcal{D}$ in a non-ambiguous context.

If L is a language (included in Σ^*) and $\mathcal{D}$ a distribution over Σ^*, $Pr_{\mathcal{D}}(L) = \sum_{x \in L} Pr_{\mathcal{D}}(x)$.

Two distributions $\mathcal{D}$ and $\mathcal{D}'$ are equal (denoted by $\mathcal{D} = \mathcal{D}'$) if $\forall w \in \Sigma^* : Pr_{\mathcal{D}}(w) = Pr_{\mathcal{D}'}(w)$.

A *sample* S is a multiset of strings; as a sample is usually built through sampling, one string may appear more than once. When considering the sample size, we note the difference between notation $|S|$, which indicates the number of (not necessarily different) strings in S, and $\|S\|$, which is the total sum of lengths of the strings in S. We also write $x \in S$ to indicate that string x is represented in the sample.

Probabilistic Automata and Languages

Probabilistic languages are generated by probabilistic automata.

Definition 3. *A* PFA *is a tuple* $\mathcal{A} = \langle Q_{\mathcal{A}}, \Sigma, \delta_{\mathcal{A}}, I_{\mathcal{A}}, F_{\mathcal{A}}, P_{\mathcal{A}} \rangle$, *where:*

- $Q_{\mathcal{A}}$ *is a finite set of states;*
- Σ *is the alphabet;*
- $\delta_{\mathcal{A}} \subseteq Q_{\mathcal{A}} \times \Sigma \times Q_{\mathcal{A}}$ *is a set of transitions;*
- $I_{\mathcal{A}} : Q_{\mathcal{A}} \to \mathbb{Q}^+$ *(initial-state probabilities);*
- $P_{\mathcal{A}} : \delta_{\mathcal{A}} \to \mathbb{Q}^+$ *(transition probabilities);*
- $F_{\mathcal{A}} : Q_{\mathcal{A}} \to \mathbb{Q}^+$ *(final-state probabilities).*

$I_{\mathcal{A}}$, $P_{\mathcal{A}}$ *and* $F_{\mathcal{A}}$ *are functions such that:*

$$\sum_{q \in Q_{\mathcal{A}}} I_{\mathcal{A}}(q) = 1,$$

and

$$\forall q \in Q_{\mathcal{A}}, \ F_{\mathcal{A}}(q) + \sum_{a \in \Sigma, \ q' \in Q_{\mathcal{A}}} P_{\mathcal{A}}(q, a, q') = 1.$$

$P_{\mathcal{A}}$ is extended with $P_{\mathcal{A}}(q, a, q') = 0$ for all $(q, a, q') \notin \delta_{\mathcal{A}}$. Also, the subscript $\mathcal{A}$ is dropped when there is no ambiguity.

The above automata definition corresponds to models that are *generative* in nature. This is in contrast with the standard definition of automata in the conventional (nonprobabilistic) formal language theory, where strings are generated by *grammars* while the automata are the *accepting* devices. From a probabilistic point of view, the process of (randomly) accepting a *given* string is essentially different from the process of generating a (random) string. Probabilistic acceptors are defined in Fu [27], but they have not been as popular in both syntactic pattern recognition and formal language theory.

Figure 8.1 shows a *graphical representation* of a PFA with four states, $Q = \{q_0, q_1, q_2, q_3\}$, only one initial state, q_0, and a four-symbol alphabet, $\Sigma = \{a, b, c, d\}$. The rational numbers in the states and in the arrows are the final state and the transition probabilities, respectively.

Deterministic Probabilistic Finite-State Automata (DPFA)

Definition 4. *A* PFA $\mathcal{A} = \langle Q, \Sigma, \delta, I, F, P \rangle$ *is a DPFA, if:*

- $\exists q_0 \in Q$ *(initial state), such that* $I(q_0) = 1$;
- $\forall q \in Q, \ \forall a \in \Sigma, \ | \{q' : (q, a, q') \in \delta\} | \leq 1$.

In a $DPFA$, a transition (q, a, q') is completely defined by q and a, and a $DPFA$ can be more simply denoted by $\langle Q, \Sigma, \delta, q_0, F, P \rangle$.

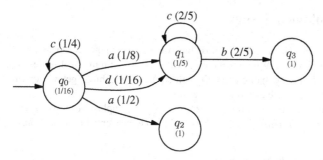

Fig. 8.1. Graphical representation of a PFA.

Distribution Modeled by a PFA

PFA generate strings of finite length. Given a PFA $\mathcal{A}$, a string is generating by randomly choosing (with respect to a distribution I over the initial states) one state q_0 in Q as the initial state. Call q this state. Then iteratively decide whether to *halt*, with probability $F(q)$, or to produce a *move* (q, a, q') with probability $P(q, a, q')$ where $a \in \Sigma$ and $q' \in Q$ in which case a symbol a is emitted and the current state is set to q'.

It should be noticed that this generative process facilitates only generating a string but not computing the probability of a given string, which can be generated in different ways or *paths*. Dynamic programming techniques are used for this computation.

If $\sum_x Pr_{\mathcal{A}}(x) = 1$, then $\mathcal{A}$ defines a distribution $\mathcal{D}$ on Σ^*.

Definition 5. *A distribution is* regular *if it can be generated by some PFA.*

An alternative definition could be used: a regular distribution is a probabilistic distribution on a regular language. However, we do not assume this definition because it would present the following problem: there would exist regular distributions that could not be generated by any PFA. This result can be easily derived from Wetherell [91].

Definition 6. *A distribution is* regular deterministic *if it can be generated by some $DPFA$.*

Definition 7. *Two PFAs are* equivalent *if they generate the same distribution.*

From the definition of PFA and $DPFA$ the following hierarchy follows:

Proposition 1. *A regular deterministic distribution is also a regular distribution.*

We do not provide here the definition of context-free stochastic (or probabilistic) grammars, which results from a combination of the definitions of context-free grammars and that of stochastic automata. These have been studied in a variety of works, including [16, 21, 39, 50].

Questions Relating to Stochastic Languages

Following the Chomsky hierarchy, it is possible to extend the previous definitions to cope with stochastic tree languages defined by stochastic tree automata or stochastic context-free grammars.

Parsing issues have also been well studied. If the deterministic case is easy to solve, a number of dynamic programming techniques have been used for the nondeterministic setting.

Equivalence of PFA is decidable, but the exact complexity is not known. More than the question of equivalence, the one of the *closeness* (How close is one distribution to another?) is a hard question, to which only partial answers have been given [62].

8.4 Topological Issues

The way the set of instances or of possible examples is organized depends on the topology that is used on this space. Whereas metrics over vectors and numerical representations are fairly well known and obey mathematically well-studied laws, things get harder when dealing with structured objects such as strings or trees.

Distances can be used to organize the set of examples, but also, sometimes, the set of possible classes. We discuss both types of distance measures in this section.

8.4.1 Distances Between Strings

Given two strings x and y, a distance can be computed in several different ways. In a broad sense the possibilities are:

- To compute the minimal number of operations needed to transform x into y. This is the principle of the *edit* or Levenshtein distances [3, 89].
- To compute some similarity measure $S(x, y)$ between the two strings, and then, with an adequate function ($2^{-S(x,y)}$) convert it into a distance.
- To select a set of measurable features over the strings and to use these to associate with each string a vector in $\mathbb{R}^n$. The vectors can then be compared by standard metrics.

In practice all three ideas have their advantages and their disadvantages.

- The edit distance is certainly the most natural form of distances on strings. But the computation of this distance in quadratic in the length of the strings and many reasonable operations (such as searching for the center of a set of strings [22]) can be intractable.
- Similarity measures abound: an easy distance based on this principle consists in computing the length of the longest common prefix and using this as $S(x, y)$. Yet convincing similarity measures have not been produced.
- Finding a finite set of features over strings and using numerical representations is a standard technique: n-grams are a typical way of doing this. But the intrinsic structure of the string is usually lost.

8.4.2 Distances Between Languages

In the nonstochastic setting (when languages are just sets of strings), comparison is done by usual set-theoretic tools. It should be noticed that without a distribution of probabilities over the strings, the number of strings in the symmetric difference between two sets is not a valid indicator, as it can easily be infinite.

The usual setting to study distances between languages is therefore the stochastic one. Defining similarity measures between distributions is the most natural way of comparing them. In tasks involving the learning of PFA or $DPFA$, one wants to measure the quality of the result or of the learning process. When learning takes place from a sample, measuring how far the learned automaton is from the sample can also be done by comparing distributions since a sample can easily be encoded as a $DPFA$.

There are two families of distance measures: those that are true distances, and those that measure a cross-entropy.

Distances Between Distributions

All the definitions hereafter are seen as definitions of distances between distributions over Σ^*. In doing so they implicitly define distances between automata, but also between automata and samples, or even between samples.

- The most general family of distances are referred to as the Minkowski distances or distances for the norm L_n. The general definition is as follows:

$$d_n(\mathcal{D}, \mathcal{D}') = \left(\sum_{x \in \Sigma^*} |Pr_{\mathcal{D}}(x) - Pr_{\mathcal{D}'}(x)|^n \right)^{\frac{1}{n}}.$$

- The following distance is used in [7] (under the name d_* or distance for the L_∞ norm):

$$d_{\max}(\mathcal{D}, \mathcal{D}') = \max_{x \in \Sigma^*} |Pr_{\mathcal{D}}(x) - Pr_{\mathcal{D}'}(x)|.$$

Entropy-Based Measures

Based on entropy definitions we can use the well-known Kullback-Leibler divergence:

$$d_{KL}(\mathcal{D}, \mathcal{D}') = \sum_{x \in \Sigma^*} Pr_{\mathcal{D}}(x) \cdot \log \frac{Pr_{\mathcal{D}}(x)}{Pr_{\mathcal{D}'}(x)}.$$

We set in a standard way $0 \log 0 = 0$ and $\frac{0}{0} = 1$.

In the case where some string has a null probability in $\mathcal{D}'$, but not in $\mathcal{D}$, then the Kullback-Leibler divergence is infinite.

Rewriting the Kullback-Leibler divergence as

$$d_{KL}(\mathcal{D}, \mathcal{D}') = \sum_{x \in \Sigma^*} (Pr_{\mathcal{D}}(x) \cdot \log Pr_{\mathcal{D}}(x) - Pr_{\mathcal{D}}(x) \cdot \log Pr_{\mathcal{D}'}(x)),$$

one can note the first term is the entropy of $\mathcal{D}$, and does not depend on $\mathcal{D}'$ and the second term is the cross-entropy of $\mathcal{D}$ given $\mathcal{D}'$. From the information theory interpretation [17], the first term measures the optimal number of bits needed to encode $\mathcal{D}$ and the second one measures the cost (in number of bits of encoding) of estimating $\mathcal{D}$ using $\mathcal{D}'$.

Computing Distances

The computation of distance d_n and d_{max} has been studied for hidden Markov models in [53], where it is shown that only for even values of n is the computation possible. Similar results hold for $DPFA$ [62]. The computation of d_{KL} is possible in polynomial time for $DPFA$ [12].

8.5 How Data Complexity Can Affect Grammatical Inference

We now turn to the question of data complexity. As discussed earlier, we discuss three aspects of the problem: the one specific to the data, the one concerning the classes, and the third one which interrelates strings and classes.

8.5.1 Problems Concerning the Data

Strings and trees are nontrivial structures. Their typical definitions are recursive, and they allow for complex extensions (infinite strings, unordered trees). For a number of reasons in grammatical inference, some basic operations over strings and trees are needed, and are not always simple:

- Distances have to be computed. In section 8.4.1 we reviewed some of the typical distances that could be used over strings, and noticed that the computation issues were not trivial.
- Finding patterns in strings [3] is a tricky issue also, for which elaborate algorithms have been built.
- Comparing strings (or trees): is a string a substring of another? A number of algorithms have been proposed for these tasks, but time complexity can be high.

All this has consequences when wanting to use traditional pattern analysis techniques (such as a nearest neighbours approach) in an application where the data is described by strings and requires specific heuristics [61, 73].

8.5.2 Problems Concerning the Languages

Formal language theory has been built on the Chomsky hierarchy which defines classes of languages through the restrictions that one can make to the type of grammar that is admitted [2]. Moreover, recursivity is central to this theory, which gives it elegance but also may not help our understanding of it. A typical example of this is the intuitive distance that there can be between a language and a grammar that generates it.

These definitions have another drawback: small changes made on the grammar (or the automaton) are likely to affect, in an important way, the language that is generated. The converse also holds, as modifying in a very small way a language can easily lead to the construction of a new grammar quite unrelated to the first one. The consequences of this is that the concept classes are very sensitive to noise. Even a very small amount of noisy data in the learning process affects what is being induced. Grammatical inference, because of this data complexity issue, is quite incapable of dealing with noisy data. As in practice, noisy data is abundant; this is a real problem for the field.

The question has probably not yet been explored in a systematic way, and there is still much to argue about this. The point we raise here is simply that (and in contrast to other fields in pattern recognition or machine learning) the topological theories over strings and the formal language theories do not match.

Knowing if two representations of classes are equivalent is a central question both in formal language theory and in learning. Indeed if the problem is intractable, then one should not expect learning to be feasible:

- This may mean that the characteristic sets needed to learn are of a size that one cannot expect to reach in reasonable time [19].
- This also means that learning from membership queries only is not tractable. If not, one could use both grammars as black boxes and learn independently from each, and at the end compare the results.

8.5.3 Problems Concerning the Relationship Between Strings and Languages

When considering strings on their own, we have a problem with the complexity of the data. When considering the classes and their representations, we have another. What happens when we consider both issues together is that new hard problems arise. We mention some of them now.

Negative Results Concerning the Combinatorics

A typical way of considering a classification task from both examples and counter-examples is to find some representation of a class consistent with the observed data. In grammatical inference, in general, this is insufficient, as any finite set of strings is a regular or a context-free language. In that case, theory teaches us that it is a good policy to find a simplest consistent class. This obeys the Occam's razor principle.

Gold [32] proves that the problem of finding the smallest DFA consistent with a given set of strings is NP-hard. Angluin [4] proves that this is the case even when the target automaton only has two states (this peculiar result is quoted by Pitt and Warmuth [70]), or even when only a very small fraction of all the strings up to length n, where n is the size of the target, is absent. Trakhtenbrot and Barzdin [84] had shown previously that when all such strings were present the problem was tractable.

There are several negative consequences of these combinatorical results. This is not enough to obtain a direct proof that learning in polynomial time is impossible, but Angluin proves the hardness of the task even using *membership queries* [6] (a string can be proposed to the oracle who must answer if the string belongs or not to the target language) or *equivalence queries* [8] (a grammar is proposed to the oracle, who answers yes if the hypothesis is equivalent to the target, and provides a counterexample if not). In the second case Angluin introduced the combinatorial notion of *approximate fingerprints* of independent interest, which correspond to a subset of hypotheses out of which only a small fraction can be excluded, given any counterexample, resulting in the necessity of using an exponential number of equivalence queries to isolate a single hypothesis. Gavaldà [30] studies this notion with care. Pitt [68] uses this result to prove the intractability of the task of identifying DFA with a polynomial number of mind changes only (i.e., the number of times the online learning algorithm changes its hypothesis should be polynomial in the size of the target DFA). The problem is proved to be hard [69], and by typical reduction techniques [90] is proved complete (hardest) in its class. But Pitt's model may be itself too demanding, as it is closely linked with Littlestone's learning model [52].

Problems with Approximation

The combinatorical results above imply that finding the exact solution is too hard, but there could be hope for approximately learning. The probably approximately correct (PAC) paradigm has been widely used in machine learning to provide a theoretical setting for this. But even for the case of DFA, most results are negative, Kearns and Valiant [41] linked the difficulty of learning DFA with that of solving cryptographic problems believed to be intractable (a nice proof is published in Kearns and Vazirani's book [42]).

Another point of view on the hardness of approximation can be seen through the different competitions that have been organized for grammatical inference. In 1997, the ABBADINGO competition [47] raised interest in the problem of DFA inference, and although a neural network technique seemed to do well, at the end, an *evidence-driven* technique developed by Price, based on classical state merging, won (Lang et al., [48]). The idea was to try different merges but keep the one that had the highest score. A (cheap) alternative to evidence-driven heuristics is data-driven heuristics (de la Higuera et al., [23]), where the idea is to try merging those states through which most information is known. Some problems from that competition are still open.

Learning with Noise

As a consequence of the above observations, learning in a noisy setting is very hard. Whereas in other areas of machine learning and pattern recognition there are many methods and results allowing us to work on cases where the data may be imperfect, this is not the case in grammatical inference. One of the few hopes of doing anything of use in this case is to learn stochastic automata [14, 83].

8.6 Conclusion

Grammatical inference is faced with a number of intrinsic difficulties that differentiate the field from other fields in pattern recognition or machine learning. These correspond to the specific recursive unbounded structure of strings and trees, the special way languages are defined, which is not some extension of well-known classes over vectors, and the combined complexity of strings and languages when considering parsing issues.

When faced with these hardness questions a number of answers seem possible:

- Modifying the internal structure of the data offers only limited possibilities. Windowing the data or associating to strings a finite number of characteristics has been done, but there is necessarily a price to pay in terms of representation;
- Finding novel ways of defining languages that do not obey to the Chomsky hierarchy would certainly be a good choice; for instance, different forms of *pattern languages* [5, 9, 25] have been studied and in certain areas, such as computational biology, are indeed of use.
- Finally the inherent difficulties should not force researchers to abandon the idea of learning languages from strings of trees. The successes of grammatical inference show that there still is a lot of room for new profound and useful results.

Acknowledgments

The author is grateful to Rafael Carrasco, Francisco Casacuberta, Rémi Eyraud, Jean-Christophe Janodet, Thierry Murgue, Jose Oncina, Franck Thollard, and Enrique Vidal, for discussions and previous related work that fostered the ideas in this chapter.

References

[1] P. Adriaans, H. Fernau, M. van Zaannen, eds. *Grammatical Inference: Algorithms and Applications, Proceedings of ICGI '02*, volume 2484 of *LNAI*. Berlin, Heidelberg: Springer-Verlag, 2002.

[2] A. Aho, J. D. Ullman. *The Theory of Parsing, Translation and Compiling, Vol 1: Parsing.* Englewood Cliffs, NJ: Prentice-Hall, 1972.

[3] A .V. Aho. Algorithms for Finding Patterns in Strings. *Handbook of Theoretical Computer Science*, pages 290–300. Amsterdam: Elsevier, 1990.

[4] D. Angluin. On the complexity of minimum inference of regular sets. *Information and Control*, 39, 337–350, 1978.

[5] D. Angluin. Finding patterns common to a set of strings. In *Conference record of the eleventh annual ACM Symposium on Theory of Computing*, pages 130–141. New York: ACM Press, 1979.

[6] D. Angluin. Queries and concept learning. *Machine Learning Journal*, 2, 319–342, 1987.

[7] D. Angluin. Identifying languages from stochastic examples. Technical Report YALEU/DCS/RR-614, Yale University, March 1988.

[8] D. Angluin. Negative results for equivalence queries. *Machine Learning Journal*, 5, 121–150, 1990.

[9] A. Brazma, I. Jonassen, J. Vilo, E. Ukkonen. Pattern discovery in biosequences. In Honavar and Slutski [37], pages 257–270.

[10] H. Bunke, A. Sanfeliu, eds. *Syntactic and Structural Pattern Recognition, Theory and Applications*, volume 7 of *Series in Computer Science*. Singapore: World Scientific, 1990.

[11] J. Calera-Rubio, R.C. Carrasco. Computing the relative entropy between regular tree languages. *Information Processing Letters*, 68(6), 283–289, 1998.

[12] R.C. Carrasco. Accurate computation of the relative entropy between stochastic regular grammars. *RAIRO (Theoretical Informatics and Applications)*, 31(5), 437–444, 1997.

[13] R.C. Carrasco, J. Oncina, eds. *Grammatical Inference and Applications, Proceedings of ICGI '94*, number 862 in LNAI, Berlin: Springer, 1994.

[14] R.C. Carrasco, J. Oncina. Learning stochastic regular grammars by means of a state merging method. In ICGI'94 [13], pages 139–150.

[15] R.C. Carrasco, J. Oncina, J. Calera-Rubio. Stochastic inference of regular tree languages. *Machine Learning Journal*, 44(1), 185–197, 2001.

[16] Z. Chi, S. Geman. Estimation of probabilistic context-free grammars. *Computational Linguistics*, 24(2), 298–305, 1998.

[17] T. Cover, J. Thomas. *Elements of Information Theory.* New York: John Wiley, 1991.

[18] C. de la Higuera, J-C. Janodet. Inference of ω-languages from prefixes. *Theoretical Computer Science*, 313(2), 295–312, 2004.

[19] C. de la Higuera. Characteristic sets for polynomial grammatical inference. *Machine Learning Journal*, 27, 125–138, 1997.

[20] C. de la Higuera. Current trends in grammatical inference. In F.J. Ferri et al., eds. *Advances in Pattern Recognition, Joint IAPR International Workshops SSPR+SPR 2000*, volume 1876 of *LNCS*, pages 28–31. New York: Springer-Verlag, 2000.

[21] C. de la Higuera, P. Adriaans, M. van Zaanen, J. Oncina, eds. *Proceedings of the Workshop and Tutorial on Learning Context-free grammars.* ISBN 953-6690-39-X, 2003.

[22] C. de la Higuera, F. Casacuberta. Topology of strings: median string is NP-complete. *Theoretical Computer Science*, 230, 39–48, 2000.

[23] C. de la Higuera, J. Oncina, E. Vidal. Identification of DFA: data-dependent versus data-independent algorithm. In Miclet and de la Higuera [59], pages 313–325.

[24] A. de Oliveira, ed. *Grammatical Inference: Algorithms and Applications, Proceedings of ICGI '00*, volume 1891 of *LNAI*, Berlin: Springer, 2000.

[25] T. Erlebach, P. Rossmanith, H. Stadtherr, A. Steger, T. Zeugmann. Learning one-variable pattern languages very efficiently on average, in parallel, and by asking queries. In M. Li, A. Maruoka, eds. *Proceedings of ALT '97*, volume 1316 of *LNCS*, pages 260–276, Berlin: Springer, 1997.

[26] H. Fernau. Learning tree languages from text. In J. Kivinen, R.H. Sloan, eds. *Proceedings of COLT 2002*, number 2375 in LNAI, pages 153–168, Berlin: Springer, 2002.

[27] K.S. Fu. *Syntactic Methods in Pattern Recognition*. New York: Academic Press, 1974.

[28] K.S. Fu, T.L. Booth. Grammatical inference: Introduction and survey. Part I and II. *IEEE Transactions on Syst. Man. and Cybern.*, 5, 59–72, 409–423, 1975.

[29] P. García, J. Oncina. Inference of recognizable tree sets. Technical Report DSIC-II/47/93, Departamento de Lenguajes y Sistemas Informáticos, Universidad Politécnica de Valencia, Spain, 1993.

[30] R. Gavaldà. On the power of equivalence queries. In *Proceedings of the 1st European Conference on Computational Learning Theory*, volume 53 of *The Institute of Mathematics and its Applications Conference Series, new series*, pages 193–203. Oxford: Oxford University Press, 1993.

[31] J.Y. Giordano. Inference of context-free grammars by enumeration: Structural containment as an ordering bias. In Carrasco and Oncina [13], pages 212–221.

[32] E.M. Gold. Complexity of automaton identification from given data. *Information and Control*, 37, 302–320, 1978.

[33] R. Gonzalez and M. Thomason. *Syntactic Pattern Recognition: an Introduction*. Reading MA: Addison-Wesley, 1978.

[34] A. Habrard, M. Bernard, F. Jacquenet. Generalized stochastic tree automata for multi-relational data mining. In Adriaans et al. [1], pages 120–133.

[35] M. H. Harrison. *Introduction to Formal Language Theory*. Reading, MA: Addison-Wesley, 1978.

[36] V. Honavar, C. de la Higuera. Introduction. *Machine Learning Journal*, 44(1), 5–7, 2001.

[37] V. Honavar, G. Slutski, eds. *Grammatical Inference, Proceedings of ICGI '98*, number 1433 in LNAI, Berlin: Springer-Verlag, 1998.

[38] J.E. Hopcroft, J.D. Ullman. *Introduction to Automata Theory, Languages, and Computation*. Reading, MA: Addison-Wesley, 1979.

[39] A. Jagota, R.B. Lyngsø, C.N.S. Pedersen. Comparing a hidden Markov model and a stochastic context-free grammar. In *Proceedings of WABI '01*, number 2149 in LNCS, pages 69–74, Berlin: Springer-Verlag, 2001.

[40] T. Kammeyer, R.K. Belew. Stochastic context-free grammar induction with a genetic algorithm using local search. In R.K. Belew, M. Vose, eds. *Foundations of Genetic Algorithms IV*, San Mateo, CA: Morgan Kaufmann, 1996.

[41] M. Kearns, L. Valiant. Cryptographic limitations on learning boolean formulae and finite automata. In *21st ACM Symposium on Theory of Computing*, pages 433–444, 1989.

[42] M. Kearns and U. Vazirani. *An Introduction to Computational Learning Theory*. Cambridge, MA: MIT press, 1994.

[43] T. Knuutila, M. Steinby. Inference of tree languages from a finite sample: an algebraic approach. *Theoretical Computer Science*, 129, 337–367, 1994.

[44] T. Koshiba, E. Mäkinen, Y. Takada. Inferring pure context-free languages from positive data. *Acta Cybernetica*, 14(3), 469–477, 2000.

[45] S.C. Kremer. Parallel stochastic grammar induction. In *Proceedings of the 1997 International Conference on Neural Networks (ICNN '97)*, volume I, pages 612–616, 1997.

[46] S.S. Kwerk. Colt: Computational learning theory. http://www.learningtheory.org, 1999.

[47] K. Lang, B.A. Pearlmutter. The Abbadingo one DFA learning competition, 1997.

[48] K.J. Lang, B.A. Pearlmutter, R.A. Price. Results of the Abbadingo one DFA learning competition and a new evidence-driven state merging algorithm. In Honavar and Slutski [37], pages 1–12.

[49] P. Langley, S. Stromsten. Learning context-free grammars with a simplicity bias. In *Proceedings of ECML 2000, 11th European Conference on Machine Learning,*, volume 1810 of *LNCS*, pages 220–228. New York: Springer-Verlag, 2000.

[50] K. Lari, S.J. Young. The estimation of stochastic context free grammars using the inside-outside algorithm. *Computer Speech and Language*, 4, 35–56, 1990.

[51] S. Lee. Learning of context-free languages: A survey of the literature. Technical Report TR-12-96. Cambridge, MA: Center for Research in Computing Technology, Harvard University Press, 1996.

[52] N. Littlestone. Learning quickly when irrelevant attributes abound: a new linear threshold. *Machine Learning Journal*, 2, 285–318, 1987.

[53] R.B. Lyngsø, C.N.S. Pedersen. The consensus string problem and the complexity of comparing hidden markov models. *Journal of Computing and System Science*, 65(3), 545–569, 2002.

[54] E. Mäkinen. A note on the grammatical inference problem for even linear languages. *Fundamenta Informaticae*, 25(2), 175–182, 1996.

[55] O. Maler, A. Pnueli. On the learnability of infinitary regular sets. In *Proceedings of COLT*, pages 128–136, San Mateo, CA: Morgan Kaufmann, 1991.

[56] F. Maryanski, M. G. Thomason. Properties of stochastic syntax-directed translation schemata. *International Journal of Computer and information Science*, 8(2), 89–110, 1979.

[57] L. Miclet. *Structural Methods in Pattern Recognition*. New York: Chapman and Hall, 1986.

[58] L. Miclet. *Syntactic and Structural Pattern Recognition, Theory and Applications*, In *Grammatical Inference*. pages 237–290. Singapore: World Scientific, 1990.

[59] L. Miclet, C. de la Higuera, eds. *Proceedings of ICGI '96*, number 1147 in LNAI, Berlin, Heidelberg: Springer-Verlag, 1996.

[60] T. M. Mitchell. *Machine Learning*. New York: McGraw-Hill, 1997.

[61] F. Moreno-Seco, L. Micó, J. Oncina. A modification of the LAESA algorithm for approximated k-nn classification. *Pattern Recognition Letters*, 24(1-3), 47–53, 2003.

[62] T. Murgue, C. de la Higuera. Distances between distributions: Comparing language models. In A. Fred, T. Caelli, R. Duin, A. Campilho, D. de Ridder, eds. *Structural, Syntactic and Statistical Pattern Recognition, Proceedings of SSPR and SPR 2004*, volume 3138 of *LNCS*, pages 269–277. New York: Springer-Verlag, 2004.

[63] B.L. Natarajan. *Machine Learning: a Theoretical Approach*. San Mateo, CA: Morgan Kaufmann, 1991.

[64] H. Ney. Stochastic grammars and pattern recognition. In P. Laface, R. De Mori, eds. *Proceedings of the NATO Advanced Study Institute*, pages 313–344. New York: Springer-Verlag, 1992.

[65] J. Oncina, P. García. Identifying regular languages in polynomial time. In H. Bunke, ed. *Advances in Structural and Syntactic Pattern Recognition*, volume 5 of *Series in Machine Perception and Artificial Intelligence*, pages 99–108. Singapore: World Scientific, 1992.

[66] R. J. Parekh, C. Nichitiu, V. Honavar. A polynomial time incremental algorithm for learning DFA. In Honavar and Slutski [37], pages 37–49.

[67] A. Paz. *Introduction to Probabilistic Automata*. New York: Academic Press, 1971.

[68] L. Pitt. Inductive inference, DFA's, and computational complexity. In *Analogical and Inductive Inference*, number 397 in LNAI, pages 18–44. Berlin, Heidelberg: Springer-Verlag, 1989.

[69] L. Pitt, M. Warmuth. Reductions among prediction problems: on the difficulty of predicting automata. In *3rd Conference on Structure in Complexity Theory*, pages 60–69, 1988.

[70] L. Pitt, M. Warmuth. The minimum consistent DFA problem cannot be approximated within any polynomial. *Journal of the Association for Computing Machinery*, 40(1), 95–142, 1993.

[71] M.O. Rabin. Probabilistic automata. *Information and Control*, 6, 230–245, 1966.

[72] J.R. Rico-Juan, J. Calera-Rubio, and R.C. Carrasco. Stochastic k-testable tree languages and applications. In Adriaans et al. [1], pages 199–212.

[73] J. R. Rico-Juan, L. Micó. Comparison of AESA and LAESA search algorithms using string and tree-edit-distances. *Pattern Recognition Letters*, 24(9-10), 1417–1426, 2003.

[74] Y. Sakakibara. Learning context-free grammars from structural data in polynomial time. *Theoretical Computer Science*, 76, 223–242, 1990.

[75] Y. Sakakibara. Efficient learning of context-free grammars from positive structural examples. *Information and Computation*, 97, 23–60, 1992.

[76] Y. Sakakibara. Recent advances of grammatical inference. *Theoretical Computer Science*, 185, 15–45, 1997.

[77] Y. Sakakibara, M. Kondo. Ga-based learning of context-free grammars using tabular representations. In *Proceedings of 16th International Conference on Machine Learning (ICML-99)*, pages 354–360, 1999.

[78] Y. Sakakibara, H. Muramatsu. Learning context-free grammars from partially structured examples. In de Oliveira [24], pages 229–240.

[79] A. Saoudi, T. Yokomori. Learning local and recognizable ω-languages and monadic logic programs. In *Proceedings of EUROCOLT*, LNCS, pages 157–169. New York: Springer-Verlag, 1993.

[80] J. M. Sempere, P. García. A characterisation of even linear languages and its application to the learning problem. In Carrasco and Oncina [13], pages 38–44.

[81] Y. Takada. Grammatical inference for even linear languages based on control sets. *Information Processing Letters*, 28(4), 193–199, 1988.

[82] Y. Takada. A hierarchy of language families learnable by regular language learners. In Carrasco and Oncina [13], pages 16–24.

[83] F. Thollard, P. Dupont, C. de la Higuera. Probabilistic DFA inference using Kullback-Leibler divergence and minimality. In *Proc. 17th International Conf. on Machine Learning*, pages 975–982. San Francisco, CA: Morgan Kaufmann, 2000.

[84] B. Trakhtenbrot, Y. Barzdin. *Finite Automata: Behavior and Synthesis*. Amesterdam: North Holland, 1973.

[85] M. van Zaanen. The grammatical inference homepage. http://eurise.univ-st-etienne.fr/gi/gi.html, 2003.

[86] K. Vanlehn, W. Ball. A version space approach to learning context-free grammars. *Machine Learning Journal*, 2, 39–74, 1987.

[87] E. Vidal, F. Thollard, C. de la Higuera, F. Casacuberta, R. C. Carrasco. Probabilistic finite state automata – part I. *Pattern Analysis and Machine Intelligence*, 27(7), 1013–1025, 2005.

[88] E. Vidal, F. Thollard, C. de la Higuera, F. Casacuberta, R. C. Carrasco. Probabilistic finite state automata – part II. *Pattern Analysis and Machine Intelligence*, 27(7), 1026–1039, 2005.

[89] R. Wagner, M. Fisher. The string-to-string correction problem. *Journal of the ACM*, 21, 168–178, 1974.

[90] M. Warmuth. Towards representation independence in *pac*-learning. In K. P. Jantke, ed. *Proceedings of AII'89*, volume 397 of *LNAI*, pages 78–103. New York: Springer-Verlag, 1989.

[91] C. S. Wetherell. Probabilistic languages: a review and some open questions. *Computing Surveys*, 12(4), 361–379, 1980.

[92] T. Zeugmann. Alt series home page. http://www.tcs.mu-luebeck.de/pages/thomas/WALT/waltn.jhtml, 1999.

Part II

Applications

Simple Statistics for Complex Feature Spaces

George Nagy and Xiaoli Zhang

Summary. We study the constraints that govern the distribution of symbolic patterns (letters, numerals, and other glyphs used for communication) and natural patterns in high-dimensional feature spaces, with a view to gaining insight into the complexity of classification tasks. Pattern vectors from several data sets of printed and hand-printed digits are standardized to identity covariance matrix variables via principal component analysis, shifting to zero mean and scaling. The probability density of the radius of the set of patterns (their distance from the origin) is computed and shown to predict accurately the observed average radius for a wide range of features and dimensionality. We predict further that the class centroids of symbolic patterns will form the vertices of a regular simplex (i.e., a d-dimensional tetrahedron). The observed pairwise distances of the 45 class centroids in ten-class problems are shown to be almost equal to the value predicted from the average radius of the class centroids. The class-conditional distributions of the patterns are compared using two measures of divergence. The difference between the distributions of the same class with different feature sets is found to be larger than the difference between the distributions of different classes with the same feature set. This suggests that the correlation among features of patterns of one class can predict the correlation among features of patterns in another class. The amount of within-source consistency in a data set is quantified using an entropy measure that takes into account small-sample effects. The statistical dependence between the features of same-source patterns of different classes is measured by mutual information applied to the discrete distributions resulting from quantization of the style assignments. If these observations are supported by further studies of symbolic and natural patterns with diverse data sets, they may eventually lead to improved classification methods for same-source ensembles of symbolic patterns.

9.1 Introduction

Better understanding of the disposition of patterns in feature space may help predict the difficulty and complexity of diverse classification tasks. To further this goal, we compute simple statistics of collections of patterns in several domains of numeral recognition. We focus on metrics that scale well with the number of samples and with the number of features. Unlike the metric properties in Ho and Basu [1], these metrics describe only global aspects of the class and style distributions, and neglect fine geometric details of the class boundaries.We compute metrics only on the feature space, as opposed to the data space of bitmaps.

Statistical classification algorithms are often based on the assumption of multimodal mixtures of multivariate Gaussian distributions in feature space. Such distributions can be uniquely specified by their first- and second-order statistics. For d features (i.e., a d-dimensional feature space), there are $O(d)$ first-order statistics (mean vectors) and $O(d^2)$ second-order statistics (covariance matrices). With values of d in the 10 to 256 range and tens of thousands of samples per class, complete higher-order statistics cannot be estimated reliably. Furthermore, there is a dearth of parametric multivariate distributions that can be specified in terms of arbitrary frequencies of triples of variables, because there is no convenient structure, analogous to the covariance matrix, for estimating and specifying $O(n^3)$ dependences among n variables. Therefore, we confine our attention to metrics that can be expressed in terms of only first- and second-order population, class, and subclass statistics, i.e., conditional means and covariance matrices.

We apply the proposed metrics to a set of 30,000 printed digits of six fonts, scanned at 300 dpi (Fig. 9.1), and to two sets of hand-printed digits (Fig. 9.2), SD3 (42,698 samples) and SD7 (11,495) samples), from the National Institute of Standards and Technology (NIST). For most of the analysis, SD3 and SD7 were merged to assure stable estimates of the distributions of the entire sample set and of each class. The features are localized, directional, blurred feature vectors [2], with 64 and 100 dimensions, respectively. These time-tested features are based on eight chain-coded, directional edge-detectors applied in each of a set of rectangular overlapping zones superimposed on the size-normalized bitmaps of the patterns.

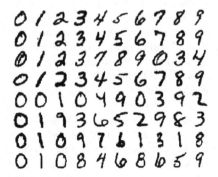

```
0 1 2 3 4 5 6 7 8 8
0 1 2 3 4 6 6 7 8 9
0 1 2 3 4 5 6 7 8 8
0 1 2 3 4 5 6 7 8 8
0 1 2 3 4 5 6 7 8 9
0 1 2 3 4 5 6 7 8 9
```

Fig. 9.1. Samples from machine-printed numeral database (originals printed at 6 pt, scanned at 300 dpi).

Fig. 9.2. Samples from handwritten numeral database. Each row corresponds to a different writer. The top four writers are from SD3 and the bottom four from SD7.

To remove the effects of the arbitrary means, variances, and statistical correlation of these features, the printed and hand-printed feature data are separately subjected to principal components analysis (PCA). The original features are projected on the eigenvectors, then shifted and scaled, resulting in 64-dimensional and 100-dimensional distributions with zero means and identity covariance matrices. The order of the eigenvalues is retained; in experiments on lower-dimensional feature spaces, we select the PCA features with the largest eigenvalues.

The above preprocessing scheme is illustrated in Figure 9.3. It allows comparing data with continuous-valued features from different application areas. The preprocessing does not require labeled data and is applied to the entire data set, regardless of any subsequent separation into training and test data. In the standard configuration, all features have zero mean

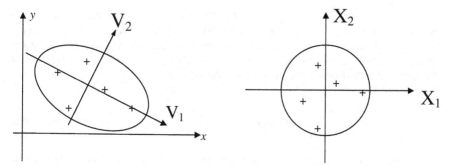

Fig. 9.3. Normalization of feature space. The feature vectors (shown as +) are projected onto the eigenvectors (V_1, V_2) of the overall covariance matrix. Then they are standardized to unit variance, and translated to have mean zero. Hence the resulting feature vectors (X_1, X_2) have mean zero and identity covariance matrix.

and unit variance, and they are uncorrelated. Differences between data sets are revealed by the class- and subclass-conditional distributions.

The means and covariance matrices of the class distributions are obtained by straightforward maximum likelihood estimation. The corresponding style labels are the font labels for the printed data. Each font has the same number of samples. The hand-printed digits were clustered into three clusters per class by the Matlab K-means routine with Euclidian metric. (Expecting three styles in each class is simply an act of faith; in hand printing, stylistic variations form a continuum. We restricted the number of clusters to three to ensure that each cluster has enough samples for stable estimates. Given a fixed number of clusters, it would probably be better not to assign them to classes uniformly.) Here the style labels are the arbitrary cluster labels. The best of ten runs with different random initializations was retained. Table 9.7 in section 9.5 shows the sizes of the resulting clusters for each class.

In section 9.2, we examine the surprisingly predictable configuration of the class centroids. In section 9.3, we observe relative concentrations and volumes of samples, expressed in terms of either the determinants of covariance matrices, or the average distance of patterns from their centroid. Section 9.4 is an attempt to discover systematic departures from the symmetries imposed by the Gaussian assumption. Sections 9.5 and 9.6 posit multiple sources of patterns that give rise to correlations across patterns that we call style. We ignore throughout statistical dependence between the labels of adjacent patterns, known in character and speech recognition as language context.

9.2 Average Radius of the Patterns

We first show that after the standardization described in section 9.1, most of the patterns occupy a relatively thin spherical shell centered on the origin. Assume that the individual features are Gaussian. Consider the probability density function (pdf) of the distance from the origin, R_i, of a single sample X_i, with features $x_{i,j}$. R_i can be expressed as the sum of the squares of the d feature values of sample X_i:

$$R_i^2 = \sum_{j=1}^{n} x_{i,j}^2 \qquad (9.1)$$

The pdf $f_{R^2}(r^2)$ has mean $\mu_{R^2} = d$ and variance $\sigma^2_{R^2} = 2d$, because the sum of the squares of d samples from an independent identically distributed (*i.i.d.*), unit-variance Gaussian distribution is Chi-square with d degrees of freedom. PCA guarantees only uncorrelated rather than independent features, but uncorrelated Gaussian variables are independent. The sum is over the features (dimensions), not the samples.

$$f_R(r) = \frac{r^{d-1}e^{-r^2/2}}{2^{\frac{d-2}{2}}\Gamma(d/2)}, \text{ with mean } \mu_R = \frac{\sqrt{2\pi}1 \cdot 3 \cdot 5 \dots (d-1)}{(d/2-1)!2^{d/2}}, \text{for } d \text{ even} \qquad (9.2)$$

The pdf of R, obtained by a transformation of variable from the χ^2 distribution, is plotted in Figure 9.4 for several even values of d. For $d = 8$, $\mu_R = 2.74$, which is in good agreement with the observed average values of 2.75 and 2.78, respectively, over all the samples of the two data sets. (Lower-case r is the instantiated value of the random variable R. The formula for odd values of d is slightly more complicated because the gamma function is not reduced to a factorial.)

pdf of R

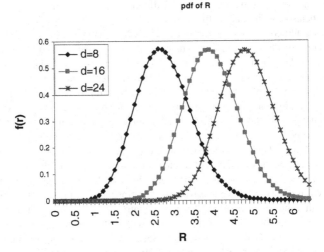

Fig. 9.4. Probability density function of radius of samples. As explained in the text, the pdf is related to the Chi-square density. The average distance of the samples from the origin increases with dimensionality, but the spread of the radii about their average value increases only slowly. The combined effect means that, at high dimensions, most of the samples are located in a thin spherical shell.

From the expressions for μ_R and μ_{R^2}, we can see that when $d \to \infty$, $\mu_{R^2}/(\mu_R)^2 \to 1$; therefore, the thickness-to-radius ratio σ_R/μ_R of the shell containing the samples converges to zero. The central limit theorem also justifies this asymptotic result. However, the Gaussian assumption on the features is necessary for computing the variance of the radius (i.e., the thickness of the shell) for finite dimensions. Table 9.1 shows expected value μ_R, the sample average radius $\langle R \rangle$ of the samples, and the observed standard deviation $\sqrt{\langle R^2 \rangle - \langle R \rangle^2}$ as a function of d for both sets of samples. The unexpected increase in the variance with dimen-

Table 9.1. Predicted and observed values of the average radius R of the samples. The observed average values of R agree well with the values predicted by the pdfs of Figure 9.4.

	Theory		Experiment			
			Machine print		Hand print	
d	μ_R	σ_R	Average sample radius	Standard deviation	Average sample radius	Standard deviation
8	2.74	0.70	2.75	0.65	2.78	0.51
16	3.94	0.70	3.94	0.67	3.94	0.71
24	4.84	0.70	4.84	0.76	4.82	0.88
50	7.03	0.71	6.98	1.13	6.96	1.23

sionality is puzzling. We will next make use of the predicted and observed regularity of the average radius to predict the configuration of the class centroids.

Before considering the class centroids, we discuss the difference between symbolic and natural patterns. Symbolic patterns are interpreted according to some alphabet intended for communicating messages. Examples are printed and hand-printed digits and letters of alphabetic scripts (Roman, Cyrillic, Hangul), shorthand alphabets, glyphs designed specifically for ease of machine reading (OCR fonts and Apple-Newton Graffiti), and the phoneme repertory of various languages. Communication symbols have either evolved, or were engineered, to maintain high separation between classes. We have no reason to believe that natural objects exhibit this property.

Given finite resources for producing each symbol (size and stroke-width limitations for print [3], limited ability to manipulate a stylus for hand print [4, 5, 6], energy budget, and a fixed articulatory musculature for phonemes [7]), we would expect the distance between any pair of classes to be approximately the same. (If it weren't, then it would be possible to modify the symbols to further separate the closest pair of classes at the cost of reducing the separation between distant pairs.) "Appropriate" features would maintain this equidistance property. The ten digits in a variety of scripts suggest that in a given alphabet most pairs are, in fact, roughly equally distinguishable (Fig. 9.5). Exceptions may occur for very high frequency symbols, such as 0, 1, and 2 (according to Benson's law, these digits account for 60% of all the leading digits in numerical fields [8, 9]), e in written English, and schwa in many spoken languages. An information-theoretic justification based on maximal entropy would, of course, also have to take into account linguistic context.

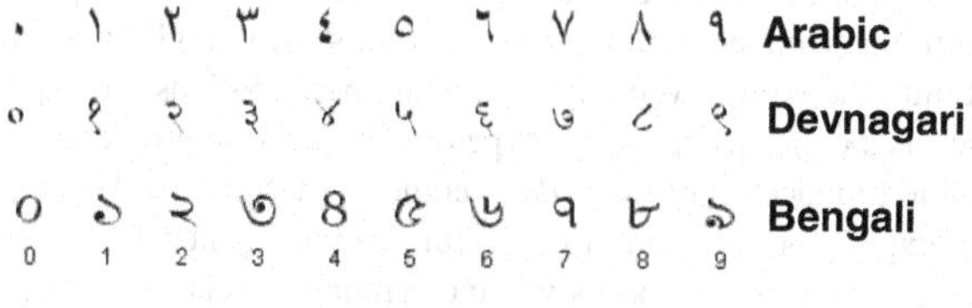

Fig. 9.5. Digits of different scripts.

If most of the samples were confined to a thin spherical shell, as argued above, then we would expect that the class centroids will be nearly equidistant from the origin. (The radii R_c of the class centroids are slightly smaller than the average sample radius $\langle R \rangle$ because the spread of the samples is orthogonal to the radii of the class centroids.) Further, if the c class means are equidistant from each other and are at the same radius $\langle R_c \rangle$ from the origin in

d-dimensional space, then they must form a c-dimensional regular tetrahedron with edges of length e_d:

$$e_d = \frac{\langle R \rangle \sin\left(\arccos d^{-1}\right)}{\sin\left(\pi - 1/2(\arccos d^{-1})\right)}, \text{ where } e_d \xrightarrow[d \to \infty]{} \sqrt{2}\langle R_c \rangle \quad (9.3)$$

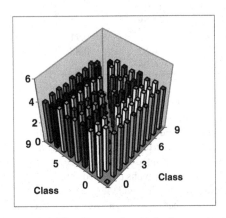 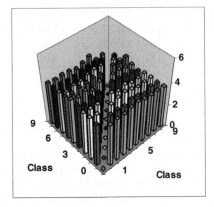

Fig. 9.6. The distance between class centroids is uniform. Machine-printed data on the left, hand-printed on the right. The distance between same-class pairs is zero.

Figure 9.6 is a plot of the intercentroid distances in 50-dimensional space. There appears to be little variation between them. Figure 9.7 shows the ratio of the difference between the largest and smallest interclass distances (i.e., the Euclidian distances between the 45 pairs of class centroids), divided by the median interclass distance. This ratio is a very rigorous measure of uniformity. We see that for $d = 50$, the largest deviation from the median value is less than 20% in both hand-printed and machine-printed data.

The average values of R_c for the ten classes are 2.51 and 2.75, respectively, for the two data sets ($d = 50$). From these values we can predict an interclass separation e_d of 3.58 and 3.92, whereas the observed average values are 3.75 and 4.10, respectively. Although the observed pairwise distances are slightly larger than predicted (because the class centroids are not all at exactly the same distance from the origin), it is clear that the pairwise distances are quite uniform in high dimensions. This confirms our tetrahedral assumption. Note that while the convergence of the sample configuration to a thin shell in high dimensions is a universal law (the central limit theorem) given random feature perturbations, the equidistance property of the class means is a consequence of the type of classification problem that we have posed.

It is impossible to place more than $(d+1)$ equidistant points in d-dimensional space. We therefore cannot expect the tetrahedral conjecture to be satisfied for $d < 9$. With increasing d, the class separation grows and its variance among the class-pairs decreases. However, the rate of increase in the separation of the classes tapers off as more features are added, in conformance with the Hughes phenomenon [10].

Since the radius of the samples about their class centroid is also the sum of independent variables, each class distribution is also a thin shell, with an average radius of r_c about the class centroid. The radius vector R_c to each class centroid is orthogonal to the subspace spanned by the samples in the remaining dimensions, and therefore obeys the Pythagorean equality $R^2 = r_c^2 + R_c^2$. The pairwise distance e_d is given by equation (9.33). Therefore,

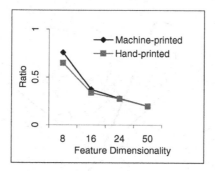

Fig. 9.7. Ratio of range of distances between class centroids to their median distance. The range is the difference between the maximum and the minimum separation of the 45 pairs of class centroids. The ratio of this range over the median interclass distance is plotted as a function of feature-space dimensionality. A low ratio means that the class centroids are located near the vertices of a regular simplex.

Table 9.2. Comparison of predicted and observed values of sample radii.

			Machine-printed				Hand-printed			
d	μ_R	σ_R	$\langle R_c \rangle$	$\langle r_c \rangle$	$\sqrt{\langle R_c \rangle^2 + \langle r_c \rangle^2}$	$\langle R \rangle$	$\langle R_c \rangle$	$\langle r_c \rangle$	$\sqrt{\langle R_c \rangle^2 + \langle r_c \rangle^2}$	$\langle R \rangle$
8	2.74	0.70	2.31	1.44	2.73	2.75	1.99	1.90	2.75	2.78
16	3.94	0.70	2.58	2.95	3.92	3.94	2.31	3.16	3.91	3.94
24	4.84	0.70	2.65	4.02	4.81	4.84	2.41	4.15	4.80	4.82
50	7.03	0.71	2.75	6.39	6.96	6.98	2.51	6.49	6.96	6.96

d *dimensionality*
μ_R theoretical mean radius
σ_R theoretical stardard deviation of radius
$\langle R_c \rangle$ average centroid radius of each class
$\langle r_c \rangle$ average radius of samples of each class about class centroid
$\langle R \rangle$ average radius of all the samples about the grand centroid

in standardized feature space, any of three single parameters can describe the configuration: (1) the average distance $\langle R_c \rangle$ of the class centroids from the grand (overall) centroid, or (2) the average distance $\langle r_c \rangle$ of the samples from their own class centroid, or (3) average separation $\langle e_c \rangle$ of the class centroids. These parameters depend on the features used. Once we know any one of them, we can compute the average separation of the class centroids and the average overlap of the class shells. These relations hold up surprisingly well across a broad range of dimensionality for both hand-printed and machine-printed data (Table 9.2). Figure 9.8 illustrates the putative d-dimensional configuration.

The disposition of the subclass centroids about the class centroids is not tetrahedral, as can be observed from Figures 9.9a and 9.9b. This is not surprising, because for communication purposes there is no real premium in being able to recognize style. Nevertheless, there are secondary problems like font and writer recognition where it is desired to discriminate styles

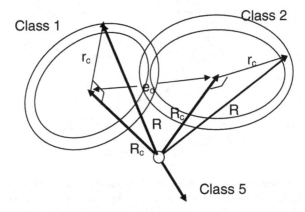

Fig. 9.8. Class configurations in feature space. The radii of the samples from their class centroids are orthogonal to the radii of the class centroids from the origin. The pairwise distance between class centroids can be computed from either.

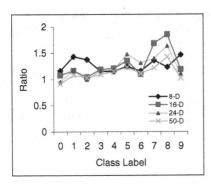

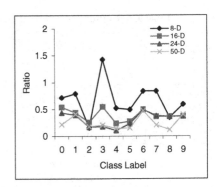

Fig. 9.9a. Ratio of range of distances between cluster centroids to their median distance (machine-printed digits). The range is the difference between the maximum and the minimum separation of the 3 pairs of cluster centroids. The ratios are high relative to those of Figure 9.6 because separation between cluster centroids varies much more than between class centroids.

Fig. 9.9b. Ratio of range of distances between cluster centroids to their median distance (hand-printed digits). The separation of the cluster centroids is not even approximately constant as in the machine-printed data.

rather than classes. We have found that the principal components that discriminate between classes are also most effective in separating styles [11].

Our observations are summarized in Table 9.3, which shows the parameters that character-ize our data sets in low-dimensional and in high-dimensional feature space. Table 9.3 indicates clearly that the separation of the class centroids is higher, and the class distributions are more compact, for machine print than for handprint.

Table 9.3. Parameters for two data sets in 8-d and in 50-d.

Data	d	$\langle R \rangle$	$\langle R_c \rangle$	$\langle r_c \rangle$	$\langle e \rangle$
MP	8	2.7	2.3	1.4	3.5
HP	8	2.7	2.1	1.9	3.0
MP	50	7.0	2.8	6.4	4.7
HP	50	7.0	2.5	6.5	3.7

9.3 Class Distributions

The determinant of the covariance matrix is a measure of the volume of a distribution. If the Gaussian assumption held, then the square root of the determinant would be proportional to the volume of the feature space that holds all the samples within one standard deviation of the mean. For a 1-d spherical distribution, 50% of the samples are within 0.6 standard deviations from the mean. For 8-d, 16-d, and 24-d, the corresponding values are 2.7, 3.9, and 4.8 standard deviations. We have computed the determinants of classes and subclasses in both data sets. We also recorded the average distance $\langle r_c \rangle$ and mean square distance $\langle r_c^2 \rangle$ of the samples from their class centroid.

If the class distributions were spherical like the overall distribution, then the expected squared radius $\mu_{r_c^2}$ of the samples could be computed from $|\Sigma_c|$, the determinant of their covariance matrix, and vice versa. As was seen in section 9.2, the expected squared radius of a zero-mean d-variant spherical distribution with components of variance σ^2 is $\mu_{r^2} = d\sigma^2$. Also $\sigma^2 = |\Sigma|^{1/d}$. Therefore $\sqrt{\mu_{r_c^2}} = \sqrt{d}|\Sigma_c|^{1/2d}$. Figure 9.10 plots $\sqrt{\langle r_c^2 \rangle}/\sqrt{d}\langle|\Sigma_c|\rangle^{1/2d}$ against d for both data sets. (The average is taken over all samples and classes and that of the determinants over the classes.) The ratio is greater than unity; therefore, the class distributions must be somewhat flattened. A more detailed examination shows that the above ratio is similar for all classes, with less than 5% difference for $d = 50$. The flattening increases with the dimensionality. We may imagine the class distributions as saucers of approximately the same size located at the vertices of a tetrahedron (Fig. 9.8).

Feature space, like the physical Universe, is very sparsely populated. We observed three volumes spanned by all the samples, by the class distributions, and by the subclass (class-style) distributions. Each distribution is assumed to have hyperellipsoidal equiprobability contours. The volume of the hyperellipsoid at a given probability density is proportional to the square root of the determinant of the corresponding covariance matrix. We compared three measures: the volume of all the samples, the sum of the volume of samples from each class, and the sum of the volume of samples from each subclass represented by the square root of the grand covariance matrix, the sum of the square roots of determinants of the class-conditional covari-ance matrix, and the sums of the square roots of the determinants of the subclass-conditional covariance matrices respectively. The values in Table 9.4 are the ratios of these different mea-

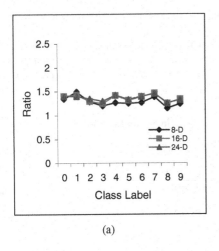
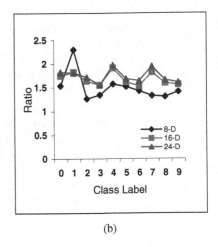

(a)   (b)

Fig. 9.10. The ratio of mean-square radius of the samples (distance from their class centroid) to value predicted under the spherical assumption from the determinant of the class covariance matrix. (a) Machine-printed samples. (b) Hand-printed samples.

sures in 8-dimensional feature space. Ratios of the same order of magnitude are obtained by computing the volumes of hyper-spheres according to the average radii. We conclude that there is a lot of empty space between classes, but much less between sub-classes.

Table 9.4. The ratios of the square roots of determinants of different covariance matrices.

Data	$\sqrt{|\Sigma_g|}/\sum_{c=1}^{C}\sqrt{|\Sigma_c|}$	$\sum_{c=1}^{C}\sqrt{|\Sigma_c|}/\sum_{c=1}^{C}\sum_{k=1}^{K}\sqrt{|\Sigma_{c,k}|}$
MP	8.7	1.4
HP	283	3.5

Σ_g grand covariance matrix
Σ_c class-conditional covariance matrix
$\Sigma_{c,k}$ class-style-conditional covariance matrix

The grand covariance matrix is the sum of the covariance matrices of the class mean vectors and of all the class-conditional covariance matrices. Similarly, for each class, the class-conditional covariance matrix is the sum of the covariance matrix of the subclass mean vectors and of all the subclass-conditional covariance matrices. These relationships are schematically illustrated in Figure 9.11. This figure portrays the relationship of equiprobability density contours of 3 classes and 12 subclasses in two dimensions.

Classes are of course most clearly distinguished from one another by their mean vectors. But are their covariance matrices also highly class-dependent? To answer this question, we compared pairs of estimated class-conditional covariance matrices under the assumption that they specify the feature dependences completely, i.e., that they induce Gaussian feature densities. For these comparisons we used two common similarity measures for probability densities,

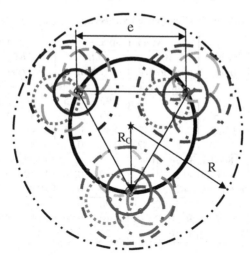

Fig. 9.11. Diagram of class and subclass geometry. The large solid circle passes through the three class centroids, located at the apexes of an equilateral triangle. The small solid circles pass through the centroids of the four subclasses of each class. The dotted and dashed circles represent equiprobability contours corresponding to the overall, class, and subclass covariance matrices.

specialized to Gaussian densities: the Bhattacharyya [12] and the Kullback-Leibler divergence [10].

The **Bhattacharyya (Bhatt)** distance between two distributions $p(X)$ and $q(X)$ is defined as

$$D_B(p(X); q(X)) = -\ln \int_\varphi [p(X)q(X)]^{\frac{1}{2}} dX \qquad (9.4)$$

where φ is the feature space containing all samples.

Between two Gaussian distributions, $p(X) = N(X; \mu_p, \Sigma_p), q(X) = N(X; \mu_q, \Sigma_q)$, it is

$$DB_N(\mu_p, \Sigma_p; \mu_q, \Sigma_q) = \frac{1}{8}(\mu_p - \mu_q)^T [\frac{\Sigma_p + \Sigma_q}{2}]^{-1}(\mu_p - \mu_q) + \frac{1}{2}\ln\frac{|\frac{\Sigma_p + \Sigma_q}{2}|}{\sqrt{|\Sigma_p||\Sigma_q|}} \qquad (9.5)$$

The **Kullback-Leibler (KL)** divergence for two distributions $p(X)$ and $q(X)$ is

$$KL(p(X); q(X)) = \int_\varphi p(X) \ln \frac{p(X)}{q(X)} dX \qquad (9.6)$$

and for two Gaussian distributions, $p(X) = N(X; \mu_p, \Sigma_p), q(X) = N(X; \mu_q, \Sigma_q)$, it is

$$KL_N(\mu_p, \Sigma_p; \mu_q, \Sigma_q) = \frac{1}{2}\ln\frac{|\Sigma_q|}{|\Sigma_p|} + \frac{1}{2}Tr(\Sigma_q^{-1}\Sigma_p) + \frac{1}{2}(\mu_p - \mu_q)^T \Sigma_q^{-1}(\mu_p - \mu_q) - \frac{d}{2} \qquad (9.7)$$

Table 9.5 shows the KL and Bhattacharyya distances (computed from the sample means and sample covariance matrices) between class-conditional distributions of selected sets of features for both hand-printed and machine-printed data. Comparing the low values of the distances in the top part of the table to the high values in the two bottom parts, it appears

Table 9.5. Divergence by class and by feature set.

| Configuration | Feature pairs | Machine-print | | | | Hand-print | | | |
| | | KL divergence | | Bhatt divergence | | KL divergence | | Bhatt divergence | |
		mean	std dev	mean	std dev	mean	std dev	mean	std dev
Different class	**1-8**	8.30	7.72	1.00	0.25	4.60	2.40	0.70	0.22
Same features	**9-16**	3.80	2.38	0.60	0.19	2.30	1.30	0.40	0.13
	17-24	3.20	2.12	0.50	0.15	1.60	0.91	0.30	0.10
	43-50	1.20	0.82	0.20	0.12	0.60	0.39	0.10	0.07
Same class	**1-8 9-16**	35.70	10.99	1.80	0.22	10.50	5.51	0.90	0.26
Different features	**1-8 17-24**	50.20	18.22	2.10	0.30	10.50	4.26	1.00	0.21
	1-8 43-50	54.20	23.10	2.20	0.25	10.80	3.72	0.10	0.20
Different class	**1-8 9-16**	43.50	26.13	1.90	0.45	10.10	6.02	0.90	0.29
Different features	**1-8 17-24**	56.90	35.28	2.10	0.50	11.80	7.82	1.00	0.36
	1-8 43-50	57.50	36.21	2.20	0.55	12.30	7.29	1.00	0.37

that the covariance matrix depends more on the feature set than on the class. With a given feature set, all of the classes will have similar covariance matrices. Therefore, a good estimate of the covariances can be obtained by pooling samples from all classes, while estimating the variances separately for each class. This may explain the relative success of classifiers based on an average covariance matrix and on covariance matrix regularization [13].

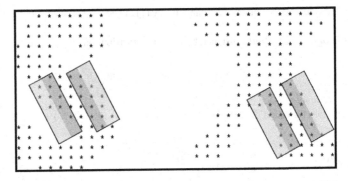

Fig. 9.12. The co-occurrence of two shapes, which leads to positive correlation between the corresponding features, depends more on the nature of the features than of the classes.

Figure 9.12 suggests why the covariance matrices depend more on the feature set than on the individual classes. Two features are shown, both responses to directional edge detectors. Such complementary gradients are likely to be present or absent at the same time, regardless of the class. Similar arguments can be made for many other types of features.

9.4 Departures from the Gaussian Model

The patterns are not distributed symmetrically about their class means. The usual measure of asymmetry is the *coefficient of skew* of the distribution. It is zero for a Gaussian. We project the patterns of each class onto the vector from the grand centroid (origin) to the class centroid. Figure 9.13 shows the distribution of these projected patterns in each class. Table 9.6 lists the coefficient of skew of these patterns. The negative values indicate a long tail towards the grand centroid. The machine-printed data also exhibit negative, though smaller, coefficients of skew.

Table 9.6. Coefficients of skew for hand-printed data.

Class	0	1	2	3	4	5	6	7	8	9	Features
Skew	−0.46	−0.91	0.03	−0.83	−0.27	0.18	−0.47	−0.55	−0.76	−0.38	2
	−0.66	−0.67	−0.09	−0.56	−0.43	−0.58	−1.03	−0.80	−0.45	−1.08	8
	−0.78	−0.95	−0.29	−0.46	−0.65	−0.72	−0.59	−0.13	−0.30	−0.80	16
	−0.93	−0.79	−0.36	−0.28	−0.48	−0.68	−0.40	−0.19	−0.29	−0.89	24
	−0.87	−1.08	−0.32	−0.46	−0.45	−0.84	−0.53	−0.55	−0.32	−0.68	50

Figure 9.14 shows some samples near the median and at the extreme values of the class distribution projected onto the vector from the origin to the class centroid. The variability of the patterns closer to the grand centroid is greater than that of the patterns far away. We have observed earlier that the error rate of a quadratic discriminant varies by a factor of five depending on which half of the patterns of each class is used for estimating the class-conditional covariance matrices [11]. These observations may eventually also lead to improved methods of regularization for estimating covariance matrices.

9.5 Single-Class Style

We now consider patterns labeled by source as well as by class. Instead of the distribution of all the samples of a class, we observe class- and source-conditional properties. We have already observed in section 9.3 that the volume occupied by samples partitioned either by clustering or by font is much less than the volume spanned by all the samples.

In this section we use *entropy* as a more precise measure of source consistency. *Single-class style* is the shape consistency of a single class among the samples from each source. For handwriting, sources usually correspond to writers, so in the rest of this section we refer specifically to writers rather than to generic sources. Our handwritten data sets contain about 100 isolated digits from each of 500 writers. They were partitioned, as mentioned, into three clusters for each class. How consistent are the writers? Do most of the digits of each writer tend to fall into a single cluster, indicating strong single-class style?

Note that style is not a property of a single writer, but of a whole group of writers. Even if a single writer always wrote a particular digit in the same way, without looking at the other writers we could not know whether it was the only way of writing this digit. If 90% of the writers always cross their sevens, then there is less style than if each writer is completely consistent, but half cross their sevens and half don't. The proposed measure reflects this consideration.

Quantification of Single-Class Style

To quantify single-class style, we first cluster the N feature vectors of M writers of a single digit class c into K clusters. (We do not use a subscript to denote the class, because all

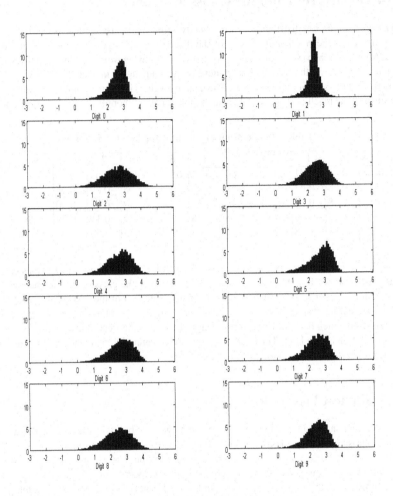

Fig. 9.13. Histogram of the distribution of the patterns of each class projected onto the vector from the grand centroid to the class centroid in 50-dimension feature space. The horizontal axes are labeled in units of standard deviation of the overall standardized sample distribution.

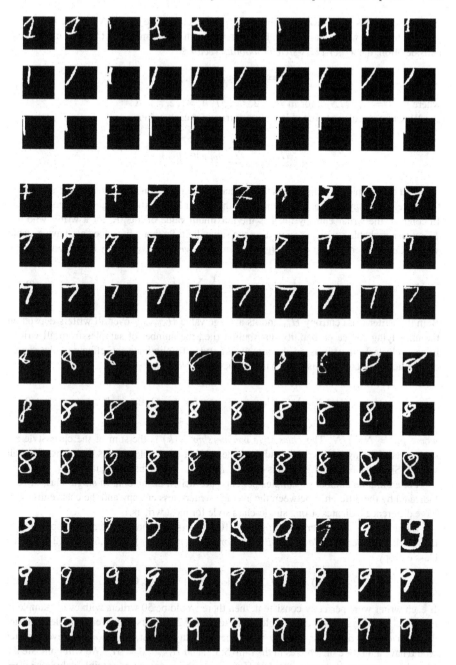

Fig. 9.14. For each class, from top to bottom: patterns nearest the grand centroid, near the class median sample, and farthest from the grand centroid. The patterns on the "outside" appear much more consistent. The patterns near the origin, and therefore near other classes, are more likely to be confused.

of the calculations are performed separately for each class.) We record $N_{m,k}$, the number of samples for each writer and cluster. For writer m with N_m samples of the digit class under consideration, the *writer-class-style probability vector* is

$$\mathbf{p}_m = (p_{m,1}, p_{m,2}, \ldots, p_{m,K}) \tag{9.8}$$

where $p_{m,k} = N_{m,k}/N_m$, for $m = 1, 2, \ldots, M$, $k = 1, 2, \ldots, K$.

We can now calculate the writer-class entropy for each writer:

$$H_m = -\sum_{k=1}^{K} p_{m,k} \log p_{m,k} \tag{9.9}$$

If all the samples of a digit class for a specific writer are assigned to the same cluster, then this writer's entropy is zero. That means that this writer has maximal single-class consistency. In contrast, the writer entropy reaches the maximum value of $\log_2 K$ for a writer who has K equally probable variations in writing the same digit. Such a writer does not have a stable single-class style for the observed digit. The *average writer-class entropy* is defined as

$$H_{average} = \frac{1}{M} \sum_{m=1}^{M} H_m \tag{9.10}$$

Both the writer-class entropy H_m and its average value $H_{average}$ over all writers depend on the underlying source probability distribution (i.e., the number of samples from all writers in each cluster), as well as on the amount of style. To eliminate the effects of the source distributions, we compute as a normalizing factor the *class entropy* H_c:

$$H_c = -\sum_{k=1}^{K} p_k \log_2 p_k \qquad \text{for } k = 1, 2, \ldots, K \tag{9.11}$$

where $p_k = N(k)/N$. The *class-style membership* $N(k)$ is the sum of the class-style assignments $N_{m,k}$ over all writers, and N is the number of samples of this digit class from all writers. Since the entropy function is convex, $H_{average}$ is less than or equal to H_c.

For an infinite number of samples per class per writer, the amount of single-class style is indicated by the difference between the average writer-class entropy and the class entropy. A large difference indicates strong single-class style for most writers.

Suppose that we cluster the samples of 100 writers into three clusters corresponding to their styles. The *class-style probability vector* $\mathbf{p} = (p_1, p_2, p_3) = (0.5, 0.3, 0.2)$, and the class entropy is

$$H_c = -(0.5 \log_2 0.5 + 0.3 \log_2 0.3 + 0.2 \log_2 0.2) = 1.49 \tag{9.12}$$

If each writer were perfectly consistent, then there would be 50 writers with every sample in cluster 1, 30 writers with every sample in cluster 2, and 20 writers with every sample in cluster 3. The average writer-class entropy would be zero. In contrast, with no style, every writer would have a mixture of samples in the ratio 5:3:2, and $H_{average} = H_c$. We will compare the empirically computed average entropy $H_{average}$ with its maximum possible value, the class entropy H_c, as a measure of single-class consistency.

However, first we must compensate for small-sample effects. With a finite number of samples, even if the writers did not exhibit single-class style, the cluster assignments would not all be exactly proportional to the elements of the class-style probability vector because of sampling fluctuations. These sampling fluctuations decrease the average entropy and may result in a significant difference between the average entropy and the class entropy even in the complete absence of single-class style. To account for the finite sample size (10 samples per class per writer), we compute the *expected class entropy* E[H] under the multinomial sampling distribution $P[n_1, n_2, \ldots, n_K; p_1, p_2, \ldots, p_K]$:

$$P[n_1, n_2, \ldots, n_K; p_1, p_2, \ldots, p_K] = \frac{n!}{\prod_{k=1}^{K} n_k!} \prod_{k=1}^{K} p_k^{n_k} \quad p_k = \frac{N(k)}{N}, n = \sum n_k = \frac{N}{M}$$

(9.13)

where $N(k)$ and N are the cluster and class memberships defined earlier.

We consider all the cases of the partitioning of n samples among K clusters and obtain the class entropy for each case:

$$H[n_1, n_2, \ldots, n_K] = - \sum_{k=1}^{K} \frac{n_k}{n} \log_2 \frac{n_k}{n}$$

(9.14)

The expected class entropy is then obtained by summing the product of the multinomial probability and the class entropy for every possible cluster assignment vector:

$$E[H] = \sum_{n_1=0}^{n} \sum_{n_2=0}^{n-n_1} \cdots \sum_{n_K=0}^{n-n_1-\cdots-n_{K-1}} P[n_1, n_2, , n_K; p_1, p_2, \ldots, p_K] H[n_1, n_2, \ldots, n_K]$$

(9.15)

Table 9.7. Expected and average entropy for all classes of hand-printed digits. If there were no single-class style, the ratio of the average entropy to the expected entropy would be near 1. (The entropies are normalized by dividing them by $log_2 3$, but this does not affect their ratio.)

Class c	Cluster Membership			E[H]	$H_{average}$	$\dfrac{H_{average}}{E[H]}$
	N(1)	N(2)	N(3)			
0	1179	1874	1391	0.89	0.52	0.58
1	2818	1393	625	0.77	0.39	0.51
2	1088	1459	1723	0.89	0.60	0.67
3	1100	1699	1701	0.89	0.58	0.65
4	1512	1822	769	0.85	0.45	0.54
5	912	1488	1312	0.87	0.48	0.55
6	950	1706	1547	0.88	0.47	0.54
7	811	1960	1710	0.85	0.49	0.57
8	1548	1344	1345	0.91	0.50	0.56
9	843	1672	1668	0.86	0.49	0.57

The expected entropy predicts the average entropy when there is no single-class style. We can judge how much single-class style is present in a data set according to the ratio of the average entropy to the expected entropy. If there were no single-class style, we would expect the average entropy to be close to the expected entropy. We have verified that when the writer identities of the samples are shuffled randomly, their ratio is over 0.98 for all classes. In contrast, the actual ratios are between 0.5 and 0.7, as seen from Table 9.7, which lists the average and expected entropy for $K = 3$ and 400 writers in the NIST SD3 data set. We also see from the table that "1" has least entropy while "2" has most. This means that individual writers exhibit more variability in writing the digit "2" than "1." We summarize this section with a diagram:

$$\underline{\text{Writer statistics}} \quad \underline{\text{Cluster statistics}}$$

$$H_m \qquad H_C$$
$$\Downarrow \qquad \quad \Downarrow$$
$$H_{average} \quad E[H]$$
$$\Downarrow \quad \Downarrow$$
$$1 - \frac{H_{average}}{E[H]} = \text{amount of single-pattern style}$$

9.6 Multiclass Style

Multiclass style derives from the correlation between the features of different samples, of the same or different class, from the same source. For now, consider only two patterns at a time, although the concept of multiclass style can be extended to an arbitrary number of patterns. We assume that all the samples have been clustered, as in the previous section. Now observe the cluster assignments of *pairs* of samples from the same writers. If the cluster assignments for samples of class i and class j of the same writer are statistically independent, then we can affirm that there is no multiclass style for class-pair (i, j).

Table 9.8 shows a toy example for the digits 5 and 6 with only ten writers and three clusters. There are exactly ten samples per class per writer. It is clear that writers who favor cluster 2 for digit 5 tend to favor cluster 3 for digit 6, while writers whose 5 usually falls into cluster 3 tend to write a 6 that often falls into cluster 1. Finally, fives of cluster 1 often happen to be associated with sixes of cluster 2. The numbering of the clusters is completely arbitrary.

A convenient measure of nonlinear statistical dependence is the *mutual information* (*MI*) between two variables X and Y with joint discrete probability distribution $P_{X,Y}(x, y)$. (Consider X the cluster assignment for the digit 5, and Y the cluster assignment for digit 6. For each writer, X and Y can each take on one of three possible values.) The marginal distributions $P_X(x)$ and $P_Y(y)$ can be computed by summation. Then

$$MI_{X,Y} = \sum_{x,y} P_{X,Y}(x, y) \log_2 \frac{P_{X,Y}(x, y)}{P_X(x) P_Y(y)} \tag{9.16}$$

We assign to every writer a cluster assignment vector (X, Y), $X = 1, 2,$ or 3; $Y = 1, 2,$ or 3, according to where (in which cluster) most of that writer's digits 5 and digits 6 fall. We count the number of each of the nine possible (x, y) combinations. Dividing these sums by the number of writers yields estimates of the probabilities $P_{X,Y}(x, y)$ required to compute the mutual information. Note that here again we have dropped the class subscripts, because the mutual information for every pair of classes is computed independently.

Table 9.8 shows cluster probabilities for each writer and the resulting style assignments. As mentioned, in this example, the cluster assignments are based simply on the dominant cluster of each writer and class, i.e., the cluster with the largest number of samples. Ties are broken randomly. The marginal and joint probabilities of X and Y, and the terms of the MI, are displayed below. The value 0.97 for the MI in this example is the sum of the individual terms. The minimum value of MI, when X and Y are independent, is 0. The maximum value of MI is $min[H_X, H_Y]$, which is $\log_2 3 = 1.6$ when all the cluster assignments are equally probable.

Table 9.8. An example of two-pattern style for digits 5 and 6.

	Writer specific cluster membership, probability, and assignment																	
	Number of samples falling in each cluster						Writer-specific cluster probability						Writer-specific cluster assignments					
Class	5			6			5			6			5			6		
Cluster	1	2	3	1	2	3	1	2	3	1	2	3	1	2	3	1	2	3
Writer 1	1	8	1	2	0	8	0.1	0.8	0.1	0.2	0.0	0.8	0	1	0	0	0	1
Writer 2	7	2	1	1	6	3	0.7	0.2	0.1	0.1	0.6	0.3	1	0	0	0	1	0
Writer 3	0	1	9	8	1	1	0.0	0.1	0.9	0.8	0.1	0.1	0	0	1	1	0	0
Writer 4	2	1	7	7	3	0	0.2	0.1	0.7	0.7	0.3	0.0	0	0	1	1	0	0
Writer 5	1	9	0	1	2	7	0.1	0.9	0.0	0.1	0.2	0.7	0	1	0	0	0	1
Writer 6	6	3	1	0	10	0	0.6	0.3	0.1	0.0	1.0	0.0	1	0	0	0	1	0
Writer 7	3	7	0	1	0	9	0.3	0.7	0.0	0.1	0.0	0.9	0	1	0	0	0	1
Writer 8	8	1	1	2	8	0	0.8	0.1	0.1	0.2	0.8	0.0	1	0	0	0	1	0
Writer 9	1	0	9	0	10	0	0.1	0.0	0.9	0.0	1.0	0.0	0	0	1	0	1	0
Writer 10	10	0	0	9	1	0	1.0	0.0	0.0	0.9	0.1	0.0	1	0	0	1	0	0
	39	32	29	31	41	28	0.39	0.32	0.29	0.31	0.41	0.28	4	3	3	3	4	3

Marginal probability P(x), P(y) and joint probabilities P(x,y)				
Joint probability P(x,y)	P(y)-Class 6			P(x) (Class 5)
X-Class 5	1	2	3	
1	0.1	0.3	0.0	0.4
2	0.0	0.0	0.3	0.3
3	0.2	0.1	0.0	0.3
P(y) (Class 6)	0.3	0.4	0.3	1.0

Mutual Information $MI = 0.97$			
P(x,y)logP(x,y)/[P(x)P(y)]	1	2	3
1	−0.02	0.27	0
2	0	0	0.52
3	0.23	−0.03	0

It is possible to quantize the cluster assignments more finely. Even for only pairs of samples, the number of combinations of the values of X and Y grows quadratically. One soon reaches the point where there are not enough samples for accurate estimates of the joint probabilities.

Table 9.9. Observed MI for hand-printed class pairs.

Class MI	0	1	2	3	4	5	6	7	8	9
0	2.29	0.49	0.26	0.34	0.41	0.26	0.52	0.49	0.34	0.49
1		1.93	0.31	0.44	0.63	0.29	0.52	0.60	0.44	0.69
2			2.31	0.25	0.21	0.13	0.24	0.30	0.18	0.24
3				2.31	0.37	0.17	0.30	0.44	0.28	0.39
4					2.21	0.24	0.42	0.50	0.37	0.61
5						2.32	0.24	0.25	0.23	0.22
6							2.25	0.53	0.34	0.50
7								2.19	0.33	0.65
8									2.37	0.35
9										2.24

Table 9.9 shows the observed values of the MI for every pair of classes in SD3. We generated 64 possible cluster assignments for each digit-pair by quantizing the cluster probabilities at two levels each, resulting in eight assignments per writer per class. Many of these assignments never occur in our data. The quantization threshold was the corresponding cluster probability. More than one style can be assigned to a writer if he is inconsistent. We observe that the values on the diagonal, i.e., for same class pairs, deviate from their maximum possible value of $\log_2 8 = 3.0$ because the clusters don't contain the same number of samples. We have verified that when the data is shuffled to eliminate multiclass style, the values of the MI are always less than 0.1.

9.7 Conclusion

We discussed the configuration of symbolic patterns in feature space. Our conjectures are based on relatively broad assumptions about sets of independent samples of several classes generated by multiple sources (i.e., *source-conditional independence* between the observable attributes of the patterns). They are supported only by statistics collected on specific features extracted from scanned printed and hand-printed numerals. We now summarize our findings, subject to this caveat.

1. Standardizing the pattern vectors to zero mean, identity covariance variables facilitate comparing data sets, within or across domains, with different patterns, features, and dimensionality.

2. In a standardized feature space, the average radius (distance from the origin) of the patterns depends only on the number of features. The mean of the radius can be predicted accurately based on the dimensionality alone. The mean increases faster with dimensionality than the standard deviation. Therefore, in any standardized high-dimensional feature space, most of the samples will be contained in a thin spherical shell even if the sample density is highest at the origin. This phenomenon is a direct consequence of well-known statistical facts. The optimal decision boundaries, therefore, intersect at the origin of the standardized feature space.

3. When the feature dimensionality exceeds the number of classes, the centroids of *symbolic* patterns are located at the vertices of a regular simplex. The observed distribution of pairwise distances is very peaked and its average value can be predicted accurately from the

average radius of the class centroids. This can be explained only by the evolution of symbolic patterns toward maximum discriminability, and may not hold for *natural* patterns. The equidistance of class centroids may serve as an indication of the merit of a feature set, without resorting to actual classification.

4. The pairwise distances between subclass centroids obtained by clustering the feature vectors of each class, or by typeface designations, are *not* approximately equal, even in high dimensions, nor could one expect it. Some pairs of styles are likely to be more similar than others if style labels reflect shape.

5. The average distance of the samples from their own class centroids is about 50% higher than predicted from the determinants of their covariance matrices under a spherical (identity covariance matrix) assumption. The class distributions, therefore, are somewhat "flattened." However, the ratio of the predicted distances to observed distances is fairly uniform across classes, suggesting that the distributions may be similar, except for scale.

6. The divergence between pattern distributions of the same class with different feature sets is significantly larger than between different classes with the same feature set. We expect the class-conditional correlation matrices to be quite similar in any given feature space, because they are determined more by the feature set than by the class. This holds for both *Kullback-Leibler* and *Bhattacharyya* distance, although these two measures of the similarity of two pdfs are not highly correlated. These observations bear on the *regularization* of covariance matrices in small-sample conditions.

7. The class-conditional distributions of symbolic features are asymmetric. In training a classifier, one may safely ignore samples on the "far" side of their class centroids, which exhibit less variation. Support vector machines, of course, do just that.

8. The amount of single-class style in a data set, i.e., within-source consistency, can be quantified by comparing the observed average entropy of style assignments to the expected entropy of an appropriate multinomial distribution. Single-class style can be exploited for classification through adaptation [14, 15, 16].

9. The amount of multiclass style, i.e., the statistical dependence between features extracted from samples of different classes from the same source, can be quantified by the mutual entropy of the style assignments. Multiclass style can be exploited through style-consistent classification [17, 18].

We intend to conduct similar measurements on natural patterns. We hope that a growing collection of such measurements on diverse multisource collections of samples will provide insight into the intrinsic complexity of classification tasks.

Acknowledgments

We are indebted to Rensselaer Polytechnic Institute graduate student Srinivas Andra for his help in some of the calculations, and we are most grateful for many excellent suggestions by a conscientious and perspicacious referee.

References

[1] T.K. Ho, M. Basu. Complexity measures of supervised classification problems. *IEEE Transactions on Pattern Analysis & Machine Intelligence*, 24(3), 289–300, 2002.

[2] C.L. Liu, H. Sako, H. Fujisawa. Performance evaluation of pattern classifiers for handwritten character recognition. *International Journal on Document Analysis and Recognition*, 4(3), 191–204, 2002.

[3] R. McLean. *Typography*. London: Thames & Hudson, 1980.

[4] R. Plamondon. A kinematic theory of rapid human movements, part I. *Biological Cybernetics*, 72(4), 295–307, 1995.

[5] R. Plamondon. A kinematic theory of rapid human movements, part II. *Biological Cybernetics*, 72(4), 309–320, 1995.

[6] R. Plamondon. A kinematic theory of rapid human movements, part III. *Biological Cybernetics*, 78, 133–145, 1999.

[7] J. Greenberg. *Universals of Human Language*, vol. 2. Stanford, CA: Stanford University Press, 1978.

[8] R. Raimi. The first digit problem. *American Mathematical Monthly*, 83, 521–538, 1976.

[9] M.J. Nigrini. "I've got your number" – CPA use of Benford's law of mathematics in discovering fraud: how a mathematical phenomenon can help CPAs uncover fraud and other irregularities. *Journal of Accountancy*, 79–80, May 1999.

[10] R.O. Duda, P.E. Hart. *Pattern Classification and Scene Analysis*. New York: John Wiley and Sons, 1973.

[11] G. Nagy, S. Veeramachaneni. A ptolemaic model for OCR. *Procs. ICDAR-03*, Edinburgh, August 2003, pp. 1060–1064.

[12] K. Fukunaga. *Introduction to Statistical Pattern Recognition*. New York: Academic Press, 1972.

[13] G.J. McLachlan. *Discriminant Analysis and Statistical Pattern Recognition*. New York: Wiley Series in Probability and Mathematical Statistics, 1992.

[14] G. Nagy, G.L. Shelton. Self-corrective character recognition system. *IEEE Transactions on Information Theory*, 12(2), 215–222, 1966.

[15] S. Veeramachaneni, G. Nagy. Adaptive classifiers for multi-source OCR. *International Journal on Document Analysis and Recognition*, 6(3), 154–166, 2004.

[16] G. Nagy. Classifiers that improve with use. In *Procs. Conference on Pattern Recognition and Multimedia*, Tokyo, Februrary 2004, IEICE, pp. 79–86.

[17] P. Sarkar, G. Nagy. Style consistent classification of isogenous patterns. *IEEE Transactions on Pattern Analysis & Machine Intelligence*, 27(1), 88–98, 2005.

[18] S. Veeramachaneni, G. Nagy. Style context with second-order statistics. *IEEE Transactions on Pattern Analysis & Machine Intelligence*, 27(1), 14–22, 2005.

List of Symbols

C	The number of classes
$D_B(\cdot)$	Bhattacharyya distance between two distributions $p(X)$ and $q(X)$
$D_{BN}(\cdot)$	Bhattacharyya distance between two Gaussian distributions
$E[H]$	Expected class entropy for samples of a class sampled from multinomial distribution
$H_{average}$	Average writer-class entropy
H_c	Class entropy
H_m	Writer-class entropy for writer m
$H[n_1, n_2, \ldots, n_K]$	Class entropy for a cluster assignment vector $[n_1, n_2, \ldots, n_K]$
K	Number of styles
$KL(\cdot)$	Kullback-Leibler divergence for two distributions $p(X)$ and $q(X)$
$KL_N(\cdot)$	Kullback-Leibler divergence for two Gaussian distributions
M	Number of writers
$MI_{X,Y}$	Mutual information between two variables x and y
N	Number of patterns of a class from all writers
$N(X; \mu, \Sigma)$	Normal distribution with mean μ and covariance matrix Σ
N_m	Number of patterns within a class for writer m
$N_{m,k}$	Number of patterns within a class for writer m and class-style k
$N(k)$	Class-style membership for class-style k
P	Class-style probability vector
$P_X(x)$	Marginal probability for variable X
$P_{X,Y}(x, y)$	Joint discrete probability distribution between variable X and Y
R_i	Distance of pattern X_i from the origin
R_c	Radius of centroid of class c
X_i	Instance of the ith random d-dimensional singlet-pattern feature vector
c	Instance of a class label
d	Dimensionality of the singlet-pattern feature space
e_d	Length of edges of c-dimensional regular tetrahedron
k	Instance of a style label
m	Instance of a writer
n	Average number of patterns within a class for each writer
n_k	Number of patterns of class-style k for each writer
$[n_1, n_2, \ldots, n_K]$	Class-cluster assignment vector
$p(\cdot)$	Distribution of samples
p_k	Probability for class-style k
$\mathbf{p}_m$	Writer-class-style probability vector for writer m
$p_{m,k}$	Writer-class-style probability for writer m and class-style k
r_c	Radius of samples of class c from class centroid
r_c^2	Square radius of samples of class c from class centroid
$x_{i,j}$	The jth feature component of a feature vector X_i
Σ_c	Class covariance matrix
$\Sigma_{c,k}$	Class-style covariance matrix
Σ_g	Grand covariance matrix
φ	The feature space of all samples
μ	Mean
σ	Standard deviation
$<>$	Average operation
$\lvert \cdot \rvert$	Determinant of a matrix

10

Polynomial Time Complexity Graph Distance Computation for Web Content Mining

Adam Schenker, Horst Bunke, Mark Last, and Abraham Kandel

Summary. Utilizing graphs with unique node labels reduces the complexity of the maximum common subgraph problem, which is generally NP-complete, to that of a polynomial time problem. Calculating the maximum common subgraph is useful for creating a graph distance measure, since we observe that graphs become more similar (and thus have less distance) as their maximum common subgraphs become larger and vice versa. With a computationally practical method of determining distances between graphs, we are no longer limited to using simpler vector representations for machine learning applications. We can perform well-known algorithms, such as k-means clustering and k-nearest neighbors classification, directly on data represented by graphs, losing none of the inherent structural information. We demonstrate the benefits of the additional information retained in a graph-based data model for web content mining applications. We introduce several graph representations for capturing web document information and present some examples of our experimental results, which compare favorably with traditional vector methods.

10.1 Introduction

In this chapter we consider applying data mining algorithms, such as the k-nearest neighbors classification algorithm and k-means clustering algorithm, to web document content; this is known as *web content mining*. Content-based classification of web documents is useful because it allows users to more easily navigate and browse collections of documents [1, 2]. Such classifications are often costly to perform manually, as it requires a human expert to examine the content of each web document. Due to the large number of documents available on the Internet in general, or even when we consider smaller collections of web documents, such as those associated with corporate or university web sites, an automated system that performs web document classification is desirable in order to reduce costs and increase the speed with which new documents are classified. Clustering is an unsupervised method that attempts to organize data items into similar groups, while classification is a supervised learning technique that aims to assign a specific label to each data item. In web content mining, clustering is performed in order to arrange web documents into related groups, such as by the topic of the documents. This has benefits when the classes are not known a priori, such as in web search engines [3], since it allows systems to display results grouped by clusters (topics), in comparison to the usual "endless" ranked list, making browsing easier for the user. Using classification techniques with these types of systems is difficult due to the highly dynamic nature of the Internet; creating and maintaining a training set would be challenging and costly. Similarly, for clustering methods, cluster centers, or other representatives used for the clusters, are required to change over time to reflect the Internet's constant and rapid influence on language and emerging new concepts. This process occurs, for example, because the topic associated with a cluster representative takes on new meanings (e.g., "Java"), or because new concepts are created that previously had no clusters related to them (e.g., "blogs"). With the arrival of new training examples, we can create new clusters or update existing ones using methods of incremental clustering (see [4]).

Traditionally, data mining methods have represented document content with a vector model, which utilizes a series of numeric values associated with each document. Each value is associated with a specific term (word) that may appear on a document, and the set of possible terms is shared across all documents. The values may be binary, indicating the presence or absence of the corresponding term. The values may also be nonnegative integers, which represent the number of times a term appears on a document (i.e., term frequency). Nonnegative real numbers can also be used, in this case indicating the importance or weight of each term. These values are derived through a method such as the popular inverse document frequency model [5], which reduces the importance of terms that appear on many documents. Regardless of the method used, each series of values represents a document and corresponds to a point (i.e., vector) in a Euclidean feature space; this is called the vector-space model of information retrieval. This model is often used when applying data mining techniques to documents, as there is a strong mathematical foundation for performing distance measure and centroid calculations using vectors. However, this method of document representation does not capture important structural information, such as the order and proximity of term occurrence, or the location of term occurrence within the document.

To overcome this limitation, we have introduced several methods of representing web document content using graphs instead of vectors, and have extended existing data mining methods to work with these graphs. Graphs are important and effective mathematical constructs for modeling relationships and structural information. Graphs (and their more restrictive form, trees) are used in many different problems, including sorting, compression, traffic/flow analysis, resource allocation, etc. [6] Utilizing graphs allows us to keep the inherent structural information of the original web document without having to discard information as we do with a vector model representation. However, until recently, we have not had available to us mathematical techniques for determining distance between graphs as we have had with vectors. Thus data mining techniques such as clustering and classification could not be applied to graphs without creating new mathematical frameworks for dealing with the graphs.

In this chapter we show how the determination of the maximum common subgraph between a pair of graphs can lead to a numerical distance measure between the graphs [7]. A problem with computing the maximum common subgraph is that this is an NP-complete problem in the general case. However, it has been shown that when the nodes in the graphs have unique labels associated with them, the time complexity of finding the maximum common subgraph becomes polynomial [8]. We introduce several methods of representing web document content by graphs with unique node labels. We then proceed to describe how these graphs may be clustered or classified by straightforward extensions to well-known machine learning algorithms such as k-means or k-nearest neighbors when utilizing graph distance measures. We also show some examples of some experimental results obtained from using our graph-based methods.

The remainder of the chapter is organized as follows. In section 10.2 we discuss the complexity issues related to using graphs in machine learning. We show how the maximum common subgraph of a pair of graphs can be used to derive a distance measure between the graphs, and how this computation of the maximum common subgraph can be performed in polynomial time when the graphs have unique node labels. We describe our graph representations of web document content, which make use of the unique node label property, in section 10.3. Versions of the k-means clustering and k-nearest neighbors classification algorithms that utilize graphs and graph distance measures are presented in Section 10.4. Section 10.5 presents some examples of results obtained when using these algorithms to perform web content mining on graph-based data. Conclusions are presented in section 10.6.

10.2 Graph Complexity

10.2.1 Basic Definitions

In this subsection we present some basic definitions related to graph theory. Practically speaking, *graphs* are used to model some system of entities such that the entities are represented by *nodes* in the graph and the relationships present between the entities are reflected in the *edges* connecting the nodes. Formally, we define a graph as follows:

Definition 1. *A graph G is a 4-tuple: $G = (V, E, \alpha, \beta)$, where V is a set of nodes (also called vertices), $E \subseteq V \times V$ is a set of edges connecting the nodes, $\alpha: V \rightarrow \Sigma_V$ is a function labeling the nodes, and $\beta: V \times V \rightarrow \Sigma_E$ is a function labeling the edges (Σ_V and Σ_E being the sets of labels that can appear on the nodes and edges, respectively). For brevity, we may abbreviate G as $G = (V, E)$ by omitting the labeling functions.*

A graph that is contained within another graph is called a *subgraph*. Conversely, a graph that contains another graph is also called a *supergraph*. Formally, subgraphs and supergraphs are defined as follows:

Definition 2. *A graph $G_1 = (V_1, E_1, \alpha_1, \beta_1)$ is a subgraph of a graph $G_2 = (V_2, E_2, \alpha_2, \beta_2)$, denoted $G_1 \subseteq G_2$, if $V_1 \subseteq V_2$, $E_1 \subseteq E_2 \cap (V_1 \times V_1)$, $\alpha_1(x) = \alpha_2(x) \ \forall x \in V_1$, and $\beta_1((x, y)) = \beta_2((x, y)) \ \forall (x, y) \in E_1$. Conversely, graph G_2 is also called a supergraph of G_1.*

When we say that two graphs are *isomorphic*, we mean that the graphs contain the same number of nodes and there is a direct 1-to-1 correspondence between the nodes in the two graphs such that the edges between nodes and all labels are preserved.

Definition 3. *Formally, a graph $G_1 = (V_1, E_1, \alpha_1, \beta_1)$ and a graph $G_2 = (V_2, E_2, \alpha_2, \beta_2)$ are said to be isomorphic, denoted $G_1 \cong G_2$, if there exists a bijective function $f: V_1 \rightarrow V_2$ such that the following conditions are met:*

1. $\forall x \in V_1: \ \alpha_1(x) = \alpha_2(f(x))$
2. $\forall (x, y) \in E_1: \ (f(x), f(y)) \in E_2 \text{ and } \beta_1((x, y)) = \beta_2((f(x), f(y)))$
3. $\forall (f(x), f(y)) \in E_2: \ (x, y) \in E_1 \text{ and } \beta_2((f(x), f(y))) = \beta_1((x, y))$

Such a function f is also called a graph isomorphism between G_1 and G_2.

There is also the notion of *subgraph isomorphism*, meaning that a graph is isomorphic to a part of (i.e., a subgraph of) another graph:

Definition 4. *Given a graph isomorphism f between graphs G_1 and G_2 as defined above and another graph G_3, if $G_2 \subseteq G_3$, then f is a* subgraph isomorphism *between G_1 and G_3.*

Graph isomorphism was one of the earliest approaches to *graph matching*, the procedure of determining if two graphs are identical to each other. It is not known whether graph isomorphism is an NP-complete problem; however, subgraph isomorphism is NP-complete [9]. Clearly, as the number of nodes in the graphs increase, the number of possible matchings to be checked increases combinatorally. A general procedure for determining subgraph isomorphism is given in Ullman [10]. The naive algorithm for graph isomorphism is to maintain a matrix that indicates which nodes in each graph are compatible; it can require all possible permutations of matchings to determine if there is an isomorphism. The procedure in Ullman [10] improves the complexity by pruning the search space.

Graph isomorphism tells us only that there exists an exact match between two graphs (i.e., that they are identical). It does not give us any indication of similarity between graphs, only whether they are isomorphic or not. Subgraph isomorphism tells us if one graph appears as part of another graph. More relaxed approaches to graph matching, *inexact graph matching* and *graph distance*, have been proposed [11, 12]. Inexact graph matching attempts not to find if two graphs are identical, but rather attempts to find a mapping between the nodes of two graphs that achieves maximum similarity (a "best" matching). Graph distance approaches provide a numerical value that approximates the dissimilarity (distance) between two graphs.

Such new methods have become very important for pattern recognition and machine learning, as they allow us to deal with more robust graph-based data in a manner similar to those used for simpler vector models. Specifically, they permit algorithms to better tolerate noise and imperfect data in the graphs. For example, a missing node or edge caused by noise is not acceptable under graph isomorphism, but may still achieve good results using an inexact matching approach.

10.2.2 Maximum Common Subgraph

A popular method for determining graph distance is the *graph edit distance* approach. *Edit distance* is a method that is used to measure the difference between symbolic data structures such as trees [13] and strings [14]. It is also known as the *Levenshtein distance*, from early work in error-correcting/detecting codes that allowed insertion and deletion of symbols [15]. The concept is straightforward. Various operations are defined on the structures, such as deletion, insertion, and renaming of elements. A cost function is associated with each operation, and the minimum cost needed to transform one structure into the other using the operations is the distance between them. Edit distance has also been applied to graphs, as graph edit distance [16, 17]. The operations in graph edit distance are insertion, deletion, and relabeling of nodes and edges. The distance between two graphs is thus the minimum cost needed to edit one graph into the other by adding, deleting, and renaming nodes and edges.

It has been shown that there is a direct relationship between graph edit distance and the maximum common subgraph between two graphs [7]. Specifically, the two are equivalent under certain restrictions on the cost functions. The *maximum common subgraph* of two graphs is the largest graph the two graphs have in common, and is defined as follows:

Definition 5. *A graph g is a* maximum common subgraph (mcs) *of graphs G_1 and G_2, denoted $mcs(G_1, G_2)$, if: (1) $g \subseteq G_1$ (2) $g \subseteq G_2$ and (3) there is no other subgraph g' ($g' \subseteq G_1$, $g' \subseteq G_2$) such that $|g'| > |g|$.*

In definition 5 above, $|g|$ is usually taken to mean $|V|$, i.e., the number of nodes in the graph; it is used to indicate the "size" of a graph. However, in this chapter we use a different definition of graph size that also takes into account the contribution of the edges in the graphs (see equation (10.5)). Otherwise, with the traditional definition, a sparsely connected graph with many nodes is considered larger than a graph with a few nodes but many edges.

Similar to the maximum common subgraph, there is the complementary idea of minimum common supergraph:

Definition 6. *A graph g is a* minimum common supergraph (MCS) *of graphs G_1 and G_2, denoted $MCS(G_1, G_2)$, if: (1) $G_1 \subseteq g$ (2) $G_2 \subseteq g$ and (3) there is no other supergraph g' $(G_1 \subseteq g', G_2 \subseteq g')$ such that $|g'| < |g|$.*

One method for determining the maximum common subgraph is given in Levi [18]; this approach is to create a compatibility graph for the two given graphs, and then find the largest clique within it. Another approach involves backtracking search [19].

Following the observation that the size of the maximum common subgraph is related to the similarity between two graphs, a graph distance measure based on the maximum common subgraph has been introduced [20]:

$$d_{MCS}(G_1, G_2) = 1 - \frac{|mcs(G_1, G_2)|}{\max(|G_1|, |G_2|)}, \qquad (10.1)$$

where $\max(x, y)$ is the usual maximum of two numbers x and y, and $|\ldots|$ indicates the size of a graph (see above). The concept behind this distance measure is that as the size of the maximum common subgraph of a pair of graphs becomes larger, the more similar the two graphs are (i.e., they have more in common). The larger the maximum common subgraph, the smaller $d_{MCS}(G_1, G_2)$ becomes, indicating more similarity and less distance. If the two graphs are in fact identical, their maximum common subgraph is the same as the graphs themselves, and thus the size of all three graphs is equal: $|G_1| = |G_2| = |mcs(G_1, G_2)|$. This leads to the distance, $d_{MCS}(G_1, G_2)$, becoming 0. Conversely, if no maximum common subgraph exists, then $|mcs(G_1, G_2)| = 0$ and $d_{MCS}(G_1, G_2) = 1$. This distance measure has been shown to be a metric [20], and produces a value in $[0, 1]$. This distance measure has four important properties. First, it is restricted to producing a number in the interval $[0, 1]$. Second, the distance is 0 only when the two graphs are identical. Third, the distance between two graphs is symmetric. Fourth, it obeys the triangle inequality, which ensures that the distance measure behaves in an intuitive way. For example, if we have two dissimilar objects (i.e., there is a large distance between them) the triangle inequality implies that a third object that is similar (i.e., has a small distance) to one of those objects must be dissimilar to the other. The advantage of this approach over the graph edit distance method is that it does not require the determination of any cost coefficients or other parameters. However, the metric as it is defined in (10.1) may not be appropriate for all applications; for example, the size of the smaller graph in d_{MCS} makes no contribution to the value of the distance measure, which may be useful to consider in some instances. Thus other distance measures based on the size of the maximum common subgraph or minimum common supergraph have been proposed.

A second distance measure that has been proposed by Wallis et al. [21], based on the idea of graph union, is

$$d_{WGU}(G_1, G_2) = 1 - \frac{|mcs(G_1, G_2)|}{|G_1| + |G_2| - |mcs(G_1, G_2)|}. \qquad (10.2)$$

By "graph union" we mean that the denominator represents the size of the union of the two graphs in the set theoretic sense; specifically adding the size of each graph ($|G_1| + |G_2|$)

and then subtracting the size of their intersection ($|mcs(G_1, G_2)|$) leads to the size of the union (the reader may easily verify this using a Venn diagram). This distance measure behaves similarly to d_{MCS}. The motivation for using graph union in the denominator is to allow for changes in the smaller graph to exert some influence over the distance measure, which does not happen with d_{MCS}, as mentioned above. This measure was also demonstrated to be a metric, and creates distance values in $[0, 1]$.

Fernández and Valiente [22] have proposed a distance measure based on both the maximum common subgraph and the minimum common supergraph:

$$d_{MMCS}(G_1, G_2) = |MCS(G_1, G_2)| - |mcs(G_1, G_2)|, \qquad (10.3)$$

where $MCS(G_1, G_2)$ is the minimum common supergraph of graphs G_1 and G_2. The concept that drives this distance measure is that the maximum common subgraph provides a "lower bound" on the similarity of two graphs, while the minimum common supergraph is an "upper bound." If two graphs are identical, then both their maximum common subgraph and minimum common supergraph are the same as the original graphs and $|G_1| = |G_2| = |MCS(G_1, G_2)| = |mcs(G_1, G_2)|$, which leads to $d_{MMCS}(G_1, G_2) = 0$. As the graphs become more dissimilar, the size of the maximum common subgraph decreases, while the size of the minimum common supergraph increases. This in turn leads to increasing values of $d_{MMCS}(G_1, G_2)$. For two graphs with no maximum common subgraph, the distance will become $|MCS(G_1, G_2)| = |G_1| + |G_2|$. d_{MMCS} has also been shown to be a metric, but it does not produce values normalized to the interval $[0, 1]$, unlike d_{MCS} or d_{WGU}. Note that if it holds that $|MCS(G_1, G_2)| = |G_1| + |G_2| - |mcs(G_1, G_2)| \ \forall G_1, G_2$, we can compute $d_{MMCS}(G_1, G_2)$ as $|G_1| + |G_2| - 2|mcs(G_1, G_2)|$. This is much less computationally intensive than computing the minimum common supergraph.

10.2.3 Graphs with Unique Node Labels

As mentioned above, the subgraph isomorphism problem is NP-complete. As finding the maximum common subgraph requires determining subgraph isomorphism, it is also an NP-complete problem [8]. However, recently it has become known that for certain classes of graphs the maximum common subgraph, and thus the graph distance, can be determined in polynomial time. Specifically, graphs whose node labels are unique can have their maximum common subgraphs computed in $O(n^2)$ time, where n is the number of nodes in the graph [8]. Formally, a graph has unique node labels according to the following definition:

Definition 7. *A graph $G = (V, E, \alpha, \beta)$ has unique node labels if for $\forall v_1, v_2 \in V, \alpha(v_1) \neq \alpha(v_2)$ unless $v_1 = v_2$.*

Note that the elements of set V, i.e., the nodes, are always uniquely defined. However, in the general case, i.e., in a graph without any restrictions, different nodes may carry the same label. For example, the field of chemistry uses graphs to represent molecules; nodes correspond to atoms and edges to bonds formed between atoms. A water molecule (H_2O) would have a graph with three nodes: one for oxygen (labeled "O") and two for hydrogen (both labeled "H").

The above result follows from the fact that determining the nodes of the maximum common subgraphs between two graphs, $G_1 = (V_1, E_1, \alpha_1, \beta_1)$ and $G_2 = (V_2, E_2, \alpha_2, \beta_2)$, each with unique node labels, reduces to the problem of finding the intersection of two sets, namely $GL_1 = \{\alpha_1(v)|\forall v \in V_1\}$ and $GL_2 = \{\alpha_2(v)|\forall v \in V_2\}$. Similarly the minimum common supergraph can be computed by taking the union of these two sets. The actual procedure can be performed as follows:

1. Determine the set of labels that each of the two original graphs have in common, GL_{mcs}, by computing the intersection of sets GL_1 and GL_2 (see above), i.e., $GL_{mcs} = GL_1 \cap GL_2$.
2. For each label $L \in GL_{mcs}$, create a new node N in V_{mcs} labeled such that $\alpha_{mcs}(N) = L$.
3. Determine the edges of the maximum common subgraph E_{mcs} by examining all pairs of nodes in V_{mcs} and add edges to E_{mcs} that connect pairs of nodes in both of the original graphs and that have matching edge labels; the added edge in the maximum common subgraph will have the same label.

We see that the complexity of this method is $O(|V_1| \cdot |V_2|)$ for step 1, since we need only compare each node label from one graph to each node label of the other and determine whether there is a match or not. Thus the maximum number of comparisons is $|V_1| \cdot |V_2|$, and since each node has a unique label we need to consider each combination only once. For step 2, the complexity is $O(|V_{mcs}|)$. The complexity is $O(|V_{mcs}|^2)$ for step 3, since we have $|V_{mcs}|$ nodes and we look at all combinations of pairs of nodes to determine if an edge should be added between them or not:

$$\binom{|V_{mcs}|}{2} = \frac{|V_{mcs}|!}{(|V_{mcs}| - 2)! \cdot 2!} = \frac{|V_{mcs}| \cdot (|V_{mcs}| - 1)}{2} < |V_{mcs}|^2. \tag{10.4}$$

Thus the overall complexity is $O(|V_1| \cdot |V_2| + |V_{mcs}| + |V_{mcs}|^2) \leq O(|V|^2 + |V_{mcs}|^2) = O(|V|^2)$ if we substitute $V = \max(|V_1|, |V_2|)$. Note that the case of the minimum common supergraph is the same, except we change the intersection in step 1 to a union.

Given this result, we introduce graph representations of data that utilize unique node labels to take advantage of the improved time complexity for determining the maximum common subgraph, which, in turn, allows for graph distance to be calculated in polynomial time. Our application domain is web content mining, and our graph representations of web documents are given in the next section.

10.3 Graph Representations for Web Document Content

In this section we describe methods for representing web document content using graphs with unique node labels instead of the vector representations that are traditionally used. All representations are based on the adjacency of terms in a web document. These representations are named *standard*, *simple*, *n-distance*, *n-simple distance*, *raw frequency*, and *normalized frequency*.

Under the *standard* method each unique term (word) appearing in the document, except for *stop words* such as "the," "of," and "and," which convey little information, becomes a node in the graph representing that document. Each node is labeled with the term it represents. Note that we create only a single node for each word even if a word appears more than once in the text. Also, if word a immediately precedes word b somewhere in a "section" s of the document, then there is a directed edge from the node corresponding to term a to the node corresponding to term b with an edge label s. We take into account certain punctuation (such as periods) and do not create an edge when these are present between two words. Sections we have defined for the standard representation are *title*, which contains the text related to the document's title and any provided keywords (meta-data); *link*, which is text that appears in hyperlinks on the document; and *text*, which comprises any of the visible text in the document (this includes text in links, but not text in the document's title and keywords). Next we remove the most infrequently occurring words in each document, leaving at most m nodes per graph (m being a user-provided parameter). This is similar to the dimensionality reduction process for vector representations [5]. For the final step in our graph creation process, we perform a simple stemming method and *conflate* words (an information-retrieval term for merging multiple word forms so they are represented by a single entity) to the most frequently occurring form by relabeling nodes and updating edges as needed.

An example of this type of graph representation is given in Figure 10.1. The ovals indicate nodes and their corresponding term labels. The edges are labeled according to *title* (TI), *link* (L), or *text* (TX). The document represented by the example has the title "YAHOO NEWS," a link whose text reads "MORE NEWS," and text containing "REUTERS NEWS SERVICE REPORTS." A brief point of clarification is necessary concerning the *link* section. We do not examine the URLs of the hyperlinks to create the graphs; instead we are examining the text that labels the hyperlink itself and appears on the web document for the user to click. Note that there is no restriction on the form of the graph, and that cycles are allowed. If pairs of terms appear adjacent in more than one section, we add an edge for each occurrence, labeled appropriately.

While this approach to document representation appears superficially similar to the bi-gram, trigram, or N-gram methods, those are statistically oriented approaches based on word occurrence probability models [23]. The methods presented here, with the exception of the frequency representations described below, do not require or use the computation of term probability relationships.

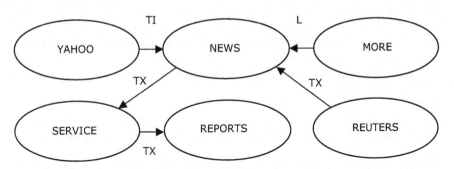

Fig. 10.1. Example of a *standard* graph representation of a document.

The second type of graph representation we will look at is what we call the *simple* representation. It is basically the same as the standard representation, except that we look at only the visible text on the page, and do not include title and meta-data information (the *title* section). Further, we do not label the edges between nodes, so there is no distinction between *link* and *text* sections. An example of this type of representation is given in Figure 10.2.

The third type of representation is called the *n-distance* representation. Under this model, there is a user-provided parameter, n. Instead of considering only terms immediately following a given term in a web document, we look up to n terms ahead and connect the succeeding terms with an edge that is labeled with the distance between them (unless the words are separated by certain punctuation marks). For example, if we had the following text on a web page, "AAA BBB CCC DDD," then we would have an edge from term AAA to term BBB labeled with a

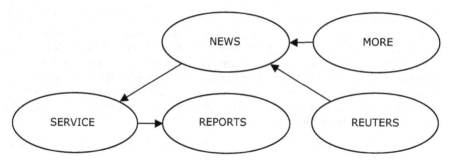

Fig. 10.2. Example of a *simple* graph representation of a document.

1, an edge from term AAA to term CCC labeled 2, and so on. The complete graph for this example is shown in Figure 10.3.

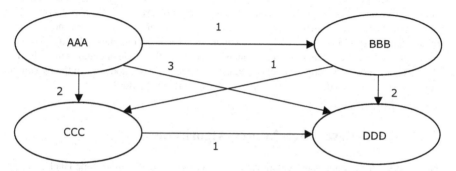

Fig. 10.3. Example of an *n-distance* graph representation of a document.

Similar to n-distance, we also have the fourth graph representation, *n-simple distance*. This is identical to n-distance, but the edges are not labeled, which means we only know that the distance between two connected terms is not more than n.

The fifth graph representation is what we call the *raw frequency* representation. This is similar to the simple representation (adjacent words, no section-related information), but each node and edge is labeled with an additional frequency measure. For nodes this indicates how many times the associated term appeared in the web document; for edges, this indicates the number of times the two connected terms appeared adjacent to each other in the specified order. The raw frequency representation uses the total number of term occurrences (on the nodes) and co-occurrences (edges).

A problem with this representation is that large differences in document size could lead to skewed comparisons, similar to the problem encountered when using Euclidean distance with vector representations of documents. Under the *normalized frequency* representation, instead of associating each node with the total number of times the corresponding term appears in the document, a normalized value in $[0, 1]$ is assigned by dividing each node frequency value by the maximum node frequency value that occurs in the graph; a similar procedure is performed for the edges. Thus each node and edge has a value in $[0, 1]$ associated with it, which indicates the normalized frequency of the term (for nodes) or co-occurrence of terms (for edges).

Previously we stated that the "size" of a graph, $|G|$, is usually defined as the number of nodes in the graph. However, for our particular representations of web documents it is detrimental to ignore the contribution of the edges, which indicate the number of phrases (term adjacencies) identified in the document content. Further, it is possible to have more than one edge between two nodes for certain representations. Thus we will use the following definition of graph size for all representations except the frequency representations (the size of a graph under the frequency representations will be described below). Formally, the size of a graph $G = (V, E, \alpha, \beta)$, denoted $|G|$, is defined as

$$|G| = |V| + |E|. \tag{10.5}$$

Thus we will take the size to be the sum of the number of vertices and edges in the graph for the standard, simple, n-distance, and n-simple distance representations.

However, under the raw frequency and normalized frequency representations the graph size is defined as the total of the node frequencies added to the total of the edge frequencies. We need this modification to reflect the frequency information in the graph size. As an example, consider two raw frequency graphs each with a node "A"; however, term "A" appears two times in one document and 300 in the other. This difference in frequency information is not captured under equation (10.5). Further, when we compute the maximum common subgraph for these representations, we take the minimum frequency element (either node or edge) as the value for the maximum common subgraph. To continue the above example, node "A" in the maximum common subgraph would have a frequency of 2, which is $\min(2, 300)$.

10.4 Graph-Based Web Mining Algorithms

Now that we have graph representations of web documents with unique node labels, we can compute the distance between two web documents in polynomial time. This allows us to retain the graph representations for use in various machine learning methods. The main benefit of this approach is that the additional structural information captured in the graphs is maintained, unlike other methods where we need to discard the structural information to arrive at a vector representation.

In this section we describe two classical machine learning algorithms, k-means and k-nearest neighbors, and show how they can be extended in a straightforward manner to utilize graphs and graph distance.

10.4.1 k-Means Clustering with Graphs

The k-means clustering algorithm is a simple and straightforward method for clustering data [24]. The basic algorithm is given in Figure 10.4. Traditionally, each item to be clustered is represented as a vector in the Euclidean space $\Re^m$, and a vector distance measure such as Jaccard is used [5]:

$$dist_{JAC}(\mathbf{x}, \mathbf{y}) = 1 - \frac{\sum_{i=1}^{n} x_i y_i}{\sum_{i=1}^{n} x_i^2 + \sum_{i=1}^{n} y_i^2 - \sum_{i=1}^{n} x_i y_i}, \tag{10.6}$$

where x_i and y_i are the ith components of vectors $\mathbf{x}$ and $\mathbf{y}$, respectively.

For our graph-based approach, instead of vectors we will represent web document content using graphs, as discussed in section 10.3. To compute distances, we simply use one of the

Inputs:	the set of n data items and a parameter, k, defining the number of clusters to create
Outputs:	the centroids of the clusters and for each data item the cluster (an integer in [1,k]) it belongs to
Step 1.	Assign each data item randomly to a cluster (from 1 to k).
Step 2.	Using the initial assignment, determine the centroids of each cluster.
Step 3.	Given the new centroids, assign each data item to be in the cluster of its closest centroid.
Step 4.	Re-compute the centroids as in Step 2. Repeat Steps 3 and 4 until the centroids do not change.

Fig. 10.4. The basic k-means clustering algorithm.

methods described in section 10.2.2. However, note that the k-means algorithm, like many clustering algorithms, requires not only the computation of distances, but also of cluster representatives. In the case of k-means, these representatives are called centroids. Thus we need a graph-theoretic version of the centroid, which itself must be a graph, if we are to extend this algorithm to work with graph representations of web documents. Our solution is to compute the representatives (centroids) of the clusters using *median graphs* [25]. Formally, the median of a set of graphs S is a graph $g \in S$ ($S = \{G_1, G_2, \ldots, G_n\}$) such that g has the lowest average distance to all graphs in S:

$$g = \arg \min_{\forall s \in S} \left(\frac{1}{|S|} \sum_{i=1}^{|S|} dist(s, G_i) \right). \tag{10.7}$$

The median of a set of graphs is the graph from the set that has the minimum average distance to all the other graphs in the set. Here the distance is computed with the graph-theoretic distance measures mentioned in section 10.2.2. The procedure is fairly straightforward, though the equation may seem complex at first. We start by selecting some specific graph, let us call it s, and then compute the distances between s and all other graphs in a pair-wise fashion. These distances are summed and then divided by the total number of graphs to calculate an average distance between s and all the other graphs. This number is saved and associated with graph s; we repeat the above process with all the graphs, taking each one in turn to be "s." The median graph is then selected by finding the graph that has the minimum distance.

We wish to clarify here a point that may cause some confusion. Clustering with graphs is well established in the literature. However, with those methods the entire clustering problem is treated as a graph, where nodes represent the items to be clustered and the weights on the edges connecting the nodes indicate the distance between the objects the nodes represent. The goal is to partition this graph, breaking it up into several connected components that represent clusters. The usual procedure is to create a minimal spanning tree of the graph and then remove the remaining edges with the largest weight until the number of desired clusters is achieved [26]. This is very different from the technique we described in this section, since it is the data (in this case, the web documents) themselves that are represented by graphs, not the overall clustering problem.

10.4.2 k-Nearest Neighbors Classification with Graphs

In this section we describe the k-nearest neighbors (k-NN) classification algorithm and how we can easily extend it to work with the graph-based representations of web documents described above. The basic k-NN algorithm [24] begins with a set of training examples; in the traditional k-NN approach these are numerical feature vectors. Each of these training examples is associated with a label that indicates to what class the example belongs. Given a new, previously unseen input instance, we attempt to estimate which class it belongs to. Under the k-NN method this is accomplished by looking at the k training examples closest (i.e., with least distance) to the input instance. Here k is a user-provided parameter and distance is computed with a vector distance measure, such as equation (10.6).

Once we have found the k nearest training examples using some distance measure, we estimate the class by the majority among the k training examples. This class is then assigned as the predicted class for the input instance. If there are ties due to more than one class having equal numbers of representatives among the nearest neighbors, we can either choose one class randomly or break the tie with some other method, such as selecting the tied class that has the minimum distance neighbor. For the experiments in this chapter we will use the latter method, which in our experiments has shown a slight improvement over random tie breaking.

To extend the k-NN method to work with graph representations of web documents instead of vector representations, we need only utilize one of the graph distance measures presented in section 10.2.2 in place of the traditional vector distance measures. Then we may use graphs in place of vectors with no further changes to the algorithm.

10.5 Experimental Results

10.5.1 Data Sets

To evaluate the performance of the graph-based k-means and k-NN algorithms as compared with the traditional vector methods, we performed experiments on two different collections of web documents, called the *F-series* and the *J-series* [27]. The data sets are available under these names at ftp://ftp.cs.umn.edu/dept/users/boley/PDDPdata/. These two data sets were selected because of two major reasons. First, all of the original HTML documents are available, which is necessary if we are to represent the documents as graphs; many other document collections provide only a preprocessed vector representation, which is unsuitable for use with our method. Second, ground truth assignments are provided for each data set, and there are multiple classes representing easily understandable groupings that relate to the content of the documents. Some web document collections are not labeled or are presented with some task in mind other than content-related classification (e.g., building a predictive model based on user preferences).

The F-series originally contained 98 documents belonging to one or more of 17 subcategories of four major category areas: *manufacturing, labor, business and finance*, and *electronic communication and networking*. Because there are multiple subcategory classifications from the same category area for many of these documents, we have reduced the categories to just the four major categories mentioned above in order to simplify the problem. There were five documents that had conflicting classifications (i.e., they were classified to belong to two or more of the four major categories) that we removed in order to create a single class classification problem, which allows for a more straightforward way of assessing classification accuracy. The J-series contains 185 documents and ten classes: *affirmative action, business capital, information systems, electronic commerce, intellectual property, employee rights, materials processing, personnel management, manufacturing systems*, and *industrial partnership*. We have not modified this data set. Additional results on a third, larger data set can be found elsewhere [28, 29, 30].

For the vector representation experiments, which are presented as a baseline for comparison purposes, there were already several precreated term–document matrices available for our experiments at the same location where we obtained the two document collections. We selected the matrices with the smallest number of dimensions. For the F-series documents there are 332 dimensions (terms) used, while the J-series has 474 dimensions. We performed some preliminary experiments and observed that other term-weighting schemes (i.e., inverse document frequency, see [5]) improved the accuracy of the vector-model representation for these data sets either only very slightly or in many cases not at all. Thus we have left the data in its original format.

10.5.2 Experimental Details

For our experiments we use a maximum graph size of 30 nodes per graph, which corresponds to setting $m = 30$ (see section 10.3). This parameter value was selected based on previous experimental results, and has been shown to work adequately for both data sets (further results with other graph sizes are omitted for brevity). We select a single value for m to be used by all graphs for experimental consistency. However, the value of m could be different for each graph, which would allow for more flexibility than vector-space models, since they require a fixed number of dimensions for every document. The graph model can allow for a different representation size for each document, which would require some method of selecting a "good" value of m for each document. This is part of the more general *keyphrase extraction* problem [31], which does not have a trivial solution; describing methods for dealing with it is beyond the scope of this chapter. Note that it is also possible to reduce the size of the graphs by examination of graph-theoretic features, such as focusing on large connected components, nodes with high edge degrees, or components with certain topologies.

The d_{MCS} distance measure (10.1) was used to compute graph distance for both algorithms. For the "distance" related graph representations, n-distance and n-simple distance, we used $n = 5$ (i.e., 5-distance and 5-simple distance). The vector representation results reported for comparison reflect using a distance measure based on Jaccard similarity, equation (10.6). We used Jaccard distance because this was consistently the best performing vector distance measure in our experimental results. Euclidean distance is generally not used for information retrieval tasks and performs poorly because it lacks a length-invariance property. With Euclidean distance, large variations in overall document size cause large distances between their representative vectors, even though the two documents may be about identical topics; the document content is ideally described by vector direction, not length. (For further discussion of this topic, see [5, 32].)

Clustering performance is measured using two performance indices that indicate the similarity of obtained clusters to the "ground truth" clusters. The first performance index is the *Rand index* [33], which is computed by examining the produced clustering and checking how closely it matches the ground truth clustering. It produces a value in the interval [0, 1], with 1 representing a clustering that perfectly matches ground truth. The second performance index we use for measuring clustering performance is *mutual information* [34], which is an information-theoretic measure that evaluates the overall degree of agreement between the clustering under consideration and ground truth, with a preference for clusters that have high purity. Higher values of mutual information indicate better performance. The clustering experiments were repeated ten times to account for the random initialization of the k-means algorithm, and the average of these experiments is reported. Classification accuracy was assessed by the leave-one-out method, where we use all but one of the instances in the data set as training examples and attempt to classify the remaining input instance. The procedure is carried out using each instance in the data set as the input instance once, and the overall accuracy is reported.

10.5.3 Examples of Results

The performance of clustering the F and J data sets, as measured by the Rand index when compared with ground truth, after applying k-means clustering, is given in Figure 10.5. Similarly, the performance as measured by mutual information is given in Figure 10.6. The figures compare the performance obtained when using the different graph representations presented in section 10.3. These are, from left to right, standard, simple, 5-distance, 5-simple distance, raw frequency, and normalized frequency. The final column is the accuracy of the vector representation approach using a distance based on the Jaccard similarity [5], which is the best performing vector distance measure we have worked with. The white bars correspond to the F-series data set, whereas the black bars are the J-series. On our system, a 2.6 GHz Pentium 4 with 1 gigabyte of memory, the average time to create clusters for the F-series using the graph-based method and the standard representation was 22.7 seconds, whereas it took 59.5 seconds on average for the J-series.

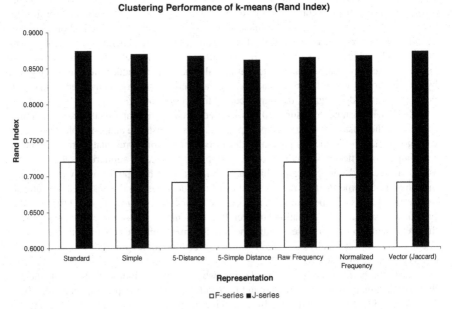

Fig. 10.5. Performance of k-means clustering on F and J data sets as measured by the Rand index.

The results for the k-nearest neighbors classification experiments are given in Figures 10.7 and 10.8 for the F and J data sets, respectively. Similar to the clustering results, the various representations are compared. The different bars in each group correspond to different values of k (the number of nearest neighbors). The white bars correspond to $k = 1$, the gray bars are for $k = 3$, the striped bars indicate $k = 5$, and the black bars are $k = 10$. The graph-based k-NN method took an average of 0.2 seconds to classify a document for the F-series, and 0.45 seconds for the J-series, both when using $k = 1$ and the standard representation.

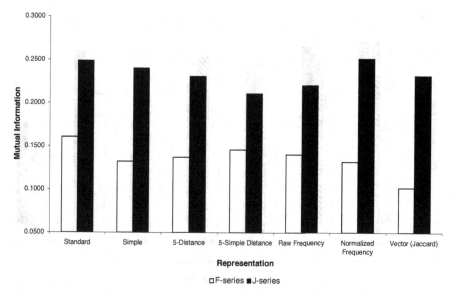

Fig. 10.6. Performance of k-means clustering on F and J data sets as measured by mutual information.

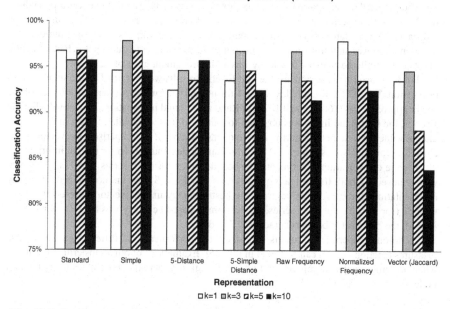

Fig. 10.7. Performance of k-nearest neighbors classification for the F-series data set with accuracy measured using leave-one-out.

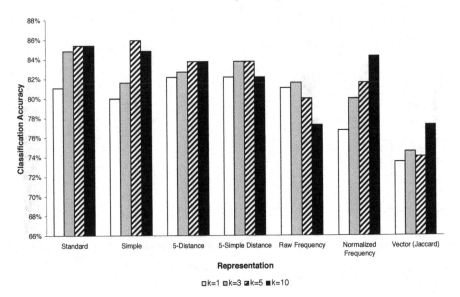

Fig. 10.8. Performance of k-nearest neighbors classification for the J-series data set with accuracy measured using leave-one-out.

The standard representation, in all experiments, exceeded the equivalent vector procedure. In 11 out of 12 experiments, the simple representation outperformed the vector model. The 5-distance representation was better in eight out of 12 experiments. The 5-simple distance representation was an improvement in nine out of 12 cases. Raw frequency was better in eight of 12 cases, while normalized frequency was an improvement in 11 of 12 cases.

For the clustering experiments, the best F-series results were attained by the standard representation (0.7202 for Rand index; 0.1604 for mutual information). The performance of the vector approach was 0.6899 and 0.1020 for Rand and mutual information, respectively. For the J-series, the best Rand index was obtained for standard (0.8741) while the best mutual information value was attained for normalized frequency (0.2516). In comparison, the vector-based clustering for the J-series achieved 0.8717 for Rand index and 0.2316 for mutual information.

For the classification experiments, the best accuracy for the F-series was 97.85%, which was achieved by both the simple representation (for $k = 3$) and the normalized frequency representation (for $k = 1$). In contrast, the best accuracy using a vector representation was 94.62% (for $k = 3$). For the J-series, the best graph-based accuracy was 85.95% (for simple, $k = 5$); the best vector-based accuracy was 77.30%.

Additional experimental results comparing the performance of different graph distance measures (section 10.2.2) can be found in [28, 35]. Evaluations of other clustering algorithms when utilizing graphs are reported in [30, 36]. Creation of classifier ensembles using random node selection for graphs is described in [37].

10.6 Conclusion

We have demonstrated how using graphs with unique node labels reduces the complexity of the maximum common subgraph problem to polynomial time, and how utilizing the maximum common subgraph allows us to calculate a graph distance measure. Such graph distance measures are useful for allowing clustering and classification algorithms to work with graph representations of data, which contain additional structural information when compared to their vector counterparts. We introduced several methods of representing web document content using graphs with unique node labels. We also presented graph-based versions of the k-means and k-nearest neighbors algorithms, and showed some examples of experimental results when applying these methods to web document collections. The results show our graph-based approach can outperform traditional vector models for both clustering and classification.

Acknowledgments

This work was supported in part by the National Institute for Systems Test and Productivity at the University of South Florida under U.S. Space and Naval Warfare Systems Command Contract No. N00039–02–C–3244.

References

[1] C. Apte, F. Damerau, S.M. Weiss. Automated learning of decision rules for text categorization. *ACM Transactions on Information Systems*, 12, 233–251, 1994.

[2] S. Dumais, H. Chen. Hierarchical classification of web content. In *Proceedings of SIGIR-00, 23rd ACM International Conference on Research and Development in Information Retrieval*, pages 256–263, 2000.

[3] O. Zamir, O. Etzioni. Web document clustering: a feasibility demonstration. In *Proceedings of the 21st Annual International ACM SIGIR Conference on Research and Development in Information Retrieval*, pages 46–54, 1998.

[4] A.K. Jain, M.N. Murty, P.J. Flynn. Data clustering: a review. *ACM Computing Surveys*, 31(3), 264–323, 1999.

[5] G. Salton. *Automatic Text Processing: The Transformation, Analysis, and Retrieval of Information by Computer*. Reading, MA: Addison-Wesley, 1989.

[6] T.H. Cormen, C.E. Leiserson, R.L. Rivest. *Introduction to Algorithms*. Cambridge, MA: MIT Press, 1997.

[7] H. Bunke. On a relation between graph edit distance and maximum common subgraph. *Pattern Recognition Letters*, 18, 689–694, 1997.

[8] P.J. Dickinson, H. Bunke, A. Dadej, M. Kraetzl. Matching graphs with unique node labels. *Pattern Analysis and Applications*, 7(3), 243–254, 2004.

[9] M.R. Garey, D.S. Johnson. *Computers and Intractability: A Guide to the Theory of NP-Completeness*. New York: W. H. Freeman, 1979.

[10] J.R. Ullman. An algorithm for subgraph isomorphism. *Journal of the Association for Computing Machinery*, 23, 31–42, 1976.

[11] J.T.L. Wang, K. Zhang, G.-W. Chirn. Algorithms for approximate graph matching. *Information Sciences*, 82, 45–74, 1995.

[12] B.T. Messmer, H. Bunke. A new algorithm for error-tolerant subgraph isomorphism detection. *IEEE Transactions on Pattern Analysis and Machine Intelligence*, 20(5), 493–504, 1998.

[13] K.-C. Tai. The tree-to-tree correction problem. *Journal of the Association for Computing Machinery*, 26(3), 422–433, 1979.

[14] R.A. Wagner, M.J. Fischer. The string-to-string correction problem. *Journal of the Association for Computing Machinery*, 21, 168–173, 1974.

[15] V. Levenshtein. Binary codes capable of correcting deletions, insertions, and reversals. *Soviet Physics-Doklady*, 10, 707–710, 1966.

[16] A. Sanfeliu, K.S. Fu. A distance measure between attributed relational graphs for pattern recognition. *IEEE Transactions on Systems, Man, and Cybernetics*, 13, 353–363, 1983.

[17] H. Bunke, G. Allermann. Inexact graph matching for structural pattern recognition. *Pattern Recognition Letters*, 1(4), 245–253, 1983.

[18] G. Levi. A note on the derivation of maximal common subgraphs of two directed or undirected graphs. *Calcolo*, 9, 341–354, 1972.

[19] J.J. McGregor. Backtrack search algorithms and the maximal common subgraph problem. *Software Practice and Experience*, 12, 23–34, 1982.

[20] H. Bunke, K. Shearer. A graph distance metric based on the maximal common subgraph. *Pattern Recognition Letters*, 19, 255–259, 1998.

[21] W.D. Wallis, P. Shoubridge, M. Kraetz, D. Ray. Graph distances using graph union. *Pattern Recognition Letters*, 22, 701–704, 2001.

[22] M.-L. Fernández, G. Valiente. A graph distance metric combining maximum common subgraph and minimum common supergraph. *Pattern Recognition Letters*, 22, 753–758, 2001.

[23] C.-M. Tan, Y.-F. Wang, C.-D. Lee. The use of bigrams to enhance text categorization. *Information Processing and Management*, 38, 529–546, 2002.

[24] T.M. Mitchell. *Machine Learning*. New York: McGraw-Hill, 1997.

[25] X. Jiang, A. Muenger, H. Bunke. On median graphs: properties, algorithms, and applications. *IEEE Transactions on Pattern Analysis and Machine Intelligence*, 23(10), 1144–1151, 2001.

[26] C.T. Zahn. Graph-theoretical methods for detecting and describing gestalt structures. *IEEE Transactions on Computers*, C-20, 68–86, 1971.

[27] D. Boley, M. Gini, R. Gross, et al. Partitioning-based clustering for web document categorization. *Decision Support Systems*, 27, 329–341, 1999.

[28] A. Schenker, M. Last, H. Bunke, A. Kandel. Classification of documents using graph matching. *International Journal of Pattern Recognition and Artificial Intelligence*, 18(3), 475–496, 2004.

[29] A. Schenker, M. Last, H. Bunke, A. Kandel. Classification of web documents using a graph model. In *Proceedings of the 7th International Conference on Document Analysis and Recognition*, pages 240–244, 2003.

[30] A. Schenker, M. Last, H. Bunke, A. Kandel. A comparison of two novel algorithms for clustering web documents. In *Proceedings of the 2nd International Workshop on Web Document Analysis*, pages 71–74, 2003.

[31] P.D. Turney. Learning algorithms for keyphrase extraction. *Information Retrieval*, 2(4), 303–336, 2000.

[32] A. Strehl, J. Ghosh, R. Mooney. Impact of similarity measures on web-page clustering. In *AAAI-2000: Workshop of Artificial Intelligence for Web Search*, pages 58–64, 2000.

[33] W.M. Rand. Objective criteria for the evaluation of clustering methods. *Journal of the American Statistical Association*, 66, 846–850, 1971.

[34] T.M. Cover, J.A. Thomas. *Elements of Information Theory*. New York: Wiley, 1991.

[35] A. Schenker, M. Last, H. Bunke, A. Kandel. Comparison of distance measures for graph-based clustering of documents. In E. Hancock, M. Vento, eds. *Proceedings of the 4th*

IAPR-TC15 International Workshop on Graph-based Representations in Pattern Recognition, volume 2726 of *Lecture Notes in Computer Science*, pages 202–213. New York: Springer-Verlag, 2003.

[36] A. Schenker, M. Last, H. Bunke, A. Kandel. Comparison of algorithms for web document clustering using graph representations of data. In A. Fred, T. Caelli, R.P.W. Duin, A. Campilho, D. de Ridder, eds. *Proceedings of the Joint IAPR Workshop on Syntactical and Structural Pattern Recognition*, volume 3138 of *Lecture Notes in Computer Science*, pages 190–197. New York: Springer-Verlag, 2004.

[37] A. Schenker, H. Bunke, M. Last, A. Kandel. Building graph-based classifier ensembles by random node selection. In F. Roli, J. Kittler, T. Windeatt, eds. *Proceedings of the 5th International Workshop on Multiple Classifier Systems*, volume 3077 of *Lecture Notes in Computer Science*, pages 214–222. New York: Springer-Verlag, 2004.

11

Data Complexity in Clustering Analysis of Gene Microarray Expression Profiles

Feng Luo and Latifur Khan

Summary. The increasing application of microarray technology is generating large amounts of high dimensional gene expression data. Genes participating in the same biological process tend to have similar expression patterns, and clustering is one of the most useful and efficient methods for identifying these patterns. Due to the complexity of microarray profiles, there are some limitations in directly applying traditional clustering techniques to the microarray data. Recently, researchers have proposed clustering algorithms custom tailored to overcome their limitations for microarray analysis. In this chapter, we first introduce the microarray technique. Next, we review seven representative clustering algorithms: K-means, quality-based clustering, hierarchical agglomerative clustering, self-organizing neural network-based clustering, graph-theory-based clustering, model-based clustering, and subspace clustering. All these algorithms have shown their applicability to the microarray profiles. We also survey several criteria for evaluating clustering results. Biology plays an important role in the evaluation of clustering results. We discuss possible research directions to equip clustering techniques with underlying biological interpretations for better microarray profile analysis.

11.1 Introduction

Understanding the system-level characteristics of biological organization is a key issue in the post-genome era. In every living organism, subsets of its gene expressions differ across types, stages, and conditions. Given a specific condition and stage, there are particular genes that are expressed. Measuring these gene expression levels across different stages in different tissues or cells, or under different conditions, is very important and useful for understanding and interpreting biological processes. For a long time, biologists dreamed of getting information about all genes in a genome and the ability to study the complex interplay of all genes simultaneously. The emergence of the microarray technique [26, 35] has brought this to realization. The microarray technology enables the massively parallel measurement of expressions of thousands of genes simultaneously. There are many potential applications for the microarray technique, such as identification of genetic diseases [32], discovery of new drugs [10], toxicology studies [31], etc.

The application of microarray technology now generates very large amounts of gene expression data. One microarray chip has anywhere from thousands to tens of thousands of genes on it. Thus a series of microarray experiments will generate ten thousand to a million data points. As a result, there is an increasing need for technologies that can extract useful and rational fundamental knowledge of gene expression from the microarray data.

The biological system, like many other engineering synthetic systems, is modular [19]. The expression patterns of genes inside the same module are similar to each other. Thus, the genes can be grouped according to their gene expressions. Clustering analysis is one of the most useful methods for grouping data in large data sets. It has been shown that the clustering techniques can identify biologically meaningful gene groups from microarray profiles.

However, due to the complexity of biological systems, the microarray data are also very involved. Conventional clustering algorithms may have some limitation to deal with such intricacies and need modifications. First, the size of the data is large. A typical microarray data set will have thousands to ten thousands of data series and up to millions of data points. So the computation time for clustering is definitely an important issue. Second, although the experiments in a microarray profile may relate to each other, like a time series experiments of cell cycle or stress response, the degree of expression in different experiments can be dramatically different. Furthermore, in many cases, there is seldom a correlation between the experiments in a microarray data set, like microarray experiments of a set of mutants or microarray experiments of tumor cell and normal cell in cancer research; or there are even several kinds of experiments in one microarray profile. Usually, microarray profiles by nature are multidimensional. Third, for one specific experimental condition, not every gene is expressed. The microarray expression data of these genes are more like random outliers. Either some preprocessing of the microarray data set is needed to remove the outliers as much as possible or the clustering algorithms themselves need to have some mechanism to handle these outliers. All these characteristics of microarray data need to be considered for successful clustering.

In this chapter, we review clustering analysis for microarray profiles. First, we introduce the microarray technology. Second, we present some traditional and newly developed clustering algorithms that have been applied to microarray profile analysis. Third, we describe some methods to evaluate the clustering results. Finally, we provide some discussions.

11.2 Microarray technology

The microarray technology refers to the use of the microarray chips to measure gene expressions. Microarray chips are commonly small slides that are made of chemically coated glass, nylon membrane, or silicon, onto which a matrix of spots are printed. Each spot on a microarray chip is less than 250 μm in diameter and contains millions of identical DNA molecules (probes). The number of spots on a single microarray chip ranges from thousands to tens of thousands, which depends on the size of the chip and the spotting technique used. In each spot there are only specific kinds of DNA sequences that correspond to a specific gene. The hybridization between the DNA sequence and the complement DNA (cDNA) that represent the messenger RNA (mRNA) from test samples (targets) is quantified by the signal of labeling molecules bound to cDNA, which is the essential principle employed by the microarray technology to measure the gene expression level of the targets.

There are two major types of microarray technology. One is the cDNA microarray [35]; the other is the oligonucleotide microarray [26]. Although there are some differences in the details of experiment protocols, the gene expressions measured by the cDNA microarray and the oligonucleotide microarray have the same biological meanings. A typical microarray experiment consists of four basic steps [40]:

Target preparation: Extract mRNA from both the test and the control samples. Then transcribe the mRNA to cDNA in the presence of nucleotides that are labeled with fluorescent dyes or radioactive isotopes. For cDNA microarray, the test and reference cDNA are labeled differently. For oligonucleotide microarray, this differential labeling is not necessary.

Hybridization: The labeled test and control cDNA samples are mixed in equal amounts and incubated with a microarray slide for hybridization for a given time. Then the microarray slide is washed to get rid of the surplus cDNA.

Scanning: Once the hybridized microarray is ready, the expression level of genes is detected by monitoring the intensity of the labeling fluorescent or radioactive molecules. For fluorescence labeling, a laser beam is used to excite the fluorescent dyes and the degree of fluorescence correlates with the abundance of target molecules at a specific spot. The fluorescent emission is monitored by a scanner, which also produces a digital image file to store signals.

Normalization: To correct the differences in overall array intensity, such as background noise and different efficiency in detection, the raw signal intensity, either from cDNA or from oligonucleotide microarray, must be normalized to a common standard. The normalization can make the gene expression profile from different experiments comparable. After normalization, the final gene expression levels are presented as an expression ratio of test versus control sample and are ready for further analysis.

A typical microarray gene expression profile is represented by a real matrix E, *the expression matrix*. Each cell e_{ij} of the expression matrix E represents an expression value of a gene (row) in a certain experiment (column). Generally, there is no biological difference between the expression profiles measured by cDNA microarray and those measured by oligonucleotide microarray. In this chapter, the term *microarray* means both cDNA and oligonucleotide microarray.

11.3 Introduction to Clustering

Clustering is defined as a process of partitioning a set of data $S = \{D_1, D_2 \dots D_n\}$ into a number of subclusters $C_1, C_2 \dots C_m$ based on a measure of similarity between the data (distance based) or based on the probability of data following certain distribution (model-based). For a survey of clustering analysis techniques, see Jain et al. [23]. The distance-based clustering techniques are broadly divided into hierarchical clustering and partitioning clustering. As opposed to partitioning clustering algorithms, the hierarchical clustering can discover trends and subtle common characteristics, and thus can provide more useful information for biologists. Hierarchical clustering algorithms are further subdivided into agglomerative algorithms and divisive algorithms. Recently, as more and more high-dimensional microarray expressions data become available, subspace clustering algorithms have been developed to find clusters in the subdimension of the whole space.

11.3.1 Similarity Measurements of Microarray Profiles

The similarity measurement is essential for the clustering analysis, which controls the definition of a cluster. Different similarity measurement may generate widely different values for the same set of data. Most commonly used similarity measurements for microarray profiles are Euclidean distance and Pearson correlation coefficient.

The Euclidean distance actually measures the geometric distance between data points. The distance between expression E_i of gene g_i and expression (E_j) of gene g_j in D-dimensions is defined as

$$Euclidean(E_i, E_j) = \sqrt{\sum_{d=1}^{D} (E_{id} - E_{jd})^2} \qquad (11.1)$$

The Euclidean distance is simple and works well when a data set has "compact" or "isolated" clusters. However, the distances can be greatly affected by differences in scale among the dimensions from which the distances are computed. To make the distance insensitive to the absolute level of expression and sensitive to the degree of change [14], the microarray expression profiles are always standardized by z-score normalization (zero mean and unit variance) [39] before the distance is computed.

The Pearson correlation coefficient measures the strength and direction of a *linear* relationship between two data. It assumes that both data are approximately normally distributed and their joint distribution is bivariate normal. The Pearson correlation coefficient between expression (E_i) of gene g_i and expression (E_j) of gene g_j in D-dimensions is defined as

$$Pearson(E_i, E_j) = \frac{1}{D} \sum_{d=1,D} (\frac{E_{id} - M_{E_i}}{\sigma_{E_i}})(\frac{E_{jd} - M_{E_j}}{\sigma_{E_j}}) \qquad (11.2)$$

where M_{E_i}, M_{E_j} are the average gene expression level of gene g_i and gene g_j, respectively, and $\sigma_{E_1}, \sigma_{E_j}$ are the standard deviation of the gene expression level of gene g_i and gene g_j, respectively. The Pearson correlation ranges from +1 to −1. A correlation of +1 means a perfect positive linear relationship between two expressions.

Although the Pearson correlation coefficient is an effective similarity measure, it is sensitive to outlier expression data. Especially if the number of data of two data series is limited, the effects of outlier points become more significant. Heyer et al. [22] observed that if the expression of two genes has a high peak or valley in one of the experiments but is unrelated in all others, the Pearson correlation coefficient still will be very high, which results as a false positive. To remove the effect of a single outlier, Heyer et al. proposed a similarity measurement called the Jackknife correlation, which is based on the Jackknife sampling procedure from computational statistics [13]. The Jackknife correlation between expression (E_i) of gene g_i and expression (E_j) of gene g_j in D-dimensions is defined as

$$Jackknife(E_i, E_j) = \min\{P_{ij}^1, \dots P_{ij}^d, \dots, P_{ij}^D\} \qquad (11.3)$$

where P_{ij}^d is the Pearson correlation coefficient between expression E_i and expression E_j with d th experiment value deleted. More general Jackknife correlation by deleting every subset of size n will be robust to n outliers, but they become computationally unrealistic to implement.

11.3.2 Missing Values in Microarray Profiles

There may be some missing expression values in the microarray expression profiles. These missing values may have been caused by various kinds of experimental errors. When calculating the similarity between two gene expressions with missing values, one way is to consider only the expressions present in both genes. The other way is to replace the missing value with estimated values. Troyanskaya et al. [43] evaluated three estimation methods: singular value decomposition based method, weighted K-nearest neighbors, and row average. Based on the robust and sensitive test, they demonstrated that the weighted K-nearest neighbors method is the best one for missing value estimation in microarray expression profiles.

11.4 Clustering Algorithms

In this section, we present several representative clustering algorithms that have been applied to gene expression analysis.

11.4.1 K-Means Algorithms

The K-means algorithm [30] is one of the most popular partitioning clustering methods. The K-means partition the data set into predefined K clusters by minimizing the average dissimilarity of each cluster, which is defined as

$$E = \sum_{k=1}^{K} \sum_{C(i)=k} ||x_{ik} - \bar{x}_k||^2 \quad where \quad \bar{x}_k = \frac{1}{N_k} \sum_{i=1}^{N} x_{ik} \tag{11.4}$$

$\bar{x}_k$ is the mean of all data belonging to the k th cluster, which represents the centroid of the cluster. Thus, the K-means algorithm tries to minimize the average distance of data within each cluster from the cluster mean. The general K-means algorithm is as follows [23]:

1. Initialization: Choose K cluster centroids (e.g., randomly chosen K data points).
2. Assign each data-point to the closest cluster centroid.
3. Recompute the cluster centroid using the current cluster memberships.
4. If the convergence criterion is not met, go to step 2.

The K-means algorithm converges if every data-point is assigned to the same cluster during iteration, or the decrease in squared error is less than a predefined threshold. In addition, to avoid the local suboptimal minimum, one should run the K-means algorithm with different random initializing values for the centroids, and then choose the one with the best clustering result (smallest average dissimilarity). Furthermore, since the number of clusters inside the data set is unknown, to find the proper number of clusters, one needs to run the K-means algorithm with different values of K to determine the best K value.

Tavazoie et al. [39] selected the most highly expressed 3000 yeast genes from the yeast cell cycle microarray profiles and applied the K-means algorithm to cluster them into 30 clusters. They successfully found that some of the clusters were significantly enriched with homo functional genes, but not all clusters showed the presence of functionally meaningful genes. This is because some clusters of genes participate in multiple functional processes, or some clusters of genes are not significantly expressed, and the number of clusters (30) may also not be the optimal one.

The K-means algorithm is most widely used because of its simplicity. However, it has several weak points when it is used to cluster gene expression profiles. First, it is sensitive to outliers. As there are a lot of noise and experimental errors among the gene expression data, the clustering result produced by K-means algorithms may be difficult to explain. Second, since not every gene expresses significantly under certain conditions, the expressions of this kind of genes do not have a clear pattern but are more likely to have random patterns. This kind of gene must be considered as noisy and should not be assigned to any cluster. However, the K-means algorithm forces each gene into a cluster, which decreases the accuracy of the clusters and renders some of the clusters meaningless and not suitable for further analysis.

11.4.2 Quality-Based Clustering

Recently, several quality-based clustering algorithms have been proposed to overcome the drawbacks of K-means. These kinds of algorithms attempt to find quality-controlled clusters from the gene expression profiles. The number of clusters does not have to be predefined and is automatically determined during the clustering procedure. Genes whose expressions are not similar to the expressions of other genes will not be assigned to any of the clusters.

Heyer et al. [22] proposed a new quality clustering algorithm called *QT_Clust*. They used the QT_Clust to cluster 4169 yeast gene cell cycle microarray expression profiles and discovered 24 large quality clusters. The *QT_Clust* algorithm uses two steps to produce quality clusters: (1) For each gene, a cluster seeded by this gene is formed. This is done by iteratively adding genes to the cluster. During each iteration, the gene that minimizes the increase in cluster diameter is added. The process continues until no gene can be added without surpassing the predefined cluster diameter threshold. After the first step, a set of candidate clusters is created. (2) Quality clusters are selected one by one from the candidates. Each time, the largest cluster is selected and retained. Then the genes that belong to this cluster are removed from the other clusters. This procedure continues until a certain termination criterion is satisfied. One criterion suggested by Heyer et al. is the minimum number of clusters. The total number of clusters is controlled by the termination criterion and is not required to be predefined like K-means algorithm. The quality of the clusters in *QT_Clust* is controlled by the cluster diameter, which is a user-defined parameter. However, determination of this parameter is not an easy task. It may need either the biological knowledge of the data set to evaluate the clustering result, or use of some cluster validation criterion to evaluate the clustering result. In either case one may need to use the clustering algorithm several times to obtain a proper clustering result. Furthermore, as pointed out by Smet et al. [37], the diameter threshold may also be different for each cluster. Then, one cluster diameter cannot be proper for all clusters.

Smet et al. [37] proposed a new heuristic adaptive quality-based clustering algorithm called *Adap_Cluster* to improve the method proposed by Heyer et al. The *Adap_Cluster* algorithm constructs clusters sequentially with a two-step approach. In the first step (quality-based step), the algorithm finds a cluster center $\mathbf{C}_K$ using a preestimated radius ($\mathbf{R}_K$_**PRELIM**) with a method similar to the algorithm proposed by Heyer et al. If the size of the cluster is less than a user-defined parameter **MIN_NR_GENES,** the clustering result is discarded. Otherwise, a second step (adaptive step) is invoked. The adaptive step uses an expectation maximization (EM) algorithm to optimize the radius $\mathbf{R}_K$ of the cluster center $\mathbf{C}_K$ for a certain significant level **S**. The significant level is the probability that a gene belongs to a cluster. The default value of the significant level is 95%, which means that a gene has less than a 5% probability of being a false positive. The significant level can determine the number of genes that belong to the cluster. Then, the significant level **S** is the quality-control criterion. All clusters have the same significant level. However, the cluster radius may differ among the clusters. The advantage of using a significant level as a quality-control criterion is that it has easy-to-understand statistical meaning and is independent of the data set. Smet et al. applied the *Adap_Cluster* to 3000 yeast gene cell cycle microarray expression profiles. Compared to the result of K-means, the result of *Adap_Cluster* has a higher degree of enrichment based on the P-value significant measure (see section 11.5) and is more biologically consistent.

11.4.3 Hierarchical Agglomerative Clustering (HAC) Algorithm

The HAC algorithm is a classical and most commonly used hierarchal clustering algorithm. The HAC algorithm iteratively joins the closest subelements into a hierarchical tree. The general HAC algorithm is as follows:

1. Put each data element into a singleton cluster; compute a list of intercluster distances for all singleton cluster; then sort the list in ascending order.
2. Find a pair of clusters having the most similarity; merge them into one cluster and calculate the similarity between the new cluster and the remaining clusters.
3. When there is more than one cluster remaining, go to step 2; otherwise stop.

Based on the calculation of similarity between the nonsingleton clusters, a variety of hierarchical agglomerative techniques have been proposed. Single-link, complete-link, and group-average-link clustering are commonly used. In the single-link clustering the similarity between two clusters is the maximum similarity of all pairs of data that are in different clusters. In the complete-link clustering the similarity between two clusters is the minimum similarity of all pairs of data that are in different clusters. In the group-average-link clustering the similarity between two clusters is the mean similarity of all pairs of data that are in different clusters [45]. Lance and Williams [25] show that many HAC algorithms can be derived from the following general combinatorial formula:

$$d_{k,i\cup j} = \alpha_i.d_{k,i} + \alpha_j.d_{k,j} + \beta.d_{i,j} + \gamma.|d_{k,i} - d_{k,j}| \qquad (11.5)$$

where $i\cup j$ is a cluster constructed by merging cluster i and cluster j and $d_{k,i\cup j}$ is the distance between cluster $i\cup j$ and an existing cluster k. The α, β, γ parameters characterize the different HAC algorithms [25].

The single-link and complete-link clustering simply use the similarity information of minimum or maximum of a cluster; therefore, these methods perform less well than the group-average-link clustering. But the simple-link algorithm is easier to implement, has some theoretical characteristic, and has been widely used. The single-link clustering tends to build a long chaining cluster, which makes it suitable for delineating ellipsoidal clusters but not suitable for poorly separated clusters.

The clustering result of HAC can be represented by a dendrogram, which provides a natural way to graphically represent the data set. Eisen et al. [14] used the average-link HAC algorithm to analyze the human gene growth response and the yeast cell cycle microarray expression profiles. They also proposed using a colored matrix to visualize the clustering result. Each row of the matrix represents expressions of a gene. Each column of the matrix represents the expressions of an experiment. Each cell of the matrix is colored according to the expression ratio. Expressions of log ratio equal to 0 are colored black, increasingly positive ratios are colored with increasing intensity of reds, and increasingly negative ratios are colored with increasing intensity of greens. The rows in the matrix are ordered based on the dendrogram of the clustering result, so that genes with similar expressions patterns are adjacent in the matrix. This graphical view presents an intuitive understanding of the clustering result of the data set, which is most favored by biologists. A program called TreeView is available on Eisen's web site [15].

Although the HAC algorithm has been widely used for clustering gene microarray expression profiles, it has several drawbacks. First, as Tamayo et al. [38] have noted, HAC suffers from a lack of robustness when dealing with data containing noise, so that preprocessing data to filter out noise is needed. Second, unlike the division hierarchical clustering algorithm (such as SOTA and DGSOT in section 11.4) that can stop the hierarchical tree construction in any level, HAC needs to construct the hierarchical tree that includes the whole data set before extracting the patterns. This becomes very computationally expensive for a large data set when only the brief upper level patterns of the data set are needed. Third, since HAC is unable to reevaluate the results, some clusters of patterns are based on local decisions that will produce difficult-to-interpret patterns when HAC is applied to a large array of data. Fourth, the number of clusters is decided by cutting the tree structure at a certain level. Biological knowledge may be needed to determine the cut.

11.4.4 Self-Organizing Neural Network-Based Clustering Algorithm

Self-Organizing Map (SOM)

The SOM is a self-organizing neural network introduced by Kohonen [24]. It maps the high-dimensional input data into the low-dimensional output topology space, which usually is a two-dimensional grid. Furthermore, the SOM can be thought of as a "nonlinear projection" of probability density function $p(x)$ of the high-dimensional input data vector x onto the two dimensional display. This makes SOM optimally suitable for applying to the problem of the visualization and clustering of complex data.

Each SOM node in the output map has a reference vector w. The reference vector has the same dimension as the feature vector of input data. Initially the reference vector is assigned random values. During the learning process an input data vector is randomly chosen from the input data set and compared with all w. The *best matching node* c is the node that has the minimum distance with the input data:

$$c : ||x - w_c|| = \min_i \{||x - w_i||\} \qquad (11.6)$$

Then, equation (11.7) is used to update the reference vectors of the best matching node and its neighboring nodes, which are topologically close in the map. In this way, eventually neighboring nodes will become more similar to the best match nodes. Therefore, the topologically close regions of the output map gain an *affinity* for clusters of similar data vectors [24]:

$$\Delta w_i = \eta(t) \times \Lambda(i, c) \times (x - w_i) \qquad (11.7)$$

where i, t, and $\eta(t)$ denote the neighboring node, discrete time coordinate, and learning rate function, respectively. The convergence of the algorithm depends on the proper choice of η. At the beginning of the learning process, η should be chosen close to 1. Thereafter, it should decrease monotonically. One choice can be $\eta(t) = 1/t$. Note that in equation (11.7), the $\Lambda(i, c)$ is the neighborhood function. A Gaussian function can be used to define $\Lambda(i, c)$:

$$\Lambda(i, c) = \exp(-\frac{||r_i - r_c||^2}{2\sigma(t)^2}) \qquad (11.8)$$

where $|| \ r_i - r_c \ ||$ denotes the distance between the best match node and the neighboring node i and $\sigma(t)$ denotes the width of the neighbor. At the beginning of the learning process the width of the neighborhood is fairly large, but it decreases during the learning process. Therefore, $\sigma(t)$ decreases monotonically with t. Thus the size of the neighborhood also monotonically decreases. At the end of learning, only the best match node is updated. The learning steps will stop when the weight update is insignificant.

Finally, each data-point is assigned to its best match node to form final clusters. Furthermore, there is a geometrical relationship between the clusters. Clusters that are close to each other in the output grid are more similar to each other than those that are further apart. This makes it easy to find some cluster relationship during the visualization of the SOM. Tamayo et al. [38] applied the SOM to analyze yeast gene cell cycle and different human cell culture microarray expression profiles. The SOM successfully identified the predominant gene expression pattern in these microarray expression profiles.

Self-Organizing Tree Algorithm (SOTA)

Dopazo et al. [11] introduced a new unsupervised growing and tree-structured self-organizing neural network called self-organizing tree algorithm (SOTA) for hierarchical clustering. SOTA is based on Kohonen's [24] self-organizing map (SOM) and Fritzke's [16] growing cell structures. The topology of SOTA is a binary tree.

Initially the system is a binary tree with three nodes (Fig. 11.1a). The leaf of the tree is called a *cell* and internal node of the tree is called a *node*. Each cell and node has a reference vector w. The values of the reference vector are randomly initialized. In SOTA only cells are used for comparison with the input data. The procedure that distribute all data into cells is called a *cycle*. Each adaptation *cycle* contains a series of *epochs*. Each *epoch* consists of presentation of all the input data, and each presentation has two steps. First, the best match cell, which is known as the *winning cell*, is found. This is similar to the SOM. The cell that has the minimum distance from the input data is the best match cell/winning cell. The distance between the cell and data is the distance between the data vector and the reference vector of the cell. Once the *winning cell* of a data is found, the data is assigned to the cell. Second, update the reference vector w_i of the winning cell and its neighborhood using the following function:

$$\Delta w_i = \varphi(t) \times (x - w_i) \tag{11.9}$$

where $\varphi(t)$ is the learning function:

$$\varphi(t) = \alpha \times \eta(t) \tag{11.10}$$

where $\eta(t)$ is the function similar in SOM and α is a learning constant. For different neighborhoods α has different values. Two different neighborhoods are here. If the sibling of the winning cell is a cell, then the neighborhood includes the winning cell, the parent node, and the sibling cell. Otherwise, it includes only the winning cell itself [11] (Fig. 11.1b). Furthermore, parameters α_w, α_m, and α_s are used for the winning cell, the ancestor node, and the sibling cell, respectively. For example, values of α_w, α_m, and α_s can be set as 0.1, 0.05, and 0.01, respectively. Note that the parameter values are not equal. These nonequal values are critical to partition the input data set into various cells. A *cycle* converges when the relative increase in total error falls below a certain threshold.

After distributing all the input data into two cells, the cell that is most heterogeneous will be changed to a node and two descendent cells will be created. To determine heterogeneity, the *resource* of a cell is introduced. The *resource* of a cell i is the average of the distances between the input data assigned to the cell and the cell:

$$Resource_i = \sum_{i=1}^{D} \frac{d(x_i, w_i)}{D} \tag{11.11}$$

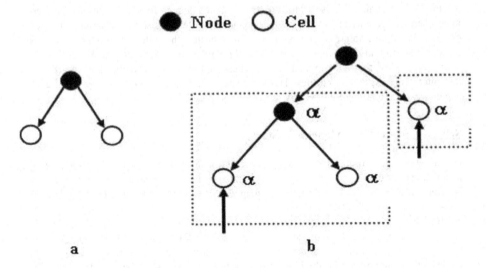

Fig. 11.1. (a) Initial architecture of SOTA. (b) Two different reference vector updating schemas.

where D is the total number of input data associated with the cell. A cell that has the maximum *resource* will expand. Therefore, the algorithm proceeds through the *cycle* until each input data-point is associated with a single cell or it reaches the desired level of heterogeneity.

SOTA uses a neural network mechanism and it is robust to noisy data. The time complexity of SOTA is O(N log N), where N is the number of genes. If only upper-level patterns are needed, the heterogeneity threshold can be set to a larger value and the SOTA can stop in the early stages. Then, the time complexity of SOTA can be reduced to $O(N)$, namely approximately linear. Herrero et al. [20] applied SOTA to cluster 800 yeast gene microarray expression profiles. An online web site tool is also available [21].

DGSOT Algorithm

Nearly all hierarchical clustering techniques that include the tree structure have two shortcomings: (1) they do not properly represent hierarchical relationships, and (2) once the data are assigned improperly to a given cluster, they cannot later be reevaluated and placed in another cluster. Recently, Luo et al. [27, 28] proposed a new tree-structured self-organizing neural network, called the dynamically growing self-organizing tree (DGSOT) algorithm, to overcome these two drawbacks of hierarchical clustering.

DGSOT is a tree-structured self-organizing neural network designed to discover the proper hierarchical structure of the underlying data. DGSOT grows vertically and horizontally. In each vertical growth, DGSOT adds two children to the leaf whose heterogeneity is greater than a threshold and turns it into a node. In each horizontal growth, DGSOT dynamically finds the proper number of children (subclusters) of the lowest-level nodes. Each vertical growth step is followed by a horizontal growth step. This process continues until the heterogeneity of all leaves is less than a threshold T_R. During vertical and horizontal growth, a learning process similar to SOTA is adopted. Figure 11.2 shows an example of DGSOT algorithm in action. Initially there is only one root node (Fig. 11.2a). All the input data are associated with the

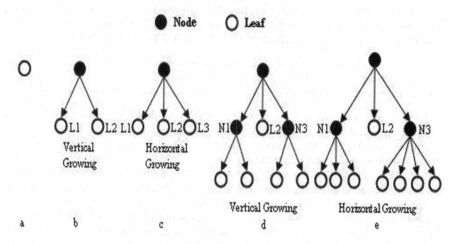

Fig. 11.2. Illustration of the DGSOT algorithm.

root, and the reference vector of the root node is initialized with the centroid of the data. When vertical growth is invoked, two children are added to the root node. All input data associated with the root node are distributed between these children by employing a learning process (Fig. 11.2b). Following vertical growth, horizontal growth is invoked to determine the proper number of children for the root. In this example, three leaves are used (Fig. 11.2c). After this, the heterogeneities of the leaves are checked to determine whether or not to expand to another level. The answer is yes in this example, and a new vertical growth step is invoked. Two children are added to the leaves (L1, L3) whose heterogeneity are greater than the threshold (Fig. 11.2d) and are turned to nodes (N1, N3). All the input data are distributed again with the learning process, and a new horizontal growth begins (Fig. 11.2e). This process continues until the heterogeneity of all the leaves (indicated by the empty cycle in Fig. 11.2) are less than the threshold.

The DGSOT algorithm combines the horizontal growth and vertical growth to construct a multlifurcating hierarchical tree from top to bottom to cluster the data. If the number or the size of the clusters and subclusters of the data set are not even, for example, there is a very large cluster in the data set, the combination of horizontal growth and vertical growth lets the DGSOT algorithm find the proper hierarchical structure of the underlying data set, and then find a more reasonable final clustering result. The harmonization of the vertical growth and the horizontal growth is important in the DGSOT algorithm to find the proper structure of the underlying data set. The balance of vertical and horizontal growth is controlled by the clustering validation criterion, which determines the number of horizontal growth. Therefore, the cluster validation criterion is critical in the DGSOT algorithm. In DGSOT, the cluster validation criterion is used to determine the proper number of clusters in each hierarchical level rather than in the whole data set. For a data set containing an even number of clusters along with similar size, a proper cluster validation criterion must not allow the horizontal growth to continue forever without the vertical growth. On the other hand, for a data set containing an uneven number of clusters or an uneven size of clusters, a proper cluster validation criterion must be able to detect that uneven behavior and find the best representation in each hierarchical level.

To improve the clustering accuracy, Luo et al. [27, 28] proposed a K-level up distribution (KLD) mechanism. For KLD, data associated with a parent node will be distributed among its children leaves and also among its neighboring leaves. The following is the KLD strategy:

- For a selected node, its K level up ancestor node is determined.
- The subtree rooted by the ancestor node is determined.
- Data associated with the selected node is distributed among all leaves of the subtree.

The KLD scheme increases the scope in the hierarchy for data distribution, which will give the data mis-clustered at an early stage a chance to be reevaluated. The DGSOT algorithm combined with the KLD mechanism overcomes the drawbacks of the traditional neural tree-based hierarchical clustering algorithms.

In DGSOT, each leaf represents a cluster that includes all data associated with it. The reference vector of a leaf is the centroid of all data associated with it. Therefore, all reference vectors of the leaves form a *Voronoi* set of the original data set, and each internal node represents a cluster that includes all data associated with its leaf descendants. The reference vector of an internal node is the centroid of all data associated with its leaf descendants. The internal nodes of each hierarchical level also form a *Voronoi* set of the data set with a different resolution.

The DGSOT algorithm is applied to cluster the same 3000 yeast gene cell cycle microarray expression data that Tavazoie et al. [39] used. The clustering results of DGSOT are compared with SOTA when both have 25 clusters. For these low-level resolution clustering results, DGSOT, with the multipartition strategy, can successfully establish the hierarchical structure of these data, and then get more reasonable results than those obtained by SOTA, which is a pure bipartitions method. This is more drastic if the structure and substructure of the data contains an uneven number of clusters and subclusters or contains dramatically different sizes of clusters and subclusters [28]. Furthermore, the biological functionality enrichment in the clustering result of DGSOT is considerably higher in the degree of enrichment based on the P-value significant measure (see section 11.5) than the clustering result of SOTA and the K-means [28].

11.4.5 Graph-Based Clustering Algorithm

Given a set of gene expression data profiles $D = \{d_i\}$, we can define a weighted undirected complete graph $G = (V, E)$ to represent it. Each vertex in graph represents a gene. And each edge $(u, v) \in E$ has a weight that represents the similarity (or distance) between u and v. The graph-based clustering algorithms solve the problem of clustering a data set based on some graph theoretical problems, such as finding the minimum cut and finding the maximal cliques, or according the properties of the graph, such as the minimum spanning tree of graph G.

CLICK (CLuster Identification via Connectivity Kernels)

The CLICK algorithm [36] recursively partitions the graph G into highly connected subgraphs, which represent clusters. The partition that removes a subset of edges in the graph to disconnect the graph is called a cut, **C**. Shamir and Sharan [36] defined the weight of the edge (v, u) as the probability that vertices u and v are in the same cluster. Then, the weight of **C** is the sum of the weights of its edges. And a minimum weight cut in G is a cut with the minimum weight. The CLICK algorithm recursively finds the minimum cut in the graph and partitions the current graph into two subgraphs. After each cut, a stopping criterion is used to check the subgraph. If the subgraph satisfies the stopping criterion, then it is a kernel, and no more split is needed. Otherwise, the partitioning procedure is continued. The full CLICK algorithm also has two postprocessing steps to improve the clustering results. The adoption step adds the singletons into the cluster if the similarity between the singleton and the cluster is beyond a predefined threshold. The merging step merges two cluster that are similar. Shamir and Sharan [36] applied the CLICK to two gene expression profiles. The clustering results of CLICK are shown to perform better in homogeneity and separation than the result of SOM and HAC on two expression profiles, respectively.

CAST (Cluster Affinity Search Technique)

Ben-Dor et al. [4] proposed a corrupted clique graph model. In this model, a cluster can be represented by a clique graph, which is a disjoint union of complete graphs. The true clusters of genes are denoted by the clique graph H. Then, the input graph G of gene expression profiles can be obtained from H by flipping each edge/non-edge with probability α. Therefore, the clustering procedure can be translated into obtaining a clique graph as good as true clique graph H with high probability from the input graph G.

Based on the corrupted graph model, Ben-Dor et al. [4] proposed a theoretical algorithm that can discover the clusters with high probability and practical heuristic algorithm called CAST that can run in polynomial time. The input of CAST is a complete graph G. The weight of the edge is the similarity between two gene expressions. Ben-Dor et al. defined the *affinity value* $a(v)$ of a vertex v with respect to a cluster C as $a(v) = \sum_{u \in C} S(u, v)$. The CAST constructs one cluster at a time. When data have not been clustered, the CAST algorithm randomly picks up a data-point and starts a new cluster. Then, a free data-point whose affinity is greater than a predefined affinity threshold t is added to the cluster, and a data-point in the cluster whose affinity is less than t is removed from the cluster. This process continues until it is stabilized, and one cluster is created. Ben-Dor et al. applied CAST to several gene expression profiles and showed very promising results.

Minimum Spanning Tree (MST)-Based Clustering Algorithm

A spanning tree, T, of a weighted undirected graph G is a minimal subgraph of G, which connects all vertices. A MST is the spanning tree with the smallest total weight. The MST can represent the binary relationship of vertices in the graph. Xu et al. [46] observed that the tree edges connecting data of the same cluster are short whereas the tree edges linking different cluster are long. Based on this observation, Xu et al. defined the separation condition of a cluster as follows: "*Let D be a data set and s represent the distance between two data in D. Then, $C \subseteq D$ forms a cluster in D only if for any partition $C = C_1 \cup C_2$, the closest data point d to C_1, $d \in D - C_1$, is from C_2.*" Then any cluster C corresponds to a subtree of its MST. That is, "*if $d1$ and $d2$ are two points of a cluster C, then all data points in the tree path P, connecting $d1$ and $d2$ in the MST, must be from C.*"

Based on above cluster definition of the MST framework, Xu et al. [46] proposed three clustering algorithms according to different objective functions. The first objective function is to minimize the total edge weight of all K subtrees when partitioning MST into K subtrees. This can be easily realized by finding the $K - 1$ longest MST-edges and by cutting them. If there is an outlier data-point that is far away from any cluster, this simple algorithm will identify the outlier data-point as a cluster and fail to identify real clusters when the number K

is chosen improperly. The second objective function minimizes the total distance between the data in each cluster and its center:

$$\sum_{i=1}^{K} \sum_{d \in C_i} dist(d, center(C_i)) \tag{11.12}$$

Xu et al. proposed an iterative algorithm for this objective function. Initially, the MST is randomly partitioned into K subtrees. Then two adjacent clusters are selected and merged into one cluster. Through all the edges in the merged cluster, the edge that is cut will optimize the objective function and the merged cluster is partitioned into two clusters again. This process continues until it converges.

The third objective function i minimizes the distance between the data in a cluster and its representative points.

$$\sum_{i=1}^{K} \sum_{d \in C_i} dist(d, represent(C_i)) \tag{11.13}$$

A dynamic programming approach is used by Xu et al. [46] to find the optimal K clusters and their K representative data. All these algorithms are implemented in a software package called EXCAVATOR and tested for three microarray expression profiles.

11.4.6 Model-Based Clustering Algorithm

Unlike the distance (similarity)-based algorithm, the model-based algorithms assume a strong structure of the underlying data set, provided that each cluster of the underlying data set is generated from a probability distribution. In the mixture model, the likelihood that data in the set x belong to these K distributions is defined as

$$L_{MiIX}(\theta_1, \ldots \theta_K | x) = \prod_{i=1}^{n} \sum_{k=1}^{K} \tau_k f_k(x_i, \theta_k) \tag{11.14}$$

where τ_k is the probability that data x_i belong to the kth cluster; $f_k(x_i, \theta_k)$ is the probability density function (PDF) of the kth cluster in the data. θ_k is the parameter of the probability density function. The model-based algorithms try to maximize the likelihood function over the model parameter θ_k and the hidden parameter τ_k. Generally, the parameters θ_k and τ_k are estimated by the EM algorithm.

Usually, multivariate Gaussian distribution with mean vector u_k and covariance matrix Σ_k:

$$f_k(x_i | u_k, \Sigma_k) = \frac{\exp\{-\frac{1}{2}(x_i - u_k)^T \sum_k^{-1} (x_i - u_k)\}}{\sqrt{\det(2\pi \Sigma_k)}} \tag{11.15}$$

The covariance matrix Σ_k controls the geometric feature of the underlying cluster. Banfield and Raftery [2] proposed a general representation of the covariance matrix through the eigenvalue decomposition:

$$\Sigma_k = \lambda_k D_k A_k D_k^T \tag{11.16}$$

where D_k is the orthogonal matrix of eigenvectors, and A_k is a diagonal matrix whose elements are proportional to the eigenvalue of λ_k. The matrix D_k determines the orientation of the cluster, A_k determines its shape, and λ_k determines its volume. The variation of parameters in equation 11.16 will lead to various models with different characteristics. For the equal volume spherical model, in which each cluster in the data set is spherically symmetric, the covariance matrix can be simplified to $\Sigma_k = \lambda I$, where I is an identity matrix. If each spherical cluster has different volume, the covariance matrix is $\Sigma_k = \lambda_k I$. A different λ_k is used to control each cluster. The variation of parameters of general covariance matrix provides the flexibility to generate different models for different kinds of data set.

Yeung et al. [47] applied different models to cluster ovarian cancer microarray profiles and yeast cell cycle microarray profiles. The clustering results were shown to be comparable to the result of heuristic graph-based algorithm CAST. The advantage of model-based algorithms is that they provide a statistical framework to understand the underlying structure of the gene expression profiles. However, the assumption of model-based clustering that data fit in a specific distribution may not be true in some cases. For example, Yeung et al. [47] found that gene expression data fit the Gaussian model poorly. Finding a more proper model for gene expression data is still an ongoing effort.

11.4.7 Subspace Clustering

As the increased application of microarray technologies is generating a huge amount of data, it is easy to collect hundreds or even thousands microarray gene expression experiment data for one genome. For these kinds of high-dimensional gene expression profiles, all the above clustering algorithms that group data based on all dimensions become extremely difficult to implement. First, as the dimensions increase, the irrelevance between dimensions also increases, which will mask the true cluster in noise and eliminate the clustering tendency. Second, there is the *curse of dimensionality*. In high dimensions, the similarity measures become increasingly meaningless. Beyer et al. [6] showed that the distance to the nearest neighbor becomes indistinguishable from the distance to the majority of the points. Then, to find useful clusters, the clustering algorithm must work only on the relevant dimensions. At the same time, it is well known in biology that only a small subset of the genes participates in a certain cellular process. Then, even for a subset of the experiments, only parts of expressions are meaningful. Furthermore, one single gene may participate in multiple processes and can be related to different genes at different process. Thus, it can join different clusters at different processes. So, clustering on all dimensions of high-dimension microarray expression profiles is not meaningful. Recently, several subspace clustering algorithms [33] have been proposed to fit the requirement of mining high-dimensional gene expression profiles.

The subspace clustering concept was first introduced by Agrawal et al. [1] in a general data mining area. In their CLIQUE algorithm, each dimension is divided into a number of equal-length intervals ξ, and a unit in subspaces is the intersection of intervals in each dimension of sub spaces. A unit is dense if the number of points in it is above a certain threshold τ. The CLIQUE discovers the dense units in k-dimension subspaces from the dense units in $k-1$ dimensional subspaces. Next, a cluster is defined as a maximal set of connected dense units. The results of CLIQUE are a series of clusters in different subspaces. The CLIQUE is the first algorithm that combined the clustering with the attribute selection and provides a different view of the data.

A number of subspace clustering algorithms have been proposed to discover subclusters (high coherence submatrix) within high-dimensional gene expression profiles. Here, we only introduce two pioneering works. For more subspace clustering algorithms on gene expression profiles, a detail review is available in [29].

Coupled Two-Way Clustering (CTWC)

For a microarray expression profile with features F and objects O, where F and O can be both genes and experiments, Getz et al. [17] proposed a coupled two-way clustering (CTWC) algorithm to find a stable subset $(F_i$ and $O_j)$ of these profiles. A stable subset means that the O_j will be significant according to some predefined threshold when using only the features F_i to clustering objects O_j. The CTWC algorithm iteratively processes two-way clustering to find the stable subset. A clustering algorithm based on the Pott model of statistical physics called the superparamagnetic clustering algorithm (SPC) [7] is used for two-way clustering. Initially, two-way clustering is applied to the full gene expression matrix and generates a set of gene clusters (g_i^1) and a set of sample clusters (e_j^1). Then, the two-way clustering is applied to submatrices defined by the combination of one of the previously generated gene clusters with one of the previously generated sample clusters. This iteration continues until no new clusters satisfy some predefined criterion.

Getz et al. [17] applied the CTWC algorithm to an acute leukemia microarray profile and a colon caner microarray profile. For the first data set, the CTWC discovered 49 stable gene clusters and 35 stable sample clusters in two iterations. For the second data set, 76 stable sample clusters and 97 stable gene clusters were generated. Several conditionally related gene clusters have been identified, which cannot be identified when all of the samples are used to cluster genes. However, the CTWC also generated some meaningless clusters.

Biclustering

Given a gene expression profile A with a set of X genes and a set of Y samples, Cheng and Church [8] defined a submatrix $A_{I,J}(I \subset X, J \subset Y)$ in A with a high similarity score as a *bicluster*. Cheng and Church introduce the *residue* to measure the coherence of the gene expression. For each element a_{ij} in the submatrix $A_{I,J}$, its mean-squared residue (MSR) is defined as:

$$r\_a_{ij} = a_{ij} - a_{iJ} - a_{Ij} + a_{IJ} \tag{11.17}$$

where a_{iJ} is the mean of the ith row in the $A_{I,J}$, a_{Ij} is the mean of the jth column of $A_{I,J}$, and a_{IJ} is the mean of all elements in the $A_{I,J}$. The value of the MSR indicates the coherence of an expression relative to the remaining expressions in the bicluster $A_{I,J}$ given the biases of the relevant rows and the relevant columns. The lower the residue is, the stronger the coherence will be. Next, the MSR of the submatrix $A_{I,J}$ can be defined as:

$$MSR\_A_{IJ} = \frac{1}{|I||J|} \sum_{i \in I, j \in J} (MSR\_a_{ij})^2 \tag{11.18}$$

A submatrix $A_{I,J}$ is called a δ-bicluster if $MSR\_A_{IJ} \leq \delta$ for some $\delta \geq 0$.

Cheng and Church [8] showed that finding the largest square δ-bicluster is NP-hard and proposed several heuristic greedy row/column removal/addition algorithms to reduce the complexity to polynomial time. The single node deletion algorithm iteratively removes the row or column that gives the most decrease in mean-squared residue. The multiple node deletion algorithm iteratively removes the rows and columns whose mean-squared residues are greater than $\alpha \times msr\_A_{IJ}$, where $\alpha > 1$ is a predefined threshold. After the deletion algorithm terminates, a node addition algorithm adds rows and columns that do not increase the mean-squared residue of the bicluster. The algorithm finds one bicluster at a time. After a bicluster is found, the elements of the bicluster are replaced by random values in the original expression matrix. Each iteration bicluster is processed on the full expression matrix. The process will continue until K prerequired biclusters are found. Masking elements of already-identified biclusters by random noise will let the biclusters that are already discovered not be reported again. However, highly overlapping biclusters may also not be discovered.

Cheng and Church [8] demonstrated the biclustering algorithm on yeast microarray profiles and a human gene microarray profiles. For each data set, 100 biclusters were discovered.

11.5 Cluster Evaluation

The cluster validation evaluates the quality of the clustering result, and then finds the best partition of the underlying data set. A detail review of cluster validation algorithms appears in [18]. An optimal clustering result can be evaluated by two criteria [5]. One is compactness; the data inside the same cluster should be close to each other. The other is separation; different clusters should be separated as wide as possible. Generally, three kinds of approaches have been used to validate the clustering result [41]: the approach based on external criteria, the approach based on internal criteria, and the approach based on relative criteria.

The clustering validation using external criteria is based on the null hypothesis, which represents a random structure of a data set. It evaluates the resulting clustering structure by comparing it to an independent partition of the data built according to the null hypothesis of the data set. This kind of test leads to high computation costs. Generally, the Monte Carlo techniques are suitable for the high computation problem and generate the needed probability density function. The clustering validation using internal criteria is to evaluate the clustering result of an algorithm using only quantities and features inherent to the data set [18]. Internal criteria can be applied to two cases when the cluster validity depends on the clustering structure: one is the hierarchy of clustering schemes, and the other is the single clustering scheme [18].

Because of their low computational cost, the clustering validation using relative criteria is more commonly used. Usually the procedure of identifying the best clustering scheme is based on a validity index. In the plotting of validity index versus the number of clusters N_c, if the validity index does not exhibit an increasing or decreasing trend as N_c increases, the maximum (minimum) of the plot indicates the best clustering. On the other hand, for indices that increase or decrease as N_c increases, the value of N_c at which a significant local change takes place indicates the best clustering. This change appears as a "knee" in the plot, and it is an indication of the number of clusters underlying the data set. Moreover, the absence of a knee may be an indication that the data set has no cluster type structure.

For gene expression profile clustering, there is a fourth clustering validation approach that is based on the biological significance of the clustering results. Several clustering validity indices are presented here.

11.5.1 Dunn Indices

Dunn [12] proposed a cluster validity index to identify clusters. The index for a specific number of clusters is defined as

$$
D_{N_c} = \min_{i=1,\ldots N_c} \left\{ \min_{j=1,\ldots N_c} \left\{ \frac{d(c_i, c_j)}{\max_{k=1,\ldots N_c} diam(c_k)} \right\} \right\}
\tag{11.19}
$$

where $d(c_i, c_j)$ is the dissimilarity function between two clusters c_i and c_j defined as

$$d(c_i, c_j) = \min_{x \in c_i, y \in c_j} d(x, y) \tag{11.20}$$

and $diam(c)$ is the diameter of a cluster c, which measures the dispersion of clusters. The diameter of cluster c can be defined as

$$diam(c) = \max_{x, y \in c} d(x, y) \tag{11.21}$$

For compact and well-separated clusters, the distance between the clusters will be large and the diameter of the clusters will be small. Then, the value of the Dunn index will be large. However, the Dunn index does not exhibit any trend with respect to the number of clusters. Thus, the maximum value in the plot of the D_{N_c} versus the number of clusters indicate the number of compact and well-separated clusters in the data set.

11.5.2 The Davies-Bouldin (DB) Index

Davies and Bouldin proposed a similarity measure R_{ij} between clusters C_i and C_j based on a dispersion measure s_i of a cluster and a dissimilarity measure, d_{ij}, between two clusters. The R_{ij} index is defined to satisfy the following conditions [9]:

- $R_{ij} \geq 0$
- $R_{ij} = R_{ji}$
- If $s_i = 0$ and $s_j = 0$ then $R_{ij} = 0$
- If $s_j > s_k$ and $d_{ij} = d_{ik}$ then $R_{ij} > R_{ik}$
- If $s_j = s_k$ and $d_{ij} < d_{ik}$ then $R_{ij} > R_{ik}$

A R_{ij} that statisfes the above condition is nonnegative and symmetric. A simple choice for R_{ij} can be [9]

$$DB_{N_c} = \frac{1}{N_c} \sum_{i=1}^{N_c} R_i \qquad R_i = \max_{i,j=1,...N_c, i \neq j} R_{ij} \tag{11.22}$$

The above definition of DB_{N_c} is the average similarity between each cluster $C_i, i = 1, \ldots, N_c$ and its most similar one. Similar to Dunn index, the DB_{N_c} index exhibits no trends with respect to the number of clusters. The minimum value of DB_{N_c} in its plot versus the number of clusters indicates the best clustering.

11.5.3 Gap Statistics

Tibshirani et al. [42] proposed estimating the number of clusters in a data set via the gap statistic, which compares the change in within-cluster dispersion with that expected under an appropriate null distribution. The complete description of the gap statistic is as follows:

- Cluster the observed data, calculate the within-dispersion measure W_k for varying number of clusters $k = 1, 2, \ldots K$.

The W_k is defined as

$$W_k = \sum_{k=1}^{K} \frac{1}{2|C_k|} \sum_{i,j \in C_k} d_{ij} \tag{11.23}$$

- Generate B reference data sets, using the uniform prescription, and cluster each one giving within-dispersion measures W_{kb}^*, $b = 1, 2, \ldots B$, $k = 1, 2, \ldots K$. Compute the (estimated) gap statistic:

$$Gap(k) = (1/B) \sum_b \log(W_{kb}^*) - \log(W_k) \qquad (11.24)$$

- Let $\bar{l} = (1/B) \sum_b \log(W_{kb}^*)$, compute the standard deviation

$$sd_k = \left[(1/B) \sum_b (\log(W_{kb}^*) - \bar{l})^2 \right]^{\frac{1}{2}},$$

and define $s_k = sd_k \sqrt{1 + 1/B}$. Finally, choose the number of clusters via:

$$\hat{k} = smallest\ k\ such\ that\ Gap(k) \geq Gap(k+1) - s_{k+1} \qquad (11.25)$$

Average Silhouette

It has been proposed (see [34, 44]), using average silhouette as a composite index to reflect the compactness and separation of the clusters. A silhouette value $s(i)$ of data i that belong to cluster A is defined as follows

$$s(i) = \frac{b(i) - a(i)}{\max\{a(i), b(i)\}} \qquad (11.26)$$

The $a(i)$ is the average distance between data i and other data in the same cluster A:

$$a(i) = \frac{1}{|A| - 1} \sum_{j \in A, j \neq i} d(i, j) \qquad (11.27)$$

where $d(i, j)$ is the distance between data i and j and $|A|$ is the number of data in cluster A.

The $b(i)$ is the minimum value of average distance of data i to data in any cluster C other than cluster A.

$$b(i) = \min_{C \neq A} \{d(i, C)\} \qquad (11.28)$$

and

$$d(i, C) = \frac{1}{|C|} \sum_{j \in C} d(i, j) \qquad (11.29)$$

The average silhouette is the average of the silhouette value of all data in the cluster. The value of the average silhouette lies between -1 and 1. If the average silhouette is great than 0, the cluster is valid. If it is less than 0, the data in this cluster on average are closer to members of some other clusters, making this cluster invalid.

11.5.4 Biological Significance-Based on P-Value

Tavazoie et al. [39] proposed evaluating the clustering result based on the biological significance of each category. First, genes are assigned categories based on gene ontology or based on the categories of some public database. Then, for each cluster, a P-value can be calculated, which is the probability of observing the frequency of genes in a particular functional category in a certain cluster, using the cumulative hypergeometric probability distribution [39]. The P-value of observing k genes from a function category within a cluster of size n is

$$P = 1 - \sum_{i=0}^{k-1} \frac{\binom{f}{i}\binom{g-f}{n-i}}{\binom{g}{n}} \tag{11.30}$$

where f is the total number of genes within that functional category and g is the total number of genes within the genome (for yeast, n equals to 6220). The lower the P-value is, the higher the biological significance of a cluster.

11.6 Discussion

In this chapter, we reviewed clustering analysis for the gene expression profiles. The list of clustering algorithms presented is very limited but representative. Because of the fact that the research in this area is very active, a list of all algorithms developed for clustering gene expression profiles will be prohibitively long.

For biologists, clustering analysis is only the first step. Biologists want the results from the clustering to provide clues for the further biological research. Because false information will cost a lot of time and money for wet experiments, more accurate results are an absolute necessity. Since only a portion of the genes are expressed under most experimental conditions, to obtain a biologically meaningful result the clustering algorithms need to artificially assign a threshold for controlling the quality of the clusters. To determine the threshold, biological knowledge is needed. For some biological organisms, like yeast, *E coli*, and *Caenorhabditis elegans,* knowledge of the genes may be enough to determine the threshold. But for most biological organisms knowledge of the genes is limited, so the threshold is determined artificially. The threshold may be either too spurious, which may produce false information, or too strict, which may cause the loss of true information. Moreover, the changing of the threshold will result in different clusters of modules [3]. Finding an objective criterion for deciding what is a biologically meaningful cluster is certainly one of the most important open problems.

With the wide application of the microarray technology, more genome-size gene expression experimental data for an organism are becoming available. Because of the *curse of dimensionality*, traditional clustering algorithms are not suitable for analyzing these high-dimensional data sets. Subspace clustering, which tries to find density sub-"blocks" in the high-dimensional data, is not only appropriate for the purpose of mining high-dimensional large gene expression profiles but also consistent with the knowledge from biology that only part of the genes is expressed at certain experimental conditions. Designing an efficient subspace clustering algorithm that can discover biologically meaningful clusters still is an important research direction.

One other important issue in clustering analysis is how to visualize the clustering result. A good clustering algorithm without a good method to visualize the result will limit its usage. The reason that hierarchical agglomerative clustering is most commonly used in biological data analysis is that it can be visualized by dendrography, which is easily understood by biologists. Developing new methods and tools for visualization of clustering result of biological data can lead to widespread application of the clustering algorithms.

References

[1] R. Agrawal, J. Gehrke, D. Gunopulos, P. Raghavan. Automatic subspace clustering of high dimensional data for data mining applications. In *Proceedings ACM SIGMOD International Conference on Management of Data*, pages 94–105, 1998.

[2] J. Banfield, A. Raftery. Model based Gaussian and non-Gaussian clustering. *Biometrics*, 49, 803–821, 1993.

[3] A-L. Barabasi, Z.N. Oltvai. Network biology: understanding the cell's functional organization. *Nature Review*, 5, 101–114, 2004.

[4] A. Ben-Dor, R. Shamir, Z. Yakhini. Clustering gene expression patterns. *Journal of Computational Biology*, 6, 281–297, 1999.

[5] M.J.A. Berry, G. Linoff. *Data Mining Techniques For Marketing, Sales and Customer Support*. New York: John Wiley & Sons, USA, 1996.

[6] K.S. Beyer, J. Goldstein, R. Ramakrishnan, U. Shaft. When is "nearest neighbor" meaningful? In *Proceedings of the 7th ICDT*, Jerusalem, Israel, pages 217–235, 1999.

[7] M. Blat, S. Wiseman, E. Domany. Superparamegnetic clustering of Data, *Physical Review Letters*, 76(18), 3252–3254, 1996.

[8] Y. Cheng, G.M. Church. Biclustering of expression data. *In Proceedings of ISMB 2000*, pages 93–103, 2000.

[9] D.L. Davies, D.W. Bouldin. A Cluster separation measure. *IEEE Transactions on Patten Analysis and Machine Intelligence*, 1(2), 224–227, 1979.

[10] C. Debouck, P.N. Goodfellow. DNA microarrays in drug discovery and development. *Nature Genetics supplement*, 21, 48–50, 1999.

[11] J. Dopazo, J.M. Carazo. Phylogenetic reconstruction using an unsupervised growing neural network that adopts the topology of a phylogenetic Tree. *Journal of Molecular Evolution*, 44, 226–233, 1997.

[12] J.C. Dunn. Well separated clusters and optimal fuzzy partitions. *J. Cybern.*, 4, 95–104, 1974.

[13] B. Efron, T. Jackknife. The Bootstrap, and Other Resampling Plans. *CBMS-NSF Regional Conference Series in Applied Mathematics*, 38, 1982.

[14] M.B. Eisen, P.T. Spellman, P.O. Brown, D. Botstein. Cluster analysis and display of genomewide expression patterns. *Proc. Natl. Acad. Sci.*, 95, 14863–14868, 1998.

[15] http://rana.lbl.gov/EisenSoftware.htm.

[16] B. Fritzke. Growing cell structures— a self-organizing network for unsupervised and supervised learning. *Neural Networks*, 7, 1141–1160, 1994.

[17] G. Getz, E. Levine E. Domany. Coupled two-way clustering analysis of gene microarray data. *Proc. Natl. Acad. Sci.*, 97, 22, 12079–12084, 2000.

[18] M. Halkidi, Y. Batistakis, M. Vazirgiannis. On clustering validation techniques. *Journal of Intelligent Information Systems*, 17, 107–145, 2001.

[19] L.H. Hartwell, J.J. Hopfiled, S. Leibler, A.W. Murray. From molecular to modular cell biology. *Nature*, 402, C47–C52, 1999.

[20] J. Herrero, A. Valencia, J. Dopazo. A hierarchical unsupervised growing neural network for clustering gene expression patterns. *Bioinformatics*, 17, 126–136, 2001.

[21] J. Herrero, F.A. Shahrour, R.D. Uriarte et al. GEPAS: a web-based resource for microarray gene expression data analysis. *Nucleic Acids Research*, 31(13), 3461–3467, 2003.

[22] L.J. Heyer, S. Kruglyak, S. Yooseph. Exploring expression data: identification and analysis of coexpressed Genes. *Genome Research*, 9, 1106–1115, 1999.

[23] A.K. Jain, M.N. Murty, P.J. Flynn. Data clustering: a review. *ACM Computing Surveys*, 31(3), 264–323, 1999.

[24] T. Kohonen. *Self-Organizing Maps*. 2nd. New York: Springer 1997.

[25] G.N. Lance, W.T. Williams. A general theory of classificatory sorting strategies: 1. Hierarchical systems. *Computer Journal*, 9, 373–380, 1966.

[26] D.J. Lockhart, H. Dong, M.C. Byrne, et al. Expression monitoring by hybridization to high-density oligonucleotide arrays. *Nature Biotechnology*, 14, 1675–1680, 1996.

[27] F. Luo, L. Khan, F. Bastani, I.L. Yen. *A dynamical growing self-organizing tree (DG-SOT)*. Technical Report, University of Texas at Dallas, 2003.

[28] F. Luo, L. Khan, I.L. Yen, F. Bastani, J. Zhou. A dynamical growing self-organizing tree (DGSOT) for hierarchical clustering gene expression profiles. *Bioinformatics*, 20(16), 2605–2617, 2004.

[29] S.C. Madeira, A.L. Oliveira. Biclustering algorithm for biological data analysis: a survey. *IEEE/ACM Transactions on Computational Biology and Bioinformatics*. 1(1), 1–30, 2004.

[30] J.B. McQueen. Some methods for classification and analysis of multivariate observations. In *Proceedings of the Fifth Berkeley Symposium on Mathematical Statistics and Probability*, volume 1, pages 281–297, University of California, Berkeley, 1967.

[31] J.M. Naciff, G.J. Overmann, S.M. Torontali, et al. Gene expression Pro.le induced by 17α-ethynyl estradiol in the prepubertal female reproductive system of the rat. *Toxicological Science*, 72, 314–330, 2003.

[32] S.T. Nadler, J.P. Stoehr, K.L. Schueler, et al. The expression of adipogenic genes is decreased in obesity and Diabetes mellitus. *Proc. Natl. Acad. Sci.*, 97, 1371–11376, 2002.

[33] L. Parsons, E. Haque, H. Liu. Subspace clustering for high dimensional data: a review. *SIGKDD Explorations, Newsletter of the ACM Special Interest Group on Knowledge Discovery and Data Mining*, 2004.

[34] P.J. Rousseeuw. Silhouettes: a graphical aid to the interpretation and validation of cluster analysis. *Journal of Computational and Applied Mathematics*, 20, 53–65, 1987.

[35] M. Schena, D. Shalon, R. Davis, P. Brown.. Quantitative monitoring of gene expression patterns with a compolementatry DNA microarray. *Science*, 270, 467–470, 1995.

[36] R. Shamir, R. Sharan. Click: a clustering algorithm for gene expression analysis. In *Proceedings of ISMB 2000*, pages 307–316, 2000.

[37] F. Smet, J. Mathys, K. Marchal, G. Thijs, Y. Moreau. Adaptive quality-based clustering of gene expression profiles. *Bioinformatics*, 18, 735–746, 2002.

[38] P. Tamayo, D. Slonim, J. Mesirov, et al. Interpreting patterns of gene expression with self-organizing maps: methods and application to hematopoietic differentiation. *Proc. Natl. Acad. Sci.*, 96, 2907–2912, 1999.

[39] S. Tavazoie, J.D. Hughes, M.J. Campbell, et al. Systematic determination of genetic network architecture. *Nature Genetics*, 22, 281–285, 1999.

[40] A. Tefferi, M. E. Bolander, S. M. Ansell, et al. Primer on medical genomics part III: microarray experiments and data Analysis. *Mayo Clinic Proc.*, 77, 927–940, 2002.

[41] S. Theodoridis, K. Koutroubas. *Pattern Recognition*. New York: Academic Press, 1999.

[42] R. Tibshirani, G. Walther, T. Hastie. Estimating the number of clusters in a data set via the gap statistic. *Journal of the Royal Statistical Society*, Series B, 63, 411–423, 2001.

[43] O. Troyanskaya, M. Cantor, G. Sherlock, et al. Missing value estimation methods for DNA microarrays. *Bioinformatics*, 17(6), 520–525, 2001.

[44] J. Vilo, A. Brazma, I. Jonssen, A. Robinson, E. Ukkonen. Mining for putative regulatory elements in the yeast genome using gene expression data. *Proceedings of ISMB 2000*, 384–394, 2000.

[45] E.M. Voorhees. Implementing agglomerative hierarchic clustering algorithms for use in document retrieval. *Information Processing & Management*, 22(6), 465–476, 1986.

[46] Y. Xu, V. Olmam, D. Xu. Clustering gene expression data using a graph-theoretic approach: an application of minimum spanning trees. *Bioinformatics*, 18, 536–545, 2002.

[47] K.Y. Yeung, C. Fraley, A. Murua, A.E. Raftery, W.L. Ruzzo. Model-based clustering and data transformations for gene expression data. *Bioinformatics*, 17, 977–987, 2001.

Complexity of Magnetic Resonance Spectrum Classification

Richard Baumgartner, Tin Kam Ho, Ray Somorjai, Uwe Himmelreich, Tania Sorrell

Summary. We use several data complexity measures to explain the differences in classification accuracy using various sets of features selected from samples of magnetic resonance spectra for two-class discrimination. Results suggest that for this typical problem with sparse samples in a high-dimensional space, even robust classifiers like random decision forests can benefit from sophisticated feature selection procedures, and the improvement can be explained by the more favorable characteristics in the class geometry given by the resultant feature sets.

12.1 Introduction

Biomedical spectra obtained by magnetic resonance (MR) spectroscopy are characterized by (a) high dimensionality and (b) a typically small number of available samples. A statistically meaningful analysis of a limited number of high-dimensional data points presents a serious challenge, due to the extreme sparsity of samples in high-dimensional spaces [13]. Dimensionality reduction techniques using feature selection and extraction provide a natural way to address this problem [10, 11, 14]. Interpretable feature selection is especially desirable in disease profiling applications when using biomedical data such as spectra or gene microarrays [8, 9, 14], because they provide hypotheses for the domain experts for further corroboration. The main goal of this chapter is to explore the utility of data complexity measures [6] in assessing several feature selection and extraction procedures in a real-world two-class discrimination problem using MR spectra.

Robust classifiers are needed to generalize the class boundary from severely limited training samples in a high-dimensional problem. Questions remain on how such classifiers interact with dimensionality reduction techniques. Recently, in the application of handwritten word recognition it has been demonstrated that feature selection and extraction can be beneficial for the random subspace method (RSM) [2]. In addition, a successful, standard application of RSM has been reported in disease profiling applications using high-dimensional gene microarray data, where the combination of feature selection and extraction with RSM was proposed as a topic for further research [1]. Motivated by the observations in [1] and [2], we use RSM classification accuracy as a guide for comparing features extracted by our algorithms.

12.2 Materials, Methods, and Data

Conventional biochemical techniques frequently have difficulty identifying closely related species or subspecies of fungi or yeasts. At best, the procedures are time-consuming. In contrast, MR spectroscopy, combined with multivariate classification methods, has proven to be very powerful. As a typical application of the methodology, we have used MR spectra of isolates of two pathogenic yeast species, *Candida albicans* and *Candida parapsilosis* [3].

The yeast colonies were suspended in phosphate-buffered saline made up with deuterated water. The suspension was immediately transferred to a 5-mm NMR tube (Wilmad Glass Co., Buena, NJ). The ^{1}H MR spectra were acquired at 37degC on a Bruker Avance 360-MHz MR spectrometer using a 5-mm ^{1}H, [1]3C inverse-detection dual-frequency probe. The following acquisition parameters were used: frequency 360.13 MHz, pulse angle 90deg, repetition time 2.3 s, spectral width 3600 Hz. For a more specific description of the technical details of the acquisition procedure, see [3]. Spectra were processed using the Xprep software (IBD, Winnipeg, Manitoba). The feature extraction and classification methods were carried out on the magnitude spectra. The dimensionality of the spectra was 1500, corresponding to intensity values in the range of 0.35 to 4.00 ppm. A typical spectrum is shown in Figure 12.1. The training set contained 124 spectra (62 in each class). The independent test set not used for classifier development contained 73 spectra (35 in class 1, *Candida albicans*, and 38 in class 2, *Candida parapsilosis*).

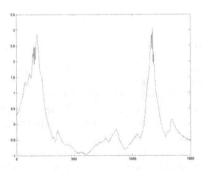

Fig. 12.1. A example of a magnetic resonance spectrum.

12.3 Dimensionality Reduction Techniques

Components of the raw spectral feature vectors are ordered by the channel frequencies. Because many spectral peaks and valleys have a naturally occurring width, intensity values in neighboring channels are expected to be correlated to some extent. To quantify this, we computed the 1500×1500 correlation coefficient matrix using the training set. Figure 12.2 shows the heat-map representation of this correlation matrix. We can clearly recognize the bands or clusters of highly correlated intervals of adjacent-neighboring features formed along the main diagonal. The motivation for the dimensionality reduction techniques under investigation is to take advantage of this structure in both an unsupervised and a supervised manner.

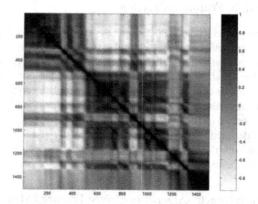

Fig. 12.2. Heat-map representation of the correlation matrix computed from the training set. The bands of highly correlated neighboring features are clearly recognizable.

In particular, let a sample in the original 1500-dim ($p_{dim} = 1500$) feature space be represented by a $1 \times p_{dim}$ row vector $s_{original}$. The dimensionality reduction is achieved using a $p_{dim} \times n_{feat}$ matrix B so that the sample in the reduced n_{feat}-dimensional space is given by the row vector $s_{reduced}$, where

$$s_{reduced} = s_{original} B.$$

The columns of the matrix B represent the basis functions onto which the data are projected. In the two feature extraction procedures we used, the new features are averages over intervals of neighboring features in the original spectrum. Thus, each column in the matrix B represents a basis function with nonzero values in some of the p_{dim} positions where the orignial features are to be averaged.

Averaging highly redundant features also has a smoothing effect and improves the signal-to-noise ratio. An example of a column of the matrix B is shown in Figure 12.3, where the feature interval 200 to 300 is averaged.

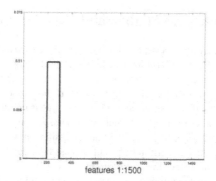

features 1:1500

Fig. 12.3. An example of a basis function that averages the intensity values in the spectral interval 200 to 300.

12.3.1 Unsupervised Feature Extraction

In unsupervised feature selection, we determine the set of features to be averaged from the training set using a sequential clustering algorithm. Clusters of features are defined as intervals of neighboring frequency channels for which the pairwise correlation coefficient is not lower than a specific threshold. We start with the feature at position 1 and keep adding the neighboring features to the current feature cluster, as long as their correlation coefficients with the first feature are at or above the chosen threshold. If the criterion is violated, the current feature cluster is assumed to be complete. The (last) feature that caused the violation of the cluster criterion is declared the first feature of a new cluster and the procedure is repeated. The procedure ends with the last feature (at position p_{dim}). The number of feature clusters identified gives the dimensionality of the reduced space.

12.3.2 Supervised, Genetic-Algorithm-Driven Feature Extraction

Alternatively, features can be selected with some regard to their discriminating power for the two classes. The feature selection algorithm we have used for supervised feature extraction is the near-optimal region selector (ORS) [8, 10]. ORS searches for intervals of neighboring features that are maximally discriminatory. ORS is guided by a genetic algorithm (GA), explicitly optimized for preprocessing spectra. GA is particularly appropriate for spectra, since the latter are naturally representable as "chromosomes," vectors of length p_{dim}, with 1's indicating the presence and 0's the absence of features. The GA's input includes (1) n_{feat}, the maximum number of features, which is the number of distinct spectral subregions required in the type of dimensionality reduction operation/transformation to be carried out (averaging of the spectral windows); (2) the population size; (3) the number of generations; and (4) two random seeds. The operations comprise the standard GA options: mutation and crossover. To achieve robust classification, the number of desired features is typically kept much smaller than the sample size. GA_ORS begins by searching the entire feature space, i.e., the complete spectrum. The output is the set of (averaged) feature intervals that optimally separate the classes. GA_ORS is applied as a wrapper, for which the search of the feature space is guided by the leave-one-out accuracy of a linear discriminant analysis (LDA). Once n_{feat} ($\ll p_{dim}$) good features have been found, the results are validated using an independent test set that was not used in the feature extraction procedure.

12.4 Random Subspace Method and Decision Forests

The random subspace method (RSM)[4] is known to produce robust classifiers for many high-dimensional problems. The method combines the decision of a large number of classifiers with sufficient differences in the generalization power [7]. Each classifier is trained to perfection, but uses only a randomly selected subset of features. If the classes are unambiguous in the chosen subspace, the classifier is perfect and at the same time is insensitive to differences in the unselected features. As a result, it has some built-in generalization power to avoid overtraining.

RSM often performs better than any individual classifier in its collection. The individual classifiers are best taken to be decision trees, but success has been reported on nearest neighbor classifiers [5], pseudo-Fisher linear discriminants [12], and support vector machines [1]. The built-in defense against overtraining has made RSM useful in problems involving a large number of features where some may be redundant. Thus RSM appears to be promising in classifying MR spectra that typify such problems.

In RSM the degree of improvement over individuals varies with the specifics of the individual classifiers. There are variations between different fractions of features chosen to use, or between different realizations of the random projections. In the case of decision trees, variations are also observed between different types of splitting hyperplanes used in the trees. Such variations have not been thoroughly analyzed, but a large range usually means that the discriminating power is concentrated in a small number of features, so that their presence in the chosen set is important.

In our experiments we use RSM with decision trees that use oblique or axis-parallel splits. In oblique trees, at each internal node the tree splits the data set using a linear function of the features obtained by a simplified Fisher's procedure, central axis projection [4]. In axis-parallel trees, each node splits the data set using the feature that maximizes information gain. The classifier that uses RSM on decision trees is also called a random decision forest.

In Table 12.1 we report the test set accuracies when the random decision forest is applied to several feature sets resulting from variations of the two feature extraction procedures. For comparison, we also show the accuracies of a nearest-neighbor classifier using Euclidean distance, and the two types of decision trees applied individually without participating in an RSM ensemble. The feature sets are

- original: the 1500 dimensional vector containing the raw spectrum;
- GA averaged: the three features that are average intensities in three spectral regions selected by the genetic algorithm;
- GA regions: the concatenation of the intensity values in the three spectral regions selected by the genetic algorithm (channel 82–96, 908–933, and 1080–1242);
- corr 0.90: averages of 90 spectral windows selected by correlation coefficient clustering with a threshold at 0.9;
- corr 0.99: averages of 330 spectral windows selected by correlation coefficient clustering with a threshold at 0.99;
- corr 0.998: averages of 849 spectral windows selected by correlation coefficient clustering with a threshold at 0.998.

Table 12.1. Nearest neighbor, single decision trees, and random decision forest accuracies (% correct on the test set) using different sets of selected features.

Feature set	Original	GA averaged	GA regions	corr 0.90	corr 0.99	corr 0.998
Dimensionality	1500	3	204	90	330	849
1-nearest neighbor	91.78	91.78	79.45	86.30	87.67	91.78
1 oblique tree	82.19	87.67	75.34	78.08	84.93	82.19
1 axis-pl. tree	73.97	86.30	83.56	78.08	83.56	75.34
Random decision forest	94.52	95.89	90.41	90.41	94.52	91.78

This problem demonstrates an extreme case where only a few of a large number of features are relevant for discrimination, and the number of available training samples is very small compared to the feature space dimensionality. In such a space, many single classifiers would suffer from overtraining, as we can see from single tree accuracies in Table 12.1. But the RSM ensembles are robust and are able to take advantage of the large number of features. Nevertheless, applying sophisticated feature selection techniques is still important, as evidenced by the accuracy improvement achieved by the feature set GA-averaged on the RSM ensemble, as well as on the single tree classifiers. Moreover, with better features to train on, RSM also shows less performance variation among different training options.

12.5 Evaluation of the Feature Set Complexity

To find explanations for the differences in classification accuracies using these feature sets, we computed the values of several measures of classification complexity as described in [6]. More details about these measures can be found in other chapters in this volume. The measures used in this experiment are

1. `boundary`: length of the class boundary estimated by the fraction of points on a class-crossing edge in a minimal spanning tree
2. `intra-inter`: ratio of average intra-class nearest-neighbor distance to average inter-class nearest-neighbor distance
3. `pretop`: fraction of points with the maximal within-class covering ball not fully contained in other balls
4. `overlap`: overlap volume of the class bounding boxes
5. `maxfeaeff`: maximum feature efficiency, or the largest fraction of points classified by a single feature
6. `nonlin-NN`: nonlinearity of nearest neighbor classifier
7. `nonlin-LP`: nonlinearity of linear classifier minimizing error distance

Table 12.2 lists the values of these measures computed from the training samples (TR) and the test samples (TE) represented by each feature set. There are some indications that the GA-averaged feature set makes the classification problem easier in at least three ways: (1) it puts fewer points on boundary, (2) the classes have less spread (lower `intra-inter` ratio), and (3) the classes are more spherical (smaller `pretop` value). Two of the metrics, volume of `overlap` and maximum feature efficiency, are heavily affected by the orientation angle of the class gap, and are thus not too revealing in this problem. The nonlinearity of the nearest neighbor classifier is relatively low for the GA-averaged feature set, suggesting that with this feature set, the nearest neighbor boundary can largely avoid cutting off part of the convex hulls of the two classes to the wrong side of the decision surface. On the other hand, the nonlinearity of the linear classifier is actually higher for the GA-averaged feature set while being zero for all others. This suggests that linear separability by itself does not necessarily give an easily learnable problem; sparse samples in a high-dimensional space have a higher chance to be linearly separable, but severe overtraining may prevent the learning algorithms from yielding a satisfactory classifier.

12.6 Conclusion

We described a study of MR spectra classification where two feature selection and extraction procedures were used to derive several feature sets representing the problem. We applied decision forests constructed with the random subspace method to each feature set, and observed that the averaged intensity values in three frequency windows selected by a genetic algorithm yielded the most accurate classifier. We further attempted to explain the superiority of this feature set using several measures of data complexity, and observed that its higher utility in classification is consistent with favorable values with three measures most relevant to the class geometry.

We expect that more studies along this line will lead to a way of using the data complexity measures to guide feature selection for classification. In this methodology, feature selection procedures may be designed for minimizing classification complexity, as measured by the most useful descriptors of the class geometry.

Table 12.2. Complexity measures of the feature sets on the training sample (TR) or test sample (TE).

		Original	GA averaged	GA regions	corr 0.90	corr 0.99	corr 0.998
boundary	TR	0.25	0.16	0.40	0.26	0.27	0.27
	TE	0.27	0.22	0.40	0.32	0.37	0.33
intra-inter	TR	0.59	0.41	0.69	0.64	0.62	0.61
	TE	0.58	0.46	0.66	0.64	0.63	0.60
pretop	TR	0.98	0.91	1.00	1.00	1.00	0.99
	TE	1.00	0.93	0.99	0.99	1.00	1.00
overlap	TR	0.00	0.38	0.00	0.00	0.00	0.00
	TE	0.00	0.29	0.00	0.00	0.00	0.00
maxfeaeff	TR	0.27	0.14	0.19	0.23	0.26	0.27
	TE	0.52	0.23	0.40	0.49	0.52	0.52
nonlin-NN	TR	0.05	0.02	0.11	0.07	0.06	0.06
	TE	0.05	0.08	0.14	0.07	0.06	0.05
nonlin-LP	TR	0.00	0.01	0.00	0.00	0.00	0.00
	TE	0.00	0.03	0.00	0.00	0.00	0.00

References

[1] A. Bertoni, R. Folgieri, G. Valentini. Bio-molecular cancer prediction with random subspace ensembles of support vector machines. *Neurocomputing*, 63C, 535–539, 2005.

[2] S. Gunter, H. Bunke. Feature selection algorithms for the generation of multiple classifier systems and their application to handwritten word recognition. *Pattern Recognition Letters*, 25(11), 1323–1336, 2004.

[3] U. Himmelreich, R.L. Somorjai, B. Dolenko B, et al. Rapid identification of Candida species by using nuclear magnetic resonance spectroscopy and a statistical classification strategy. *Applied and Environmental Microbiology* 69(8), 4566–4574, 2003.

[4] T.K. Ho. The random subspace method for constructing decision forests. *IEEE Transactions on Pattern Analysis and Machine Intelligence*, 20(8), 832–844, 1998.

[5] T.K. Ho. Nearest neighbors in random subspaces. In *Proceedings of the 2nd International Workshop on Statistical Techniques in Pattern Recognition*, Sydney, Australia, August 11–13, 1998, pages 640–648.

[6] T.K. Ho, M. Basu. Complexity measures of supervised classification problems. *IEEE Transactions on Pattern Analysis and Machine Intelligence*, 24(5), 289–300, 2002.

[7] E.M. Kleinberg. Stochastic Discrimination. *Annals of Mathematics and Artificial Intelligence*, 1, 207–239, 1990.

[8] C.L. Lean, R.L. Somorjai, I.C.P. Smith, P. Russell, C.E. Mountford. Accurate diagnosis and prognosis of human cancers by proton MRS and a three stage classification strategy. *Annual Reports on NMR Spectroscopy* 48, 71–111, 2002.

[9] C. Mountford, R. Somorjai, P. Malycha, et al. Diagnosis and prognosis of breast cancer by magnetic resonance spectroscopy of fine-needle aspirates analyzed using a statistical classification strategy. *British Journal of Surgery*, 88(9), 1234–1240, 2001.

[10] A. Nikulin, B. Dolenko, T. Bezabeh, R. Somorjai. Near optimal region selection for feature space reduction: novel preprocessing methods for classifying MR spectra. *NMR in Biomedicine*, 11, 209–216, 1998.

[11] S. Raudys, A. Jain. Small sample size effects in statistical pattern recognition: recommendation for practitioners. *IEEE Transaction on Pattern Analysis and Machine Intelligence*, 13(3), 252–264, 1998.

[12] M. Skurichina, R.P.W. Duin. Bagging, boosting, and the random subspace method for linear classifiers. *Pattern Analysis and Applications*, 5(2), 121–135, 2002.

[13] R. Somorjai, B. Dolenko, R. Baumgartner. Class prediction and discovery using gene expression and proteomics mass spectroscopy data. Curses, caveats, cautions. *Bioinformatics*, 19, 1484–1491, 2003.

[14] R. Somorjai, B. Dolenko, A. Nikulin, et al. Distinguishing normal from rejecting renal allografts: application of a three-stage classification strategy to MR and IR spectra of urine. *Vibrational Spectroscopy*, 28, 97–102, 2002.

13

Data Complexity in Tropical Cyclone Positioning and Classification

Chi Lap Yip, Ka Yan Wong, and Ping Wah Li

Summary. Tropical cyclones (TCs), life-threatening and destructive, warrant analysis and forecast by meteorologists so that early warnings can be issued. To do that, the position of a TC should be located and its intensity classified. In this chapter, we briefly introduce the problem of TC positioning and classification, discuss its associated data complexity issues, and suggest future research directions in the field.

13.1 Introduction

A tropical cyclone (TC) is a synoptic-scale[1] to mesoscale[2] low-pressure system over tropical or subtropical waters with organized convection and definite cyclonic (anticyclonic in Southern Hemisphere) surface wind circulation [18, 25]. Figures 13.1(a) and 13.1(b) show the structure of a typical tropical cyclone. In appearance, a TC resembles a huge whirlpool — a gigantic mass of revolving moist air. It has a disk-like shape with a vertical scale of tens of kilometers against horizontal dimensions of hundreds of kilometers [35]. The center of circulation, or the "eye," of a TC is the low-pressure center around which organized convection occurs and low-level cloud lines spiral. It is also the warmest part of a TC. An eye is bounded by the "eye wall," a ring-shaped region where maximum winds are found. The eye is typically of the order of tens of kilometers in diameter, and most of the heavy rain occurs near it and along the spiral rain bands [44]. A dramatic fall and rise in wind strength and pressure occur during the passage of TC eye, which is shown in Figure 13.1(c). According to the National Oceanic and Atmospheric Administration (NOAA) [6], the average annual frequency of named TCs over the globe from 1968 to 2003 is 87.7, and 30.4% of them occur in the Western North Pacific Ocean basin [26]. Figures 13.2(a) and 13.2(b) show tracks of TCs that occurred over the Western North Pacific and the South China Sea in 2003 and the distribution (average number and percentage)[3] of TCs over the globe from 1986 to 2003, respectively.

Since TCs often cause significant damage and loss of lives in affected areas, to reduce the loss, weather warning centers normally issue early warnings based on the forecasted TC track

---

[1] Synoptic-scale systems are continental or oceanic in scale, such as fronts and tropical high pressure areas [7].

[2] Mesoscale weather systems are phenomena of 2 to 2000 km, such as thunderstorms.

[3] Since some TC tracks stride more than one basin, the total percentage is larger than 100%.

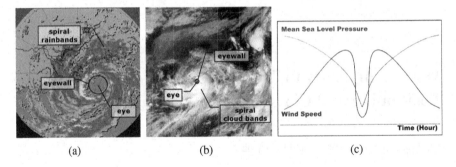

(a)   (b)   (c)

Fig. 13.1. Tropical cyclone (TC) structure. (a) Typhoon York, 1999-09-16 0300 Hong Kong
Time (HKT), Radar reflectivity data. (b) Typhoon York, 1999-09-16 0200 HKT, GMS-5 visible light data. (c) Typical variations of pressure and wind speed during the passage of TC eye.

Data sources: (a, b): Tai Mo Shan Doppler weather radar of the Hong Kong Observatory (HKO) [4].
(c): The Geostationary Meteorological Satellite (GMS-5) of the Japan Meteorological Agency (JMA) [5].

Figure 13.2(c). Two steps, namely positioning and classification, are required for TC analysis
before a TC forecast can be done. In the positioning step, an accurate location of the eye of the
TC is found by applying eye fix techniques. This allows the movement of the TC to be tracked,
and is normally done by the analysis of data from remote sensors or numerical models. In the
classification step, the intensity of a TC is determined. Depending on its intensity, a TC can
normally be categorized as a tropical depression, tropical storm, severe tropical storm, and
typhoon or hurricane. The classification step allows forecasters to know whether the TC is
strengthening or dissipating. In this chapter, we focus on the analysis steps of positioning and
classification. The forecasting issues will only be touched briefly when we discuss numerical
weather prediction (NWP).

Traditionally, a TC eye is fixed manually by a forecaster. This is done by identifying the
center of rotation from a sequence of radar or satellite images, or overlaying templates onto
a printed image. Since these traditional methods require human recognition of cloud shapes
or eye location, they are not totally objective. The results from the same set of data may not
be consistent when they are analyzed by different forecasters. With the availability of more
powerful computers in recent years, computer-assisted analysis becomes possible. Algorithms
have been designed for positioning the TC eye and classifying its intensity in a more objective
and efficient way.

In the following sections, we first introduce the data sources that are often used for the
positioning and classification problems. Then, a brief survey of the developments in the field
is given, highlighting the issues associated with these seemingly simple problems. After that,
a discussion of data complexity issues associated with the problem is given, followed by a
discussion of the future direction of research and development, and conclusions.

13.2 Data Sources

There are four major types of weather data used for automated TC eye fix: radar reflectivity
data, Doppler velocity data, satellite images, and numerical weather prediction (NWP) data.
Since these data are collected or generated by different sensors, each of which focuses on

different aspects of the atmosphere, specialized algorithms for processing and analysis are needed to handle each of these data types. Indeed, the results of an eye fix of the same TC at the same time period using different data or by different people could be different. A brief description of each type of data is provided in this section.

Radar reflectivity and Doppler velocity data are obtained from weather radars, most of which are fixed on earth. Weather radars send out microwave signals to the atmosphere and collect the reflected signals. Radar reflectivity values show the intensity of the echos reflected from rain, snow, ice, or hail aloft. Doppler velocity data show the radial velocities of these water species with respect to the radar. The reflected signals are processed to extract the relevant slices suitable for analysis. Radar data at 3 km from sea level, called the 3-km constant altitude plan position indicator (CAPPI), is often used for the TC eye fix. The range of weather radars are normally limited to a few hundred kilometers, and their data are updated at intervals of a few minutes. With a high resolution of a few hundred meters, they are ideal for observing precipitation near the station. Figures 13.3(a) and 13.3(b) show two radar images.

Meteorological satellites carry sensors that point to the ground to obtain a bird's view of the earth. Images of the earth at different wavelengths from infrared (IR) to visible light (VIS) are captured in different channels. Satellites can be polar-orbiting or geostationary. Polar-orbiting satellites are relatively low-flying (400–900 km) and take images of the portion of the earth below it when it orbits from pole to pole. In contrast, geostationary satellites usually take much higher orbits (35,800 km) and fly above the equator at the same angular velocity as the earth's rotation, and thus appear stationary to the ground. They normally transmit data in intervals ranging from 1 to 12 hours. The resolutions of weather satellites typically range from 1 to 5 km. Figure 13.3(c) shows an IR image of Southeast Asia from NOAA's Geostationary Operational Environmental Satellite-9 (GOES-9).

In contrast to radars and satellites, NWP data are obtained from a model of the physics of the atmosphere. NWP models can be based on grid point values or spectral representations of the atmosphere. Gas laws, energy conservation laws, laws of motion, laws of thermodynamics, water vapor equations, and continuity equations are used to model the atmosphere. Given an initial condition, the atmospheric parameters at particular time instances in the future can be computed numerically. In NWP, the initial conditions are seeded by observed and interpolated values of atmospheric parameters. Elements such as temperature, pressure, and wind components are used. Resolutions of NWP models range from a few to tens of kilometers, usually in time steps of minutes. Though data intensive and computationally expensive, numerical modeling allows future values of the atmospheric parameters to be simulated, and is thus adopted by many weather centers in forecasting operations. NWP models can be categorized as global or regional. The former covers the whole globe and the latter a geographical region. An example of regional NWP model is the Operational Regional Spectral Model (ORSM) [20] used at the Hong Kong Observatory. Figure 13.4 shows two visualizations of NWP results, the model domains and grids for ORSM. Other examples of NWP models include Japan Meteorological Agency (JMA) Global Spectral Model [8], European Centre for Medium-Range Weather Forecast (ECMWF) global atmospheric model [2], the Fifth-Generation National Center for Atmospheric Research (NCAR)/Penn State Mesoscale Model (MM5) [3], and Coupled Ocean/Atmosphere Mesoscale Prediction System (COAMPS) [1].

13.3 TC Eye-Fix Algorithms

13.3.1 Traditional Eye Fix Techniques

As mentioned in section 13.1, a TC is a low-pressure system that has a rain-free circulation center where spiral rain bands whirl. TC eye-fix methods mainly focus on locating the low-pressure center, wind center, or rain-free center. The traditional manual eye-fix process is still important. It can be categorized into identification of the low pressure or wind center, template matching, remote sensing sequence analysis, and the extrapolation method.

Tsui [48] discusses the methods for locating the low-pressure center and wind center. To locate the low-pressure center, one can examine the pressure profile of a TC and pick the local minimum point with acute rise in pressure on the sides. To determine the wind center, one can assume a symmetrical wind profile and the constant inflow angle of 20 degrees. Figure 13.5(a) illustrates the method. With the wind directions (arrows in Fig. 13.5(a)) obtained from different observations, straight lines are drawn from these points at an angle of 110 degrees plus the angle of wind direction. The centroid of the polygon formed by these straight lines is then regarded as the TC center. To use these methods, information about pressure and wind directions are needed. However, this information depends on the reports by ships or land stations. Unless the TC comes close to these stations, this information may not be available.

Manual eye-fix methods that make use of remote sensing data are also used in practice. Since the rainband of a TC is of spiral shape, one can overlay spiral templates onto a remote sensing image for the best match to determine the position of the rain-free center on the radar [46]. Alternatively, by playing back a sequence of remote sensing images in a loop, forecasters can trace the movement of spiral rain bands by identifying the cyclonic rotations. Extrapolation eye-fix methods that make use of previous eye-fix results are also used. Linear, spline, or cycloid extrapolation can be applied [21].

Though time-honored, the techniques just mentioned often require subjective and fuzzy matching by experienced meteorologists. Thus, they are error-prone, especially for weaker TCs such as tropical depressions and even some tropical storms. Automated eye-fix techniques, in contrast, employ objective measures, and in theory could give unbiased results.

13.3.2 Automated Eye-Fix Techniques

Two main approaches of automated TC eye fix are wind field analysis and pattern matching. For wind field analysis, the TC center is fixed by analyzing the motion field constructed from a sequence of remote sensing images. Since the quality of the motion field determines the quality of the result, a motion field construction algorithm, image preprocessing, and vector field postprocessing are all critical in this approach. For pattern matching, which can be applied on a single image as well as a sequence, a TC eye is fixed by finding the best match between predefined TC models and the observed atmospheric data. Research issues in this paradigm include model design, image preprocessing and transformation, and efficiency of matching algorithms.

Motion Field Construction

A number of methods have been developed to construct motion fields from a sequence of remote sensing images. Schemetz et al. [43] derived cloud motion winds (CMW) by finding cross-correlation values on three successive infrared (IR) satellite images. With the use of three successive images, a symmetry check of the two corresponding vectors can be done so that they agree within certain limits with respect to speed and direction. The same idea is also applied on satellite images on the visible spectrum (VIS) to derive cloud motion winds (VIS-CMW) [36].

In another study, cloud features are tracked using massively parallel semifluid motion analysis (MPSMA) [17]. The dynamic cloud motion is represented by a semifluid motion model. Non-rigid motion vectors are estimated using satellite images [37, 38], which can then be used for the analysis of wind fields within the inner core and the eye of TCs.

To construct motion fields from radar data, the tracking radar echoes by correlation (TREC) algorithm is developed [42]. In TREC, two scans of plan position indicator (PPI) reflectivity data measured at the same elevation angle, a few minutes apart, are used. The analysis proceeds by dividing the first scan into a number of equal-sized two dimensional arrays of pixels. Each array is correlated with the possible arrays of the same size in the second scan to find the best matching (the one with highest correlation) second array. The location of the second array determines the end point of motion vector. As the radar reflectivity echo patterns circulate about the eye, the motion field built using TREC is considered as the horizontal winds of a tropical cyclone [49]. The TREC algorithm has been adopted in weather analysis and forecasting systems such as SWIRLS [33] for tropical cyclone observation [23], short-range precipitation forecasting [32], and other applications. Figure 13.5(c) shows the motion field constructed using the TREC algorithm of the SWIRLS system used by the Hong Kong Observatory.

Motion Field Analysis

A TC center can be fixed by analyzing the motion fields. One possibility is to extract and characterize critical points such as swirls, vortices, sinks, or sources by analyzing the field mathematically [10, 11]. The idea is to represent a vector field as the sum of a solenoidal and an irrotational field, which can be obtained by techniques such as two-dimensional Fourier transform. The stream function and velocity potential are then found from these fields, and a complex potential function of the flow is constructed. An assumption that the field follows the Rankine model is then made [11]. The model approximates the velocity field of a vortex as a vector field with constant curl value and zero vorticity inside a circular area around it. The velocity is also modeled to decrease inverse squarely with the radius. With this model, the field can be analyzed mathematically and the critical points located by finding the local extrema of the complex potential function. Alternatively, as in [45], critical points are classified by examining the linear phase portrait matrix [63]. Vortex centers can then be regarded as TC centers.

Besides TC eye-fix, motion field analysis is also used in other meteorological applications, such as cloud structure and height estimation [60, 61, 62]. Yet these techniques mandate the use of a sequence of images for the construction of the vector field. Hence, they may not be suitable if the image is sampled infrequently, partly missing, of low quality, or when the TC moves fast. Pattern matching, in contrast, can be performed using only a single image and even on partially available data.

Pattern Matching

To fix the eye of an ideal TC, Wood [56] uses an axisymmetric hurricane vortex flow model. Using Doppler velocity data, a TC is found by locating areas with cyclonic shear, and its center located by the identification of extreme Doppler velocity values.

Recently, the idea of automatic spiral template matching has been used in a number of works. In Wang et al. [51], a rain band of a TC is modeled as a logarithmic helix (spiral) with the equation $\rho = e^{a(\theta + \theta')}$, where a is the obliquity parameter and θ' is the initial rotary angle of the helix. The method of least squares is applied to find the parameters of the equation from cloud features extracted from satellite images. The center of the helix thus gives the initial center of the TC. An extrapolation method is then applied to improve the precision of the located centers by adjusting the center location obtained using past results.

The automatic spiral template matching method is also used in microwave and IR satellite images for eye fix [53]. A 10-degree log spiral is matched against the curve bands of a TC. The image gradient and a spiral-shaped unit vector field are used in the process. To increase the precision, the Hough transform is applied to determine the optimal position and the size of circle that fits the gradient map of the region around the eye.

A more recent work based on pattern matching focuses on the processing of radar data [55]. In this work, a spiral model of a TC is designed based on the requirement that the eye should be relatively cloud-free, and the rain bands follow a spiral equation $r = ae^{\theta \cot \alpha}$. The parameters a and α are estimated from the radar data by a number of image processing and transformation operations at different coordinates (lon, lat). The eye-fix results are smoothed using Kalman filter [34, 52] to reduce sensitivies due to intrinsic errors and noise.

To assess the performance of an eye-fix algorithm, it is customary to compare the results with best-track data [18]. Best track is the track of the center of a TC determined after the event with the benefit of all available data and the wisdom of hindsight. This postanalysis data is often used for verification since no real-time ground truth is available. This verification enables easy comparison with subjective forecast for evaluation of the accuracy of an eye-fix algorithm. Using the algorithm suggested in [55], an average error of about 0.16 degrees on a Mercator projected map with respect to best-track data was reported. The authors subsequently modified the model to a six-parameter one by limiting the extent of rain bands, allowing the eye to vary in size during the TC's lifetime, and modeling the eye wall as well [57, 58]. Figure 13.5(b) shows the TC model. Genetic algorithm is used to speed up the convergence process of the searching algorithm. With different parameter settings, errors ranges from 0.139 to 0.257 degrees were obtained with a tenfold improvement in speed. This pattern matching method can fix the TC center using only a single image as soon as the data is available. Results from individual images are then smoothed to form the estimated track. Figure 13.6(a) shows the five best templates overlaid on a preprocessed radar image. A comparison between the best track and estimated track for Typhoon Yutu (2001-07-24 2000 HKT to 2001-07-25 1954 HKT, 240 radar images at 6-minute intervals) found by the above-mentioned algorithm is shown in Figure 13.6(b).

Pattern matching requires only a single image and thus could be effectively applied even if the image is sampled infrequently, or when the TC moves fast. However, the TC must have the features (e.g., rain band or eye wall) that resemble those defined in the TC model. Motion field analysis, in contrast, requires at least two images for the analysis, and exploits both spatial and temporal information. It could be used even if the TC is dissipating or partially out of the image. These two approaches in a certain sense are complementary to each other and thus could be used to handle different types and stages of TCs.

13.3.3 Dvorak Analysis

One of the most important use of the eye-fix results is intensity classification, or the estimation of TC intensity. This is traditionally done by Dvorak analysis [13, 14, 15], which employs pattern-matching techniques and empirically derived rules to obtain an estimation of TC intensity in terms of T-numbers. The parameter T-number is used to represent a simple model of TC evolution such that T-number increments correspond to a change in intensity. The initial step of Dvorak analysis is a manual TC eye fix using satellite images. Forecasters then observe the cloud shapes shown on satellite images and search for the most similar pattern against a swatch of more than 60 templates. Figures 13.7(a) and 13.7(b) show some of the templates and example satellite images used in Dvorak analysis. An initial estimation of TC intensity is then made according to the best matched pattern. An intricate process of adjustments to the estimated intensity is then done by examining measurements such as satellite readings and cloud features, after which a final intensity value is determined and the TC classified.

The Dvorak analysis is not completely objective. For example, different forecasters may give different answers according to their own judgments. To eliminate the subjectiveness, the objective Dvorak technique (ODT) is designed to automate some of the steps [59]. Infrared (IR) satellite data, which provide information of temperatures of cloud top, sea surface, and land, are used. In ODT, once the eye is fixed, a search is done to find the warmest pixel temperature within a 40-km radius of the chosen storm center on the IR image. This eye temperature, which is the warmest part of the TC, together with the surrounding temperature readings, are used to estimate the TC intensity through a table lookup. In a later work, the techniques were modified so that cloud patterns can be categorized [50]. The relationship between cloud pattern, temperature at the storm center, and temperature of the convective cloud environment are used for cloud pattern classification. The cloud categories include eye, central dense overcast (CDO), embedded center, and shear. The eye is the warmest part of a TC. CDO occurs when a dense, solid-looking mass of clouds with cold cloud tops occluding the warm eye is observed in a visible satellite image. The embedded center pattern, on the other hand, occurs when the cloud system center is within a cold overcast and is observable in IR satellite images. A shear pattern is observed when the cold clouds move to one side of the cyclone, developing a sharp edge. By examining the histogram of cloud top temperature of the IR image, together with a Fourier analysis for eye and surrounding cloud region, cloud patterns are classified.

Attempts to completely automate Dvorak analysis on satellite images can be found in [27] and [29], where an elastic graph dynamic link model, based on elastic contour matching, is used. The method integrated traditional dynamic link architecture for neural dynamics and the active contour model for contour extraction of TC patterns. By elastic graph matching between the query pattern and all the Dvorak templates in the database, the best match template is found, and its eye position is taken as the closest approximation of the center location of the query pattern. An overall recognition rate of 97% for eye positions with respect to the template-defined center was reported with the use of enhanced infrared (EIR) satellite images. The authors also proposed a method that uses a neural oscillatory elastic graph matching model [28] and reported an eye position recognition rate of 99%.

Researchers have also designed some algorithms, such as Fourier-based contour analysis [12], different cloud classifiers [39], or the use of fuzzy mathematical morphological operators [40], to automate the process of TC extraction from satellite images. Such automation could allow the TC eye fix to be done more easily. The TC pattern-matching approaches were also used in a typhoon image database for content-based image retrieval [21, 22].

13.4 Data Complexity Issues

The seemingly simple TC positioning and classification problems are practically difficult for a number of reasons. Besides the technical ones mentioned in the previous sections, such as the lack of objective best-match measures, some of the complexities are due to the specific nature of the data used. The complexity manifests itself as incomplete and noisy data, indirect measurements, and spatially and temporally scarce observations. Moreover, there is a lack of a "universal truth" for evaluation. Also, the best tracks from different weather centers are given at different intervals, which often do not concur. These problems are discussed in this section.

As discussed in section 13.2, meteorological data are often collected by remote sensing instruments. Data for the cloud top (satellite data) or a few kilometers from sea level (radar data at a certain CAPPI) are often used for the TC eye fix. For radar data, the low altitude radar measurements are often affected by sea clutter (Fig. 13.8(a)), terrains, and man-made structures, which cause difficulties in analysis. Moreover, TC data may be out of range (Fig. 13.8(b)) or incomplete (Fig. 13.8(c) and 13.8(d)). In contrast to weather radars, which provide volume data of the atmosphere, satellites view the earth from above and provide data for the cloud top. However, in practice, we are more concerned about finding the eye location of the TC at sea level, as it is where we inhabit. The TC eye location a few kilometers above sea level may not be the same as that at sea level. This would not be a problem for TCs with little vertical wind shear. For weak TCs and those with significant vertical wind shear, the TC eye may be obscured by high-level clouds and the eye-fix results may not be usable.

For practical TC eye fix, observations from sources other than remote sensing are often used as well. These sources include observations from ships and aircrafts, as well as weather stations on ground or on islands. However, these are not easily obtained, as reports from ships and aircrafts are incidental, and weather stations based at sea or on islands are few. Weather centers mostly have to rely on remote sensing measurements or aircrafts and ships passing by for observation over the ocean. This is one of the reasons that even for the same TC, different weather centers give different results.

The use of remote sensing data also means that measurements such as wind speed and precipitation are indirect. Besides, these data are available only at particular intervals in time, for example, minutes for radars and hours for satellites. For data that are available only a few times a day, such as those from polar-orbiting satellites, automated techniques that track objects, such as motion estimation, may not be applicable because of the low correlation between frames of data. Not many methods beyond simple extrapolation could be used in these situations.

Automated TC eye-fix systems are often evaluated against best track results. Best tracks are the (usually hourly) TC locations issued by a TC warning center. They are determined after the event by forecasters using all the observations available. Although the error calculations tend to be straightforward, for reasons discussed above, different weather centers could give best tracks of the same TC that differ in the order of 0.3 degrees on a Mercator projected map [24]. Besides, different weather centers often also give best track locations at different time intervals. Some would give hourly values, and some give values every 3 or 6 hours. For radar-based automated TC methods where an eye location is given every few minutes (e.g., six for the Hong Kong Observatory), the use of these relatively infrequent best track locations for evaluation means that these values have to be interpolated before use. This introduces another layer of uncertainly since the use of different interpolation algorithms may affect the evaluation results.

Since the goal of NWP is to predict the state of the atmosphere given an initial condition, problems related to data density and acquisition do not seem to apply. With NWP data, the location of a TC center could be relatively easily located by finding local pressure minima. However, the use of NWP has its own set of problems. First, as initial conditions of the models are seeded by actual observed values, interpolation is inevitable. This is because most earthbound weather stations are scattered over the ground. Interpolation introduces error that may propagate into the prediction. Second, the set of equations and boundary conditions used in the model could affect the accuracy of the prediction. We can never describe all the intricacies of the atmosphere in a model. Complex models require a lot of computational power to be practical, but simple models could be inaccurate when the forecast time is long. Third, the resolution of grid points or spectral representations of the atmosphere also affect the results. Models with a fine resolution capture more local atmospheric phenomena, but they require more detailed topographical information and smaller time steps in calculations, and would often make the model run much slower. Fourth, the values at the boundaries of regional models have to be treated with special care. Errors are often generated there because of a lack of data beyond these boundaries. To avoid this problem in practice, a regional model covering areas larger than required is commonly used, and values near the boundaries are discarded in operational environments.

13.5 Future Directions

In this section, we identify a number of issues related to the TC eye-fix problem that are worthy of further studies. They include algorithmic improvements, ensemble forecasting, and application of data mining in meteorology.

13.5.1 Algorithmic Improvements

In the techniques described in section 13.3.2, a TC eye is fixed by locating the low pressure center, wind center, or rain-free center. Most of these algorithms focus on finding or matching features such as the rain band or the eye wall without regard to historical data. For example, in Dvorak analysis, previous results are not considered even if a sequence of images is given. To improve and automate these algorithms, continuous features such as the eye size, rain-band influx angle, or TC movement speed can be taken into account so that the search space can be further restricted, resulting in potentially faster algorithms and more accurate results. Smoothing algorithms that make use of past data, such as Kalman filtering, can also be used.

Many algorithms for constructing vector fields are based on block matching, a technique that has been widely adopted in video and multimedia processing. These algorithms often use the rigid body model that only approximates the real structure of a TC. To construct better motion fields, nonrigid fluid motion models could be used (e.g., as in [37]). Postprocessing algorithms to remove noises in the vector fields (e.g., that in [33]) found by these algorithms are also needed.

13.5.2 Ensemble Forecasting

To forecast the track of a TC, two common approaches adopted by weather centers are extrapolating from past eye-fix results, and approximating the future atmospheric situations using NWP models. As could be expected, different results are obtained when different extrapolation methods are used, or when the initial condition of NWP models are different. The effect is especially apparent in NWP models, as these complex models often exhibit chaotic behavior. Since the initial conditions are seeded by observed and interpolated values from measured ones, a slight error in measurements or difference in interpolation algorithm could affect the output a lot even if the same model is used. Hence, it is not reliable to make a forecast by just relying on the output of a model under one initial condition. To solve this problem practically, a forecaster refers to the results of multiple models under slightly different initial conditions. Knowledge of the pros and cons of each of the models and methods, statistics on the accuracy of past results, as well as the experience with conditions to pay attention to guide the forecaster to make a decision. This could be achieved by using ensemble forecast technique [30, 31]. The input to the ensemble forecast can be forecasts from an NWP model initialized differently, or forecasts from different NWP models.

As an example of ensemble forecast, an NWP model is run many times with slightly different initial conditions representing the uncertainties or errors in measurements. If the model outputs are similar, the forecaster could have higher confidence in the model results. Forecasting decisions can then be made by, for example, taking a majority vote. The same technique can be used on multiple models under multiple sets of initial conditions. An example of ensemble forecasting on TC track is shown in Figure 13.9. TC tracks of multiple models are shown and the line with crosses (En F/C) indicates the results of ensemble forecast. The technique can be applied in other areas such as precipitation, temperature, humidity forecast, onset and movement of fronts and troughs or other weather systems.

13.5.3 Data Mining Applications

All the approaches for TC eye fix introduced so far are goal-driven in the sense that there is a clear objective function to maximize that would give the location of an eye. For example, in template matching, the eye is where the correlation value between the template and target image is maximum. In wind field analysis, the eye is where the local extrema value of certain mathematical properties (e.g., curl, divergence, vorticity) is found. While these approaches often work well, a model that establishes the relationship between eye position and physical measurements is needed. All other relationships, if they exist, are hidden or ignored if not modeled. To unravel these hidden relationships, techniques in data mining [16, 54] could be used. For example, association rule mining can be used to establish meteorological events that happen together, spatial mining can link up events that occur in different locations, outlier analysis can help detecting abnormal phenomena, and temporal mining can help relating events that occur at different times. A wide variety of applications is possible. Recently, researchers have started to apply data mining in meteorology [19, 41] such as precipitation forecast [9, 47].

13.6 Conclusions

In this chapter, we have discussed the practical problems of tropical cyclone (TC) positioning and classification. Solving these problems require meteorological data. Four data sources have been identified: radar reflectivity data, Doppler velocity data from weather radars, satellite images, and numerical weather prediction (NWP) data. Each data source has its own characteristics, making consistent eye fix and classification difficult, as different sensors or models focus on different aspects of the atmosphere. This also means that there is no single indisputable solution to the problem, making verification difficult. Indeed, the best tracks on the same TC issued by different weather centers could differ by 0.3 degrees on the Mercator projected map.

Classification of a TC involves fixing its eye and applying methods to estimate its intensity. For eye fix, most algorithms focus on locating the low-pressure center, wind center, or rain-free center. These can be done by wind field analysis and pattern-matching methods. The former works by analyzing a vector field of wind intensities or cloud motion directions constructed from meteorological data taken close in time. The latter work on preprocessed meteorological data to find the best match to a model of TC. Wind or cloud motion field analysis methods require vector fields to work. Vector fields can be constructed using motion compensated prediction techniques used in multimedia video processing, or techniques to find cloud motion winds (CMW) from IR or VIS satellite channels. On the other hand, when the input is radar reflectivity data, the TREC method is often used to build the vector field. Though most vector field construction techniques use the rigid-body assumption on clouds, some, such as MPSMA, use the semifluid motion model. After the vector fields are constructed, motion field analysis techniques can be applied to find the TC center.

Pattern-matching methods often require a model of TC. These models include an axisymmetric hurricane vortex flow model, a simple logarithmic helix model, a fixed 10 degree log spiral rain band model, a model describing a TC with fixed eye size and spiral rain band with fixed extent, and a six-parameter model that describes a TC with variable eye size and spiral rain bands with variable extent. To optimize the accuracy and speed, methods such as extrapolation, Kalman filtering, and the use of genetic algorithms have been applied to various pattern-matching methods.

The use of eye-fix results includes forecasting the future path of a TC, and estimation of TC intensities, among others. For intensity analysis, the standard procedure is a pattern-matching method called Dvorak analysis. Attempts to partly or fully automate the process can be found in the literature. The objective Dvorak technique and the use of an elastic graph dynamic link model to match predefined templates are two examples.

In TC positioning and classification, we face a number of data complexity issues. For example, the location of the eye on the ground could be very different from that of a few kilometers above sea level. This means only a small part of the meteorological data collected is useful to solve the problem. Meteorological data near sea level are difficult to obtain by remote sensing. This is because satellites give only cloud-top data, and low-altitude radar measurements are often affected by sea clutter, terrains, and man-made structures. Also, there is a spatial bias in meteorological data sources. Weather stations on land are often clustered together, reports from ships and aircrafts are incidental, and weather stations based at sea or on islands are few. Besides, remote sensing data are often updated in intervals of minutes to hours. Successive sets of data thus may not correlate very well. This inherently limits the set of algorithms usable on them.

There are also data complexity issues regarding NWP data. The difficulties lie in the fact that the atmosphere is hard to model completely by a set of equations. To give an accurate forecast, NWP models need to be fed by the right initial boundary conditions. This is not always easy. Also, though high-resolution NWP models are desired, as they are expected to give better results, they usually run slowly and are therefore not practical. This limits their use for medium-to-long term forecasting. Nonetheless, the lack of well-defined patterns on weak TCs also compounds the problem.

In the future, we believe that algorithmic improvements and the use of new techniques could help us position and classify TCs better. For example, the use of continuous features of TCs, such as the variation of eye size, could help improving the speed and accuracy of analysis. More realistic models with better postprocessing methods can be used for vector field-based methods. Meanwhile, since some weather systems exhibit certain chaotic behavior, ensemble forecasting could be used to reduce the error due to inaccurate measurements. Finally, hidden relationships between meteorological events could be discovered by data mining techniques.

References

[1] Coupled Ocean/Atmosphere Mesoscale Prediction System (COAMPS). http://meted.ucar.edu/nwp/pcu2/coamps/index.htm.

[2] European Centre for Medium-Range Weather Forecast (ECMWF) global atmospheric model. http://www.ecmwf.int/products/forecasts/guide/.

[3] The fifth-generation NCAR/Penn State Mesoscale Model (MM5). http://www.mmm.ucar.edu/mm5/overview.html.

[4] Hong Kong Observatory. http://www.hko.gov.hk/.

[5] Japan Meteorological Agency. http://www.jma.go.jp/.

[6] National Oceanic and Atmospheric Administration (NOAA). http://www.noaa.gov/.

[7] J.M. Moran, M.D. Morgan, P.M. Pauley. *Meteorology: The Atmosphere and the Science of Weather*, Englewood Cliffs, NJ: Prentice-Hall, 5th ed., 1997.

[8] Japan Meteorological Agency. Outline of the operational numerical weather prediction at the Japan Meteorological Agency. In *WMO Numerical Weather Prediction Progress Report*, chapter appendix. March 2002. http://www.jma.go.jp/JMA_HP/jma/jma-eng/jma-center/nwp/.

[9] M.A. Bramer. *Knowledge Discovery and Data Mining*. Institution of Electrical Engineers, 1999.

[10] T. Corpetti, É. Mémin, P. Pérez. Dense motion analysis in fluid imagery. In *Proceedings of the 7th European Conference on Computer Vision (ECCV-2002)*, volume 2350 of *LNCS*, pages 676–691, Copenhagen, New York: Springer-Verlag, 2000.

[11] T. Corpetti, É. Mémin, P. Pérez. Extraction of singular points from dense motion fields: an analytic approach. *Journal of Mathematical Imaging and Vision*, 19, 175–198, 2003.

[12] F. Dell'Acqua, P. Gamba. A novel technique for hurricane detection in Meteosat images by means of contour analysis. In *Proceedings of the International Symposium on Geoscience and Remote Sensing*, Sydney, Australia, volume 3, pages 1512–1514, July 2001.

[13] V.F. Dvorak. A technique for the analysis and forecasting of tropical cyclone intensities from satellite pictures. Technical Report NESS 45, National Oceanic and Atmospheric Administration (NOAA), US Department of Commerce, 1973. 19 pages.

[14] V.F. Dvorak. Tropical cyclone intensity analysis and forecasting from satellite imagery. *Monthly Weather Review*, 103, 420–430, 1975.

[15] V.F. Dvorak. Tropical cyclone intensity analysis using satelite data. Technical Report NESDIS 11, National Oceanic and Atmospheric Administration (NOAA), US Department of Commerce, 1984. 47 pages.

[16] J. Han, M. Kamber. *Data mining: concepts and techniques*. San Francisco, CA: Morgan Kaufmann, 2001.

[17] A.F. Hasler, K. Palaniappan, C. Kambhammetu, P. Black, E. Uhlhorn, D. Chesters. High resolution wind fields within the inner-core and eye of a mature tropical cyclone from GOES one-minute images. *Bulletin of the American Meteorological Society*, 79(11), 2483–2496, 1998.

[18] G.J. Holland, ed. *Global Guide to Tropical Cyclone Forecasting*. Number WMO/TC-No. 560, Report No. TCP-31. Bureau of Meteorology Research Centre, Melbourne, Victoria, Australia. http://www.bom.gov.au/bmrc/pubs/tcguide/.

[19] R. Honda, S. Wang, T. Kikuchi, O. Konishi. Mining of moving objects from time-series images and its application to satellite weather imagery. *Journal of Intelligent Information Systems*, 19(1), 79–93, 2002.

[20] Hong Kong Observatory. Operational Regional Spectral Model (ORSM). Web page. http://www.hko.gov.hk/wservice/tsheet/nwp.htm.

[21] A. Kitamoto. The development of typhoon image database with content-based search. In *Proceedings of the 1st International Symposium on Advanced Informatics*, Chiyodaku, Tokyo, pages 163–170, March 9-10, 2000.

[22] A. Kitamoto. Data mining for typhoon image collection. In *Proceedings of the 2nd International Workshop on Multimedia Data Mining*, San Francisco, CA, pages 68–77, August 26-29, 2001.

[23] E.S.T. Lai. TREC application in tropical cyclone observation. In *ESCAP/WMO Typhoon Committee Annual Review*, pages 135–139, 1998.

[24] C.Y. Lam. Operational tropical cyclone forecasting from the perspective of a small weather service. In *Proceedings of ICSU/WMO International Symposium on Tropical Cyclone Disasters*, Beijing, pages 530–541, October 1992.

[25] C. Landsea, S. Goldenberg. Tropical Cyclone FAQ. Web page, 13 August 2004. Version 4.0, http://www.aoml.noaa.gov/hrd/tcfaq/A1.html.

[26] C. Landsea, S. Goldenberg. Tropical Cyclone FAQ. Web page, 13 August 2004. Version 4.0, http://www.aoml.noaa.gov/hrd/tcfaq/E10.html.

[27] R.S.T. Lee, J.N.K. Liu. An elastic graph dynamic link model for tropical cyclone pattern recognition. In *Proceedings of the 6th International Conference on Neural Information Processing (ICONIP-1999)*, Perth, Australia, volume 1, pages 177–182, November 16-20, 1999.

[28] R.S.T. Lee, J.N.K. Liu. Tropical cyclone identification and tracking system using integrated neural oscillatory elastic graph matching and hybrid RBF network track mining. *IEEE Transactions on Neural Networks*, 11(3), 680–689, 2000.

[29] R.S.T. Lee, J.N.K. Liu. An elastic contour matching model for tropical cyclone pattern recognition. *IEEE Transactions on Systems, Man and Cybernetics — Part B: Cybernetics*, 31(3), 413–417, 2001.

[30] T.C. Lee, M. Leung. Performance of multiple-model ensemble techniques in tropical cyclone track prediction. The 35th session of the Typhoon Committee, November 2002.

[31] T.C. Lee, M.S. Wong. The use of multiple-model ensemble techniques for tropical cyclone track forecast at the Hong Kong Observatory. In *Proceedings of the WMO Commission for Basic Systems Technical Conference on Data Processing and Forecasting Systems*, Cairns, Australia, December 2-3, 2002.

[32] P.W. Li, S.T. Lai. Short range quantitative precipitation forecasting in Hong Kong. *Journal of Hydrology*, 288, 189–209, 2004.

[33] P.W. Li, W.K. Wong, K.Y. Chan, E.S.T. Lai. SWIRLS – an evolving nowcasting system. Technical Report 100, Hong Kong Observatory, 1999.

[34] P.S. Maybeck. *Stochastic models, estimation, and control*, volume 1 of *Mathematics in Science and Engineering*. New York: Academic Press, 1979.

[35] The Hong Kong Observatory. Nature and structure of tropical cyclones. Web page, 13 May 2003. http://www.hko.gov.hk/informtc/nature.htm.

[36] A. Ottenbacher, M. Tomassini, K. Holmlund, J. Schmetz. Low-level cloud motion winds from Meteosat high resolution visible imagery. *Weather and Forecasting*, 12, 175–184, 1997.

[37] K. Palaniappan, C. Faisal, M. Kambhamettu, A.F. and Hasler. Implementation of an automatic semi-fluid motion analysis algorithm on a massively parallel computer. In *Proceedings of the 10th International Parallel Processing Symposium*, Honolulu, Hawaii, pages 864–872, April 15-19, 1996.

[38] K. Palaniappan, C. Kambhamettu, A.F. Hasler, D.B. Goldgof. Structure and semi-fluid motion analysis of stereoscopic satellite images for cloud tracking. In *Proceedings of the 5th International Conference on Computer Vision (ICCV-1995)*, Boston, MA, pages 659–665, June 20-23, 1995.

[39] G.S. Pankiewicz. Pattern recognition techniques for the identification of cloud and cloud systems. *Meteorological Applications*, 2, 257–271, 1995.

[40] J.C.H. Poon, C.P. Chau, M. Ghadiali. Using fuzzy mathematical morphology for locating tropical cyclones in satellite imagery. In *Proceedings of the International Circuits and Systems Symposium*, Hong Kong, pages 1353–1356, June 1997.

[41] R. Ramachandran, J. Rushing, H. Conover, S. Graves, K. Keiser. Flexible framework for mining meteorological data. In *Proceedings of the 19th Conference on Interactive Information and Processing Systems for Meteorology, Oceanography, and Hydrology*, February 2003.

[42] R.E. Rinehart. Internal storm motions from a single non-Doppler weather radar. Technical Report TN-146+STR, National Center for Atmospheric Research, 1979. 262 pp.

[43] J. Schemetz, K. Holmlund, J. Hoffman, B. Strauss, B. Mason, V. Gaertner, A. Koch, L. Van De Berg. Operational cloud-motion winds from Meteosat infrared images. *Journal of Applied Meteorology*, 32, 1206–1225, 1993.

[44] H.V. Senn, H.W. Hiser. On the origin of hurricane spiral rain bands. *Journal of Meteorology*, 16, 419–426, 1959.

[45] C.F. Shu, R.C. Jain. Vector field analysis for oriented patterns. *IEEE Transactions on Pattern Analysis and Machine Intelligence*, 16(9), 946–950, 1994.

[46] M.V. Sivaramakrishnan, M. Selvam. On the use of the spiral overlay technique for estimating the center positions of tropical cyclones from satellite photographs taken over the Indian region. In *Proceedings of the 12th Conference on Radar Meteorology*, Norman, OK, pages 440–446, October 17-20, 1966.

[47] T.B. Trafalis, M.B. Richman, A. White, B. Santosa. Data mining techniques for improved WSR-88D rainfall estimation. *Computers and Industrial Engineering*, 43(4), 775–786, 2002.

[48] K.S. Tsui. Tropical cyclone tracking and forecasting, parts I and II. The WMO Regional Training Seminar for National Meteorological Instructors of RAs II & V, November 1982.

[49] J. Tuttle, R. Gall. A single-radar technique for estimating the winds in tropical cyclones. *Bulletin of the American Meteorological Society*, 80(4), 653–668, 1999.

[50] C.S. Velden, T.L. Olander, R.M. Zehr. Development of an objective scheme to estimate tropical cyclone intensity from digital geostationary satellite infrared imagery. *Weather and Forecasting*, 13, 172–186, 1998.

[51] Y. Wang, H. Wang, H. Chen, W-C. Sun. Tropical cyclone center location with digital image process. In *Proceedings of the International Conferences on Info-tech and Info-net*, volume 3, pages 563–567, Beijing, November 2001.

[52] G. Welch, G. Bishop. An introduction to the Kalman filter. In *Proceedings of the ACM Computer Graphics Conference (SIGGRAPH-2001)*, Los Angeles, CA, August, 2001.

[53] A. Wimmers, C. Velden. Satellite-based center-fixing of tropical cyclones: New automated approaches. In *Proceedings of the 26th Conference on Hurricanes and Tropical Meteorology*, May 3-7, Miami, FL, 2004.

[54] I.H. Witten, E. Frank. *Data Mining: practical machine learning tools and techniques with Java implementations*. San Francisco, CA: Morgan Kaufmann, 2000.

[55] K.Y. Wong, C.L. Yip, P.W. Li, W.W. Tsang. Automatic template matching method for tropical cyclone eye fix. In *Proceedings of the 17th International Conference on Pattern Recognition (ICPR-2004)*, volume 3, pages 650–653, Cambridge, UK, August 2004.

[56] V.T. Wood. A technique for detecting a tropical cyclone center using a Doppler radar. *Journal of Atmospheric and Oceanic Technology*, 11, 1207–1216, October 1994.

[57] C.L Yip, K.Y. Wong. Efficient and effective tropical cyclone eye fix using genetic algorithms. In *Proceedings of the 8th International Conference on Knowledge-Based Intelligent Information and Engineering Systems (KES-2004)*, Lecture Notes in Artificial Intelligence LNAI, pages 654–660, Wellington, New Zealand, New York: Springer-Verlag, 2004.

[58] C.L. Yip, K.Y. Wong. Tropical cyclone eye fix using genetic algorithm. Technical Report TR-2004-06, Department of Computer Science, The University of Hong Kong, 2004.

[59] R. Zehr. Improving objective satellite estimates of tropical cyclone intensity. In *Proceedings of the 18th Conference on Hurricanes and Tropical Meteorology*, San Diego, CA, pages J25–J28, May 16-19,1989.

[60] L. Zhou, C. Kambhamettu, D.B. Goldgof. Extracting nonrigid motion and 3D structure of hurricanes from satellite image sequences without correspondences. In *Proceedings of the IEEE Conference on Computer Vision and Pattern Recognition (CVPR-1999)*, Fort Collins, USA, June 1999.

[61] L. Zhou, C. Kambhamettu, D.B. Goldgof. Fluid structure and motion analysis from multi-spectrum 2D cloud image sequences. In *Proceedings of the IEEE Conference on Computer Vision and Pattern Recognition (CVPR-2000)*, Los Alamitos, June 2000.

[62] L. Zhou, C. Kambhamettu, D.B. Goldgof, K. Palaniappan, A.F. Hasler. Tracking nonrigid motion and 3D structure of hurricanes from satellite image sequences without correspondences. *IEEE Transactions on Pattern Analysis and Machine Intelligence*, 23(11), 1330–1336, 2001.

[63] D.G. Zill. *Differential Equations with Computer Lab Experiments.*2nd ed. Monterey, CA: Brooks/Cole, 1998.

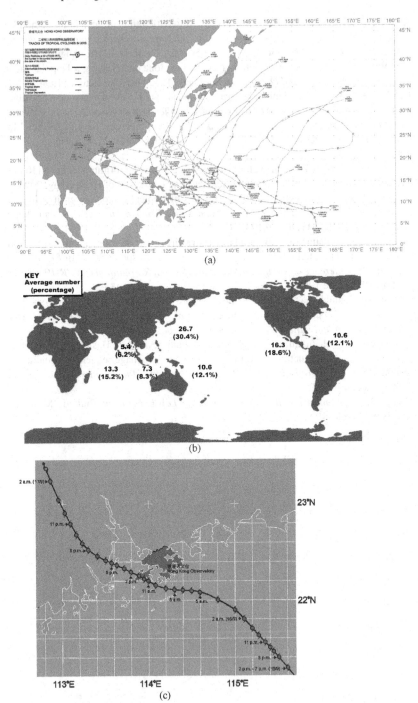

Fig. 13.2. Tropical Cyclones (TC) tracks. (a) TCs occurred over the Western North Pacific and the South China Sea in 2003. (b) Distribution (average number and percentage) of TCs over the globe. (c) TC track of Typhoon York (1999-09-16).

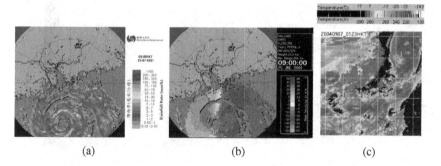

(a)   (b)   (c)

Fig. 13.3. Remote sensing data for eye fix. (a) Radar reflectivity data. (b) Doppler velocity data. (c) GOES-9 satellite data (IR).

Data sources: (a, b): Tai Mo Shan Doppler weather radar of the Hong Kong Observatory.
(c): GOES-9 of National Oceanic and Atmospheric Administration (NOAA).

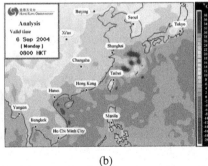

(a)   (b)

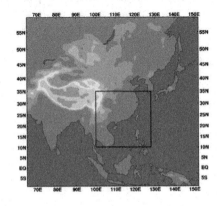

(c)

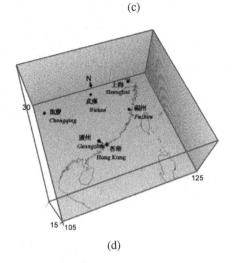

(d)

Fig. 13.4. Operational Regional Spectral Model (ORSM). (a) Surface wind field from ORSM.
(b) Temperature field from ORSM. (c) Model domains for 60 km ORSM (outer) and 20 km
ORSM (inner). (d) 20 km × 20 km ORSM grids.

Data sources: (a, b): Operational Regional Spectral Model (ORSM) of the Hong Kong Observatory.

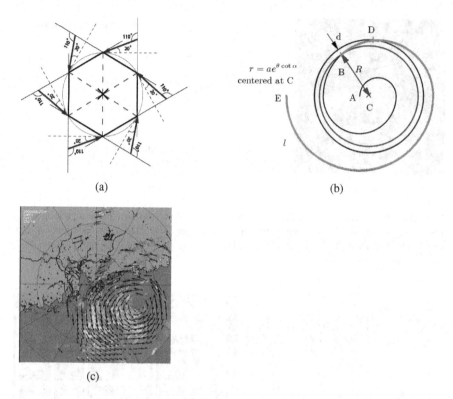

(a)

$$r = ae^{\theta \cot \alpha}$$
centered at C

(b)

(c)

Fig. 13.5. Determining the wind center. (a) Illustration of the eye fix method discussed in [48]. (b) TC model discussed in [57]. (c) TREC analysis for Typhoon Maria, 2000-08-31 2200 HKT.

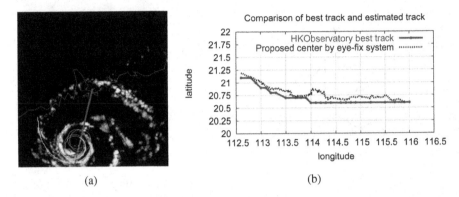

(a)   (b)

Fig. 13.6. Pattern matching results of reference [57]. (a) Results of pattern matching using genetic algorithm. (b) Comparison between best track and estimated track for Typhoon Yutu (2001-07-24 2000 HKT to 2001-07-25 1954 HKT, 240 radar images at 6-minute intervals).

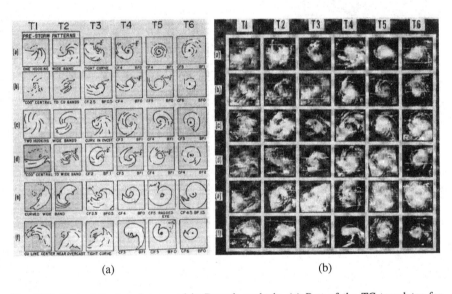

(a)   (b)

Fig. 13.7. Part of the templates used in Dvorak analysis. (a) Part of the TC templates for the Dvorak analysis. (b) Example of TC patterns (satellite images) that match with the set of templates. (Image source: "TC Intensity Analysis and Forecast for Satellite Imagery," Monthly Weather Review, American Meteorological Society [14]).

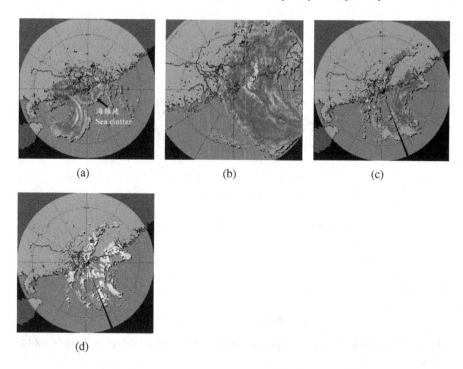

(a)   (b)   (c)

(d)

Fig. 13.8. Radar data affected by sea clutter, incomplete radar data, and typhoon data out of radar range. (a) Radar data affected by sea clutter, Typhoon Imbudo, 2003-07-24 0617 HKT. (b) Out of range radar reflectivity data, Typhoon Dujuan, 2003-09-02 1230 HKT. (c) Incomplete radar reflectivity data (missing data at 5 o'clock position), Typhoon Utor, 2001-07-05 1805 HKT. (d) Incomplete Doppler velocity data (missing data at 5 o'clock position), Typhoon Utor, 2001-07-05 1805 HKT.

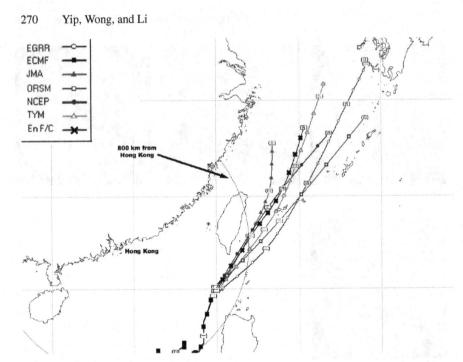

Fig. 13.9. Ensemble TC track of Typhoon Conson, 2004-06-03 0000 UTC to 2004-06-08 1200 UTC.

14

Human–Computer Interaction for Complex Pattern Recognition Problems

Jie Zou and George Nagy

Summary. We review some applications of human–computer interaction that alleviate the complexity of visual recognition by partitioning it into human and machine tasks to exploit the differences between human and machine capabilities. Human involvement offers advantages, both in the design of automated pattern classification systems, and at the operational level of some image retrieval and classification tasks. Recent development of interactive systems has benefited from the convergence of computer vision and psychophysics in formulating visual tasks as computational processes. Computer-aided classifier design and exploratory data analysis are already well established in pattern recognition and machine learning, but interfaces and functionality are improving. On the operational side, earlier recognition systems made use of human talent only in preprocessing and in coping with rejects. Most current content-based image retrieval systems make use of relevance feedback without direct image interaction. In contrast, some visual object classification systems can exploit such interaction. They require, however, a domain-specific visible model that makes sense to both human and computer.

14.1 Introduction

The goal of visual pattern recognition during the past 50 years has been the development of automated systems that rival or even surpass human accuracy, at higher speed and lower cost. However, many practical pattern recognition applications involve random noise and systematic variations in the patterns, inaccurate and incomplete prior information, limited and unrepresentative training samples, the mostly invincible challenge of segmentation, non-discriminating and unreliable features, many classes, as well as complex decision boundaries. Therefore, automatic recognition systems often require years of research and development in order to achieve fast and accurate classification. Some applications, e.g., optical character recognition, fingerprint identification, and target recognition, have met with modest success after decades of research and development, but many theoretical and practical problems remain. Face recognition has been intensively studied since 1960s, but is still considered unsolved [43]. Automated recognition in many other domains, such as petroglyphs, shards, arrowheads, flowers, birds, skin diseases, and so on, requires too much development for a limited market, or is too complex to be accommodated by the current methodologies.

A divide-and-conquer strategy for visual recognition should partition such domains into components that are relatively easier for both human and machine. There are pronounced differences between human and machine cognitive abilities. Humans excel in gestalt tasks, like object-background separation. We apply to recognition a rich set of contextual constraints and superior noise-filtering abilities. Computer vision systems, on the other hand, still have difficulty in recognizing "obvious" differences and generalizing from limited training sets [25]. We can also easily read degraded text on which the best optical character recognition systems produce only gibberish [1, 15].

Computers, however, can perform many tasks faster and more accurately. Computers can store thousands of images and the associations between them, and never forget a name or a label. They can compute geometrical properties like higher-order moments, whereas a human is challenged to determine even the centroid of a complex figure. Spatial frequency and other kernel transforms can be easily computed to differentiate similar textures. Computers can count thousands of connected components and sort them according to various criteria (size, aspect ratio, convexity). They can quickly measure lengths and areas. They can flawlessly evaluate multivariate conditional probabilities, decision functions, logic rules, and grammars. On the other hand, the study of psychophysics revealed that humans have limited memory and poor absolute judgment [30].

There is a growing consensus among experts to advocate interactive approaches to difficult pattern recognition problems. As early as 1992, a workshop organized by the U.S. National Science Foundation in Redwood, California, stated that "computer vision researchers should identify features required for *interactive image understanding,* rather than their discipline's current emphasis on automatic techniques" [27]. A more recent panel discussion at the 27th Applied Imagery Pattern Recognition (AIPR) workshop also emphasized "... the needs for computer-assisted imagery recognition technology" [29].

We concur with the suggestions of combining human and computer cognitive abilities to cope with the complexity of practical pattern recognition problems. To lay down some guidelines for integrating human–computer interaction with pattern recognition, we first briefly review human and machine visual perception and selected findings in psychophysics. We then discuss three human–computer interaction methodologies used in pattern recognition and image retrieval: exploratory data analysis (EDA), relevance feedback for content-based image retrieval, and Computer-Assisted Visual InterActive Recognition (CAVIAR) for visual pattern classification.

Our conjectures on what aspects of visual pattern recognition are easy and difficult for humans and computers are set forth in Table 14.1. The remainder of this chapter attempts to justify some of these conjectures and explores their implications for the design of pattern recognition systems.

14.2 Human and Machine Visual Perception

Visual perception is defined as: "the process of acquiring knowledge about environmental objects and events by extracting information from the light they emit or reflect" [33].

Visual perception has been studied separately by psychologists, performing experiments on sighted organisms; computer scientists, writing programs that extract and transform optical information; and neuroscientists, studying the structure and function of the visual nervous system. Recently, these three approaches converged to form a central idea of visual perception: *visual perception is a kind of computation.* In living organisms, eyes and brains perform visual

Table 14.1. Comparison of relative strength of human and machine in diverse aspects of visual pattern recognition.

Human	Machine
Dichotomies	Multicategory classification
Figure–ground separation	
Part–whole relationships	
Salience	
	Nonlinear, high-dimensional classification boundaries
Extrapolation from	
limited training samples	
Broad context	
	Store and recall many labeled reference patterns
	Accurate estimation of statistical parameters
	Application of Markovian properties
	Estimation of decision functions from training samples
	Evaluation of complex sets of rules
	Precise measurement of individual features
	Enumeration
Gauging *relative* size and intensity	
Detection of significant differences	
between objects	
	Computation of geometric moments
	Orthogonal spatial transforms (e.g., wavelets)
	Connected component analysis
	Sorting and searching
	Rank-ordering items according to a criterion
	Additive white noise
	Salt & pepper noise
Colored noise, texture	
Nonlinear feature dependence	
	Determination of local extrema in high-D spaces
Global optima in low dimensions	

perception through complex neural information processing, and in principle, visual perception can also be achieved by video cameras and programmed digital computers. This idea enables psychologists, computer scientists, and neuroscientists to relate their findings to each other in the common language of computation, and generates a new branch of cognitive science: vision science [33].

14.2.1 Machine Visual Perception

After Alan Turing [42] defined the fundamental model of computation, he and many others realized that it may be possible for Turing machines to simulate human intelligence. This idea gave rise to the field of artificial intelligence.

The goal of the subfield of artificial intelligence called computer vision is to develop programmed computers, that can interpret the environment visually. The mathematical approach to creating working computer vision programs was most clearly and effectively articulated by David Marr and his colleagues at the Massachusetts Institute of Technology [28]. Marr's work dominated computer vision research for the last two decades, and a great deal of progress has been made. Nevertheless, machine perception still lags far behind human visual perception with respect to the breadth of visual stimuli, perspective invariance, partial occlusion, tracking, learning, and uneven illumination (highlights and shadows).

14.2.2 Human Visual Perception

Classical psychological theories about human visual perception include structuralism, gestaltism, ecological optics, and constructivism [33]. In the field of visual pattern recognition, there are two theories: recognition by components (RBC) [8] and view-based recognition [40]. Unfortunately, they do not agree with each other. The debate centers on the form of the representation mediating three-dimensional object recognition.

Recognition by components assumes that perceptual processes derive the constituent parts of an object and represent each of those parts with a simple geometric volume, or *geon*. An object representation, or geon structural description, consists of geons corresponding to the two or three most salient parts of an object and the spatial configuration in which the geons are connected. This structural description is represented without regard for the specific viewpoint of the observer. Recognition is performed by recovering the 3D geon model from the input image.

In contrast, the key idea of the theory of view-based, or sometimes called image-based, recognition, is that object representations encode visual information as it appears to the observer from a specific vantage point.

After several years of debate between proponents of the two theories [9][10, 40], most researchers now agree that these theories can be considered as different points in a single continuum. RBC, or viewpoint-invariant theory, does depend on viewpoint to some extent because single representations normally encode only some viewpoints of an object. A number of representations may be needed to cover all possible views of the object. Similarly, view-based theory doesn't propose that all viewpoints are needed for recognition. In any case, how humans recognize objects is still not clearly understood.

14.2.3 Psychophysics

Image quality can be described in purely physical terms, but optimal image quality can be described only with reference to the performance of an imaging task. The relation between physical image quality and diagnostic performance is the borderland between physics and psychology known as psychophysics. Psychophysics is the quantitative branch of the study of perception, examining the relations between observed stimuli and responses and the reasons for those relations. Psychophysics is based on the assumption that the human perceptual system is a measuring instrument yielding results (experiences, judgments, responses) that may be systematically analyzed [6].

The psychophysical aspects of visual pattern recognition, including color, shape, perspective, and illumination, have been the objectives of sustained study for centuries. These studies revealed many facets of the amazing human capacity for visual perception, which are important guidelines for the design of systems that integrate human–computer interaction with pattern recognition.

Attneave [4] pointed out the importance of redundancy in visual stimulation. Visual perception is a kind of economical abstraction of the redundant visual stimuli. He proposed ten principles of abstraction in human visual perception, and mentioned that "information is concentrated along contours."

In a celebrated article, George A. Miller [30] summarized many psychophysical experiments and claimed that human absolute judgment is poor, limited to distinguishing only about eight categories within any single dimension: tone, loudness, taste (saltiness), length, area, hue, brightness, and curvature. He also noted that we can accommodate only about seven objects in our span of attention, and that our short-term memory is limited to about seven items. Nevertheless, we can recognize hundreds or thousands objects because we can make relatively coarse absolute judgments of several features simultaneously. We can also trick our short-term memory by recoding (so we can memorize a string of 30 zeros and ones by recoding it as seven letters).

Ashby and Perrin [3] argued that the perceptual effect of a stimulus is random, but that on any single trial it can be represented as a point in a multidimensional space. The perceived similarity is determined by distributional overlap. The perceptual space itself is fundamental. The difference is in the nature of the response function of the subject. In a recognition task, the decision process divides the space into response regions, one associated with each response. On a particular trial, the subject's response is determined by the region into which the perceptual sample falls. This theory of human recognition is analogous to the theory of statistical pattern classification.

14.3 Exploratory Data Analysis

Human–computer interaction was first exploited for pattern recognition under the term *exploratory data analysis* (EDA). The increasing use of graphical user interfaces in the 1970s attracted much research to visual data analysis for designing pattern classification systems.

The seminal works in EDA are those of Ball and Hall [5], Sammon [37], Tukey and Mosteller [31] and Tukey [41]. Chien [12] summarized early work on interactive techniques in data acquisition, pattern analysis, and the design of pattern classification schemes in a monograph, *Interactive Pattern Recognition*. Over the years, the techniques of EDA have been steadily enhanced [38, 46].

Most EDA techniques are graphical in nature, with only a few quantitative techniques. High-dimensional data is incomprehensible to humans, but we have superior ability to understand configurations of data in 1D, 2D, and 3D, and the evolution of changes over time. The primary goal of EDA is to maximize the analyst's insight into the underlying structure of a data set by projecting it into a 1D, 2D, or 3D subspace for ease of human visual assimilation. Exploratory data analysis facilitates understanding the distribution of samples in a fixed feature-space in order to design a classifier, but stops short of operational classification.

Recently, Mirage, an open source Java-based EDA software tool, was implemented at Bell Laboratories [23, 24]. Besides supporting the basic EDA functions, i.e., projecting the data into one, two, or higher dimensional subspace, and displaying them in tables, histograms, scatter plots, parallel coordinate plots, graphs, and trees, Mirage facilitates the analysis and visualization of the correlation of multiple proximity structures computed from the same data. All functions are available through an elaborate graphical user interface (GUI), but a small interpretive command language is provided for repetitive, large-scale data analysis. In Mirage, the users can also configure several plots at the same time, and perform classification manually or automatically.

14.4 Relevance Feedback in Content-Based Image Retrieval

Content-based image retrieval (CBIR) has been the subject of widespread research interest. Many prototype systems have been implemented, such as QBIC [18], Virage [7], Photobook [34], MARS [26], PicToSeek [21], PicHunter [16], Blobworld [11], and so on. Several surveys have also been published over the years [2, 32, 36, 39]. Content-based image retrieval attempts to retrieve images similar to the query image from an image database. It is motivated by the fast growth of image databases, which requires efficient search schemes.

Fully automatic content-based retrieval does not yet scale up to large heterogeneous databases. Human–computer interaction is an important component of all content-based image retrieval systems. Relevance feedback is broadly adopted in content-based retrieval systems for human–computer interaction, and has been found effective [14, 35].

A typical CBIR system with relevance feedback operates as follows: the user submits a query image, which is somewhat similar to the desired image (or a sketch of a desired image) and specifies which properties, e.g., overall color, overall texture, and so on, are important to the query. Upon seeing the query results, the user designates the retrieved images as acceptable or unacceptable matches in order to provide more information to the retrieval algorithm. This process is iterated until the user finds the desired image or gives up the task.

A major shortcoming of the above interface is that the user cannot share the computer's view of the image. Without knowing whether the query image was properly understood (processed) by the machine, the user can only wonder what went wrong when the retrieval result was unsatisfactory. The developers of Blobworld recognized this drawback, and suggested that the CBIR systems should display its representation of the submitted and returned images and should allow the user to specify which aspects of that representation are relevant to the query. In the Blobworld image retrieval system, the user composes a query by submitting an image, then views its Blobworld representation, selects the blobs to match, and finally specifies the relative importance of the blob features.

14.5 Computer-Assisted Visual InterActive Recognition

Reject correction may be the most common example of interacting with a classifier. Almost all classification algorithms admit some means of decreasing the error rate by avoiding classifying ambiguous samples. The samples that are not classified are called "rejects" and must, in actual applications, be classified by humans. Reject criteria are difficult to formulate accurately because they deal with the tails of the statistical feature distributions. Furthermore, most classifiers generate only confidence, distance, or similarity measures rather than reliable posterior class probabilities. Regardless of the nature of the classifier, at least two samples must be rejected in order to avoid a single error, because any reject region must straddle the classification boundary, near which there must be a 50-50 mixture of two classes[1] [13].

The efficiency of handling rejects is important in operational character and speech recognition systems, but does not receive much attention in the research literature. Keeping the human in the loop was recently also demonstrated in the domains of face and sign recognition (the extraction and recognition of text in natural scenes). However, it was confined

---

[1] This is a lower bound under the assumption of uniform cost of errors, because some samples may occur near the intersection of more than two regions. Therefore, error-reject curves have an initial slope of at least -0.5, which increases further as the fraction of rejects is increased to lower the error rate.

to preprocessing, i.e., establishing the pupil-to-pupil baseline [45] or a text bounding box [22, 47]. In these approaches, human intervention occurs only at the beginning or at the end of the recognition process, i.e., segmenting objects or performing other kinds of preprocessing *before* machine operations, or handling rejects *after* machine operations. There is little communication between the human and the computer.

The motivation of our recently proposed methodology for interactive visual pattern recognition, Computer-Assisted Visual InterActive Recognition (CAVIAR), is simply that it may be more effective to establish a seamless human–computer communication channel to make parsimonious use of human visual talent *throughout* the process, rather than only at the beginning or end [48, 49]. The vehicle for human-machine communication is a *visible model*.

Unlike content-based image retrieval, which is usually on a broad domain, each CAVIAR system addresses only a narrow domain. In the broad domain of content-based image retrieval, no effective way has been found so far to interact with arbitrary images. In pattern classification with CAVIAR, the domain-specific geometrical model, e.g., a set of contours and critical feature points, plays the central role in facilitating the communication (interaction) between the human and the computer. The key to effective interaction is the display of the automatically fitted adjustable model that lets the human retain the initiative throughout the classification process.

CAVIAR is designed to allow the human to quickly identify an object with a glimpse at the candidate samples that were ranked near the top by the computer. Avoiding having to look at many low-ranked classes is clearly most effective in a many-class classification problem. Because of the nature of the human–computer interaction, CAVIAR is more appropriate for low-throughput applications, where higher accuracy is required than is currently achievable by automated systems, but where there is enough time for a limited amount of human interaction.

Traditionally, visual pattern recognition includes three subtasks: segmentation, feature extraction, and classification. As mentioned, psychophysical studies suggest that the information is concentrated along object contours [4]; therefore, the pattern contours are important for classification. Locating the precise object boundary (strong segmentation) is generally considered too difficult and unreliable [39]. On the other hand, it may not even be necessary for visual pattern recognition. Several content-based image retrieval systems circumvent strong segmentation by locating only the approximate object boundary (weak segmentation). CAVIAR also gives up strong segmentation for weak segmentation based on a family of rose curves specified by six parameters. If the automatically constructed rose curve does not fit well, the user can easily adjust the model parameters by dragging a few control points. In CAVIAR, this model describes not only the object contour, but also some components of the object (petals).

In Blobworld, the Blobworld representation, which is an approximate segmentation of the object, is displayed in order to avoid misunderstandings between the human and the computer. This is much better than leaving the users to wonder what went wrong when a machine error occurs. However, apprehending the machine errors without being able to correct them is also frustrating. In CAVIAR, the user can not only *view* the machine's understanding (processing) of the image, but also *correct* the machine errors if necessary.

In CAVIAR, the first generic computer-vision task, segmentation, becomes model building. Therefore, a CAVIAR process has three subtasks: *model building*, i.e., generating a model instance, which explains the image according to the domain model; *feature extraction*, i.e., measuring discriminative object properties according to the constraints provided by the model instance; and *classification*, i.e., assigning a category label to the object.

Model building in CAVIAR-flower consists of fitting a rose curve to the flower. First a circle is fitted to the foreground (the flower to be recognized) based on the expected difference in color between flowers and background (leaves, dirt). The boundary propagates to high-gradient locations penalized according to their distance from the initial circle [50]. Finally, a rose curve is fitted to the propagated boundary (Fig. 14.1). The area delineated by the rose curve constrains feature extraction to the discriminative parts of the picture.

The model instances constructed in this manner are not always correct (Fig. 14.2). After decades of extensive research on this topic, many researchers now agree that automatic image segmentation is not likely to correspond consistently to human expectations except in narrow domains. On the other hand, humans perform image segmentation smoothly, accurately, and with little ambiguity. So we believe that model building should be, at least for now, subject to human correction.

Most laypersons don't understand computer vision features like moment invariants or wavelets. Humans find it difficult to visualize computer vision feature vectors and the geometry and topology of high-dimensional feature spaces. Furthermore, lay users are seldom familiar with all the distinguishing properties of the various classes, and therefore cannot judge the adequacy of the machine-proposed decision boundary. As mentioned, psychophysical studies also point out that human absolute judgment is poor, effective only in an approximately seven-interval scale [30]. Machines, on the other hand, can compute complicated features very accurately and very fast. So, in CAVIAR, feature extraction should be performed primarily by machine, without human intervention. However, *indirect* human refinement of feature values, by adjusting the CAVIAR model instance throughout the process, does promote faster and more accurate classification.

The whole CAVIAR process can be modeled as a finite state machine (Fig. 14.3). The computer tries its best to estimate an initial model for the unknown sample and calculate its similarity to the training samples that belong to each class. Representative training pictures are displayed in the order of computer-calculated similarities. The current model is also displayed, so that the user can correct it if necessary. Any correction leads to an update of the CAVIAR state: the remaining unadjusted model parameters are reestimated, and all the candidates are reordered. Figure 14.2 shows a difficult example, where the picture is blurred.

In summary, CAVIAR operates on four entities: (1) the unknown image, (2) the parameters of a visible geometrical model instance, (3) the feature vector extracted from the image according to the model, and (4) the list of class labels ranked according to the similarity of the corresponding reference pictures to the query picture. Interaction takes place through the model. The process terminates when the user assigns a label to the unknown image.

The *image* is a 2D color or gray-scale picture, as in the conventional visual pattern recognition systems.

The *geometrical model* consists of critical points and parametric curves, which are both abstract and visual descriptions of the contours of the pattern components and of the geometrical relations among them. The model estimation algorithm can use any segmentation algorithm (edge based, region based, hybrid optimization) to locate these critical points and curves. The human's understanding of the image can be communicated to the machine by adjusting a few critical points. The machine can then reestimate the remaining model parameters in a lower-dimensional space for improved classification.

The *feature vector* is a set of features for classifying patterns. It is extracted from a picture according to the model instance. The features, which may include shape (derived from the model parameters), color, texture, and other attributes, exist only in a high-dimensional space invisible to the user.

The *class label list* is a machine-ordered list of candidates based on the feature vector. It governs the display of reference pictures. The user assigns a particular label to the unknown object by clicking on one of the displayed reference pictures.

Fig. 14.1. Automated model construction in CAVIAR. Initial circle, detailed segmentation, and parametric rose curve segmentation of two flowers. The rose curve serves as a visible model of the computer's concept of the unknown flower. It guides the computer in the extraction of classification features.

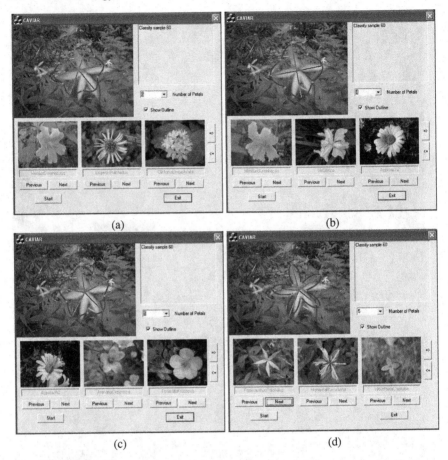

(a)   (b)

(c)   (d)

Fig. 14.2. An example of CAVIAR flower recognition. (a) The initial automatic rose curve estimation and indexing are bad because the picture is blurred: the correct candidate does not appear among the top three. (b) The user adjusts the center. (c) The user adjusts the petal number. (d) After the user adjusts the inner radius, the computer displays the correct candidate. (It is almost never necessary to make this many adjustments.)

The model parameters constitute a vector random variable. Human and machine observations of model parameters are also random variables, with human model estimates much better than machine estimates. The feature vector is related to the model parameters through a deterministic function. Human adjustments reduce the bias and variance of the feature vector by reducing the bias and variance of the model parameters. More accurate features generally improve classification.

The CAVIAR methodology has been applied to flower recognition on a database with 612 samples from 102 classes. Experiments with 36 naïve subjects show the following properties of CAVIAR systems [48, 49]:

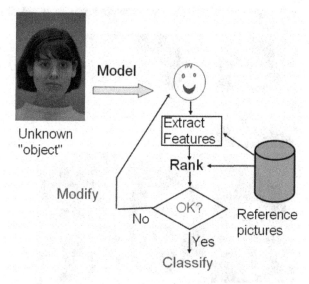

Fig. 14.3. CAVIAR Flowchart, showing transitions between automated modeling and human modification of the model, followed by browsing and classification.

- Human–computer communication through a geometrical model is effective. Combining human and machine can significantly reduce the recognition time compared to the unaided human, and significantly increase the accuracy compared to the unaided machine.
- The CAVIAR system can be initialized with a single training sample per class, but still achieve high accuracy (because there is a human in the loop).
- The CAVIAR system shows self-learning. The user classified samples, along with the user-adjusted model instances, are added to the reference set of labeled samples to effect unsupervised decision-directed approximation [17]. Although the samples may not be 100% correctly classified, automatic recognition still improves, which in turn helps users to identify the patterns faster. The performance based on just-classified samples is almost as good as with the same number of ground-truth training samples. Instead of initializing the CAVIAR system with many training samples, we can trust the system's self-learning ability (although, of course, the initial users would need more time).
- Users remember the examples to become "connoisseurs" of the specific family. With CAVIAR, laypersons need little practice to become faster than unaided "connoisseurs."

CAVIAR methodology can be applied to many other tasks. Interactive face recognition under head rotation, occlusion, and changes of illumination and facial expression is very challenging, but of great practical importance (Fig. 14.4). CAVIAR has also been ported to a stand-alone PDA, and to a pocket PC with a wireless link to a host laptop. Interaction with the visual model through a stylus is faster than with a mouse. We expect some applications, like the identification of skin diseases and other medical diagnoses based on visual observations, to be more appropriate for mobile versions of CAVIAR [51]. With mobile system, taking additional photos from a different perspective or distance, or under different illumination, could be extremely useful. Whether the resulting information should be combined at the pixel, feature, or classifier level is an unresolved research issue.

As do all classifiers, CAVIAR systems collect, in the course of operation, mostly-correctly-labeled samples. As more and more samples are accumulated, they can be used to

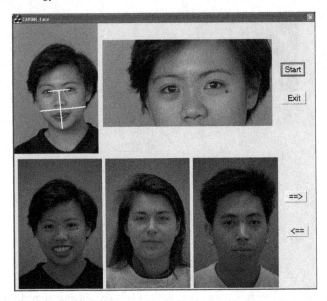

Fig. 14.4. CAVIAR-face GUI and model. The eye region is enlarged to allow accurate location of the crucial characteristic points at the pupils.

improve the machine's performance either directly, by machine learning, or by studying the accumulated training samples and upgrading the classification and learning algorithms.

CAVIAR could offer suggestions to its users. For example, it could suggest which model parameters to adjust, or request the operator to inspect further candidates because the top candidates have low confidence values. We do not allow CAVIAR to make such suggestions, because its judgment so far is worse than the human's; therefore, most of its suggestions would just annoy the user. Eventually machines may, of course, earn suggestion privileges.

14.6 Discussion

Fifty years of sustained research has increased our appreciation of the fundamental difficulty of some visual recognition tasks and our admiration for the complex, multilevel biological systems that accomplish these tasks with apparent ease. At the same time, technological developments have enabled human–computer interaction at a level that could be found earlier only in science fiction. Within the 0.5-second response time that experts consider acceptable, a laptop or a PDA can perform calculations that used to require hours or days on a mainframe, and display the results instantly at high resolution, in color, and, if need be, in motion. It is therefore now highly appropriate to seek joint human–computer solutions, at least as a temporary expedient, to recognition problems that have so far eluded an entirely algorithmic approach.

An interactive solution is not appropriate for all classification tasks. Character and speech recognition require the rapid interpretation of long pattern sequences rather than isolated patterns, while "real time" in many military applications is much less than human reaction time. But there are also many applications, like face, fingerprint, or flower recognition and medical diagnosis, where isolated patterns are recognized only sporadically, and where image acquisition takes long enough to dominate any real need for quasi-instantaneous classification. The advent of PDAs and cell phones with Internet access and plug-in cameras increases the scope for interactive personal recognition systems.

In many other fields of engineering, sophisticated and mature CAD software is widely used to mock-up proposed solutions, prepare and access test data, simulate experiments, check design constraints, perform routine calculations, and retrieve, modify, and incorporate previously designed modules. As such systems evolve, more and more intricate tasks are relegated to the computer, but the design engineer always remains in charge. In pattern recognition and machine learning, specialized computer-aided design tools have been slow to emerge. Nevertheless, interactive design and analysis tools have proved useful for improved understanding of the data even in domains where no intervention can be admitted at run time.

Interactive data analysis can lead to the selection of better features for classification, the identification of subsets of the data for which special provisions are necessary, the discovery of correlations or redundancies between features or patterns, and the detection of mislabeled items. Human–computer interaction is especially appropriate for discovering complex hidden information, and for accumulating training samples, which, according to the no-free-lunch theorem [44] and the bias-variance dilemma [19, 20], are the only two factors that can really improve classification performance.

Computer-assisted labeling has always been used to prepare training sets for classifier design, and often to classify rejects. It seems likely that with further advances in active and semi-supervised learning, these labeling operations will be more closely integrated with the algorithmic classification process itself. This may be most easily accomplished within the existing systems for exploratory data analysis.

At the operational, "real-time" level, we have seen that there are two options. The more common one, almost universally used in content-based image retrieval, is to let the computer do the best it can, and tell it where it fails. The machine then can use the set of positive and negative samples that it has just acquired to improve its next try. The information provided by the user is limited to one bit per picture, because he or she has no knowledge of how the computer made its decision and where it went wrong. Some research attempts to organize postage-stamp displays of the retrieved images in a configuration that suggests their putative relationships.

The other paradigm is CAVIAR, where users interact with the picture directly through a parametric model. Such a model must be constructed for every new application domain. For applications that justify the investment of effort, it is an effective approach to interactive classification.

The differences between peripheral and in-the-loop human intervention exist in other fields as well. In chess and checkers, relevance feedback would only tell the machine whether it has won or lost the game (which of course it can deduce by itself), while a CAVIAR approach could offer comment on every move. Although using some computer help is quite popular in the current online format of postal chess competition, much AI research runs counter to our philosophy of letting the machine help the user, rather than vice versa.

14.7 Conclusion

In some domains, the accuracy of automatic classification remains far below human performance. Human and computer abilities differ, and we are making progress in understanding the differences. A good interactive visual recognition system capitalizes on the strengths of both. It must establish effective two-way communication. In narrow domains simplified models of the real world can bridge the semantic gap between human and machine. The human must be able to exercise gestalt perception in his or her customary visual, domain which, in addition to natural scenes, includes several well-established sets of symbols. The computer should take full advantage of its almost unlimited memory and of its ability to solve huge but essentially repetitive problems. Further research is needed on how to translate complex multidimensional internal data to a form where any fallacies and failures of the current computer model can be readily apprehended and corrected.

Acknowledgments

We are grateful for the appropriate and detailed suggestions of an anonymous reviewer.

References

[1] L. von, M. Blum, J. Langford. Telling humans and computers apart automatically. *Communications of ACM*, 47(2), 57–60, 2004.

[2] P. Aigrain, H. Zhang, D. Petkovic. Content-based representation and retrieval of visual media: a state of the art review. *Multimedia Tools and Applications,* 3, 179–202, 1996.

[3] F.G.Ashby, N.A. Perrin. Toward a unified theory of similarity and recognition. *Psychological Review*, 95(1), 124–150, 1988.

[4] F. Attneave. Some informational aspects of visual perception. *Psychological Review*, 61, 183–193, 1954.

[5] G.H. Ball, D.J. Hall. Some implications of interactive graphic computer systems for data analysis and statistics. *Technometrics*, 12, 17–31, 1970.

[6] J.C. Baird, E. Noma. *Fundamentals of scaling and psychophysics.* New York: John Wiley & Sons, 1978.

[7] J. Bach, C. Fuller, A. Gupta et al. The Virage image search engine: an open framework for image management. *Proc. SPIE Storage and Retrieval for Image and Video Databases IV*, San Jose, CA, pages 76–87, 1996

[8] I. Biederman. Recognition-by-components: a theory of human image understanding. *Psychological Review*, 94, 115–147, 1987.

[9] I. Biederman, P.C. Gerhardstein. Recognizing depth-rotated objects: evidence and conditions for three-dimensional viewpoint invariance. *Journal of Experimental Psychology: Human Perception and Performance*, 19, 1162–1182, 1993.

[10] I, Biederman, P.C. Gerhardstein. Viewpoint-dependent mechanisms in visual object recognition: reply to Tarr and Bülthoff (1995). *Journal of Experimental Psychology: Human Perception and Performance*, 21, 1506–1514, 1995.

[11] C. Carson, S.Belongie, H. Greenspan, J. Malik.Blobworld: image segmentation using expection-maximization and its application to image querying. *IEEE Transactions on Pattern Analysis and Machine Intelligence*, 24(8), 1026–1038, 2002.

[12] Y.T. Chien. *Interactive Pattern Recognition*. New York: Marcel Dekker, 1970.

[13] C.K. Chow. On optimum recognition error and reject tradeoff. *IEEE Transactions Information Theory* 16, 41–46, 1970.

[14] G. Ciocca, R. Schettini. Using a relevance feedback mechanism to improve content-based image retrieval. *Proc. Visual '99: Information and Information Systems*, pages 107–114, 1999.

[15] A.L. Coates, H.S. Baird, R.J. Fateman. Pessimal print: a reverse Turing test. *Proc. Int. Conf. on Document Analysis and Recognition*, pages 1154–1159, 2001.

[16] I.J. Cox, M.L. Miller, T.P. Minka, T.V. Papathomas, P.N. Yianilos. The Bayesian image retrieval system, PicHunter: theory, implementation, and psychophysical experiments. *IEEE Transactions on Image Processing*, 9(1), 20–37, 2000.

[17] R.O. Duda, P.E. Hart, D.G. Stork. *Pattern classification*. New York: John Wiley & Sons, 2001.

[18] M. Flickner, H. Sawhney, W. Niblack. *Query by image and video content: the QBIC system. IEEE Computer*, 28(9), 23–32, 1995.

[19] J.H. Friedman. On bias, variance, 0/1-loss, and the curse-of-dimensionality. *Data Mining and Knowledge Discovery*, 1(1), 55–77, 1997.

[20] S. Geman, E. Bienenstock, R. Doursat. Neural networks and the bias/variance dilemma. *Neural Networks*, 4(1), 1–58, 1992.

[21] T. Gevers, A.W.M. Smeulders. PicToSeek, combining color and shape invariant features for image retrieval. *IEEE Transactions on Image Processing*, 9(1), 102–118, 2000.

[22] I. Haritaoglu. Scene text extraction and translation for handheld devices. *Proc. IEEE conf. on Computer Vision and Pattern Recognition*, 2, 408–413, 2001

[23] T.K. Ho. Exploratory analysis of point proximity in subspaces. *Proc. 16th Int. Conf. on Pattern Recognition*, Quebec City, Canada, 2, pages 196–199, August 11-15, 2002.

[24] T.K. Ho. Mirage: a tool for interactive pattern recognition from multimedia data. *Proc. of Astronomical Data Analysis Software and Systems XII*, Baltimore, MD, pages 339–342, October 13-16, 2002.

[25] A. Hopgood. Artificial intelligence: hype or reality? *IEEE Computer*, 36(5), 24–28, 2003.

[26] T.S. Huang, S. Mehrotra, K. Ramachandran. Multimedia analysis and retrieval system (MARS) project. *Proc. 33rd Annual Clinic on Library Application of Data Processing Digital Image Access and Retrieval*, 1996.

[27] R. Jain. US NSF workshop on visual information management systems, 1992.

[28] D. Marr. *Vision: a computational investigation into the human presentation and processing of visual information*. New York: W.H. Freeman, 1982.

[29] R.J. Mericsko. Introduction of 27th AIPR workshop - advances in computer-assisted recognition. *Proc. of SPIE 3584*, Washington, DC, October 14, 1988.

[30] G. Miller. The magical number seven plus or minus two; some limits on our capacity for processing information. *Psychological Review*, 63, 81–97, 1956.

[31] F. Mosteller, J. Tukey. *Data analysis and regression*. Reading, MA: Addison-Wesley, 1977.

[32] G. Nagy. Image database. *Image and Vision Computing*, 3, 111–117, 1986.

[33] S.E. Palmer. *Vision science, Photons to Phenomenology*. Cambridge, MA: MIT Press, 1999.

[34] A. Pentland, R.W. Picard, S. Sclaroff. Photobook: content-based manipulation of image database. *International Journal of Computer Vision*, 18(3), 233–254, 1996.

[35] Y. Rui, T.S. Huang, M. Ortega, S. Mehrotra. Relevance feedback: a power tool for interactive content-based image retrieval. *IEEE Transactions on Circuits and Systems for Video Technology*, 8(5), 644–655, 1998.

[36] Y. Rui, T.S. Huang, S.F. Chang. Image retrieval: current techniques, promising directions, and open issues. *Journal of Visual Communication and Image Representation*, 10, 39–62, 1999.

[37] J.W. Sammon. Interactive pattern analysis and classification. *IEEE Transactions on Computers*, 19, 594–616, 1970.

[38] W. Siedlecki, K. Siedlecka, J. Sklansky. An overview of mapping techniques for exploratory pattern analysis. *Pattern Recognition*, 21, 411–429, 1988.

[39] A.W.M. Smeulders, M. Worring, S. Santini, A. Gupta, R. Jain. Content-based image retrieval at the end of the early years. *IEEE Transactions on Pattern Analysis and Machine Intelligence*, 22(12), 1349–1380, 2000.

[40] M.J. Tarr, H.H. Bülthoff. Is human object recognition better described by geon-structural-descriptions or by multiple-views? comment on Biederman and Gerhardstein (1993). *Journal of Experimental Psychology: Human Perception and Performance*, 21, 1494–1505, 1995.

[41] J. Tukey. *Exploratory data analysis*. Reading, MA: Addison-Wesley, 1977.

[42] A.M. Turing. On computable numbers with an application to the entscheidungs problem. *Proc. of the London Mathematical Society*, 42, 230–265, 1936.

[43] R. Willing. Airport anti-terror systems flub tests face-recognition technology fails to flag "suspects". *USA Today*, 3A, September 2, 2003. http://www.usatoday.com/usatonline/20030902/5460651s.htm.

[44] D.H. Wolpert. The relationship between PAC, the statistical physics framework, the Bayesian framework, and the VC framework. In: D.H. Wolpert, eds. *The Mathematics of Generalization*. 117–214, Reading, MA: Addison-Wesley, 1995.

[45] J. Yang, X. Chen, W. Kunz. A PDA-based face recognition system. *Proc. the 6th IEEE Workshop on Applications of Computer Vision*, 19–23, 2002.

[46] J. Vesanto. SOM-based data visualization methods. *J. Intelligent Data Analysis*, 3, 111–126, 1999.

[47] J. Zhang, X. Chen, J. Yang, A. Waibel. A PDA-based sign translator. *Proc. the 4th IEEE Int. Conf. on Multimodal Interfaces*, pages 217–222, 2002.

[48] J. Zou. *Computer assisted visual interactive Recognition*. Ph.D. thesis, Rensselaer Polytechnic Institute, Troy, NY, 2004.

[49] J. Zou, G. Nagy. Evaluation of model-based interactive flower recognition. *Proc. of 17th Int. Conf. Pattern Recognition*, Cambridge, UK, volume 2, pages 311–314, 2004.

[50] J. Zou. A model-based interactive object segmentation procedure. *Proc. of IEEE 2005 Workshop on Applications of Computer Vision*, Breckenridge, CO, pages 522–527, 2005.

[51] J. Zou, A. Gattani. Computer-assisted visual interactive recognition and its prospects of implementation over the Internet. *IS&T/SPIE 17th Annual Symposium, Internet Imaging VI, Proceedings of the SPIE*, San Jose, CA, volume 5670, pages 76–87, 2005.

15

Complex Image Recognition and Web Security

Henry S. Baird

Summary. Web services offered for human use are being abused by programs. Efforts to defend against these abuses have, over the last 5 years, stimulated the development of a new family of security protocols able to distinguish between human and machine users automatically over graphical user interfaces (GUIs) and networks. AltaVista pioneered this technology in 1997; by 2000, Yahoo! and PayPal were using similar methods. Researchers at Carnegie-Mellon University [2] and then a collaboration between the University of California at Berkeley and the Palo Alto Research Center [9] developed such tests. By January 2002 the subject was called human interactive proofs (HIPs), defined broadly as challenge/response protocols that allow a human to authenticate herself as a member of a given group: e.g., human (vs. machine), herself (vs. anyone else), etc. All commercial uses of HIPs exploit the gap in reading ability between humans and machines. Thus, many technical issues studied by the image recognition research community are relevant to HIPs. This chapter describes the evolution of HIP R&D, applications of HIPs now and on the horizon, relevant legal issues, highlights of the first two HIP workshops, and proposals for an image recognition research agenda to advance the state of the art of HIPs.

15.1 Introduction

In 1997 Andrei Broder and his colleagues [19], then at the DEC Systems Research Center, developed a scheme to block the abusive automatic submission of URLs [7] to the AltaVista web site. Their approach was to present a potential user with an image of printed text formed specially so that machine vision [optical character reading (OCR)] systems could not read it but humans still could. In September 2000, Udi Manber, Chief Scientist at Yahoo!, challenged Prof. Manuel Blum and his students [2] at the School for Computer Science at Carnegie Mellon University (CMU) to design an easy-to-use reverse Turing test that would block bots (computer programs) from registering for services including chat rooms, mail, briefcases, etc. In October of that year, Prof. Blum asked me, at the time I was with the Palo Alto Research Center (PARC), and Prof. Richard Fateman, of the Computer Science Division of the University of California at Berkeley (UCB), whether systematically applied image degradations could form the basis of such a filter, stimulating the development of PessimalPrint [9].

In January 2002, Prof. Blum and I ran a workshop at PARC on human interactive proofs (HIPs), defined broadly as *a class of challenge/response protocols that allow a human to be authenticated as a member of a given group — an adult (vs. a child), a human (vs. machine), a particular individual (vs. everyone else), etc.* All commercial uses of HIPs known to us exploit the large gap in ability between human and machine vision systems in reading images of text.

The number of applications of vision-based HIPs to web security is large and growing. HIPs have been used to block access to many services by machine users, but they could also, in principle, be used as "anti-scraping" technologies to prevent the large-scale copying of databases, prices, auction bids, etc. If HIPs — possibly not based on vision — could be devised to discriminate reliably between adults and children, the commercial value of the resulting applications would be large.

Many technical issues that have been systematically studied by the image recognition community are relevant to the HIP research program. In an effort to stimulate interest in HIPs within the document image analysis research community, this chapter details the evolution of the HIP research field, the range of applications of HIPs appearing on the horizon, highlights of the first HIP workshop, and proposals for an image recognition research agenda to advance the state of the art of HIPs.

This chapter is an expanded and updated version of reference [5].

15.1.1 An Influential Precursor: Turing Tests

Alan Turing [33] proposed a methodology for testing whether or not a machine effectively exhibits intelligence, by means of an "imitation game" conducted over teletype connections in which a human judge asks questions of two interlocutors — one human and the other a machine — and eventually decides which of them is human. If judges fail sufficiently often to decide correctly, then that fact would be, Turing proposed, strong evidence that the machine possessed artificial intelligence. His proposal has been widely influential in the computer science, cognitive science, and philosophical communities [30] for over 50 years.

However, no machine has passed the Turing test in its original sense in spite of perenniel serious attempts. In fact it remains easy for human judges to distinguish machines from humans under Turing-test-like conditions. Graphical user interfaces (GUIs) invite the use of images as well as text in the dialogues.

15.1.2 Robot Exclusion Conventions

The Robot Exclusion Standard, an informal consensus reached in 1994 by the robots mailing list (`robots@nexor.co.uk`), specifies the format of a file (`http://.../robots.txt` file) which a web site or server may install to instruct all robots visiting the site which paths it should not traverse in search of documents. The Robots META tag allows HTML authors to indicate to visiting robots whether or not a document may be indexed or used to harvest more links (cf. `www.robotstxt.org/wc/meta-user.html`).

Many web services (Yahoo!, Google, etc.) respect these conventions. Some abuses that HIPs address are caused by deliberate disregard of these conventions. The legality of disregarding the conventions has been vigorously litigated but remains unsettled [3, 27]. Even if remedies under civil or criminal law are finally allowed, there will certainly be many instances where litigation is likely to be futile or not cost-effective. Thus there will probably remain strong commercial incentives to use technical means to enforce the exclusion conventions.

The financial value of any service to be protected against "bots" cannot be very great, since a human can be paid (or in some other way rewarded) to pass the CAPTCHA (an acronym for Completely Automated Public Turing Test to Tell Computers and Humans Apart, coined by Prof. Manuel Blum, Luis A. von Ahn, and John Langford of CMU). Of course, minimum human response times — of 5–10 seconds at least — may be almost always slower than a automated attack, and this speed gap may force reengineering of the "bot" attack pattern. Nevertheless, this may be simpler—and more stable—than actively engaging in an escalating arms race with CAPTCHA designers. There are widespread, but so far unsubstantiated, reports of systematic "farming out" of CAPTCHAs, in which humans are encouraged and rewarded (by, for example, according to an often-repeated rumor, access to porn sites) to pass CAPTCHAs [32].

15.1.3 Primitive Means

For several years now web-page designers have chosen to render some apparent text as image (e.g., GIF) rather than encoded text (e.g., ASCII), and sometimes in order to impede the legibility of the text to screen scrapers and spammers. A frequent use of this is to hide email addresses from automatic harvesting by potential spammers. To our knowledge the extent of this practice has not been documented.

One of the earliest published attempts to automate the reading of imaged text on web pages was by Lopresti and Zhou [12]. Kanungo et al. [17] reported that, in a sample of 862 sampled web pages, "42% of images contain text" and, of the images with text, "59% contain at least one word that does not appear in the ... HMTL file."

15.1.4 First Use: The Add-URL Problem

In 1997 AltaVista sought ways to block or discourage the automatic submission of URLs to their search engine. This free "add-URL" service is important to AltaVista since it broadens its search coverage and ensures that sites important to its most motivated customers are included. However, some users were abusing the service by automating the submission of large numbers of URLs, and certain URLs many times, in an effort to skew AltaVista's importance ranking algorithms.

Andrei Broder, chief scientist of AltaVista, and his colleagues developed a filter (now visible at [7]). Their method is to generate an image of printed text randomly (in a "ransom note" style using mixed typefaces) so that machine vision (OCR) systems cannot read it but humans still can (Fig. 15.1). In January 2002 Broder told me that the system had been in use for over a year and had reduced the number of spam add-URL by over 95%. (No details concerning the residual 5% are mentioned.) A U.S. patent [19] was issued in April 2001.

These efforts do not seem to present a difficult challenge to modern machine vision methods. The black characters are widely separated against a background of a uniform gray, so they can be easily isolated. Recognizing an isolated bilevel pattern (here, a single character) that has undergone arbitrary affine spatial transformations is a well-studied problem in pattern recognition, and several effective methods have been published [20, 31]. The variety of typefaces used can be attacked by a brute-force enumeration.

15.1.5 The Chat-Room Problem

In September 2000, Udi Manber of Yahoo! described this "chat-room problem" to researchers at CMU: "bots" were joining online chat rooms and irritating the people there, e.g., by pointing them to advertising sites. How could all "bots" be refused entry to chat rooms?

CMU's Manuel Blum, Luis A. von Ahn, and John Langford [2] articulated some desirable properties of a test:

Submission Code:

Enter Submission Code:

Fig. 15.1. Example of an AltaVista challenge: letters are chosen at random, then each is assigned to a typeface at random, then each letter is rotated and scaled, and finally (optionally, not shown here) background clutter is added.

- The test's challenges can be automatically generated and graded (i.e., the judge is a machine).
- The test can be taken quickly and easily by human users (i.e., the dialogue should not go on long).
- The test will accept virtually all human users (even young or naive users) with high reliability while rejecting very few.
- The test will reject virtually all machine users.
- The test will resist automatic attack for many years even as technology advances and even if the test's algorithms are known (e.g., published and/or released as open source).

Theoretical security issues underlying the design of CAPTCHAs have been addressed by Nick Hopper and Manuel Blum [15].

The CMU team developed a hard GIMPY CAPTCHA, which picked English words at random and rendered them as images of printed text under a wide variety of shape deformations and image occlusions, the word images often overlapping. The user was asked to transcribe some number of the words correctly. An example is shown in Figure 15.2.

Fig. 15.2. Example of a "hard" GIMPY image produced by the Carnegie-Mellon University CAPTCHA.

The nonlinear deformations of the words and the extensive overlapping of images are, in our opinion, likely to pose serious challenges to existing machine-reading technology. However, it turned out to place too heavy a burden on human users, also. In trials on the Yahoo! web site, users complained so much that this CAPTCHA was withdrawn.

As a result, a simplified version of GIMPY ("easy" or "EZ" GIMPY) , using only one word-image at a time (Fig. 15.3), was installed by Yahoo!, and is in use at the time of writing (visible at chat.yahoo.com after clicking on "Sign Up For Yahoo! Chat!"). It is used to restrict access to chat rooms and other services to human users. According to Udi Manber, Chief Scientist of Yahoo!, it serves up as many as a million challenges each day.

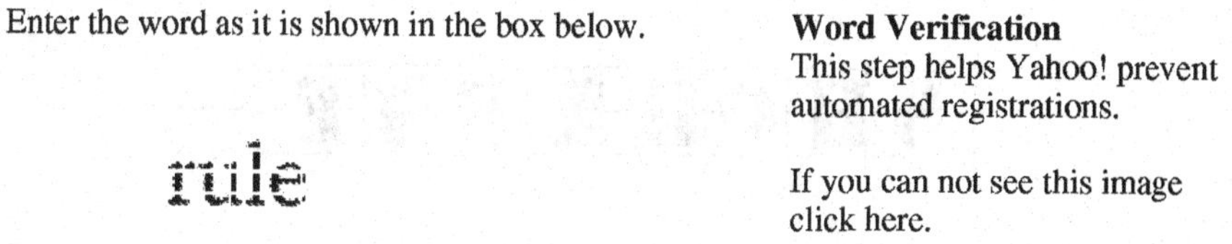

Enter the word as it is shown in the box below.

Word Verification
This step helps Yahoo! prevent automated registrations.

rule

If you can not see this image click here.

Fig. 15.3. Example of a simplified Yahoo! challenge (CMU's "EZ GIMPY"): an English word is selected at random, then the word (as a whole) is typeset using a typeface chosen at random, and finally the word image is altered randomly by a variety of means including image degradations, scoring with white lines (shown here), and nonlinear deformations.

The variety of deformations and confusing backgrounds (the full range of these is not exhibited in the figure) poses a serious challenge to present machine-vision systems, which typically lack versatility and are fragile outside of a narrow range of expected inputs. However, the use of one English word may be a significant weakness, since even a small number of partial recognition results can rapidly prune the number of word choices.

15.1.6 Screening Financial Accounts

PayPal (www.paypal.com) is screening applications for its financial payments accounts using a text-image challenge (Fig. 15.4). We do not know any details about its motivation or its technical basis.

This CAPTCHA appears to use a single typeface, which strikes us as a serious weakness that the use of occluding grids does little to strengthen.

A similar CAPTCHA has recently appeared on the Overture web site (click on "Advertiser Login" at www.overture.com).

15.1.7 PessimalPrint

A model of document image degradations [1]—approximating the physics of machine-printing and imaging of text—was used to generate the "PessimalPrint" challenges illustrated in Figure 15.5.

An experiment assisted by ten U.C. Berkeley graduate-student subjects and three commercial OCR machines located a range of model parameters in which images could be generated

As a security measure, please
enter the characters you see in the
box on the right into the box on
the left. (The characters are not
case sensitive.) Help?

Fig. 15.4. Example of a PayPal challenge: letters and numerals are chosen at random and then typeset, spaced widely apart, and finally a grid of dashed lines is overprinted.

Fig. 15.5. Example of a PessimalPrint challenge: an English word is chosen at random, then the word (as a whole) is typeset using a randomly chosen typeface, and finally the word-image is degraded according to randomly selected parameters (with certain ranges) of the image degradation model.

pseudorandomly that were always legible to the human subjects and never correctly recognized by the OCR systems. In the current version of PessimalPrint, for each challenge a single English word is chosen randomly from a set of 70 words commonly found on the Web; then the word is rendered using one of a small set of typefaces and that ideal image is degraded using the parameters selected randomly from the useful range. These images, being simpler and less mentally challenging than the original GIMPY, would in our view almost certainly be more readily accepted by human subjects.

15.1.8 BaffleText

Chew and Baird [8] noticed vulnerabilities of reading-based CAPTCHAs to dictionary and computer-vision attacks, and also surveyed the literature on the psychophysics of human reading, which suggested fresh defenses available to CAPTCHAs. Motivated by these considerations, they designed "BaffleText," a CAPTCHA that uses non-English pronounceable words to defend against dictionary attacks, and Gestalt-motivated image-masking degradations to defend against image restoration attacks. An example is shown in Figure 15.6.

Fig. 15.6. Example of a BaffleText challenge: a nonsense (but English-like) word was generated pseudorandomly, the word (as a whole) was typeset using a randomly chosen typeface, an mask was generated, and the word image was damaged using the mask.

Experiments on human subjects confirmed high human legibility and user acceptance of BaffleText images. They also found an image-complexity measure that correlated well with user acceptance and assisted the generation of challenges lying within the ability gap.

15.1.9 ScatterType

In response to reports (e.g., [10, 23]) that several CAPTCHAs in wide use could be broken by segment-then-recognize attacks, Baird et al. [4, 6] developed ScatterType, whose challenges are images of machine-print text whose characters have been pseudorandomly cut into pieces that have then been forced to drift apart. An example is shown in Figure 15.7. This scattering is designed to repel automatic segment-then-recognize computer vision attacks. Results from an analysis of data from a human legibility trial with 57 volunteers that yielded 4275 CAPTCHA challenges and responses show that it is possible to locate an operating regime—ranges of the parameters that control cutting and scattering—within which human legibility is high (better than 95% correct) even though the degradations due to scattering remain severe.

15.2 The First International HIP Workshop

The first National Science Foundation (NSF) sponsored workshop on human interactive proofs (HIPs) was held January 9-11, 2002, at the Palo Alto Research Center. There were 38 invited participants, with large representations from CMU, U.C. Berkeley, and PARC. The chief scientists of Yahoo! and Altavista were present, along with researchers from IBM Research, Lucent Bell Labs, Intertrust STAR Labs, RSA Security, and Document Recognition Technologies, Inc. Prof. John McCarthy of Stanford University presented an invited plenary talk, "Frontiers of AI".

As a starting point for discussion, HIPs were defined tentatively as

> *automatic protocols allowing a person to authenticate him/herself — as, e.g., human (not a machine), an adult (not a child), himself (no one else) — over a network without the burden of passwords, biometrics, special mechanical aids, or special training.*

Topics presented and discussed included:

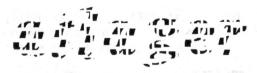

Fig. 15.7. Example of a ScatterType challenge: a nonsense (but English-like) word was generated pseudorandomly, the characters (separately) typeset using a randomly chosen typeface, an mask was generated, the character images cut into pieces, and the pieces scattered pseudorandomly.

- Completely Automatic Public Turing tests to tell Computers and Humans Apart (CAPTCHAs): criteria, proofs, and design;
- Secure authentication of individuals without using identifying or other devices;
- Catalogues of actual exploits and attacks by machines to commercial services intended for human use;
- Audio-based CAPTCHAs;
- CAPTCHA design considerations specific to East-Asian languages;
- Authentication and forensics of video footage;
- Feasibility of text-only CAPTCHAs;
- Images, human visual ability, and computer vision in CAPTCHA technology;
- Human-fault tolerant approaches to cryptography and authentication;
- Robustly nontransferable authentication; and
- Protocols based on human ability to memorize through association and perform simple mental calculations.

Some details of the HIP2002 workshop (program, participant's list, etc.) are available online at www.parc.com/istl/groups/did/HIP2002

15.3 The Second International HIP Workshop

The 2nd International Workshop on Human Interactive Proofs (HIP2005, May 19-20, Bethlehem, PA) brought together 26 researchers, engineers, and business people interested in technologies to protect networked services from abuse by programs (bots, spiders, phishers, etc.) masquerading as legitimate human users.

Attendees participated in an intensive day and a half of plenary talks, panels, and group discussions on the state of the art and identifying urgent open problems. Nine regular papers, published in the refereed, on-site, 141-page hardcopy proceedings [BL2005], established the framework of discussion, which embraced three broad topics:

- Performance analysis of HIPs and CAPTCHAs
- HIP architectures
- HIPs within security systems

Three working groups delved into the topics "Evaluation Methodologies for HIPs," "Assuring High Performance in HIPs," and "Present and Future HIP Technologies."

Dr. Patrice Simard of Microsoft Research presented an invited talk "HIP Design: Synthesis, Analysis, and Usability." At the workshop banquet, Dr. Andrei Broder of IBM Research gave the keynote address "The Story Behind Patent No. 6,195,698 (the First CAPTCHA)."

Complete lists of the participants and the regular papers, details of the program, and slides of some of the talks are available at the web site http://www.cse.lehigh.edu/prr/hip2005. Summaries of the working group discussions will be posted there.

The workshop was organized by Professors Henry Baird and Daniel Lopresti of the Computer Science and Engineering Department at Lehigh University.

15.4 Implications for Image Recognition Research

The emergence of human interactive proofs as a research field offers a rare opportunity (perhaps unprecedented since Turing's day) for a substantive alliance between the image recognition and the theoretical computer science research communities, especially theorists interested in cryptography and security.

At the heart of CAPTCHAs based on reading-ability gaps is the choice of the family of challenges: that is, defining the technical conditions under which text images can be generated that are reliably human-legible but machine-illegible. This triggers many image recognition research questions:

- Historically, what do the fields of computer vision and pattern recognition suggest are the most intractable obstacles to machine reading, e.g., segmentation problems (clutter, etc.); gestalt-completion challenges (parts missing or obscured); severe image degradation?
- What are the conditions under which human reading is peculiarly (or even better, inexplicably) robust? What does the literature in cognitive science and the psychophysics of human reading suggest, e.g., ideal size and image contrast; known linguistic context; style consistency?
- Where, quantitatively as well as qualitatively, are the margins of good performance located, for machines and for humans?
- Having chosen one or more of these "ability gaps," how can we reliably generate an inexhaustible supply of distinct challenges that lie strictly inside the gap?

It is well known in the image recognition field that low-quality images of printed-text documents pose serious challenges to current image pattern recognition technologies [28, 29]. In an attempt to understand the nature and severity of the challenge, models of document image degradations [1, 16] have been developed and used to explore the limitations [14] of image pattern recognition algorithms. These methods should be extended theoretically and be better characterized in an engineering sense, in order to make progress on the questions above.

The choice of image degradations for PessimalPrint was crucially guided by the thoughtful discussion in [28] of cases that defeat modern OCR machines, especially

- thickened images, so that characters merge together;
- thinned images, so that characters fragment into unconnected components;
- noisy images, causing rough edges and salt-and-pepper noise;
- condensed fonts, with narrower aspect ratios than usual; and
- italic fonts, whose rectilinear bounding boxes overlap their neighbors'.

Does the rich collection of examples in this book suggest other effective means that should be exploited?

To our knowledge, all image recognition research so far has been focused at applications in *nonadversarial environments*. We should look closely at new security-sensitive questions, such as:

- How easily can image degradations be normalized away?
- Can machines exploit lexicons (and other linguistic context) more or less effectively than can people?

Our familiarity with the state of the art of machine vision leads us to hypothesize that no modern OCR machine will be able to cope with the image degradations of PessimalPrint. But how can this informed intuition be supported with sufficient experimental data?

CMU's Blum et al. [2] have experimented, on their web site www.captcha.net, with degradations that not only are due to imperfect printing and imaging, but also include color, overlapping of words, nonlinear distortions, and complex or random backgrounds. The relative ease with which we have been able to generate PessimalPrint, and the diversity of other means of bafflement at hand, suggest to us that the range of effective text-image challenges at our disposal is usefully broad.

There are many results reported in the literature on the psychophysics of human reading that appear to provide useful guidance in the engineering of PessimalPrint and similar reading-based CAPTCHAs. Legge et al. [22] report on studies of the optimal reading rate and reading conditions for people with normal vision. Legge et al. [21] compare an ideal observer model quantitatively to human performance, shedding light on the advantage provided by lexical context. Human reading ability is calibrated with respect to estimates of the intrinsic difficulty of reading tasks in Pelli et al. [26], under a wide range of experimental conditions including varying image size, white noise, and contrast; simple and complex alphabets; and subjects of different ages and degrees of reading experience. These and other results may suggest which image degradation parameters, linguistic contexts, style (in)consistencies, and so forth provide the greatest advantage to human readers.

How long can a CAPTCHA such as PessimalPrint resist attack, given a serious effort to advance machine-vision technology, and assuming that the principles — perhaps even the source code — defining the test are known to attackers?

It may be easy to enumerate potential attacks on vision-based CAPTCHAs, but a close reading of the history of image pattern recognition technology [25] and of OCR technology [24] in particular support the view that the gap in ability between human and machine vision remains wide and is only slowly narrowing. We notice that few, if any, machine vision technologies have simultaneously achieved all three of these desirable characteristics: high accuracy, full automation, and versatility. Versatility — the ability to cope with a great variety of types of images — is perhaps the most intractable of these, and so it may be the best long-term basis for designing CAPTCHAs.

Ability gaps exist for other varieties of machine vision, of course, and in the recognition of nontext images, such as line-drawings, faces, and various objects in natural scenes. One might reasonably intuit that these would be harder and so decide to use them rather than images of text. This intuition is not supported by the cognitive science literature on human reading of words. There is no consensus on whether recognition occurs letter-by-letter or by a word-template model [11, 18]; some theories stress the importance of contextual clues [13] from natural language and pragmatic knowledge. Furthermore, many theories of human reading assume *perfectly formed* images of text. However, we have not found in the literature a theory of human reading that accounts for the robust human ability to read despite extreme segmentation (merging, fragmentation) of images of characters.

The resistance of these problems to technical attack for four decades and the incompleteness of our understanding of human reading abilities suggest that it is premature to decide that the recognition of text under conditions of low quality, occlusion, fragmentation, and clutter is intrinsically much easier — that is, a significantly weaker challenge to the machine vision state-of-the-art — than recognition of objects in natural scenes. There is another reason to use images of text: the correct answer to the challenge is unambiguously clear and, even more helpful, it maps into a unique sequence of keystrokes. Can we put these arguments more convincingly?

Acknowledgments

Our interest in HIPs was triggered by a question — Could character images form the basis of a Turing test? — raised by Manuel Blum of Carnegie-Mellon University, which in turn was stimulated by Udi Manber's posing the "chat-room problem" at CMU in September 2000.

References

[1] H.S. Baird. Document image defect models. In H.S. Baird, H. Bunke, K. Yamamoto, eds. *Structured Document Image Analysis*, 546–556, New York: Springer-Verlag, 1992.

[2] M. Blum, L.A. von Ahn, J. Langford. *The CAPTCHA Project*, Completely Automatic Public Turing Test to tell Computers and Humans Apart. www.captcha.net, Dept. of Computer Science, Carnegie Mellon University, and personal communication, November, 2000.

[3] D.P. Baron. eBay and Database Protection. Case No. P-33, Case Writing Office, Stanford Graduate School of Business, 518 Memorial Way, Stanford Univ., Stanford, CA, 2001.

[4] H.S. Baird, M.A. Moll, S-Y. Wang. A highly legible CAPTCHA that resists segmentation attacks. In H.S. Baird, D.P. Lopresti, eds. *Proc., 2nd Int'l Workshop on Human Interactive Proofs (HIP2005)*, May 19-20, Bethlehem, PA. Lecture Notes on Computer Science, LNCS Vol. No. 3517, Berlin: Springer-Verlag, 2005.

[5] H.S. Baird, K. Popat. Human Interactive Proofs and Document Image Analysis. *Proc., 5th IAPR Int'l Workshop on Document Analysis Systems*, Princeton, NJ. Berlin: Springer-Verlag, LNCS 2423, 507–518, August 2002.

[6] H.S. Baird, T. Riopka. ScatterType: a reading CAPTCHA resistant to segmentation attack. *Proc., IS&T/SPIE Document Recognition & Retrieval XII Conf,*, San Jose, CA, January 16-20, 2005.

[7] AltaVista's Add-URL site: altavista.com/sites/addurl/newurl, protected by the earliest known CAPTCHA.

[8] M. Chew, H.S. Baird. BaffleText: a human interactive proof. *Proc., 10th SPIE/IS&T Document Recognition and Retrieval Conf. (DRR2003)*, Santa Clara, CA, January 23-24, 2003.

[9] A.L. Coates, H.S. Baird, R. Fateman. Pessimal Print: a reverse Turing test. *Proc., IAPR 6th Intl. Conf. on Document Analysis and Recognition*, 1154–1158, Seattle, WA, September 10-13, 2001.

[10] K. Chellapilla, K. Larson, P.Y. Simard, M. Czerwinski. Building segmentation based human-friendly human interactive proofs (HIPs). In H.S. Baird, D. P. Lopresti, eds. *Proc., 2nd Int'l Workshop on Human Interactive Proofs (HIP2005)*, LNCS Vol. No. 3517, 1–26 Berlin: Springer-Verlag, May 2005.

[11] R.G. Crowder. *The Psychology of Reading*, New York: Oxford University Press, 1982.

[12] D. Lopresti, J. Zhou. Locating and recognizing text in WWW images. *Information Retrieval*, 2(2/3), 177–206, 2000.

[13] L.M. Gentile, M.L. Kamil, J.S. Blanchard. *Reading Research Revisited*. Columbus, Ohio: Charles E. Merrill Publishing, 1983.

[14] T.K. Ho, H.S. Baird. Large-scale simulation studies in image pattern recognition. *IEEE Transactions on PAMI*, 19(10), 1067–1079, 1997.

[15] N.J. Hopper, M. Blum. Secure human identification protocols. In C. Boyd. *Advances in Crypotology, Proceedings of Asiacrypt*, LNCS 2248, 52–66, Berlin: Springer-Verlag, 2001.

[16] T. Kanungo. *Document degradation models and methodology for degradation model validation*. Ph.D. Dissertation, Dept. EE, University of Washington, March 1996.

[17] T. Kanungo, C.H. Lee, R. Bradford. What fraction of images on the web contain text? *Proc., 1st Int'l Workshop on Web Document Analysis*, Seattle, WA, September 8, 2001 and also at www.csc.liv.ac.uk/~wda2001.

[18] P.A. Kolers, M.E. Wrolstad, H. Bouma. *Processing of Visible Language 2*. New York: Plenum Press, 1980.

[19] M.D. Lillibridge, M. Abadi, K. Bharat, A.Z. Broder. Method for selectively restricting Access to computer systems. U.S. Patent No. 6,195,698, Issued February 27, 2001.

[20] T. Leung, M. Burl, P. Perona. Probabilistic affine invariants for recognition. *Proc. IEEE Comput. Soc. Conf. Comput. Vision and Pattern Recogn.*, 678–684, Santa Barbara, CA, June 23-25, 1998.

[21] G.E. Legge, T.S. Klitz, B.S. Tjan. Mr. Chips: an ideal-observer model of reading. *Psychological Review*, 104(3), 524–553, 1997.

[22] G.E. Legge, D.G. Pelli, G.S. Rubin, M.M. Schleske. Psychophysics of reading: I. normal vision. *Vision Research*, 25(2), 239–252, 1985.

[23] G. Mori, J. Malik. Recognizing objects in adversarial clutter: breaking a visual CAPTCHA. *Proc., IEEE CS Society Conf. on Computer Vision and Pattern Recognition (CVPR'03)*, Madison, WI, June 16-22, 2003.

[24] G. Nagy, S. Seth. Modern optical character recognition. In *The Froehlich / Kent Encyclopaedia of Telecommunications*, 11, 473–531, New York: Marcel Dekker, 1996.

[25] T. Pavlidis. Thirty years at the pattern recognition front. King-Sun Fu Prize Lecture, 11th ICPR, Barcelona, September, 2000.

[26] D.G. Pelli, C.W. Burns, B. Farell, D.C. Moore. Identifying letters. *Vision Research*, (in press), 2006.

[27] P. Plitch. Are Bots Legal? *The Wall Street Journal*, Dow Jones Newswires: Jersey City, NJ, online.wsj.com, September 16, 2002.

[28] S.V. Rice, G. Nagy, T.A. Nartker. *OCR: An Illustrated Guide to the Frontier*, Amsterdam: Kluwer Academic Publishers, 1999.

[29] S.V. Rice, F.R. Jenkins, T.A. Nartker. The Fifth Annual Test of OCR Accuracy. *ISRI TR-96-01*, University of Nevada, Las Vegas, 1996.

[30] A.P. Saygin, I. Cicekli, V. Akman. Turing Test: 50 Years Later. In *Minds and Machines*, 10(4), Amsterdam: Kluwer, 2000.

[31] D. Shen, W.H. Wong, H.H.S. Ip. Affine-invariant image retrieval by correspondance matching of shapes. *Image and Vision Computing*, 17, 489–499, 1999.

[32] C. Thompson. Slaves to Our Machines. *Wired magazine*, 35–36, October, 2002.

[33] A. Turing. Computing Machinery and Intelligence. *Mind*, 59(236), 433–460, 1950.

Index